FROM INTERNATIONALISM
TO POSTCOLONIALISM

From Internationalism to Postcolonialism

Literature and Cinema between the Second and the Third Worlds

ROSSEN DJAGALOV

McGill-Queen's University Press

Montreal & Kingston · London · Chicago

ISBN 978-0-2280-0109-6 (cloth)
ISBN 978-0-2280-0110-2 (paper)
ISBN 978-0-2280-0201-7 (ePDF)
ISBN 978-0-2280-0202-4 (ePUB)

Legal deposit first quarter 2020
Bibliothèque nationale du Québec

Printed in Canada on acid-free paper that is 100% ancient forest free
(100% post-consumer recycled), processed chlorine free

This book has been published with the help of a grant from the American Comparative
Literature Association through the Helen Tatar First Book Subvention. Funding was also
received from the Jordan Center for the Advanced Study of Russia, New York University.

Funded by the   Financé par le
Government   gouvernement   Canadä   Canada Council   Conseil des arts
of Canada   du Canada   for the Arts   du Canada

We acknowledge the support of the Canada Council for the Arts.

Nous remercions le Conseil des arts du Canada de son soutien.

Library and Archives Canada Cataloguing in Publication

Title: From internationalism to postcolonialism : literature and cinema between the
    Second and the Third Worlds / Rossen Djagalov.

Names: Djagalov, Rossen, 1979- author.

Description: Includes bibliographical references and index.

Identifiers: Canadiana (print) 20190215976 | Canadiana (ebook) 20190216093 |
    ISBN 9780228001096 (cloth) | ISBN 9780228001102 (paper) |
    ISBN 9780228002017 (ePDF) | ISBN 9780228002024 (ePUB)

Subjects: LCSH: Developing countries–Foreign relations–Soviet Union. | LCSH: Soviet
    Union–Foreign relations–Developing countries. | LCSH: Developing countries–
    Literatures–Soviet influences. | LCSH: Motion pictures–Developing countries–Soviet
    influences. | LCSH: Soviet Union–Foreign relations–1945–1991.

Classification: LCC D888.S65 D53 2020 | DDC 327.470172/4–dc23

This book was designed and typeset by Peggy & Co. Design in 10.5/14 Minion 3.

To my family

Contents

Figures

Acknowledgments

This book was born as a paper given at Yale's Working Group on Globalization and Culture. Thanks should go to its first readers: my dissertation advisor and personal hero Michael Denning, Naomi Paik, Dan Gilbert, Amanda Ciafone, Eli Jelly-Schapiro, Christina Moon, and Ariana Paulson. The Working Group and the larger Initiative on Labor and Culture were my intellectual homes at graduate school. I always liked to think of them as the intellectual wing of the Yale graduate student union, GESO. I was also fortunate with my department, Comparative Literature, which had by that point largely shed its deconstructionist profile and was experimenting with world literature (and film) approaches, which eventually became central to this book. Katy Clark, whom I was very lucky to have as my other dissertation advisor, stayed on as the guardian angel of this project. Katie Trumpener, John MacKay, and Marci Shore were all generous and devoted teachers and I have learned much from them. The graduate school years at Yale gave me also some of my best friends and colleagues: Yasha Klots, Nora Gortcheva, Roman Uktin, Alice Lovejoy, Michael Cramer, Brais Outes, Raisa Sidenova, and many others. Ilya Kliger, who together with Tom Campbell was my first and finest GESO organizer, has remained so throughout the years and geographies, politically, intellectually, personally. Tom told me once that no single person can have all the right answers to all questions, but in life he does everything to prove this wrong.

The PhD thesis I submitted contained only one chapter of what would eventually become this book, and for a long while, I did not know what to do with them. Thanks to dissertation awards by SSRC and ACLS, however,

I had a great many notes and thoughts on Soviet–Third World cultural engagements, which I proceeded to write about in two distinct spurts. One of these took place during a postdoctoral fellowship at the Penn Humanities Forum, where I enjoyed the mentorship of Kevin Platt and the collegiality and friendship of Monica Kim, Laurent and Ece Dissard, Elidor Mëhilli, and Noah Tamarkin.

The other spurt has occurred already at my present workplace, the Department of Russian and Slavic Studies at New York University, the best department in the world, where my colleagues – Anne Lounsbery, Yanni Kotsonis, Eliot Borenstein, Anne O'Donnell, Mikhail Iampolski, Maya Vinkour, and Ilya Kliger – as well as the inimitable Leydi Ortiz – made this work possible in more ways than I can thank them for.

In between, I spent a year as a lecturer at Harvard's Program of History and Literature, which memorably coincided with the Occupy movement, and two more years teaching at Koç University during a dramatic period in Turkey's recent history. I left Istanbul with a sad heart but also with a number of colleagues, friends, and comrades: my confidante Georgia Axiotou, the leaders of the revolution Osman Şahin, Ekin Koçabas, Erdem Yöruk, among others, as well as my departmental colleagues: Meliz Ergin, Nazmi Agil, Soo Kim, Megan MacDonald, and Erik Mortenson. Throughout this postgraduate period of movement, the precious friendships of Suzanna Weygandt, Georgi Felixov, Marian Zumbulev, Kalina Hamraeva, Marijeta Bozovic, Jessie Labov, Yuliya Minkova, and many others have kept me grounded while *LeftEast*'s editorial collective gave me the chance to relive the internationalism of my characters.

In Moscow, Zhenya Trefilov and Misha Levitin's merry company made every visit a joy. The conversations with Ilya Budraitskis to this day account for most of what I know about today's Russia. Thanks to a fellowship at the Poletayev Institute for Theoretical and Historical Studies in the Humanities at the Higher School of Economics and invitations from the InterLit group (Elena Zemskova, Elena Ostrovskaya, and Natalia Kharitonova) based at the same university, I not only had a source of a visa, a dormitory, and a cafeteria but also a Russian academic institution to call home and a remarkable scholarly community with whom to share my work. Over the course of many years and many visits, archivists from RGALI, RGANI, GARF, RGAKFD, RGASPI, and VGIK have brought me countless documents on Soviet literary and cinematic internationalism. I also spoke to a number of people – scholars, translators, VGIK-trained foreign filmmakers – who had once occupied the interface of Soviet–Third World engagements. They are the real heroes of this book.

What ultimately made my interviews, archival notes, and observations into a book was the help of a growing circle of co-conspirators. First among them was Masha Salazkina. Our collaboration started with a co-written article "Tashkent '68: a Cinematic Contact Zone" (*Slavic Review* 75.2 (Summer 2016)), which not only smoothed my foray into film studies but also became the kernel out of which Chapter Four grew. Since then, Masha has read the entire book twice, on each occasion producing nine single-spaced pages of exceptionally sharp commentary. The other participants of my manuscript workshop – Margaret Litvin, Katerina Clark, Yasha Klots, Betty Banks, Anne Lounsbery, and Ilya Kliger – all offered illuminating criticism that over the ensuing months helped give the baggy monster shape, coherence, meaning. Kevin Platt's generous invitation to present chapters of the manuscript to the Penn *kruzhok* gave it another round of audience and constructive commentary. An inventory workshop co-organized at NYU's Jordan Center with the ever-generous Monica Popescu, Leah Feldman, and Duncan Yoon on the Afro-Asian Writers Association and my participation in the Postcolonialist Print Culture network have become a source of hope that this work could be of interest to scholars beyond Soviet culture. Throughout this process, Galin Tihanov has been a wise friend. At crucial moments, Alice Lovejoy, Louise Spence, Katharine Holt, Elena Razlogova, Raisa Sidenova, and Nariman Skakov read and advised me on whole chapters. From then on, my editor, Richard Ratzlaff, ably shepherded this manuscript to completion and Anna Yegorova heroically indexed it.

And finally, my family. Petia, Lilyan, Ivan Djagalovi, grandparents, uncles, and aunts gave me not only a happy childhood in an otherwise turbulent transition to capitalism in Bulgaria but constant care over the years that followed. And Asli, who joined me in life more recently, read the manuscript countless times, cheered me up with her love through the interminably long revisions, and taught me what happiness is. It is to them that this book is dedicated.

FROM INTERNATIONALISM
TO POSTCOLONIALISM

Introduction

"The Third World was not a place. It was a project."
Vijay Prashad, *The Darker Nations* (2008)

The first question I was asked upon finishing a talk on Second-to-Third-World literary engagements at the Moscow-based Institute of Oriental Studies was a very polite, but equally sincere "But who needs this?" (*A komu eto nuzhno?*). After all, "this" (the engagements) was a product of a twentieth-century political and cultural configuration that is no more. Never quick on my feet, I mumbled away an explanation, but the question has stayed with me ever since. Indeed, who needs "this"? Why study the cultural byproducts of a failed political alliance, which may once have been a source of inspiration and cultural capital but is no more? Certainly, "its" cause has not been helped by the collapse of the Soviet state and its imperial ambition to map the whole world through a powerful area studies apparatus of which post-Soviet Russia's institutes of Africa, Asia, and Latin America are but pale shadows. An amnesia has descended over this topic. Except in certain leftist quarters, academic establishments in most African, Asian, and Latin American countries seem similarly uninterested in reconstructing the story of their cultures' multiple engagements with international communism and the Second World. Ironically, but perhaps tellingly, it is postcolonial scholars and historians of Soviet internationalism based in the Western academy who have shown the greatest interest in "it." Yet even there, reconstructing Second-to-Third-World cultural networks entails overcoming not only the area studies division of labour, which has erected professional, intellectual, and linguistic barriers between the two worlds, but also the embarrassment before real or imagined cold-warriors ready to expose the Soviet trace.

Why, for example, compromise the illustrious reputations of canonical postcolonial writers such as Ngũgĩ wa Thiong'o and Faiz Ahmad Faiz or Third-Cinema filmmakers such as Sembène Ousmane and Mrinal Sen with an unsavoury association with the Soviet state? Indeed, it has been one of postcolonial studies' foundational moves to rescue the study of the contemporary cultures of Africa, Asia, and Latin America from narrow Cold War dichotomies and assert their independence. Today, however, this move obscures more than it reveals, serving as a decontextualizing force that needs to be explicitly challenged. Not only does it account for our inability to explain individual actions and preferences of Third-Worldist cultural producers and their audiences but it also keeps us blind to the larger ways in which the Second and the Third World have been mutually constitutive, up to their near-simultaneous disappearance ca 1990.

From Internationalism to Postcolonialism addresses this disconnect by demonstrating the extent to which Third-Worldist literary and cinematic platforms and networks shared the same field of political and cultural struggle with Soviet ones. The Soviet perspective provides a novel vantage point to write the history of African, Asian, and Latin American cultures, which have been almost exclusively studied on their own terms or in their relation to Western modernity. Moscow and Tashkent, Soviet society and culture, too, become less familiar places when seen through the eyes of a visiting Senegalese writer as do Cuban and Syrian cinema when viewed from the perspective of their engagement with the USSR. This book also reconfigures the relationship between Soviet and postcolonial studies: rather than using postcolonial theory to study the Russo-Soviet peripheries (East European, Caucasian, and Central Asian), it documents the multiple ways in which the Soviet experience has affected this theory and its attendant literary and cinematic production.

Drawing on the archives of the Soviet Writers and Filmmakers Unions, the Central Committee of the Communist Party of the Soviet Union (CPSU), and other cultural agencies of the Soviet state, *From Internationalism to Postcolonialism* focuses on the main organizing platforms of post-Stalin-era Soviet engagement with the literature and cinema of the Third World: the Afro-Asian Writers Association (1958–91, Chapter 2) and the biennial Tashkent Festival of Asian, African, and Latin American Film (1968–88, Chapter 4). The Cold War, which saw the peak of those engagements, is bracketed by an interwar era during which African, Asian, and Latin American writers first entered the Soviet Republic of Letters (Chapter 1) and the post-Soviet era, when that Republic and its cinematic equivalent had fallen apart, but not without leaving influential legacies (Epilogue). This excavation of cultural networks and interfaces sets the context for structural readings of dozens of postcolonial novels and films, specifically interrogating how they imagined international solidarity (Chapters 3 and 5, respectively). This resulting textual analysis uncovers both typological affinities and genetic contacts that underlay the similarities in the transnational imaginaries of Soviet and canonical Third-Worldist novels and films.[1]

Protagonists

Before we proceed, a word may be needed about the protagonists of these engagements: Third-Worldist cultural producers and audiences and their Soviet counterparts. Coined by Alfred Sauvy in 1952 to refer to the countries not aligned with the Communist USSR or the capitalist NATO bloc, the term "Third World" has since gone in multiple different directions.[2] In today's popular usage, which is the one that I will avoid, it has devolved into a pejorative synonym for "underdeveloped" (as in "a Third-World country"). Another sense in which the term "Third World" is commonly used, which I will also avoid, is as a more neutral designator of the cultural and human geographies of Africa, Asia, and Latin America, without any necessary assumption of common politics.

Drawing on Vijay Prashad's opening sentences of his magisterial *Darker Nations* (2007), "The Third World was not a place. It was a project," I will use the term in its third meaning: not a figure of backwardness, nor even a more neutral designator of a geography comprising dominated or (formerly) colonial territories of Africa, Asia, and Latin America, but rather, an emancipatory supranational movement on these continents seeking not only national independence but also the formation of socially just societies. Used in this narrower sense, Third-World (or Third-Worldist, as I will call them to avoid confusion) literatures and cinemas are those associated with that project rather than the cumulative sum of all the possible literatures and cinemas coming from three continents. Although partially institutionalized through organizations such as the Non-Aligned Movement (NAM), the Cairo-based Afro-Asian People's Solidarity Organization (AAPSO), the Havana-based Organization of Solidarity with the People of Africa, Asia, and Latin America (OSPAAAL), and others, Third-Worldism was an immensely heterogeneous phenomenon. Ideologically, it ranged widely, from progressive nationalisms and regionalisms, Nehruism, Sukarnoism, Peronism, pan-Arabism, and pan-Africanism to radical Guevarism and Maoism, in each case with their attendant cultures, and in each case opposed to Western domination of their societies. Third-Worldist formations could be genuinely non-aligned and exclude Soviet representatives, as was the case of the NAM or the numerous non-state initiatives, such as the Third-World Filmmakers Committee, or they could include Soviet participation (AAPSO, OSPAAAL, and the literary and cinematic organizations studied in this book). Like these larger Third-Worldist formations and institutions, many of the artists and audiences were attracted to the Soviet Union for four complexly intertwined reasons: commitment to Soviet-centred communism and its culture; interest in the Soviet model of industrial development and its cultural achievements without the adoption of communist ideology or geopolitical alignment; the material and symbolic resources the Soviet state could provide to their particular struggles; and as an ally in the struggle against Western (cultural) domination. While a common front against the West remained a relatively constant factor behind this alliance, over the course of the Soviet Union's seven decades, ideological affinities for it increasingly gave way to a more pragmatic appreciation for its resources. For all the rich motivations driving the cultural traffic between the Second and the Third World, *From Internationalism to Postcolonialism* seeks to demonstrate the degree of connectedness between the Soviet bloc and the Third-World project, thus putting the latter's non-alignment in question.

Neither the Soviet state nor the Soviet-aligned cultural formations examined in this book used the term "Third World." The term was expressly proscribed in the mid-1970s by the head of the International Department of CPSU's Central Committee, Boris Ponamarev (a former Comintern cadre, he rejected the possibility of a third position between capitalism and socialism), but in its place, alternative designations proliferated ("young countries," "formerly colonial and capitalist countries," "developing countries," "countries of socialist orientation," "countries of non-capitalist orientation," "countries of revolutionary democracy," and so on), signifying both the ideological uncertainty within Soviet-area studies and foreign policy but also the active debates taking place there.[3] Bandung's more neutral Afro-Asian formula (later extended to Latin America) offered a way of papering over these distinctions and was adopted by the Soviet-aligned cultural formations examined in this book, sometimes with the implicit assumption of the militant, anti-colonialist, Third-Worldist orientation of the three continents, in Vijay Prashad's "project" sense, at other times seeking the most inclusive possible formula, as in the purely geographical meaning of "Third World." Though often contested, this strategic ambiguity allowed the organizers of these cultural formations greater latitude in issuing invitations or articulating positions. The continental designators came with their own problems. In the early life of this three-continent formula, Latin America stood somewhat apart from the other two continents, owing both to its distinct history and to political considerations: the regimes ruling most of it during the Cold War were dependent on the United States and hostile to communism while many of the continent's guerrilla movements had long rejected Moscow as an ideological authority.[4] The continental designation came with certain incompatibilities: because of the Arab and Chinese vetoes, Israel and Taiwan could not be represented at such gatherings either. By contrast, Japan had to be invited to any "Afro-Asian" event despite its recent imperial history and status as a recognized economic, literary, and cinematic powerhouse, which distinguished it from most other participants. Pushing the Afro-Asian formula even further, African-Americans were sometimes invited, usually in observer status.[5]

The "Second World" is a less debatable term as its source and project nature is clearer. In comparison to "the Third World," it appears a more centralized entity with authority firmly embedded in the Communist Party of the Soviet Union.[6] In this sense, dissident or exilic authors, even though located in these countries or writing in their languages, could not be part of the Second World. Moreover, the limited autonomy in which Second-World official writers, filmmakers, and intellectuals operated between the 1930s and 1980s meant that the engagement with the cultural Third World was spearheaded by the Soviet cultural bureaucracies – a broad category that extended from the Central Committee of the Communist Party (CP) through the leaderships of the writers and filmmakers unions to the individual writers and filmmakers themselves who were employees of those unions. As contemporary scholarship on the Second World and its foreign cultural engagements has shown, however, we reduce it to "the Kremlin" at our peril. Different Soviet institutions – from the Ministry of Foreign Trade interested in foreign currency, through the Ministry of Foreign Affairs, which privileged the extension of foreign power abroad, to the ideologically-minded Central Committee's International Department – each inflected Soviet–Third-World cultural engagements with their own preoccupations, often acting at odds with each other. More importantly, it was actual Soviet writers and filmmakers who talked and walked with their Third-Worldist peers and real Soviet viewers and readers who consumed the latter's books and films. While meticulously choreographed, these encounters produced friendships, attachments, and sometimes conflicts that no one could have ever scripted. Moreover, any generalization about "Soviet internationalism" runs into the extreme variability of the Soviet(-bloc) state and society: how can 1937 or 1942 be compared to 1979 or 1986?

While their engagement with the non-Western world was cumulatively massive, this book does not do justice to the wider Second-World societies beyond the USSR: Warsaw Pact East European countries and Yugoslavia, Cuba, and China before the Sino-Soviet split. China, of course, is its own separate and big story, belonging at different points to both the Second and the Third World, and in fact contesting Soviet and NAM's claims to lead each. Seen through Soviet eyes, Maoism's revolutionary appeal, which at its peak stretched from Paris to Tanzania, from San Francisco–based Black Panthers to Naxalite rebels in India, made it at times an even more dangerous rival than the West.[7] Over the course of the 1960s, it split not only the Afro-Asian Writers movement and the first, itinerant, version of the Afro-Asian Film Festival but also dozens of Third-Worldist initiatives and communist parties worldwide into pro-Soviet and pro-Chinese versions.[8] Similarly flying high its own revolutionary flag and emphasizing anti-imperialist, global racial justice, which had been deprioritized within Soviet discourse and foreign policy, Cuba's Third-Worldist cultural outreach, institutionalized through OSPAAAL, posed a much friendlier and more loyal challenge.[9] By the end of the long 1960s, however, the Cultural Revolution had brought Chinese foreign policy to a state of solipsism and such initiatives to a halt while Cuba had entered its "grey years" of Sovietization.[10] As a whole, despite the gradual waning of its symbolic appeal, the Soviet model of cultural internationalism remained the most durable and best-resourced.

Yugoslavia, a founding member of the Non-Aligned Movement, pursued its own high-profile engagements in Africa and Asia.[11] Another early "defector" from the Soviet bloc, Albania, picked up the global Maoist flag, where China had dropped it in the mid-1970s, and under the banner of its own anti-revisionist Marxism, Hoxhaism, commanded the loyalties of small communities of Asian and Latin American communists. Warsaw Pact states were another matter. Acting within the broader parameters set by the USSR and yet with a surprising degree of autonomy, they followed its lead in accepting non-Western students, sending experts, and conducting construction and development projects, both on a commercial basis and as a form of socialist solidarity.[12] For complicated reasons that had to do with West Germany's Hallstein doctrine, East Germany maintained a particularly active (cultural) diplomacy with the non-Western world, for example becoming the main publisher of the African National Congress.[13] Thus, a number of works of politically engaged African writers such as Alex La Guma had their first publication worldwide in East Berlin, thanks to the English-language Seven Seas Publishers. Czechoslovakia was also active on that front, much more so than Romania or even Poland, opening a whole university in Prague (University of 17 November) dedicated to the education of African and Asian students. As a whole, however, the institutional forms East European countries and China developed in their outreach to the non-Western world predictably followed a Soviet grammar: writers and cinematographers unions entrusted with monitoring contemporary foreign literatures and cinemas, sending their members abroad and receiving foreign ones, individually or at literary conferences, film festivals, or coordinating meetings; literary magazines and presses charged with translating Afro-Asian literatures in the local language and vice versa; and a network of friendship societies facilitating non-commercial distribution of film and literature.

Finally, one last group will be included, if somewhat uneasily, in the Second World: mid-twentieth-century Western leftist cultural producers who served as key mediators between Soviet and non-Western cultures. While only one of them – the Dutch documentarian Joris Ivens – will feature prominently in this book, their role in passing interwar leftist cultural developments, including the Soviet avant-garde of the 1920s, to Third-Worldist cultural producers cannot be understated. Others, such as the French Communist poet Louis Aragon, helped introduce francophone Arab and African writers to Soviet cultural bureaucracies at a time when the latter lacked such direct connections.[14]

Thus defined, the available resources, structures, and internal coherence of the two parties in Second-to-Third-World cultural engagements appear highly asymmetrical. At the level of cultural producers, the Soviet side – organized into Unions of Writers and Cinematographers subordinate to the Cultural Section of the Party's Central Committee – encountered Third-World peers of a vast range of politics, styles, and political situations. It would be an error, however, to take the Soviet cultural bureaucracies' ambitions of control and leadership over the latter, codified in their archives, for an actuality. As we see again and again, the terrain of interactions allowed African, Asian, and Latin American writers and filmmakers to treat Soviet texts and initiatives as resources to be drawn from selectively, interpreted in peculiar ways, and radically repurposed for the needs of their different contexts.

The same is true to an even greater extent of cultural consumers, as *From Internationalism to Postcolonialism*'s occasional peeks into Soviet audiences illustrate. The Third-World optic complicates significantly the two categories in which scholarship has (implicitly) divided Soviet audiences – critical intelligentsia or *inakomysliashchie* (other-thinking) ones and conformists happy to read whatever the state provided for them, by focusing on the Western-centrism of the former and the latter's interest in melodrama, which Soviet film distributors satisfied with non-Western films. There was also a third type of audience – the people of Soviet Central Asia and the Caucasus – who had a much closer engagement with (post)colonial cultures. As for audiences from Africa, Asia, and Latin America, this book will limit itself to the most important ones – the writers and filmmakers themselves, who made statements about Soviet literature and film, highlighting their creative appropriations of Russian and Soviet culture and thus the sheer agency they exercised in their readings. Studying both audiences, and in particular their interest (or lack thereof) in each other's culture, offers an empirical way to examine the power and evolution of the internationalisms that linked them.

Soviet–Third World Cultural Entanglements in the Short Twentieth Century

In reconstructing the history of these engagements, this book will implicitly challenge the two dominant approaches to the history of twentieth-century colonial and postcolonial culture: on the one hand, archive-free heroic narratives focused on texts and manifestoes, which exhibit little interest in the materiality and extent of textual circulation; on the other, usually more historically grounded studies originating from the Soviet archives that treat African, Asian, and Latin American cultural producers as objects of a Soviet Cold War policy. While much more sympathetic to the former narrative and arguing against frameworks that reduce their agencies to the realpolitik of the main geopolitical confrontation of the day, *From Internationalism to Postcolonialism* challenges it by demonstrating the extent to which Third-Worldist cultural producers were imbricated in the Cold War context, and in particular, their search for Soviet recognition, audiences, and platforms. The cultural Cold War, as Monica Popescu has convincingly shown, arguing against its erasure in postcolonial scholarship, was the common field within which postcolonial cultural producers operated.[15] Moreover, that one of the superpowers happened to be the USSR injected into that field a peculiar literature- and culture-centrism. Down to its very bureaucracy, the Soviet state, as an heir to the nineteenth-century Russian intelligentsia, believed in the power of literature and culture to change hearts and minds, heavily invested in this belief, and projected it onto societies, including postcolonial ones, structured very differently from its own. By the logic of the Cold War, Soviet literary investments had to be at least reciprocated and even better – exceeded. It is impossible to imagine otherwise how such agencies as the CIA and the State Department, which had never before the Cold War (or after) shown much interest in foreign literary journals, would expend so many resources on them. The main beneficiary of this competition for "the hearts and minds" were writers, who faced significantly expanded publication possibilities, and audiences throughout the three worlds, who were given greater access to those writers.

While historians have gone much further than their literary and film studies peers in studying Soviet–Third World engagements, it is primarily *political* histories of the Comintern and the Cold War that have sought to keep Africa, Asia, and Latin America simultaneously within their purview.[16] The vast majority of culturally-attuned histories of the USSR and the Global South deal with the interactions of the former with one particular non-Western country, region, or continent, usually over a limited period of time.[17] Building upon them, *From Internationalism to Postcolonialism* offers a more composite account of the cultural relationship between the USSR and the Third World, which roughly falls into three discontinuous phases:

The Comintern phase, situated between the Second, anti-colonial, Congress of the Comintern in 1919 and the late 1930s, was a time when the formidable body of pre-1917 Marxist thought on imperialism and the colonial question began to serve as the basis for the new Soviet state's policies. These went into two very different directions: nation-building in the Caucasus and Central Asia ("the inner East" in Masha Kirasirova's words), directed by the Commissariat of the Nationalities, and support for anti-colonial struggles in the "outer East" (initially, the Asian and North African territories geographically proximate to the USSR; subsequently, as the anti-colonial and communist movements expanded, the whole of Asia, Africa, and Latin America) under the Comintern's jurisdiction.[18] "The East," of course, referred to the oppressed. For all the problems and limitations of Soviet anti-colonialism, which only grew under Stalinism, it is worth remembering that the interwar Bolshevik state was the one (major power) state that not only fought racism and imperialism at home but also took this fight internationally, a fact appreciated by anti-colonial and racial justice activists worldwide. By mapping out the cultural connectivities between these two Easts, *From Internationalism to Postcolonialism* sets into dialogue the two branches of historiography devoted to Soviet nationalities policies on one hand, and histories of the Soviet engagements with the (semi-)colonial world on the other. The connection between the two Easts, bridged in the early years of Bolshevik rule by a hoped-for but unrealized "revolution in Asia," was gradually disarticulated over the course of the 1930s, as was the larger Soviet investment in anti-colonial struggles, sacrificed to the realpolitik of the Popular Front (a de facto anti-German coalition between the Soviet Union and the major imperial powers of the United Kingdom and France) and the primacy of the European theatre in the run-up to the Second World War.

Moscow's realpolitik, however, did not straightforwardly translate into the imaginaries of leftist cultural producers and their texts. Quite a few progressive intellectuals from the (semi-)colonial world did indeed join their local communist parties, following the Comintern through its occasionally vertiginous zig-zags. Yet the vast majority of such intellectuals took the October Revolution and the Soviet cultural production it inflected and turned them into gigantic canvases onto which to project their own aspirations.[19] The distances separating them from Moscow allowed them greater leeway, politically and aesthetically. Not even in this Comintern period – when Soviet monopoly over world communism was at its height – should we mistake instructions and resolutions that Soviet cultural bureaucracies directed at Third-World cultural producers for actual outcomes.

While the colonial world ceased to be a Soviet geopolitical priority in the twenty-year hiatus between the mid-1930s and mid-1950s, it re-emerged powerfully in the years after Bandung, inaugurating the second phase of the Soviet–Third World engagements, their Cold War peak (mid-1950s to the 1980s). That period saw not only devastating proxy wars in the Global South but also a remarkably favourable environment for the flourishing of Third-World culture.[20] *From Internationalism to Postcolonialism* shows how the struggle for cultural influence between the two superpowers vastly increased the symbolic and material resources available to Third-World cultural producers: royalties, invitations, and audiences. The cultural Cold War also structurally expanded the room for manoeuvre available to them as the superpowers were forced to outbid each other for their attention. Synthesizing these interactions through a focus on the common Soviet(-aligned) networks and institutions specifically designed for non-Western cultures, *From Internationalism to Postcolonialism* demonstrates the centrality of Central Asian and Caucasian spaces and mediators in the Soviet courtship of Third-World writers, filmmakers, and audiences.

While the post-Stalin-era Soviet state continued to command the loyalties of millions in Africa, Asia, and Latin America and the sheer volume of engagements and resources it devoted to the decolonizing world steadily grew, it had lost much of the appeal it had in the interwar era. The rigidity of the Soviet version of Marxism meant that the USSR often ended up denying agency to newly assertive Third-Worldist forces, insisting on guiding, teaching, and leading them a little too much. The pursuit of a superpower status for the Soviet state (as opposed to promotion of international communism), the attendant "Soviet superiority complex," and the bureaucratization of its internationalist cadre, which reached deadening proportions under Brezhnev's stagnation too, could alienate Third-Worldist thinkers and activists.[21] Lacking the idealism, creativity, and vigorous debates that characterized the early Bolshevik years, late-Soviet Marxism all too often discouraged socialist revolutions in non-Western societies because the conditions were not "ripe," because the proletariat was not strong or numerous enough, thus denying to others the revision that Lenin had introduced in Marxism for the specific case of Russia (you do not have to wait until the conditions are "ripe").[22] At the same time, the emergence of the Non-Aligned Movement, the various region-based anti-colonial forces, and the iconic revolutions of China and Cuba all meant the loss of the earlier global monopoly the Soviet state held on state support for anti-colonialism and anti-racism. Additionally, as the small number of female names that appear in this book shows, post–Second World War Soviet internationalism was, if not a male-only affair, then at least largely unconcerned with gender equality. It was also a race-blind affair, a fact the prominence of Soviet Central Asian participants was meant to obfuscate. Soviet cultural bureaucracies of the post-Stalin era found the whole discourse of race – a subject most Third-Worldist formations were highly sensitive to – deeply worrying and perceived it as a potential threat to themselves, as a mostly white people and a former empire. As the book shows, in the eyes of Third-World artists and audiences, the red star of the October Revolution steadily dimmed over the course of the Cold War's last quarter century, only partly compensated by the increasing resources the Soviet state was investing in these engagements.

Their final, post-Soviet phase – the age of amnesia and ruins – saw not only the disappearance of the Soviet state but also the related winding-down of the Third World project and the cultural institutions that once fuelled it. What is left are fragments: memories of Indian melodramas that Soviet viewers flocked to see, Moscow-based research institutes – of Africa and Asia, of Latin America, of Oriental studies – which have clearly seen better days, and a large volume of translations from the literature of these continents, which remain stored and practically unread in Russian libraries. By the same token, in some African, Asian, and Latin American countries, one finds second-hand bookstores and libraries – private and public – with numerous volumes of Russian or Soviet literature published by the Moscow-based Progress Publishers or its local, left-wing partners and generations of readers with vivid memories of them. Numerous filmmakers from these continents were educated in Moscow's All-Soviet Institute of Cinematography between the late 1950s and 1990s. But what is past is not necessarily finished. *From Internationalism to Postcolonialism* demonstrates the continuities between canonically postcolonial literature and film and Soviet and Western leftist narrative models of the 1920s and '30s as well as between today's postcolonial theory itself and the discourses generated within Soviet-aligned Third-World cultural platforms or pre-Second World War earlier Soviet experience. Such a *longue-durée* perspective allows us to question the foreshortened, post-1978 (the year Edward Said's *Orientalism* was published) history that mainstream postcolonial studies has constructed for itself, showing the latter to be only the latest stage of a much longer tradition of critical thought on colonialism, as Marxist postcolonialists of the "Warwick School" have repeatedly argued in the debates with their poststructuralist colleagues.[23]

By juxtaposing the Second and the Third World – two geographies typically viewed either on their own terms or through their relationship to the West – *From Internationalism to Postcolonialism* offers a new perspective on both. Seen from a Third-Worldist point of view, Soviet history looks very different from the standard Western-centric or domestic narratives.

In this perspective, the main outcome of the October Revolution was not a working-class victory over the forces of capitalism, as seen by West European leftists, but the resounding call for national emancipation the Bolsheviks issued, the emergence of a model for such emancipation and development, and the only state in the world willing and able to support anti-colonial causes abroad against Western imperialism. To many non-white observers such as W.E.B. Du Bois, visiting the early Soviet Union from racially segregated societies, the interwar-era Soviet state's unique commitment to racial justice and equality trumped Stalinist authoritarianism.[24] The rise of the Third-World project deprived the Cold War–era Soviet state of this monopoly.

A Third-Worldist perspective also revises the current historiography of the USSR, shifting not only the set of crucial sites (no longer Weimer Germany but Guomindang China, no longer Czechoslovakia but Vietnam) but also the very events foundational to that historiography. Thus, for example, African(-American) activists found the sectarian Third Period that the world communist movement entered in the late 1920s and early '30s more congenial to their demands than the broad anti-fascist Popular Front phase declared by the Comintern in 1934, which enlivened communist parties in Western Europe and North America.[25] To communists in the Middle East, the 1947 Soviet vote at the United Nations in favour of partitioning Palestine, which discredited them in the eyes of Arab nationalists for decades to come, was more consequential than the contemporary repressions or anti-cosmopolitan campaigns inside the USSR, about which they knew very little. While the revelations of Khrushchev's Secret Speech in 1956 shook the faith of millions of Western communists, that same year their Arab comrades basked in the Soviet support for Nasser's Egypt, which faced a combined Anglo-French-Israeli assault over Suez. Soviet economic aid abroad trumped the persecution of its dissidents at home. Viewed from this perspective, Khrushchev's and Brezhnev's "peaceful co-existence" no longer seems a successful, or at least reasonable, strategy to avert a third world war, but rather a betrayal of anti-imperialist struggles, which the USSR was increasingly willing to sacrifice in the name of the détente. The consequent Soviet objection to guerrilla movements and other instances of what they termed "adventurism" was the main factor distancing many Third-Worldist radicals from Soviet politics and culture. Such a line of thought could also explain Fidel Castro's and Che Guevara's anger and disappointment when Khrushchev announced the removal of nuclear weapons from Cuba: rather than preventing a nuclear catastrophe, this action made them feel that they had been used as a pawn in the Global Cold War. Rather than democratizing Soviet society, perestroika and its culmination, the dissolution of the USSR, too, meant a betrayal, as they involved reneging on Soviet assurances and support to many countries of Africa, Asia, and Latin America.

A similar reinterpretation of Soviet literature, film, and culture from a Third-World point of view radically revises the all-too-familiar narrative of an immensely fertile avant-garde of the 1920s, followed by a stifling socialist realism and cultural isolation during the Stalin era, followed by a Thaw-era relaxation and opening to the West, struggles between neo-Stalinists and reformers, emergence of samizdat and tamizdat, and Western-Europe or US-based émigré culture, etc.[26] At the most basic level, the chronology of Soviet engagement with African, Asian, and Latin American culture differed from that of Soviet rapprochement with Western literary or cinematic leftists. Moreover, few readers and viewers in Africa, Asia, and Latin America were able to see Soviet culture in this sequential development, with these meanings; far more common was a decontextualized arrival of Russian and Soviet texts and films, which were then filled with completely different meanings by their audiences. Through this Third-World lens, even nineteenth-century Russian literature, interpreted through the teleology of the Bolshevik Revolution, was often read as revolutionary literature. Soviet novels or films, too, were creatively misinterpreted to fit emancipatory struggles in African, Asian, and Latin American societies.

As recent scholarship is discovering, the Soviet perspective can similarly enrich our account of African, Asian, and Latin American histories, which, too, have been viewed either on their own terms or through the prism of Western (neo-)colonialism or at least, economic and cultural domination. The scholarly reduction of the three continents' global connectivities to their tense relationship with the hegemonic West obscures the richness of global imaginaries, the powerful East–East connections, and the textual and material flows during the short twentieth century. Omitting the Second World from our studies, we might struggle to understand why so many African states called themselves "socialist," why a large number of East Europeans spent time in Mongolia, China, Vietnam, and Cuba, why throughout Africa and the Middle East we find so many Soviet, Polish, or GDR-built projects, not to mention the vast number of Soviet-bloc university graduates in the non-Western world.[27]

Contact Zones and Intermediaries

While many of the cultural encounters between the Second and the Third World happened during the act of reading, viewing, and imagining, others took place at very real and material contact zones. This concept, developed by Mary Louise Pratt to refer to the social spaces where cultures "meet, and clash, and grapple" in the highly hierarchical context of Spanish colonization of the Americas, has been applied to many other contexts, historically or in the present.[28] Its application to the relations between the Soviet cultural bureaucracies and African, Asian, and Latin American cultural producers demands its partial reworking: while highly asymmetric, restricted within the parameters of Soviet foreign policy, and heavily choreographed, these engagements lacked the obvious violence that marked the object of Pratt's original formulation.

The urban spaces and human geographies of Central Asia, and to a lesser extent the Caucasus, provided the main settings for these encounters. Having historically served as crossroads of different Asian peoples, they also exemplified the Soviet state's efforts at modernizing its peripheries. As Soviet Central Asia's biggest population centre, Tashkent was the main hub of these activities from very early on. Hosting the Central Asian Bureau of the Comintern as early as September 1920, the city became the founding site of the Indian Communist Party a few months later and the location for an Indian military school (an unsuccessful project spearheaded by the Indian Communist M.N. Roy to train a national liberation army). As hopes of anti-imperialist uprisings in Asia dimmed over the course of the early 1920s, the showcasing of economic, social, and cultural achievements of interwar-era Soviet Central Asia became primarily addressed at domestic audiences.[29]

It was only during the post-Stalin era, when the USSR began to actively court newly decolonized states, that it launched a massive campaign to communicate its achievements in developing Central Asia worldwide. While Tashkent became the main Soviet showcase city for the Third World, Alma-Ata, Samarkand and Bukhara, Tbilisi and Baku, would also serve as common destinations for countless delegations from Africa, Asia, and Latin America. Historians of the Soviet periphery have shown the degree to which the Soviet state used this earlier experience of Sovietizing Central Asia in its outreach to Afro-Asian audiences.[30] Visiting Afro-Asian writers and filmmakers often made note of these spaces, of their combination of ancient Central Asian culture and Soviet modernity, of the harmonious ethnic diversity of these cities, of the proverbially welcoming and boisterous Uzbek audiences, who flocked to see them. In sum, their perspective allows us to see Soviet Central Asia as a cosmopolitan contact zone vis-à-vis the non-Western world rather than the culturally backward (if exotic) Soviet province that the Western-centric Moscow intelligentsia saw.

Central Asia and the Caucasus were not only the main setting of these encounters but also the source of Soviet cultural intermediaries to the Afro-Asian world. The names of Sharaf Rashidov, Mirzo Tursun-Zade, Chinghiz Aitmatov, Anuar Alimzhanov, Rasul Gamzatov, Zul'fia, Kamil Yarmatov, Malik Kaiumov, and Tolomush Okeev loom large in the lists of Soviet delegations at Afro-Asian Writers' Congresses and film festivals. They were no mere puppets. They were of course acting in line with Soviet cultural policies, and their non-white bodies were meant to represent an ethnically and racially diverse Soviet Union and dispel the lingering suspicion of many African, Asian, and Latin American cultural producers that the USSR was just another white empire. What is more important, however, is that such engagements with the Third World provided Soviet Central Asian political and cultural leaders with an internationalism of their own, focused on non-Western cultures and societies. This position as key Soviet mediators allowed them to make claims on the Moscow centre. Cultural producers were the main beneficiaries of these global relations but ordinary people, too, were heavily involved as viewers, readers, and hosts of non-Western films, texts, and visitors.

There was another type of intermediary sustaining Soviet–Third World cultural engagements. Especially in the case of post–Second World War literature, these were leftist, usually communist, figures from Asia and Latin America (there were fewer Africans on the list), who had either spent time in the USSR or entered the Soviet orbit before the war: Jorge Amado in Brazil, Pablo Neruda in Chile, Nicolás Guillén in Cuba, Nâzım Hikmet in Turkey, Mulk Raj Anand in India, Faiz Ahmad Faiz in Pakistan, Mao Dun, Guo Moruo, and Emi Siao in China, and Paul Robeson in the US. Their acknowledgement as major literary figures sympathetic to the USSR during the late-Stalin period, when Soviet foreign cultural outreach was at its most constrained, meant not only that in the eyes of the Soviet public they almost single-handedly represented their respective contemporary national literatures and culture but also that they mediated those cultures with Soviet cultural bureaucracies, promoted writers (both

Soviet ones and their compatriots), forged reputations, and composed invitee lists.[31] The gradual expansion of Soviet engagements with the Third World in the post-Stalin period significantly diluted their monopoly on representation without entirely changing the logic. Some of them, such as Amado, left the Communist Party following the shocking revelations of Khrushchev's Secret Speech of 1956; others, such as Hikmet, remained faithful to the Soviet cause even if critical of its degradation; and still others, such as the Chinese writers, lost their role after the Sino-Soviet split of the 1960s.[32] New intermediaries, such as Sembène Ousmane or Alex la Guma, came to fill their shoes in the post-Stalin era although they never achieved the monopoly of representation enjoyed by their predecessors or the close connections with the Soviet cultural apparatus.

There was a third type of intermediary, especially relevant in the field of film: leftist Western European cultural producers who remained faithful to the ideals of early Soviet revolutionary art and avant-garde and developed them further at a time when that option was unavailable to official Soviet writers and filmmakers. These intermediaries account for the presence of "a Soviet trace" in non-Western cultural geographies where Soviet literary texts, films, and theories could not have possibly reached.[33] *From Internationalism to Postcolonialism*, for example, interprets the Dutch filmmaker Joris Ivens's significance for Third Cinema of the 1960s and '70s in a similar key.

The Soviet Place in Postcolonial Studies, World Literature, and World Cinema

In addition to the cultural history of Soviet–Third-World engagements, this book makes specific interventions into postcolonial studies, world literature, and world cinema, which over the last three decades have emerged as the major frameworks for reconceptualizing transnational geographies, textual dissemination, and reception in literary and film studies. A scholar interested in Russian and Soviet culture's connectivity with the rest of the world is quickly forced to discover that the spatial frameworks developed by postcolonial theorists, exclusively concerned with the relationship between "the West" and "the East," leave little space for her. To be sure, some of the more exciting scholarship in Russian, East European, and Eurasian studies in the last two decades has been a result of Slavic, East European, and Eurasian scholars adapting that theory to their specific regions and

periods, though often with different methods and results.[34] Inspired by
David Chioni Moore's call, Slavic scholars have also started illuminating
the post-Soviet condition by deploying a postcolonial optic.[35]

However, the reverse side of the (post)colonial-(post)socialist relationship – a systematic attempt to understand the implications of the October
Revolution, of Russian and Soviet culture, for postcolonial thought and
culture – has been decidedly missing. Among the very few postcolonial
theorists who have shown interest in that relationship are Robert Young and
Timothy Brennan. Young devotes several chapters of his *Postcolonialism: A
Historical Introduction* (2001) to reconstructing the pre-1917 Marxist lineage
of postcolonial thought, which the Soviet state then took up.[36] His account
also covers Lenin's, Bukharin's, and Stalin's interventions into the colonial
question in the 1910s as well as various practical initiatives undertaken
by the Bolsheviks, such as the 1920 Baku Congress of the Peoples of the
East and the 1927 Brussels Congress of the (Comintern-initiated) League
against Imperialism. In a rather more polemical spirit, Timothy Brennan
challenges certain poststructuralist claims about Marxism's Eurocentrism
by demonstrating how thinkers from the (former) colonial world creatively
absorbed and reinterpreted this political philosophy and its practitioners.
By labelling the Bolshevik Revolution "an anti-colonial revolution par
excellence," Brennan issues a call to postcolonial scholarship to re-evalu-
ate the Russian Revolution's legacy for the non-Western world.[37] Such a
re-evaluation is beginning to take place among historians of the Comintern
and the global left in general, but it has yet to find resonance among mainstream postcolonial scholars.

My two-fold argument for the relationship between the USSR and
postcolonial studies both draws on these observations and departs from
them. In the first place, while Young and Brennan show the reception of
Marxist thought and powerful impact of the Bolshevik revolution on interwar colonial thinkers, their studies are less concerned with literature and
cultural production per se, and end before the mid-twentieth century, when
Soviet cultural engagement with the Third World intensified. Secondly,
postcolonialism appears on the scene precisely at the moment when
(Soviet-aligned) Third-Worldist cultural formations such as the Afro-Asian
Writers Association and the Tashkent Film Festival entered into decline.
Spearheaded by a different cultural formation of diasporic scholars based
in Anglo-American universities, postcolonial studies performed some of
the same intellectual labour as the Festival and the Association had done

earlier – decried colonialism and celebrated non-Western cultures – introducing, of course, French poststructuralist theory and otherwise making
it acceptable in the academy. Mirroring some of the earlier anti-colonial
thinkers' conflict with Soviet Marxism, postcolonial theorists have insisted
on a culture-specific approach that places the question of race and difference at the heart of their enterprise in a way that sits uneasily with Marxist
universalism and materialism, and especially its Soviet version, the rigidity
of which did much to alienate earlier anti-colonial thinkers. For all their
immense differences, the shared histories between Soviet-aligned networks
and postcolonial studies become evident when we follow the transition
of figures such as Ngũgĩ wa Thiong'o and Sembène Ousmane from these
earlier, Soviet-aligned networks to postcolonial syllabi.

One would have thought that this blind spot in postcolonial studies
would be resolved in the wealth of scholarship currently being produced
under the headings "world literature" and "world cinema," which is well on
its way to supplanting postcolonial studies as the main approaches to trans-
nationalism in literature and film. While still in flux, the contours of this
paradigm shift have already become clear: in addition to a reconciliation
with a Western-centric perspective and abandonment of postcolonialism's
political commitments, the world literature paradigm has sidelined French
poststructuralism central to postcolonial theory and greater openness to
new geographical scenarios. (Postcolonialism has historically been most
comfortable with studies of Middle Eastern, Indian, and African cultures
and a critique of their Western perspectives.) Of particular relevance to
From Internationalism to Postcolonialism are the more critical and materialist models for world literary circulation that Franco Moretti and Pascale
Casanova developed by adapting Immanuel Wallerstein's world-systems
theory to literary scholarship. However, just as world-systems theory
had struggled to find a place for the Second World, so has Moretti's and
Casanova's impressive but woefully Eurocentric work. It is telling that out
of the fifty chapters comprising the authoritative *Routledge Companion
to World Literature* (2012), many of them devoted to the geographical
dimensions of world literature, Russia and the Soviet Union are decidedly
absent, despite the former's paradigmatic example of moving from the
literary periphery to the literary core or the latter's ambitious projects for
world literature.[38] The issue at stake here is not so much another blank spot
on the geographical and historical map of world literature – there are plenty
of these and it is uncharitable to hold any book or its author(s) responsible

for failing to provide comprehensive coverage of the whole world – but the alternative logics of textual circulation that become sidelined in the process. For example, had Moretti and Casanova considered the reception of the proletarian novel in the early twentieth century (or even of Tolstoy's and Dostoevsky's works), they would have been forced to acknowledge, respectively, that modern literary models can travel in multiple directions, not only West to East, and that competition among national literatures and individual writers is hardly the sole force that keeps the World Republic of Letters running. In this sense, this book contributes to Galin Tihanov's project of excavating twentieth-century Russian and Eastern European conceptualizations of the world literary spaces as alternatives to the liberal, Anglo-American version of world literature in fashion today.[39]

Arguably, the most significant phenomenon to emerge out of this territory was the Soviet project for world literature, perhaps the most concerted and best-resourced effort in history to transform the workings of literary production, circulation, and consumption worldwide. The first generation of works to examine its impact on the world literary system is in the process of reaching its readers. Mirroring the divide between scholarship on Comintern and on Soviet nationalities policy, these studies have gone in two distinct directions. On the one hand, Katerina Clark, the members of the Moscow-based Interlit group, and other scholars have set about reconstructing the legacy of Maxim Gorky's World Literature project, the *International Literature* magazine, and the contours of the interwar Writers International as a whole.[40] On the other hand, numerous Soviet literary historians, such as Harsha Ram, Evgeny Dobrenko, and Susanne Frank, have focused on the formation of a multilingual Soviet literature, especially as it concerned the literatures of the Caucasus and Central Asia, seeing in it a world-literature project.[41] With few exceptions, both have yet to cross the post–Second World War divide. Relying on Soviet institutional archives as well as multiple canonical postcolonial texts, *From Internationalism to Postcolonialism* brings the story up to the end of the Soviet Union. It also evaluates the aesthetics of the texts circulating through the Soviet Republic of Letters. Though "realism" ultimately remained the common screen onto which different writers projected their individual styles, the Soviet Republic of Letters was aesthetically a much broader church than Soviet literature, offering space to various species of modernism, Third-Worldism, folkloric epics, national sentimentalism, and so on.

World cinema is an even newer theoretical body, inspired in part by the booming scholarship in world literature, in part by the need to theorize commercial branding practices, and in part by the historical precedent of Third Cinema, the broad, manifesto-rich movement for political cinema in the 1960s and '70s that sought to challenge the cinematic and aesthetic dominance of Hollywood or Europe.[42] Because Sergei Eisenstein and Dziga Vertov, Mikhail Kalatozov, Andrei Tarkovsky, Alexander Sokurov, and other Soviet auteurs have firmly entered the Western cinematic canon, the place of Soviet film in non-Western, world cinema frameworks, and more particularly, its relationship with Third-Worldist cinematic formations, remains largely unexplored. Masha Salazkina's pioneering scholarship has been the main source of conceptualizing Soviet cinematic connectivities to the non-Western world.[43] Together with other recent work on Soviet cinematic internationalism, it has delineated various possibilities for direct (or Western-mediated) engagements, based on the movement of film canisters, theories, or filmmakers.[44] Following this small but growing body of work and drawing on the archives of the Soviet Union of Cinematographers, Goskino, Sovexportfilm, and the Moscow-based All-Soviet Institute for Cinematography (VGIK), where a number of non-Western filmmakers were trained, *From Internationalism to Postcolonialism* reconstructs the main contact zone between Soviet and non-Western film, the Tashkent Film Festival (1968–88), as well as the long journey of the solidarity documentary film from early Soviet cinema to Latin American Third Cinema.

Over the last several years, the traces of magma left by Soviet cultural internationalism have generated a growing interest among literary and film scholars specializing in Africa, Asia, and Latin America.[45] *From Internationalism to Postcolonialism* offers itself as a platform for this conversation between scholars of the Second and the Third World, across the dividing lines of area studies.

Though these Soviet-aligned projects for Third-World literature and cinema left a lasting impact on many national cultures, they neither vanquished nor escaped from Western hegemony. These projects – probably the most significant concerted attempt at intervention into world literature and world cinema in history – are best thought of as a challenge to the kind of world systems that Pascale Casanova and, following her, Dudley Andrew construct for their fields. Given the Wallersteinian origins of these conceptualizations, the forces moving literature and cinema in these accounts mirror the logic of global capital accumulation and circulation. In trans-lating them into the language of literary and cinema studies, we arrive at market competition (between literary and cinematic nations or individual writers and filmmakers), diffusion of narrative and genre models from the West to the East, and provincial cultural producers' desire to come closer to the Greenwich Meridian of Literature/Cinema and its ultimate aesthetic prize (modernism). Not unlike the Soviet-bloc economy, which sought to leave – or, in practice, acquire a measure of independence from – the capitalist world-system, the Soviet projects for (Third-)World literature and cinema sought to reduce non-Western cultures' dependence on the West (the literary Paris and London or the cinematic Hollywood and Cannes) for cultural imports or the very production of value by both inserting the Soviet bloc as an alternative source of such imports and fostering direct South-to-South exchanges. These projects thus aimed to replace some key operational principles of Casanova's world literature and Andrew's world cinema with their own vision of cultural circulation: Western domination with a much less hierarchical world, global markets with international institutions, competition with bureaucratic administering, and West-to-East circulation of literary and cinematic models with East-to-East (with the USSR itself as the main, but not only, source).

Imagining International Solidarity in Literature and Film

The consumption of the same literary and cinematic texts circulating within these Soviet-aligned projects was not the only source of commonality among leftist publics internationally. It very much matters what these texts were. It is by now a cliché in literary studies to say that the acts of writing and reading fiction are akin to world-making.[46] *From Internationalism to Postcolonialism* takes this cliché with a certain geographical literalness. Today literature and film can hardly compete with the news cycle in creating mental maps of the world, but we must not forget that round-the-clock, multimedia coverage in the short twentieth century, especially in Africa, Asia, and Latin America, did not yet exist. Indeed, one of David Damrosch's central claims about world literature is that – in addition to literary master-pieces – it comprises texts that offer readers windows on cultures and societies located in very different times and geographies.[47] Dudley Andrew has articulated a similar argument for world cinema.[48] The world-making we are interested in was of a more politically engaged kind than Damrosch's and Andrew's. After all, worlding was one of the Bolsheviks' operative terms: world proletariat, world revolution, world literature. Over the course of time, the power of the Bolshevik revolutionary worlding would erode, compromised by its instrumentalization in Stalinist foreign policy, by the new forces of official Soviet patriotism, and by postwar Russian nationalism. Of course, it could not simply disappear. It remained in the Trotskyist movement, which clung to international revolution as its banner, and later in transnational revolutionary movements such as Maoism, Guevarism, and even in revolutionary nationalisms of the decolonizing era, which sought to make common cause against imperialism. It remained in the USSR as well, in the form of the official and increasingly unconvincing rhetoric of Soviet internationalism. Cultural production made these worlds emotionally powerful and broad in a way that would have been impossible for political programs. But how exactly did they figure in literary and cinematic texts?

Benedict Anderson has offered probably the most convincing method of working through that question. In addition to examining the circulation of common texts and the state institutions (from school curricula to maps and censuses) that helped create national subjects, he famously analyzes the plot devices and tropes via which those national subjects were inscribed into novels, thus forcing readers to identify with the nation and experience solidarities with the millions of their countrymen they had never seen and would never see.[49] The tropes and narratives of transnational solidarity are different, often premised on distance and difference than on contiguity and similarity. International solidarity filmmakers, for example, had to show that action taken in the United States by honourable Americans could help Chinese people in their struggle against the Japanese invasion of the late 1930s. Solidarity tropes were needed for freedom fighters who had lost faith in ever winning to believe that victory and the creation of another, better world was possible, as the Chinese or Russian example showed. Films and novels also taught Third-Worldist audiences that their local struggles were a link in a gigantic chain, stretching not only across different continents but through time as well, part of the same emancipatory movement that brought out the Russian working class in 1917 and led the worldwide struggle against fascism. Solidarity could be of a negative kind, as enmity toward the often-abstract forces of capitalism and imperialism. Third-Worldist writers had to establish relationships between decisions taken in Chicago corporate boardrooms and life (and death) in Central

American banana plantations as does Miguel Asturias in his banana trilogy. *From Internationalism to Postcolonialism* examines the inscription of these transnational solidarities through tropes and narratives in a number of signature texts of postcolonial literature and Third Cinema.

While it is usually premised on overcoming a spatial separation, solidarity sometimes has a strong and often-ignored temporal dimension. For example, the attraction that Russo-Soviet culture held for non-Western audiences exhibited a major temporal lag. That is to say, all too often, the latter were interested not so much in contemporary Soviet culture as they were in that of earlier eras. Thus, despite the Soviet state's efforts to popularize post-1930 socialist-realist literature, the texts most admired by African, Asian, and Latin American writers were from nineteenth-century Russian realism as well as the works of Vladimir Mayakovsky and Maxim Gorky, which to this day constitute an obligatory element of any self-respecting leftist library in many a non-Western country. Similarly, for all the efforts to propagandize contemporary Soviet film, it was Eisenstein and Dovzhenko, Pudovkin, and Dziga Vertov whose early films and theories accounted for the lasting attraction of Third-World filmmakers to Soviet culture. This is not to say that Cold War–era Soviet culture was uninteresting to non-Western audiences: Yevgeny Yevtushenko's poetry and Chinghiz Aitmatov's prose received an enthusiastic reception in certain non-Western cultures as, occasionally, did post-Second World War Soviet films such as Grigory Kozintsev's Thaw-era *Hamlet* (1964). With the progression of the twentieth century, however, the most iconic, politically powerful cinematic images such as those of Sergei Eisenstein's films were growing older and older, giving them a somewhat nostalgic quality. The sense that inspirational nineteenth-century Russian and early Soviet literatures belonged to the past was becoming ever more palpable over the course of late socialism. The erosion of Soviet culture's affective power in the Cold War period, however, was inversely proportional to the growth of Soviet material investment in its connections with non-Western cultures.

My choice to devote comparable parts of the book to literature (Chapters 1 to 3) and film (Chapters 4 and 5) reflects the Soviet cultural bureaucracies' singling out of these two media (initially literature, subsequently film) as the main forms of cultural outreach to the societies of Asia, Africa, and Latin America. This juxtaposition allows us to study important differences and historical dynamics in the workings of world literary and world cinematic systems, which are typically studied on their own rather than comparatively. Those differences also reflect each medium's specific capacity to "cross" physical and cultural borders and "carry" politics.

On balance, such a juxtaposition reveals that literature was arguably a more familiar and comfortable terrain for Soviet cultural bureaucracies than cinema. While the value of Soviet literature was always contested by foreign critics, the combination of its predecessor – nineteenth-century Russian literature – and the resources of a superpower continued to lend the Soviet Republic of Letters indisputable cultural authority. By the Second World War, Soviet cultural bureaucracies had conceptualized alternatives to the contemporary world literary system and had even begun implementing them through international writers' congresses, visits, multilingual journals such as *International Literature*, publishing houses such as Progress, and an elaborate industry for translating foreign texts into Russian (and even into other foreign languages). This experience guided post–Stalin-era Soviet engagement with African, Asian, and Latin American cultural producers and publics.

The capital-intensive nature of film production, distribution, and exhibition and the more modest achievements and means of Soviet cinema (as opposed to Russian and Soviet literature) account for the belated and ultimately more limited character of the project for a Soviet-aligned Third-World cinema. In fact, I have purposefully avoided evoking a "Soviet Republic of Film" for the simple reason that one never quite emerged. Outside of a brief moment in the Soviet 1920s, which filmmakers worldwide have looked upon as the birth of political cinema, the Soviet state could not claim the same global cinematic pre-eminence, and in fact, distributionally and aesthetically, shared the subordinate status of African, Asian, and Latin American countries vis-à-vis Hollywood and even the Western European cinema industry. Moreover, judging by the archives they left us, Soviet cultural bureaucracies viewed cinema – unlike literature – as a profit-making industry in which Soviet films, in addition to conveying a political message to African, Asian, and Latin American audiences, were charged with earning precious foreign currency. Non-Western films – in addition to being ideologically acceptable – had to fill Soviet cinemas and thus generate revenue at the domestic box office. As a result, melodrama films that thematically had little to do with emancipatory politics reached Soviet screens and enjoyed a far greater popularity with Soviet viewers than their political counterparts, which Soviet cultural bureaucracies rhetorically championed. By contrast, most of the major Third-Worldist films and the radical (Marxist) philosophy behind them, such as Frantz Fanon's writings, were largely denied to Soviet audiences.[50]

With all these considerations in mind, *From Internationalism to Postcolonialism* proceeds though this story in chronological order. Chapter 1, "Entering the Soviet Literary Orbit, Early 1920s–Mid-1950s," offers an account of how Asian and Latin American writers entered into contact with Soviet literature in the first place. The affinities from afar, based on such writers' reading of Russo-Soviet translations and feeling a kinship with Russian writers, were harnessed by the Soviet cultural bureaucracies of the 1920 and 30s into actual engagements. The chapter examines how Comintern-affiliated institutions such as the Communist University for Toilers of the East (KUTV), the International Union of Revolutionary Writers (MORP), and its successors brought into the Soviet orbit such major writers as Nâzım Hikmet, Emi Siao, Mulk Raj Anand, and Pablo Neruda. And while the revolutionary phase of Soviet culture lasted just over a decade, soon to be replaced by a statist socialist realism, in the eyes of foreign audiences that decade lasted much longer. Radical writers and intellectuals from these societies were hardly in the business of faithfully reproducing Soviet culture; whether through creative misunderstanding or through a willful selectiveness and repurposing, they took from it what they needed for their domestic struggles.

Interrupted by the Great Terror, the devastations of the Second World War, and the earliest and sharpest phase of the Cold War with its attendant McCarthyisms and late Stalinism, Soviet literary outreach would resume only in the mid-1950s, as decolonization in Africa and Asia was gaining momentum. Chapter 2, "The Afro-Asian Writers Association (1958–1991) and Its Literary Field," follows the development of the earlier interwar-era encounters into the much more extensive and systematic Second-to-Third-World literary networks of the post-Stalin era. It offers the first historical reconstruction of the epicentre of these engagements, the Afro-Asian Writers Association, its numerous international writers congresses, the multilingual magazine *Lotus*, and literary prizes and translation initiatives, which aimed to establish direct South-to-South literary relations that would bypass the (neo-)colonial metropoles of Paris, London, or New York. Many of the writers associated with it – Sembène Ousmane, Mulk Raj Anand, Faiz Ahmad Faiz, Mahmoud Darwish, Pramoedya Toer, Ngũgĩ wa Thiong'o, and Alex La Guma – are now seen as canonical postcolonial figures and their participation in such earlier, Soviet-aligned networks has been forgotten.

Founded in 1958 in Tashkent, the Association aimed to be the literary equivalent of the Non-Aligned Movement, the Third World's main political project, except that it was very much aligned: thanks to the Central Asian writers, Soviet cultural bureaucracies were able to claim a place at the Afro-Asian table. Their efforts, however, were not supported by Soviet readers, especially the elite Western-centric intelligentsia, who showed little interest in the vast range of Russian translations of Afro-Asian literatures those bureaucracies made available to them.

If Chapter 2 concerns the geopolitics of culture and the attempt to establish (with Soviet participation) counter-hegemonic fields for the Global South, Chapter 3, "'The Links That Bind Us': Solidarity Narratives in Third-Worldist Fiction," examines the aesthetic consequences of those engagements in the realm of literature. Here, the focus is on three literary devices which the novelists of the Afro-Asian Writers Association and their Latin American peers used to textually situate their nations within a wider world. The most common device novelists resorted to in synthesizing these contradictions is the foreign-utopia topos, the novelistic evocation of foreign revolutions as an inspiration for emancipatory struggles at home. Chain narratives linking fields, mines, and factories in mid-twentieth-century Latin American novels to corporate boardrooms in Chicago or New York offer an omniscient reconstruction of a system of exploitation few readers could witness in its entirety. More limited to the realm of the nation, railway narratives in the novels of Mulk Raj Anand or Sembène Ousmane connect distant villages to provincial centres to capitals, constructing the imagined community of the new postcolonial nation and turning a technology for colonial control (the railway) into a site for emancipatory struggle. All three literary devices serve to align the emancipatory national struggles with the broader internationalism that held the political Third-World project together.

The gradual realization that film could reach even greater audiences in the non-Western world led Soviet cultural bureaucracies to invest in a similar effort in the realm of cinema. That is the subject of Chapter 4, "The Tashkent Film Festival (1968–1988) as a Contact Zone." Soviet cinema's interwar networks to the non-Western world had been much thinner and more one-sided than Soviet literature's, largely limited to the small number of Soviet films screened in a few big cities or the even smaller number of Soviet filmmakers, who shot their *kulturfilm* abroad. Inaugurated in 1968, the Tashkent Festival was meant to centralize and offer a single platform to the various institutional channels that had come to connect Soviet cultural bureaucracies and the emerging cinemas of Africa, Asia, and Latin America: Sovexportfilm's (SEF) growing network branches in the three continents, students educated at the All-Soviet Institute of Cinematography (VGIK), as well as individual filmmakers from the three continents, who professed political sympathies and cinematic debts to the USSR. The lasting legacy of the festival was that it made it possible for non-Western filmmakers to get to know each other, see each other's films, articulate a common set of grievances against the Western-dominated system of world cinema and agree on positive steps to confront it. As far as Soviet cultural bureaucracies were concerned, it also functioned as the main Soviet lens on the cinemas of the three continents, the main market where the Soviet film industry could buy films from there and sell its own, and as an opportunity to showcase its contributions to the cinemas of the three continents such as the VGIK students and graduates. Once again, the Soviet state was represented by films and filmmakers, studios and cultural bureaucrats, urban landscapes and audiences from Central Asia. However, unlike the striking success of Mexican, Egyptian, and especially Indian melodramas, political film from the three continents was either simply not purchased by Sovexportfilm or enjoyed little attention by Soviet viewers, again exposing the limits of Soviet internationalism.

Whereas Chapter 4 tells the story of the Soviet-aligned efforts to create a cinematic field for Africa, Asia, and Latin America independent of the West's, Chapter 5, "'Brothers!': Solidarity Documentary Film," seeks to establish a certain "Soviet trace" in Latin American Third Cinema of the 1960s and '70s. Following the intertwined trajectories of the Soviet Roman Karmen, the Dutch communist Joris Ivens, who developed the genre of solidarity documentary film in the battlefields of the Spanish Civil War and the Sino-Japanese War of the late 1930s, and then over the independence struggles of Indonesia, Vietnam, Cuba, and Chile, where they were joined by a younger Chris Marker, this chapter establishes a common narrative linking the Soviet and European leftist cinematic avant-garde of the 1920s and the later Third Cinema. It was in Latin America that Soviet and Western solidarity film entered into dialogue with and became a source of the cinematic practices of Santiago Álvarez, Octavio Getino, Fernando Solanas, Patricio Guzmán, and other leading representatives of the documentary Third Cinema tradition.

From Internationalism to Postcolonialism offers two conclusions. The first – more interview-based and historical – examines the place of non-Western literature and cinema in today's Russia. Contra the dominant discourses of world literature and world cinema, which focus on the emergences of novel cultural formations, the successes of transnational circulation, and the creativity of reception, it shows that, seen from the point of view of contemporary post-Soviet audiences, world literature and world cinema, which do not exist in the abstract, but are always located within a certain geographically based perspective, have dramatically shrunk over the last quarter of a century. The second conclusion – an exercise in intellectual history – addresses the largely unacknowledged ways Soviet thought and experience contributed to contemporary Anglo-American postcolonial theory. Indeed, this book ends by reversing the commonplace assertion that the post-Soviet space is postcolonial by showing the extent to which postcolonial studies is itself a post-Soviet phenomenon.

This has been a difficult book to write because of the incredible diversity of literatures, cinemas, and national traditions that fall within its purview. A single author – this one included – cannot be familiar with all of the African, Latin American, Middle Eastern, South or East Asian cultural producers who participated in these Soviet-aligned networks. The latter's institutionally structured character, on the Soviet side at least, offers a focus and coherence to this project but also makes it a somewhat one-sided one. Because the main sources of evidence have come from the Soviet archives, the cultural field reconstructed in this book risks appearing as Soviet cultural bureaucracies saw it, with all their limitations, such as growing race-blindness, lack of concern for women's representation, and a stageist understanding of historical development. These alienated a growing number of Third-Worldist cultural producers and audiences, as did those bureaucracies' efforts to control their interlocutors. As much as possible, I have sought to temper their perspective limitations using non-Soviet sources, books and films, interviews, and (auto)biographies by Third-Worldist writers and filmmakers, but it is important to acknowledge them before we begin.

Entering the Soviet Literary Orbit,
Early 1920s–Mid-1950s

He sang it with feeling,
My pal from Ukraine,
Now why should he feel
Such devotion to Spain?[1]

Mikhail Svetlov, "Grenada"

When they came to power, the Bolsheviks brought with them a whole tradition of Marxist thought on imperialism. Marx himself had left only brief and contradictory remarks on the colonial question, partly celebrating the introduction of capitalism in territories where feudalism or "the Asiatic mode of production" had reigned supreme, partly decrying "the inherent barbarism of bourgeois civilization," which truly sheds any form of respectability and bares itself fully only in the colonies.[2] Subsequent Marxist thought on the subject grew both more systematic and more unequivocal in its condemnation of imperialism. Eduard Bernstein, the famous "revisionist" of German social democracy at the turn of the century, may have famously believed in a humane "socialist colonialism," but that position was roundly denounced by the vast majority of his Marxist contemporaries, who remained committed to universalistic conceptions of equality, and hence, to anti-imperialism.[3] Thanks to Robert Young's magisterial *Postcolonialism: An Historical Introduction* (2001), we are spared the necessity of surveying the writings of the most significant pre-1917 Marxist thinkers on the colonial question, such as Rudolf Hilferding, Karl Kautsky, Rosa Luxemburg, Lev Trotsky, Nikolai Bukharin, and Vladimir Lenin.[4]

When the Bolsheviks came to power, they were in a position to transform the hitherto abstract Marxist theories on imperialism into actual policies. Their efforts went in two distinct directions: first, the Russian empire itself, that "prisonhouse of nations," as they called it, whose territories and populations they largely inherited; second, the colonial and semi-colonial societies of Africa, Asia, and Latin America. Over the course of the early years of Bolshevik power, these two sides of Soviet anti-colonialism were placed under different arms of the Soviet state (respectively, the Commissariat for the Nationalities, headed by Stalin; and the Comintern, which gradually degenerated into an arm of Soviet foreign policy), and driven by vastly different sets of political expediencies, they became increasingly decoupled. Nevertheless, their connections remained through late socialism and the Soviet state remained keen on highlighting them when it toured visitors from Africa, Asia, and Latin America through Tashkent and Alma-Ata, Samarkand and Bukhara, Tbilisi and Yerevan, touting the successes of its Asian republics, and showcasing them as a model of successful decolonization.[5] Until now, these two fields have been the provenance of two very different kinds of researchers: Soviet nationalities policy scholars and historians of Soviet foreign relations. Recent and forthcoming work by Masha Kirasirova, Artemy Kalinovsky, Adeeb Khalid, and Katerina Clark promises to bridge that gap.[6]

The Comintern remained the main site where the pre-1917 Marxist debates over imperialism continued, though now tinged with the priorities and exigencies of the Bolshevik state's politics. While the main preoccupation of the First Congress of the Comintern was the hoped-for Red Bridge over Europe, that is, a European revolution, already at the Second Comintern Congress in 1920 the colonial question absorbed a good deal of the discussion. Later that year, it would serve as the main agenda item of the Baku Congress of the Peoples of the East in September 1920.[7] With 1,891 participants drawn largely from the peoples inhabiting the neighbourhood of the Soviet Caucasus (Turks; Armenians; Russians; Iranians; Kurds; Arabs; various peoples of the Russian empire, primarily Muslim; and diverse observers such as John Reed), and famously addressed by Grigory Zinoviev, Karl Radek, and Bela Kun, this gathering was meant to consolidate Bolshevik power in the Caucasus and integrate the newly founded Turkish and Iranian communist parties into the international communist movement. Despite the misunderstandings and conflicts occasioned by the vast variety of languages, political persuasions, and nationalisms represented, by all accounts it was a momentous event that demanded nothing less than the global abolition of colonialism.[8] Examining the Congress as a linguistic attempt to rewrite the story of Babel, Nergis Ertürk has even placed it at the origin of an alternative genealogy of comparative literature.[9]

By 1922, however, the leadership of the Turkish and Iranian Communist Parties had been killed, arrested, exiled, or gone underground and no

Second Congress of the Peoples of the East was ever held.[10] Also doomed to be a one-off affair was the First Congress of Toilers of the Far East. This was a smaller, yet more coherent gathering of communists and leftist organizations from Korea, China, Japan, Mongolia, and Indonesia held in January-February of 1922 in Moscow and Petrograd, with the avowed aim of countering the division of spheres of influence in the Pacific agreed upon by the Western powers and Japan at the Washington Conference a few months earlier.[11] Indeed, as we shall see, numerous political exigencies and the sharp policy zig-zags of the Comintern meant that its initiatives and congresses, after the early wave of enthusiasm they aroused among participants, would not be followed up, dissipating the accumulated energy.

While political developments abroad would occasionally – and power-fully – reignite Soviet engagement with the non-Western world, with the dashing of hopes for a revolution in Asia and, ultimately, the rise of Stalin's "socialism in one country" thesis in the mid-1920s, the (semi-)colonial world was becoming increasingly peripheral in the eyes of the Soviet state. The fiasco suffered by the Chinese Communist Party in 1927, when its forces were massacred by the Guomindang armies, forced the Comintern to downgrade its whole involvement in Asia.[12] As the coming to power of the Nazi Party in Germany in 1933 raised the likelihood of another European war, Soviet foreign policy in the mid- and late-1930s shifted to this more pressing and existential danger at the expense of its engagements with African and Asian colonies. The final blows to Soviet anti-imperialism were dealt by the Popular-Front policy, which, among other things, called for an anti-German alliance with the two main colonial powers, Great Britain and France, and, even more dramatically, by the Great Terror of 1937–38, which de facto liquidated the Comintern and most of the platforms of Soviet cultural internationalism.[13] The domestic nationalities question, too, was "resolved" by the late 1930s with "the friendship of the peoples" formula, which reversed the earlier anti-imperialist policies of nativization and acknowledged the seniority of the older, Russian brother.[14] Thus, by the Second World War, Stalinism had blunted the two force-vectors of Bolshevik anti-imperialism.

Lest we conclude, however, purely based on Soviet historiography, that after some initial enthusiasm, the Soviet contribution to the tradition of Marxist anti-imperialism became victim to Stalinist realpolitik without yielding any fruit, let us examine it from the point of view of the colonial societies it was meant to benefit. Following what Erez Manela has called "the Wilsonian moment," the upsurge in anti-colonial activity in the years immediately following the First World War (the Revolution in Egypt, the May Fourth movement in China, and the March First uprising in Korea, all taking place in 1919, and the Non-Cooperation Movement Gandhi launched in India the following year) has been typically attributed to Wilson's promises of national self-determination and their resonance in the colonial world.[15] Independently of each other, Vijay Prashad and Stephen Smith have challenged that assertion, showing that the promises of the Declaration of the Rights of the People of Russia (2 November 1917) were not only more radical but also more influential and lasting than Wilson's:

1   Equality and sovereignty of peoples of Russia
2   Right of peoples of Russia of a free self-determination, including secession and formation of a separate state
3   Abolition of all national and religious privileges and restrictions
4   Free development of national minorities and ethnographic groups populating the territory of Russia.

In the (semi-)colonial world, as Stephen Smith has argued, this Declaration and the Appeal to the Muslims of Russia and the East, which the Bolsheviks issued a month later, resonated more powerfully than their promises of economic and social transformation. Indeed, it was the anti-imperialist commitments of the October Revolution – genuine, though decidedly secondary, as far as the Bolsheviks were concerned – that proved more resonant in the colonial world than their anti-capitalism.[16]

But the mystique and inspiration of the October Revolution – the Red Star over the Third World, as Vijay Prashad puts it – was not the only contribution the Soviet state made to the anti-colonial movement of the interwar era.[17] Toward the mid-1920s, after the successes of the international "Hands off China" and "Against the Cruelties in Syria Committee" campaigns, Willi Münzenberg's International Labour Relief (a Comintern front organization) established the League against Imperialism. That fascinating organization, whose history has been meticulously reconstructed in Fredrik Petersson's dissertation *Willi Münzenberg, the League against Imperialism, and the Comintern, 1925–1933*, represented probably the most significant attempt to unite, at least symbolically, the major anti-imperialist movements, primarily in Asia, but with some representation from Africa and the Americas.[18] The League's trajectory peaked at its first congress in Brussels in 1927, which managed to attract figures like Jawaharlal Nehru of the Indian National Congress; J.T. Gumede, president of the South African National Congress, as well as his close associate, James La Guma; Messali Hadj, of the Algerian North-African Star; Mohammad Hatta, future Indonesian Prime Minister; Ho Chi Minh; Jomo Kenyatta, Kenya's founding and long-time president; Ali Jinnah, Pakistan's first independence leader, as well as Western sympathizers such as Albert Einstein.[19] According to Petersson, the discovery of each other in Brussels, the intense conversations that took place, and the promise of future collaboration between the different anti-colonial movements left the Comintern organizers surprised and the participants euphoric.[20] Testifying to the significance of that earlier meeting, at the opening of the Bandung Conference in 1955, Sukarno would acknowledge its contribution to the anti-imperial cause, at the same time distinguishing this Comintern-led initiative from the one he was inaugurating:

> I recall in this connection the Conference of the "League Against Imperialism and Colonialism," which was held in Brussels almost thirty years ago. At that Conference many distinguished Delegates who are present here today met each other and found new strength in their fight for independence.[21]

The appeal of Soviet anti-imperialism indirectly helped the stature of Russo-Soviet literature with readers and writers from the (semi-)colonial world. As this chapter will show, however, there were more specifically literary forces that brought them into the Soviet Republic of Letters. In the first place, that was the explosive reception of Russo-Soviet literature in Asia, Africa, and Latin America in the first decades of the twentieth century and the elective affinities politically engaged writers from these continents felt for the Soviets. Over the course of the 1920s and '30s, this attraction from afar was harnessed into actual engagements. Relying largely on archival work as well as participant memoirs and biographies, this chapter delineates two transnational networks whereby writers from these continents entered the Soviet orbit. The first was a non-literary institution, the Moscow-based Communist University for Toilers of the East (KUTV, 1921–38), some of whose students, such as Nâzım Hikmet, Hamdi Selam, Emi Siao, and Jiang Guangci, would go on to become major writers and enduring liaisons between Soviet literature and their own national ones. The second were the institutions of the interwar Soviet Republic of Letters itself, the international leftist literary field that co-existed and competed with the one described by Pascale Casanova. Though aimed primarily at Western writers and readers, its force field, which took the form of international writers' congress invitations, publication opportunities at its affiliated journals and publishing houses, and ultimately, proximity to the Revolution occasionally attracted writers from the (semi-)colonial world. Thus, even before the formation of the Afro-Asian Writers movement in 1958 and a separate Second-to-Third-World literary space – the subject of Chapter 2 – Soviet cultural bureaucracies could boast a significant number of engaged African, Asian, and Latin American writers who had entered the orbit of the interwar-era Soviet Republic of Letters.

Russo-Soviet Literature in the (Post)colonial World

The story of Russian literature's reception in Africa, Asia, and Latin America in the first half of the twentieth century is too long to be meaningfully told in this section as it varied enormously depending on the state of the national literature, its connections to Russia, and political circumstances. An examination of the available scholarship, however, reveals some distinct motifs.[22] Russian literature's appeal to such audiences had as much to do with its aesthetic merits – experienced also by contemporary Western European audiences – as with factors specific to non-Western audiences. A Koreanist scholar, Heekyoung Cho, has identified the intersection of literary and geopolitical factors that made Russian literature so attractive:

> The first [reason for Russian literature's greater popularity in East Asia than any other European literature] is geographical proximity. Political and geographical contact among these countries created both the need and the opportunity to know each other's languages, causing a boom in language education ... This process drove translations of Russian literature. Another factor to consider in relation to Russian literature's popularity is that in the late nineteenth century, Russian literature entered the realm of what was known to Japanese and Koreans as world literature: an established canon of European masterpieces ... France, England, and other European countries' validation of Russian literature as "world literature" legitimated and accelerated its importation in East Asia.[23]

That is, Russia's putative "Easternness" offered the emerging Japanese, Chinese, and Korean intelligentsias a model of how to be modern without (quite) being Western, that is, without surrendering to colonialism. Though a purely extra-literary factor, the political prestige Russia gained on the diplomatic and military fields permeated the cultural field: Russia's cultural exports to Japan, such as literature, came with the imprimatur of a great Eastern power that had held its own against the Western empires. Such an image must have proven very attractive to the intelligentsias of East Asia who sought to mobilize their societies into modern nations that could face up to the threat of Western imperialism.

While the Russo-Japanese war of 1904–05 seriously diminished Russia's political stature in East Asia, the esteem enjoyed by Russian literature there seemed continually on the rise owing to the significant time lag with which the works and biographies of Tolstoy and Dostoevsky, Turgenev and Gogol reached East Asian audiences. Since the process of translation was a very indirect one, often via a European language into Japanese, and then from Japanese into Chinese and Korean, these novels came to East Asia having already been admitted into the pantheon of world literature. Thus, regardless of the Russian empire's political fortunes vis-à-vis the Western colonial powers, as far as Japanese, Chinese, and Korean audiences were concerned, Russian literature came to symbolize, among other things, the late appearance of an "Eastern" culture on the world stage and hence to acquire model status.

Even more important than this geopolitical appeal was the third reason for nineteenth-century Russian literature's popularity: its reputation for social engagement. Indeed, Chinese, Japanese, and Korean writers and intellectuals shared with their Russian counterparts a belief in literature's role as "the most effective instrument of social reform" (Liang Qichao) or "the best tool for changing Chinese national character" (Lu Xun) in an era of immense social and national upheaval.[24] "A Moral Example and Manual of Practice" is the subtitle of the main English-language study of Russian literature's reception in China.[25]

In his essay "China's Debt to Russian Literature" (1932), Lu Xun, perhaps the single most important figure in the efforts to modernize and democratize Chinese literary language, contends that:

[s]tories of detectives, adventures, English ladies and African savages can only titillate the surfeited senses of those who have eaten

and drunk their fill. But some of our young people were already
conscious of being oppressed and in pain. They wanted to struggle,
not to be scratched on the back, and were seeking for genuine
guidance. That was when they discovered Russian literature. That
was when they learned that Russian literature was our guide and
friend. For from it we can see the kindly soul of the oppressed, their
sufferings and struggles.[26]

While the truth value of such statements is beside the point, the qualities
East Asian intellectuals attributed to nineteenth-century Russian literature
ultimately reflected their own ideal of literature. The figure of Tolstoy, in
particular, acquired all the trappings of a legend. His religious-philosophical
turn after 1880 in interesting ways exemplified the Confucian ideal for a
man of letters who combines moral duty with social benevolence. The
image of the Russian writer thus came to represent the status East Asian
authors sought for themselves.

The processes of nationalization, modernization, and anti-colonial
struggle can radically reduce the autonomy of the literary field and open it
up to influence from neighbouring socio-political fields. The revolutionary
emergence of the Soviet state produced a similar effect. This extra-literary
event further bolstered Russian literature's status in the eyes of its East
Asian readers, who interpreted it teleologically, that is, as leading to, if
not causing, the Bolshevik Revolution. Seen in this light, not only the
legitimately revolutionary Gorky but also the Christian anarchist Tolstoy,
the conservative nationalist Dostoevsky, and the classical liberal Turgenev
acquired the reputation of revolutionary writers.[27]

The explosive effect of Russian literature's translation into the languages
of Africa and Asia was not solely an interwar East Asian phenomenon. The
vagaries of cultural geography, politics, and translation capacity meant that
its appeal was experienced at different times in India, the Middle East, or
Latin America. For example, even though Tolstoy and Dostoevsky and
perhaps even Soviet literature were available to elite Arab intellectuals fluent
in French or English earlier, Russian literary texts began to be translated
en masse into Arabic only in the mid-1950s and 1960s, after the successful
revolution of General Nasser's "free officers." Margaret Litvin's account
of their reception draws on contemporary critics such as Abdel Rahman
el-Abnudi:

In 1956, a new literary realism began to take shape, a school of writing that devoted itself largely to the poor the disinherited majority that had been more or less excluded from literature. Already the example of the Soviet Union as revolution, state and system of thought had exercised an influence on young writers, or, as they are called, intellectuals. Translations of Soviet books had begun to flood Egyptian bookshops, and the great Russian classics at last became available, to many of us for the first time. The great novelists and poets Dostoievski, Shulokhov [*sic*], Gorki, Pushkin, Mayakovski were, as it were, knocking on our doors ... A great wave, you could say, was breaking over the old, established literature, breaking it apart.[28]

The startling simultaneity implied in this list – the concurrent arrival of Dostoevsky's and Sholokhov's novels, Pushkin's and Mayakovsky's poetry – collapses time and situates all Russo-Soviet literature in the single historical context of the 1917 Revolution and its emancipatory promise. Indeed, the randomness and haphazardness of the reception of Russo-Soviet transla-tions, the unexpected readings that no authors could have ever foreseen, which often had more to do with Nasser-era cultural politics than with the Russian historical context, the powerful role of domestic and international affairs in the creation of literary meaning in Litvin's account typify the process through which Soviet literature reached many Afro-Asian readers. Also common was the enthusiasm about Russo-Soviet literature among left-wing writers and critics invested in literary representations of "the people" (what Abdel Rahman el-Abnudi calls "new realism").

Realism (of a socialist kind) is the common aesthetic M. Keith Booker and Dubravka Juraga identify in the Soviet and post-independence African novel. Instead of taking this comparison to denigrate both literatures, as has been done before, Booker and Juraga insist on the existence of specific aesthetic criteria different from Western ones and on the necessity of judging African or Soviet literary texts on their own terms rather than by the kind of modernist aesthetics that does not really fit them.[29] Though skipping the Soviet novel and focusing instead on nineteenth-century Russian and Cold War dissident writing (Alexander Solzhenitsyn, Milan Kundera, Czesław Miłosz, and Danilo Kiš), Monica Popescu reaches a similar conclusion about East European literature's capacity to inspire South African writers "to imagine new themes and narrative strategies or to reflect anew on the relationships between literature and society."[30] Yet, as the following quote from J.M. Coetzee's "The Essays of Joseph Brodsky" illustrates, even the East European dissidents' appeal is set in the mould of the nineteenth-century Russian writers and relies on the institutionalized literature-centrism of the Soviet(-bloc) state:

> [t]he prestige of the poet figure ... since Pushkin, the example of the great poets in keeping the flame of individual integrity alive during Stalin's dark night, as well as deeply embedded traditions of reading and memorising poetry, cheap editions of the classics, and the near-sacred status of the forbidden text in the samizdat phase ... contributed to the persistence in Russia, before the great opening up of the 1990s, of a large, committed, and informed public for poetry.[31]

Coetzee probably stands out in the above line of interpreters of Russian literature located outside of Western Europe and North America, and not only because of the later date of his statement (1996). To a far greater extent than in the West, in such literary geographies, the translation, publication, interpretation, and reading of nineteenth-century Russian and Soviet literature remained a monopoly of the political left and Solzhenitsyn never loomed as large there as he did in France, Germany, or the United States in the 1970s.

Russo-Soviet literature's appeal to Third-Worldist writers and critics was hardly a question of faulty optics. There was a historical basis to that feeling of kinship for the Russians: the sheer thinness of the layer of Western-educated, literature-centric elite ("the intelligentsia") surrounded, and in fact defined, by their dual relationships to the illiterate, largely rural populace ("the people") and to the oppressive imperial state. The ideological configurations possible in this environment and especially the writer's choice to side with the former against the latter account for the affective and elective affinities between twentieth-century (post)colonial writers and their nineteenth-century Russian predecessors. In fact, the main intellectual currents within the Russian intelligentsia of the 1840s, from the Slavophiles' insistence on Russian distinctiveness vis-à-vis the West and the Westernizers' adoption of "Europe" as the main developmental model to the later revolutionary populism of the 1870s, and subsequent avant-gardist strategies stemming from disappointment with "the going to the people," prefigure the main intellectual positions available to pre-/post-independence intellectuals in

Afro-Asian societies. Such a social structure in both cases meant a very close relationship between the intelligentsia's literary output and the political sphere. In other words, the literary fields in both nineteenth-century Russia and most early-twentieth-century African and Asian societies had not achieved the kind of autonomy they enjoyed in societies such as those in France or England on the basis of which universal literary histories are written. Literary utterance in such synthetic space could not help being political. The absence or defectiveness of institutions of representative democracy in colonial or otherwise authoritarian regimes essentially meant that literature fulfilled some of the political field's functions. The nineteenth-century Russian tradition of literary journals operating as de facto political parties became the norm in many Afro-Asian societies.

Seen in this light, Sajjad Zaheer's biographical trajectory, from a poet and co-founder of the All-India Progressive Writers Association before the 1947 Partition to the general secretary of the Pakistani Communist Party, with occasional spells in prison, appears perfectly logical.[32] Also typical of mid-twentieth-century writers from decolonizing societies was the sheer scope of his writings – poetry, novels, translations of Shakespeare into Urdu, journalism, memoirs, and Marxist theory. Not unlike their nineteenth-century Russian predecessors, most writers of fiction and poetry from the initial postcolonial period also doubled as social critics. Indeed, as the Leningrad-educated Nigerian critic Fidelis Odun Balogun observed, in such circumstances, "there is no strict professional boundary between the writer and the critic."[33]

African societies, which were for the most part the last to acquire formal political independence and national literary traditions, offer the clearest illustration of the literature–politics nexus. A mere listing of post-independence African political leaders will include a number of writers, whether poets, such as Leopold Senghor (president of Senegal), Marcelino dos Santos (vice-president of Mozambique), and Agostinho Neto (president of Angola), or political theorists and non-fiction writers, such as Kwame Nkrumah (president of Ghana), Julius Nyerere (president of Tanzania), Jomo Kenyatta (president of Kenya), Sekou Toure (president of Guinea), and Amilcar Cabral (leader of the Guinea-Bissau independence movement). One struggles to think of a single contemporary writer who occupied a similar position in a twentieth-century Western European society.[34] Even if the majority of African, Asian, and Latin American writers ultimately never served in government, owing to the relative lack of autonomy of their literary field, their voices were heard more often in the political realm than those of their Western counterparts, a position they shared with the Russians.

Communist University for Toilers of the East (KUTV)

These affinities and the consequent appeal Russo-Soviet literature exercised on many (semi-)colonial writers in the interwar period set the stage for actual engagements between them. One of the major platforms of this initial contact was KUTV, a Moscow-based university meant to prepare young people from the Soviet East for building socialism at home and students from the foreign East (Africa, Asia, and Latin America) for anti-colonial revolutions in their own society.[35] Other institutions such as the Comintern itself may have brought far greater numbers of politically engaged foreigners to the USSR, but no other institution had as great a literary significance. Founded in 1921, KUTV counted among its alumni a number of writers who not only became major figures in their own right but also served as their national literature's main liaisons with the world of Soviet letters: Nâzım Hikmet, the modernist poet and best-known Turkish writer internationally before Orhan Pamuk, as well as three of his compatriots: Vâlâ Nureddin, Nizamettin Nazif Reşat Fuat Baraner, and Zeki Baştımar; Hikmet's friend Xiao San (Emi Siao), a Chinese poet, translator of Russian literature into Chinese, and the editor of the short-lived Chinese version of the *International Literature* magazine in the 1930s; Jiang Guangci, another revolutionary Chinese writer, translator from Russian, and one of the founders of the League of Left-Wing Chinese Writers; his friend and fellow poet and translator Qu Qiubai; the Iranian poet Abdol-Hossein Hesabi, who remained in the USSR as an Iran scholar and exilic leader of his country's Communist Party before being purged, together with many fellow Moscow-based Comintern cadres, in 1938; Najati Sidqi, a Palestinian short-story writer, literary critic, and one of the translators who first introduced Maxim Gorky and Anton Chekhov to broad Arab audiences; Ho Chi Minh, maybe better known for other achievements, but also the author of the cycle *Prison Poems* written in Guomindang captivity in 1942; Hamdi Selam, who escaped his native Egypt for Moscow at the age of twenty, and spent the rest of his life in that city (except for a five-year stint in GULAG), working as a physician, a writer of proletarian novels, and one of the very few scholars of Arabic during the late-Stalin era, who helped train the much larger generation of post-Stalin-era Arabists, as well as scores of Soviet Asian writers, many of whom were foundational for their own national literary traditions.[36] Many of the latter were graduates of KUTV's literary seminar. Forgotten for many years, KUTV has recently been brought into the scholarly limelight it long deserved.[37] For the purposes of this chapter, it is in its role of attaching many Asian, Latin American, and African writers to the broader world of Soviet letters, institutionally, culturally, and sentimentally, that KUTV is most valuable. Moreover, the vast majority of them did not arrive there as writers but as youth in their late teens and early twenties and the experience of KUTV was formative in their literary trajectories. While other pathways, too, led non-Western writers to Moscow, only KUTV could provide its alumni with deep knowledge of Russian – so valuable for translation, interpretation, and cultural mediation – and lived experience of the Soviet Union. They qualitatively stand out among the cultural intermediaries between the Soviet Republic of Letters and several non-Western literatures.

KUTV's legacy extended beyond the literary. Over the course of the 1920s, the university became one of the centres for interwar Soviet area studies, eventually coming to host the Research Institute of National and Colonial Problems and publish its own scholarly review, *Revolutionary East* [*Revoliutsionnyi Vostok*], and its supplements *Materials on National and Colonial Problems* [*Materialy po national'no-kolonial'nym problemam*] and *Problems of China* [*Problemy Kitaia*].[38] The scholarship featured in these journals, of course, was in no way Weberian, but very much geared toward the needs of the Eastern Secretariat of the Comintern's Executive Committee. While there were several other centres for Oriental studies in Moscow and Leningrad, none of them had as many scholars from the societies they were studying, who would usually be selected as graduate students from among the more talented and politically reliable undergraduates. KUTV became the main Soviet hub of African scholarship, where Comintern cadres such as the Hungarian foreign minister Endre Sik; Ivan Potekhin, who would go on to become the first head of the Institute of Africa in 1959; and Alexander Zusmanovich, who would be arrested during the anti-cosmopolitan campaign of the late 1940s, taught the likes of Moses Kotane, J.B. Marks, Edwin Mofutsanyana, Albert Nzula, future leaders of South African communism and editors of *The Negro Worker*. The closure of KUTV and its affiliated research institute meant that Soviet African studies had to start virtually from scratch in the late 1950s.[39]

Figure 1.1   A group photo of KUTV students taken before 1933. Fifth from the left in the middle row is the Iranian Kudrat Ali Shakhbazov, first an undergraduate, then a graduate student, and teacher at the university.

Over the fifteen or so years of its existence, this university educated over a dozen CP general secretaries, several country leaders, as well as hundreds of martyrs for the cause, or victims of internal repressions. Its alumni populated prisons across Asia and Africa. Theirs were extraordinary lives. Ho Chi Minh's '23 and Deng Xiaoping's '25 may be better known than most but were no more unusual than the others. The Indian M.N. Roy may have been more mature than most students, having served as a founding figure for both the Mexican and, subsequently, the Indian Communist Parties, and then famously having argued against Lenin's proposal of a popular front with the colonial bourgeoisie at the Second Congress of the Comintern. Another adult student was Sen Katayama, an earlier member of the Communist Party of the United States and a co-founder of the Japanese Party. Though the Kurd Khalid Bakdash arrived at KUTV in 1933 aged only twenty-one, he was no callow youth either. He had already done time in prison in French-mandate Syria, translated *The Communist Manifesto* into Arabic, and become a communist in the process. Within two years of arriving in Moscow, he would head the Arab delegation to the

Seventh Comintern Congress; within three – the whole Communist Party of Syria, a position he would hold for nearly sixty years. Yusuf Salman Yusuf (Comrade Fahd) '37 enjoyed a briefer and more tumultuous tenure in the Iraqi Communist Party (1941–49), which he ran from prison for much of the time, before being hanged by the country's Hashemite authorities at the respectable age of forty-six. His body was left to hang on the gallows, as a warning to the restive population.

Shortly after graduating from KUTV in 1931, at the age of twenty-eight, Nikos Zachariadis was appointed the general secretary of the highly faction-alized Greek Communist Party (KKE) and embarked upon a vast expansion of its membership and representation in unions, parliament, and other social structures. Within five years, he would be arrested, spending the next decade in Greek, Italian, and German prisons and camps. Liberated from Dachau at the end of the Second World War, he returned to Greece, regrouping KKE and leading it through a bloody civil war, practically with-out Moscow's support. After its defeat in 1949, he settled with the remnants of KKE in a Tashkent exile, until 1956. That year "the Greek Stalin," "the die-hard Nikos" openly condemned revisionism, the attacks on "the cult of personality," and Khrushchev himself, following which he was forcibly removed from his position. The final seventeen years of his life he spent in Siberian exile, first in Yakutia, then in Surgut, working in the local forest department. In 1973, aged seventy, having tired of pleading to the Soviet authorities to be allowed to return to Greece, he hanged himself.

Indeed, KUTV was no mere pipeline of servile individuals always look-ing up to Moscow for instructions. The Comintern archives testify to the outspokenness within KUTV's classrooms and dormitories. In one instance, the Japanese student section launched an open letter to the university authorities demanding the revision of certain overly constricting rules (going to bed by a certain hour), the overhaul of the curriculum to better adapt it to the practical needs of launching a communist revolution in Japan, and conditions better suited to studying (no luxury, but a desk and a chair for every student). In the same letter, they also challenged the decision of the university authorities to expel their Korean classmates and countered the administration's claim that the Koreans were poor students, unsuitable to revolutionary work, with their own investigation. More than the content of these demands, what is striking is their defiant tone.[40]

But it is the postgraduate KUTV trajectories that are even more telling of their rebelliousness. Abandoning the Moscow kind of communism was fairly common, as evidenced by the future pan-Africanist thinker George Padmore and Kenya's independence leader Jomo Kenyatta. Padmore remained within the Communist movement for a few more years, as the editor of *The Negro Worker* and one of the main organizers of the International Trade Union Committee for Black Workers before he parted ways with it in 1934 over his increasing disenchantment with the Soviet reluctance to help Ethiopia, then under attack by fascist Italy.[41] His subsequent work and thought was dedicated to the elaboration of an African socialism, which his mentee, the Ghanaian president Kwame Nkrumah, sought to implement. Kenyatta was even quicker than Padmore in abandoning Comintern networks and the version of pan-Africanism he eventually came to espouse over his fourteen-year-long presidency of Kenya was shorn of Padmore's socialism. Chinese Trotskyism was born within KUTV's campus, or more precisely, at its sister institution, the University for the Toilers of China, which had initially emerged from and was subsequently reunited with KUTV.[42] Another possible trajectory was explored by Chiang Ching-kuo, Chiang Kai-shek's son, who completed KUTV in the early 1930s, remained a hostage in the USSR until 1937, and finally became president of the Republic of China (Taiwan) after his father's death.

The careers of KUTV's Soviet graduates (as we mentioned earlier, the university had two sections, one devoted to preparing cadres for the colonial world, the other for the Asian republics of the USSR and Russia's autonomous republics) were equally illustrious (and sometimes as truncated). Upon graduation, they were typically sent to populate the ranks of the communist party of their republic under the policy of nativization (*korenizatsiia*).[43] Many vertiginous careers such as that of Torekul Aitmatov '25 were cut short in 1937–38, when the purges decimated the republican and regional branches of the Party. Born in a Kyrgyz village close to the Chinese border in 1903, Aitmatov would, upon graduating KUTV at the age of twenty-five, become the head of the Council of People's Economy of the Kyrgyz Soviet Republic. At thirty, he was already the second secretary of the CP of Kyrgyzia. At thirty-four, during the Great Terror, he would be arrested for "nationalism" (the main rubric under which communist cadres and intellectuals from the republics were being purged) and shot within a year. Decades later, his son, the pre-eminent Soviet Central Asian novelist Chinghiz Aitmatov, would commemorate his death in his masterpiece *The Day Lasts Longer than a Hundred Years* (1980). Khasan Israilov '36 led the desperate Chechen insurgency during the Second World War (also known as the Rebellion of

Khasan Israilov), following which the Soviet authorities deported the whole Chechen and Ingush population to Kazakhstan. His death in December 1944, at the age of thirty-three, marked the formal end of the rebellion.

Not everybody died so young, of course. The couple Salchak Toka '29 and Khertek Anchimaa '35 served, respectively, as the prime minister and head of parliament of the Tuva People's Republic, a formally independent state but practically a Soviet satellite on the border with China (1921–44). In this role, to which she was elected at the age of twenty-eight, Khertek Anchimaa was the world's first female non-hereditary head of state until 1944, when she and her husband presided over the transformation of their country into an autonomous republic of the Russian Federation. (Another KUTV graduate, Yanjimaa Sükhbaataryn '30, became the second such woman when she was briefly president of Mongolia in 1953–54.) Upon retiring from active politics, Salchak Toka devoted himself to writing prose, becoming the chair of the Tuvan Writers Union.

For all the stellar biographies KUTV helped launch, it has received little scholarly attention. The measure of secrecy surrounding it certainly did not help. Upon arriving in Moscow, foreign students would assume a nom de guerre and practise a good deal of secrecy, for no hero's welcome awaited the Moscow-trained revolutionaries upon returning to their countries. Although many never reached the age at which memoirs are written, we still have a few autobiographical chapters about KUTV. One of these belongs to the "the enigmatic Jerusalem Bolshevik," as one article devoted to the Palestinian poet Najati Sidqi calls him, and describes how he ended up in Moscow:

> At the time [1921], I was a young man employed in the Department of Post and Telegraph in Jerusalem, which was located in the old compound of the Italian Consulate, across the street from what is Barclays Bank today [1939]. That is, it was located at the borders separating the Arab areas from the Jewish areas outside the city walls. The postal department included employees from both groups and a variety of ethnicities and life-styles ... In the department, we used to associate with Jewish immigrants, either as workmates or through socializing ... Some of these immigrants would invite me to their club behind the German hospital in Jerusalem. There I learned about the arrest of their comrades in Egypt and about the death in prison of one of the militants, a Lebanese Arab, after

a prolonged hunger strike. They used to distribute an Arabic newspaper – *al-Insaniyya* – published in Beirut by Yusif Yazbek. They also gave me a pamphlet in Arabic by Prince Kropotkin on anarchism. We used to meet alternately in the club and the Shniller forest. Occasionally, we met in the hills of Ratzbone. One day at the end of 1924, when I was only nineteen, my comrades asked me if I would be interested in traveling to Moscow to study at the university without paying for travel, education, or living expenses. I did not hesitate for a moment. They asked me to prepare for travel within six months. I started by taking private lessons in elementary Russian from a young Russian immigrant who knew some Arabic. He taught me the alphabet and some basic rudimentary conversational skills. During this period the group invited me to their youth conference in Haifa, where I was elected to the central committee of the party's youth section. That was my formal initiation into the Bolshevik movement in Palestine. From that day, I was expected to attend all the movement's clandestine meetings and to distribute the party's leaflets and brochures.[44]

Like other alumni memoirs I was able to find – "the Black Bolshevik" Harry Haywood's, Nâzım Hikmet's, Emi Siao's, Tan Malaka's, Qu Qiubai's – Sidqi's recollections focus on the lingering effects of war communism and other encounters with Russian realities, on the mesmerizing effect of Russian women on visitors, and the author's relationships with students from their (language) section.[45] Another motif common to these texts is the prevailing sense of a conscious encounter with History or at least preparation for it. In a revealing episode, for example, Haywood tells the story of a slanderous caricature hung inside KUTV, showing him surrounded by a dozen or so beautiful Russian women at the seaside and captioned: "Comrade Haywood Doing Practical Work in a Crimean Rest Home." Upset, Haywood demands that the picture be taken down and that he be told the name of its author. His first request is granted, but the most he learns about the culprit is some "young Mexican in the Spanish language section of the school."[46] Almost thirty years later, at David Siqueiros's birthday party, Haywood discovered that the world-renowned Mexican muralist had studied at KUTV at the same time,[47] and thus, the authorship of the caricature.

As this episode suggests, getting to know students from other nations was made difficult by the fact that all members of a single linguistic section studied and lived together.[48] As we learn from Najati Sidqi's memoir, there were, however, a few personalities who could not be contained within their own linguistic section:

> Each national group had its own activities. The most active was the Turkish group, which was headed by the poet Nâzım Hikmet. He was a young man of twenty-five when I met him, tall with blond hair and blue eyes and a ruddy complexion. Constantly moving and full of energy, he used to wear golf pants and a jacket almost fully buttoned up and would stand among the Turkish students declaiming revolutionary poems he had composed. The students would then move on to a comic performance ridiculing the Turkish sultans. Someone would ride around on a broomstick, saluting the people left and right, while his classmates would recite the sultan's anthem in a derisive way.
>
> When he asked me my name, I told him that my university name was Mustafa Kamil. A shudder passed through him and he said, "What?! Mustafa Kemal? Who gave you this name, who?" I told him that it was Mustafa Kamil, the Egyptian nationalist leader, not Mustafa Kemal. He still did not like the name, as he said it caused confusion between "freedom" and "despotism," and suggested that it be changed to Mustafa Sa'di to honour the Persian poet. This was how ties of friendship were established between Nâzım Hikmet and me. He invited me to visit the Turkish students often and even insisted that I join their group and attend their meetings, since both our peoples until the recent past had been living under the same despotism.[49]

Another of Hikmet's cross-sectional friendships, with the Chinese poet Emi Siao (Xiao San), the future editor of the Chinese version of the *International Literature* magazine, functions as one of the central plots of Hikmet's own semi-autobiographical novel *Life's Good, Brother* (*Yaşamak Güzel Şey Be Kardeşim*), written shortly before his death in 1962. Their friendship in the novel is mediated, or rather complicated, by a beautiful Russian blonde, Anushka, whom they both love and who appears to share their feelings. A similar love triangle structures Hikmet's narrative poem *Giaconda and Si-Ya-U* (1929).[50]

But it was KUTV's inner, that is, Soviet, section that produced the greatest number of writers. Reconstructing the literary education the university gave them is no simple matter. Certainly, the university's location in Moscow's centre – near today's Izvestia building, next to Pushkin Square – made it easy for the young men and the smaller number of women sent to the university from the distant provinces of the former Russian empire to attend literary and poetry readings and witness debates among the major participants in 1920s Russian culture. In addition to formal courses, there was a student-run literary seminar, founded by Utebai Turmanzhanov '25, who would go on to become one of the first Soviet Kazakh poets, prose-writers, folklorists, and children's writers. The seminar even published its own literary-political journal, *Star of the East* (*Zvezda Vostoka*), though I have been able to find only one issue from 1922. As nationalities were being forged in Central Asia, the Caucasus or Russian Siberia in the 1920s, they all had to have national literatures, and national writers, too. The Gorky Literary Institute, which would take on the responsibility of training them, was founded only in 1933 and did not graduate its first class until the late 1930s. In the all-important years prior to that, it was the KUTV that educated some of the poets, novelists, playwrights, folklorists, and children's writers who would help develop a national literary language and write the first novel or play in it. Much of their poetry, which moved away from older farsi, Arabic, or Ottoman conventions, bringing language closer to the local vernaculars, is a paean to Bolshevik Revolution. Many of their novels, such as Magomed Mamakaev's '30 *The Murid of the Revolution* (1963) or Anton Pyrerka's '31 *Vedo's Younger Son* (1940) deal with the arrival of Soviet power in, respectively, Chechnya and the Nenets Region (an Arctic region populated by Indigenous people). Collectively, they were part of the cohort of Soviet-educated young Caucasians and Central Asians who over the course of the 1920s and '30s displaced the older *jadids* as the main intelligentsia of their nations-in-construction.[51]

The list of domestic KUTV graduates includes other leading mid-twentieth-century Soviet Asian writers: Moldogazy Tokobaev '31 (1905–1974), one of the first Kyrgyz playwrights; Sagit Miftahov '27 (1907–1942), a Bashkir playwright; Ata Kaushutov (1903–1953), a Turkmen writer and playwright, one of the founders of modern Turkmen literature; Mazhit Davletbayev '24 (1900–1938), a pioneering Kazakh poet, prose writer, and playwright; Kasy-Maly Bayalinov '33 (1902–1979), a writer, translator, head of the Kyrgyz writers' union; Akhmed Khatkov (1901–1937), an Adyghe writer, later secretary of the Adygeian Writers union; Shigabetdin Shagar (1904–1941), a Bashkir and Tatar writer; the Chuvash Prokhor Trofimov '29 (1908–1991); Pavel Kuchiak (1895–1943), an Altai poet and playwright, founder of Altai theatre and author of it classical play *Cheynish* (1938), about the Civil War in Siberia and the Soviets coming to power; and Victor Kok-ool '32, whose time at KUTV was followed by several years at the Lunacharsky State Theatre Institute and who played a similar role in Tuvan drama. Between graduating from KUTV and launching his desperate rebellion, Khasan Israilov worked as a journalist for *The Peasant Gazette* and wrote poetry and plays on the side.[52] The hunger Soviet institutions felt for republican cadres pulled many young, ambitious, and not infrequently literarily gifted people from the provinces of Soviet Asia to KUTV and into the maelstrom of Moscow literary and political life of the 1920s and '30s.

The Interwar-era Soviet Republic of Letters

Though a well-used one, KUTV was still a back door into the interwar Soviet Republic of Letters. The front entrance was maintained by the specifically literary institutions of that Republic. Focused on Western Europe and North America as they may have been, their force-field as well as the sheer appeal of the Revolution brought many Asian and Latin American writers into the Soviet orbit. As a result, the number of such authors known to the Soviet cultural bureaucracies and texts read by Soviet readers grew steadily between the early 1920s and the early 1950s, even if they remained a marginal constituency. Over this period, the Soviet Republic of Letters developed in distinct stages (the visionary Litintern, the radical MORP, the broad anti-fascist Association for the Defence of Culture, and the early Cold War–era Peace Movement) with each one, as the rest of this chapter documents, seeing the addition of new groups of non-Western writers and their texts and the development of institutions: a permanent Bureau that would conduct day-to-day activities; international writers congresses, beginning with the 1927 Moscow Conference of Proletarian Writers; a worldwide network of literary magazines and publishing houses anchored, respectively, in Moscow's multilingual *International Literature* magazine and Co-operative Publishing Society of Foreign Workers in the USSR (ITIR) and the larger Soviet translation project; and the post-Second World War Peace Prize meant to establish an alternative literary canon.[53] Thus, the

Figure 1.2   A cover page of the first, 1932, issue of *International Literature* in English.

literatures of the USSR and Africa, Asia, and Latin America had already experienced their first encounters even before the massive Soviet outreach of the post-Stalin era.

Soviet literary internationalism was announced in the midst of the Civil War. In August 1920, during the Second Congress of the Comintern, the Temporary International Proletkult Bureau was announced, counting Comintern delegates such as the writers Anatoly Lunacharsky, John Reed, and Raymond Lefevbre among its numbers. To the best of my knowledge, it never reconvened. At the next Comintern congress, the third, in 1921, the idea of a Litintern – the literary equivalent of *The Communist International* – was broached but quickly forgotten.[54] The Fourth Comintern Congress in 1922 counted among its members Claude McKay, the Jamaica-born pioneer of the Harlem Renaissance, who famously delivered "The Report on the Negro Question." He was the first of a whole procession of African-American writers to make his pilgrimage to the land of the Bolsheviks, attracted by their promise for a worldwide struggle against class and race oppression.[55] Over the course of the several months McKay spent between Moscow and Leningrad, he met a number of Russian writers and read his poetry to Russian audiences. Even if he later recounted his Soviet experiences in

Figure 1.3   Claude McKay delivering his "Report on the Negro Question" to the
4th Congress of the Comintern, November 1922. Karl Radek, Clara Zetkin, and other
communist leaders are in the background.

essays and autobiographical texts, his disillusionment with the Soviet state
meant that he never returned to Moscow.[56] But even without making it to
the USSR, a number of African-American artists and writers of the 1920s
and '30s, whom Steven Lee has called "the ethnic avant-garde," actively
followed the Soviet avant-garde's effort to transform society.[57]

With the country's resources still absorbed by the Civil War and given
the state of international isolation, visionary initiatives such as the Litintern
were doomed to remain on paper. While remaining under the overall
auspices of the Comintern, these early plans for an international writers
organization were drawn under Proletkult, the mass organization that
envisioned the creation of proletarian culture out of the ashes of the old
bourgeois culture.[58] As of the mid-1920s, after Proletkult's decline, those
internationalist initiatives would be taken up by the Russian Association of
Proletarian writers, the notorious RAPP, which was a very different kind
of organization: smaller, highly sectarian, and more party-minded, that is,
trying to reflect and anticipate much more closely the policies of the Soviet
party-state.[59] Consequently, its vision of internationalism, of the foreign

writers, texts, and readers it would seek to connect with and the terms of that engagement, would bear these hallmarks. As RAPP was at war with Soviet futurism and insisted on realist art, for example, no foreign avant-gardist, even card-carrying party members, could pass its "revolutionary" standard. On the other end of the spectrum, RAPP's intolerance for fellow travellers meant that even realist giants broadly sympathetic to the Soviet project such as Romain Rolland would be targets of harsh criticism rather than recruitment. Henri Barbusse himself, a committed communist and a realist whose *Clarté* group (1919–21) was one of the earliest organizations of leftist literary internationalism and whose *Monde* journal served as the flagship literary journal on the French left in a later period (1929–35), would also become subject to RAPP's occasional virulent attacks.[60]

Even in the words of one of its founders and secretaries, the Moscow-based Hungarian exile, novelist, and RAPP member Bella Illes, the early efforts of the International Bureau of Revolutionary Literature (MBRL) to unite national proletarian writers' organizations worldwide were doomed because such organizations did not exist at the time.[61] For a time, the Bureau – best thought of as an organizing committee for a future proletarian writers' organization – claimed an international status thanks to a few minor foreign communist writers living in or visiting Moscow such as the (Romanian-born) German Heinrich Heinz-Kagan, the Italian Edmondo Peluso, the Romanian Al. Zalik, the Latvian Sigizmund Valaitis as well as the Bureau of National Minorities at the Moscow Association of Proletarian Writers. Some KUTV students such as Nâzım Hikmet, Hamdi Selam, and M.N. Roy would occasionally join their discussions.

MBRL thus continued to exist, mostly as an unpronounceable acronym, until 1927, when it announced itself to the broader literary world. The occasion was typical: not a Comintern Congress this time, but a more populous celebration of the tenth anniversary of the October Revolution in November 1927. The sheer number and prominence of the foreign writers in attendance, however, became an occasion for an improvised meeting of foreign and Russian writers presided over by the Commissar of the Enlightenment, Anatoly Lunacharsky. The delegates' speeches, published in a special issue of the RAPP journal *Na literaturnom postu*, were meant to offer a brief snapshot of the state of proletarian letters in each of the countries represented.[62] The event (only retrospectively called the First International Conference of Proletarian and Revolutionary Writers) apparently convinced the assembled delegates that they were witnessing the birth of an international movement. The thirty or so participants, coming from eleven countries, had only happened to be in Moscow for the festivities and represented no one in particular.[63] The non-Euro-American world was represented by Sen Katayama and the Mexican philosopher Samuel Ramos, each of whom spoke about the state of politically engaged literature in their part of the world.

The Second Conference of Proletarian Writers held in November 1930 in Kharkov was a much more ambitious and better organized affair, bringing to the Ukrainian city of Kharkov 120 writers from 22 countries. More importantly, however, these writers were already representing genuine proletarian writers' organizations, a number of which had emerged between the two conferences. This time Asian and Latin American literatures were represented by actual writers: Emi Siao, from China; the Arab Hamdi Selam (both KUTV alumni); Katsumoto Seitiro and Fudzimori Seikiti from Japan; and the Brazilian Salvador Borges (born Betsalel Borodinny, he had emigrated to Brazil from his Ukrainian shtetl on the eve of the First World War). It was in Kharkov that MBRL's mission – uniting national proletarian organizations – was formally fulfilled with the inauguration of the International Union of Revolutionary Writers (MORP).

The place of these future Third-Worldist writers, of course, was marginal in comparison to that of the more illustrious participants of that conference such as Louis Aragon, Johannes Becher, Ludwig Renn, Harold Haslop, Michael Gold, or Bruno Jasenski. Nevertheless, some lasting East-West connections were forged at Kharkov such as the decades-long friendship between Emi Siao and Anna Seghers.[64] But what is more important was that they were speaking on behalf of organized groups of proletarian/left-wing/revolutionary writers. While the literary and political powerhouses of Germany and France had the biggest proletarian writers' movements, and published important literary journals, proletarian arts organizations had also emerged in Austria, the Baltic states, Belgium, Bulgaria, Czechoslovakia, Hungary, Poland, and the USA, where the famous John Reed Clubs attracted many young and aspiring writers, such as Richard Wright.[65]

Most relevantly, proletarian writers' organizations were founded in China, Japan, and Korea, which played a significant role in the literary histories of their countries. The Soviet example was infectious, but it was an internal Chinese dynamic and initiative that led the major politically engaged writers of Shanghai – China's literary capital of the time – to establish the League of Left-Wing Writers in March 1930. Of its founding members, only "the youngsters," Qu Qiubai, Emi Siao, and Jiang Guangci, whom we met earlier as KUTV students, had spent time in the USSR and knew Russian. Even without knowing any Russian, however, the League's heavyweights, from Lu Xun, arguably the foremost figure in modern Chinese letters, to Guo Moruo, the future president of the Chinese Academy of Sciences, and Mao Dun, the PRC's future minister of culture, were translating both pre-Revolutionary Russian and Soviet literature, via Japanese, English, or French.[66] Typical of CP-affiliated organizations of Comintern's revolutionary but sectarian Third Period (1928–34), the League waged sectarian polemics over "deviations" against writers and groups who could have easily been its allies.[67] It dissolved in 1936, in response to the Popular Front policy of abandoning narrower, party-aligned forms (MORP had remained under Comintern's auspices) in favour of broader coalitions with socialists and liberals against the primary enemy (in the case of China – Japanese imperialism). However, in the six years of its existence, the League of Left-Wing Writers united hundreds of writers and millions of readers via a network of sympathetic publishing houses and literary journals, such as *Mass Literature* and *Pioneer*. The careers it launched continued to shape Chinese literature for decades to come.[68] The Moscow-based multilingual literary quarterly *International Literature*, one of the most visible platforms of the Soviet Republic of Letters, even experimented with a Chinese version in 1935 under Emi Siao's editorship.

A similar proletarian writers' organization had emerged in Japan even earlier. The Japanese Federation of Proletarian Arts (NAPF) had formed in 1928 out of the merger of two earlier writers' organizations, subsequently adding others in the realm of visual culture, Esperanto, and so on. The first issue of its main monthly magazine, *Senki* (*Battle Flag*) came out in May of that year, reaching in 1930 – the peak year of the movement, before repressions severely curtailed it – a circulation of 30,000 copies and introducing Japanese readers to the classics of Soviet and global proletarian literature. As we saw earlier, having learned of the forthcoming Kharkov conference from the pages of the German *Linkskurve* and the American *New Masses* magazines, two Japanese proletarian writers, Katsumoto and Fudzimori, showed up in Kharkov to report on the state of Japanese letters and participate in the heated discussions over an international proletarian strategy, which was extensively discussed in Japan upon their return. NAPF was not only on the receiving end of communications with other proletarian organizations worldwide. After the murder of the young Japanese proletarian writer Takiji

Kobayashi by the police in 1933, his 1929 novel *The Cannery Ship* became probably the best-known Japanese literary text abroad thanks to numerous translations by leftist publishing houses globally.[69] That this novel was not translated into Russian until 1952 was no anomaly: while Moscow was the capital of the Soviet Republic of Letters, it never fully dominated that literary field, which featured plenty of relations bypassing that city.[70]

While Soviet culture and the Bolshevik revolution were powerful, if somewhat distant, inspirations, NAPF's practical communication with MORP and Western national proletarian writers' organizations remained somewhat limited, except for its short-lived Berlin Bureau in the early 1930s.[71] NAPF's most active international vector pointed to the Korean Federation of Proletarian Art (KAPF). Those connections predated "the resolution on Japanese literature" of the Kharkov Conference, which demanded that Japanese proletarian writers devote resources to help their Korean comrades, as a result of which NAPF established a formal commission on Korea and facilitated the founding of a KAPF branch in Tokyo in 1931. Texts by Korean writers and letters from Korean readers had been a regular feature of *Senki* since its beginning.[72] This relative weakness of direct ties to MORP or other proletarian literary organizations may have produced greater ideological heterogeneity (a constant motif in the organization's self-criticism) and may in fact have helped KAPF unite a number of literary, theatrical, musical, and visual arts associations and simultaneously run several different journals at its peak in the late 1920s and early '30s.[73]

Because of the increasingly repressive Japanese rule domestically, over Korea, and after 1931, over much of China, and because of the rising number of proletarian writers killed or imprisoned, magazines closed, and books censored, by the mid-1930s, all three organizations had lost their initial momentum. In Korea alone, over 200 KAPF members were arrested by the Japanese authorities in 1934. By that time, most progressive proletarian associations that NAPF was uniting had been banned. But it was the Soviet foreign policy shift of folding proletarian front organizations in favour of broader alliances with other progressive groups that led the local communist parties to pull their support from the League of Left-Wing Writers, NAPF, and KOPF.

Each of these short-lived Japanese, Chinese, and Korean literary organizations has generated volumes of scholarship on its own because of the role it played in its respective national literature.[74] However, the links that bound them to each other and to the Moscow-based MBRL/MORP have received much less scrutiny because of their somewhat secretive nature, the languages needed for such a study, and often, the political implications of such reconstructions. The only other non-Euro-American MORP section ever mentioned in the archives was the mysteriously named Eastern section represented by the KUTV Egyptian student Hamdi Selam.

As a feature of the Third Period, MORP came to an end with it. After Comintern's abandonment of that policy in favour of the Popular Front, all of MORP's national sections were dissolved or rebranded. In the Soviet case, that process coincided with the closure of RAPP in 1932 and the formation of the Writers Union in 1934. Elsewhere, however, the transition was more jarring. In an autobiographical chapter, for example, Richard Wright recollects the abruptness with which the Party pulled its support from the John Reed Clubs, whose Chicago branch he had led, to make way for the more inclusive American League of Writers.[75] The transition coincided with a shift in focus away from cultivating young, militant, proletarian writers and toward bringing into the fold better-known progressive writers regardless of the particular brand of progressivism or degree of political involvement. If in Richard Wright's case the closure of the chapter under his leadership resulted in his alienation from the Party, elsewhere the new strategy proved generative for broader literary fronts.

The anti-fascist Association of Writers for the Defence of Culture, the international literary organization that replaced MORP, may have lasted only four years, but represented the high point of the Soviet Republic of Letters and its de facto convergence with the Paris-based one of Pascale Casanova. Indeed, looking at the composition of the Association's presidium at its inaugural congress in Paris in 1935, the list of writers who agreed to lend their name to the cause of Popular-Front literary anti-fascism reads like a Who's Who of contemporary world literature: Romain Rolland, Louis Aragon, Ernest Hemingway, Langston Hughes, Thomas Mann, Bertolt Brecht, Anna Seghers, George Bernard Shaw, E.M. Forster, Virginia Woolf, W.H. Auden, Mikhail Sholokhov, Nâzım Hikmet (*in absentia*), and Pablo Picasso. What is unusual about its participants in comparison to earlier Soviet efforts of literary internationalism is not only the fame and inclusivity of the list (Virginia Woolf was no MORP material) but also the broad geographical reach.[76]

And while the Association's history is usually told as a Euro-American history, and the Popular Front, which gave birth to it, is rightly thought as marking a decline in Soviet and Western leftist anti-colonialism, it proved

Figure 1.4   The International Congress of Writers for the Defence of Culture. Paris. June 1935. In the presidium (from left to right): the American writer Waldo Frank, Ilya Ehrenburg, Henri Barbusse, and the French philosopher and writer Paul Nizan.

surprisingly congenial for Indian writers' incorporation into the Soviet Republic of Letters. The newly discovered ecumenism of the national communist parties extended the appeal of their literary initiatives. Thus, for example, if the poet Sajjad Zaheer and fellow CP members had been trying to call into existence a proletarian writers' organization in India ever since 1930, it was not until five years later that this call materialized in the form of the All-India Progressive Writers Association (AIPWA). Under the loose self-descriptor "progressive," the Association brought together an ideologically broader multilingual constellation of Indian letters that included the Nobel Prize laureate and modernizer of Bengali literature Rabindranath Tagore, Munshi Premchand ("The Emperor among Novelists"), writing in Hindi, the Urdu poet Faiz Ahmad Faiz, and Mulk Raj Anand, India's major mid-twentieth-century English-language novelist.[77]

Mulk Raj Anand's fame following his debut novels *Untouchable* (1935) and *Coolie* (1936) and his position as a Cambridge-educated resident of Bloomsbury allowed him to serve as a liaison between Indian letters and the world of politically engaged European literature.[78] While never formally a member of the Communist Party, for most of the mid-twentieth-century, he would be the main correspondent of Soviet cultural bureaucracies and the representative writer from the subcontinent as far as the Soviet reader was concerned. His prominence in the global Soviet Republic of Letters would be recognized by his position in the International Bureau of the Association of Writers for the Defence of Culture, where he was one of just four non-Western writers, together with Pablo Neruda, Nâzım Hikmet, and Emi Siao. The only other writer from the subcontinent to achieve a similar status in the Soviet Republic of Letters was Faiz Ahmad Faiz. After India's partition in 1947, which rendered him a Pakistani citizen, Faiz would become a newspaper editor, occasional political prisoner, and most relevantly to us, his country's national poet. In this last capacity, he would receive the Lenin Peace Prize in 1962 and eventually serve as the editor of the Afro-Asian Writers' Association's literary quarterly, *Lotus.* Maybe a lesser-known writer, who did not bask in the limelight like the above two, the Urdu poet Sajjad Zaheer, whom we encountered earlier, was the driving force behind the 1935 conference and its chief chronicler. After his extradition from Pakistan in 1954, where he served as the general secretary of the Communist Party, he became one of the doyen figures of the All-India Progressive Writers Association and the Afro-Asian Writers Association, dying while attending its 1973 Alma-Ata Congress. Symbolically and practically, these men helped connect the 30,000 members of the All-India Progressive Writers Association, writing in all the Indian vernaculars to the international Soviet Republic of Letters.[79]

Other than writers from the Indian subcontinent, the other major non-European group to enter the orbit of the Soviet Republic of Letters during the Popular Front era was a whole cohort of Latin American writers. They had already started trickling in at the beginning of the 1930s, when César Vallejo, the great modernist Peruvian poet, made his pilgrimages to the USSR, during the last of which he served as a delegate to the 1931 Kharkov Writers conference. His impressions of the new Soviet society are recounted in two admiring travelogues: *Russia in 1931* (1931) and the posthumously published *Russia before the Second Five-Year Plan* (1965). Soviet readers, however, encountered Vallejo as the author of the proletarian novel *Tungsten* (1931; translated in *Literature of the World Revolution* in 1932) rather than the poetry for which he is best known today.[80] But it was the call of the Spanish Civil War, one of the most literary of all wars, that brought many of the Latin American writers to the Second Congress of the Association of Writers for the Defence of Culture, held over the course of June 1937 in Valencia, Madrid, Barcelona, and Paris: Chileans Pablo Neruda, Vicente Huidobro, and Alberto Romero; the Cubans Alejo Carpentier, Nicolás Guillén, and Juan Marinello; the Mexicans Jose Mancisidor and Carlos Pellicer; the Argentinians Raul Gonzales Tunon and Anabel Ponce; and the Peruvian César Vallejo.[81] Indeed, the Spanish Civil War helped introduce Latin American literature to Soviet literary bureaucracies, publishing houses, and readers. Thus, the involvement with the literary war effort helped José Mancisidor secure not only an invitation to the USSR in 1936, on the basis of which he wrote the travelogue *120 Days* (1937) but also an enduring reputation among Soviet readers as the leading Mexican writer of his time.[82] The 1939 Russian translation of Neruda's book of poetry *Spain Is in the Heart* by the ubiquitous Soviet internationalist Ilya Ehrenburg would be the beginning of Soviet publishers' and readers' love affair with Latin America's best-known modernist poet and Nobel Prize winner.[83] Around that time, Brazilian literature made its debut before Soviet audiences with a few poems by Octavio Brandao – a Communist Party leader and minor poet – and Mario Andrade – a much more significant modernist figure – on the pages of *International Literature* even if it was not to be until 1948 that the Soviet reader would be introduced to the novels of Jorge Amado, which went on to be printed in many editions throughout the Soviet bloc, and which still stand for Brazilian literature in the eyes of most readers from the region.[84]

The main figures on the interface of Soviet literature vis-à-vis Latin American literatures were David Vygotsky, Mikhail Kol'tsov, Fyodor Kel'in, and the above-mentioned Ilya Ehrenburg. Mikhail Kol'tsov's execution in February 1940, "the case against the translators," which resulted in Vygotsky's arrest in 1938 and subsequent death in GULAG, the overriding fact of the Second World War, which cut off most literary connections emanating from Moscow, and the general suspicion of contacts with foreigners during the anti-cosmopolitan campaign of the late 1940s and early 1950s, held back those connections. For the next twenty years, it was Ilya Ehrenburg's friendships with Neruda and Amado that represented the main axes along which authors and texts would move between Soviet, and respectively, Chilean and Brazilian literatures. Thus, the canon of contemporary Latin American literature available in Russian would remain quite narrow until the late 1950s, when a new generation of Soviet Latin Americanist scholars and translators, led by Vera Kuteishchikova, her husband Lev Ospovat, and Inna Terterian, would help translate, introduce, and establish relationships with many more Latin American writers, most prominently the magical realists.[85]

Indeed, the two decades between the late 1930s and late '50s saw the retrenchment and decomposition of the Soviet Republic of Letters. The Third Congress of the Writers for the Defence of Peace, planned for 1939 in New York, never happened, most likely owing to the combined effects of the Soviet purges, which tore at the Soviet literary interface with foreign literatures, and the Molotov-Ribbentrop pact, which diminished the number of foreign writers willing to participate in Soviet initiatives. The Second World War brought an abrupt halt to most forms of literary internationalism. The Russian version of *International Literature* was closed in 1943 while three years later the foreign ones were renamed *Soviet Literature in (English/French/Spanish) Language*, reflecting the wartime transformation of the magazine's contents. An international writers' organization presiding over the Soviet Republic of Letters did not emerge until the 1950s even if detailed plans had been put forth for an International Stalingrad Congress of Writers from the People's Democracies in October 1948, which was meant to inaugurate an international writers' organization, several new literary magazines and publication/ translation initiatives. The preparatory documents deposited in the Soviet Writers Union's archives reflect the extent to which this new writers' organization was to reflect the ideological bloc character of early Cold War Soviet internationalism. In addition to much longer lists of writers from East European countries, who constituted the bulk of the invitees, invitations were meant to go out to a small number of Western literary sympathizers as well as China's trio of Guo Moruo, Mao Dun, and Emi Siao, India's Mulk Raj Anand (badly misspelled), Chile's Pablo Neruda, and Cuba's Juan Marinello. Korea and Mexico are listed, too, but the spaces devoted to the writers' names are left blank.[86]

In the absence of an international literary organization consolidating the postwar-era Soviet Republic of Letters, the World Peace Movement fulfilled this role.[87] In fact, its creation at the initiative of the Polish Workers' Party could have been one of the reasons why the Stalingrad Writers Congress never took place. They were scheduled for the same month (August 1948) and the participants in the inaugural Wroclaw Congress of Intellectuals for the Defence of Peace heavily overlapped with those meant to be invited to the Stalingrad gathering. Although not a literary organization per se, the World Peace Movement provided the main platform through which prominent foreign writers, whether party members or at least Soviet sympathizers, could cross borders, meet, and address wider publics during the first decade or so of the Cold War. Writers constitute one of the best-represented professional groups at the multiple congresses held by the movement (Wroclaw '48, Paris and Prague '49, Sheffield and Warsaw '50, Stockholm '51, Vienna '52, Helsinki '53 and so on) and its governing body, the Presidium of the World Peace Council, whose first iteration in 1952 included writers Jean Laffitte (general secretary), Ilya Ehrenburg (vice-president), Jean-Paul Sartre, Pablo Neruda, Diego Rivera, and Louis Aragon. A fuller list of Soviet sympathizers among internationally regarded writers in the first two post-Second World War decades could be gleaned from the recipient list of the yearly International Peace Prize awarded by the World Peace Council. Forgotten now, the International Peace Prize was the Communist world's answer to the Nobel, aimed at creating an alternative, state-socialist canon of contemporary writers, painters, and peace-makers.[88] Non-Western writers such as Pablo Neruda, Nâzım Hikmet, Mulk Raj Anand, Maria Rosa Oliver, Bozorg Alavi, and Guo Moruo form a significant faction among the four dozen Peace Prize and Peace Medal recipients before their reformatting in 1957.

The Peace movement's importance peaked in the earliest and sharpest phase of the Cold War, when the necessity for alternative canons of contemporary culture, science, and history was greatest. Once the Khrushchev government adopted a policy of peaceful co-existence and the accompanying opening to the West and East, the Soviet Republic of Letters was subjected to its final major reconfiguration. In the first place, investment in literary internationalism – translation and publication, sending and hosting writers – was multiplied. Second, new, specifically literary institutions were established, extracting the Republic from the broadly public intellectual and political World Peace Movement. Third, the previously singular Republic was divided into three distinct geographical entities with the resulting division of labour: the Co-ordinating Council of the Leadership of the Writers Unions, responsible for the literatures of the Warsaw Pact; the European Association of Writers, offering a platform to Soviet literature dialogue with Western Europe; and finally, the Afro-Asian Writers Association, which will be the subject of the next chapter.

The Afro-Asian Writers Association (1958–1991) and Its Literary Field

In October 1958, over a hundred writers from Asia and the emerging African nations descended onto Tashkent, the capital of the Soviet Republic of Uzbekistan. Among the list of participants we find the nonagenarian W.E.B. Du Bois, who had just flown from Moscow, having persuaded Nikita Khrushchev to found the Institute for the Study of Africa. In Tashkent, he was joined by the major figures of the 1930s literary left outside of Europe or the Americas: the modernist Turkish poet Nâzım Hikmet, the Chinese polymath Mao Dun, as well as the founding figures of the Popular-Front-era All-India Progressive Writers Association – Mulk Raj Anand and Sajjad Zaheer. Though poorly known at the time, some of the younger delegates at that meeting would go on to become the leading literary figures of their countries: the Indonesian Pramoedya Toer, the Senegalese novelist soon-to-become filmmaker Sembène Ousmane, the poet and one of the founders of Angola's Communist Party Mario Pinto de Andrade, and his Mozambican counterpart – the poet and FRELIMO politician Marcelino dos Santos. Also in attendance were some leading Russian, Central Asian, and Caucasian writers and Writers Union officials, the formal hosts of the event: the Russians, Konstantin Simonov, Nikolai Tikhonov, and Boris Polevoi; the Dagestani, Rasul Gamzatov; the Georgian, Iraklii Abashidze; the Kazakh, Mukhtar Auezov; the Tajik, Mirzo Tursun-Zade; and the Uzbek, Kamil Yashen.

The Soviet state documented the event exhaustively: in addition to the 523-page publication of the conference proceedings and Orest Mal'tsev's *Tashkent Encounters* (1959), a highly stylized book of interviews with several

Figure 2.1   Khrushchev with writers from the United Arab Republic (Egypt and Syria) at a reception in the Kremlin Palace in honour of the Writers from the Afro-Asian Writers' Association, 1958.

Afro-Asian writers, the archives of the Foreign Section of the Soviet Writers Union contain multiple clippings from foreign newspapers with articles about the Tashkent Congress that participants published upon returning to their home countries accompanied by their Russian translations.[1] And while the vast majority of those articles represent little more than expressions of gratitude to the Soviet hosts, a few more critical ones, penned by authors less favourably disposed to the USSR, predictably concern themselves with the hosts' efforts to impose their political agenda on the Congress.

One of the latter was written by the Indian poet, playwright, and journalist Krishnalal Shridharani (1911–1960).[2] His contacts with Uzbek reality, on the one hand, and the other Afro-Asian writers, on the other, form the core of his account. Both were somewhat limited and mediated by linguistic barriers and the rigid conduct of the Soviet guides and interpreters. The latter did not share Shridharani's sightseeing priorities and only unwillingly took the foreign visitors to spaces that might have contradicted the official narrative of a modernizing Soviet Central Asia. Nevertheless, Shridharani was thankful for the chance to talk to writers from other Afro-Asian countries. Like himself, he observes in the newspaper article he wrote upon his return from Tashkent, they knew all the nuances of Western European

Figure 2.2 W.E.B. Du Bois, Shirley Graham Du Bois, Majhemout Diop, Zhou Yang, and Mao Dun at the Afro-Asian Writers Conference in Tashkent, October 1958.

Figure 2.3 Mongolian writer Tsendiin Damdinsüren (at left) and one of the founders of Soviet Buryat literature Hotsa Namsaraev at the opening of the book exhibit in the Alisher Navoi theatre in Tashkent, 1958.

Figure 2.4   Poets from different countries gathered in an informal atmosphere at the home of the writer Gafur Guliam in Tashkent, 1958.

Figure 2.5   Many delegates were wearing their own beautiful and colourful clothes, which impressed the people of Tashkent. You don't see African mantles or Indian sari on the streets of Tashkent every day. In this photo: Sembène Ousmane and Majhemout Diop heading for a session of the Afro-Asian Writer Congress, 1958.

Figure 2.6   Professor Alexander Zusmanovich and the translator of African poetry Lidia Nekrasova met with young African writers, whom they previously knew only from book and journal publications. Moscow or Tashkent, 1958. (Zusmanovich had taught in KUTV's Africa section before spending several years in the GULAG, like other interwar Soviet Africanists.)

Figure 2.7   The flowers they are holding in their hands have long withered, but the friendship they gained in Tashkent continues to flourish. Nâzım Hikmet with writers from India, Georgia, Pakistan, and Uzbekistan in Tashkent, 1958.

literatures, but had never spoken to each other. Echoing most participants' fascination with Tashkent, Shridharani also keeps returning to the city's mixture of familiar Easternness and Western modernity:

> Ask very insistently of your omni-present interpreter to take you to the old town and even to the side streets off the side of the asphalted alleys and you will see clay shacks covered with hay, mosques, and even burkas. Despite the world's biggest textile factory and straight asphalt roads ... this still remains a colourful Eastern city. ... The people! Smiling and hospitable, warm and unofficial and unforced, as any Eastern peoples. Here you can see the faces, beards, and suits that will remind you of Kashmir, Darjeeling and even Bombay.[3]

Tashkent's effect on such visitors was hardly unforeseen or unintended by the Soviet hosts. In fact, the Afro-Asian Writers Congress helped inaugurate the Uzbek capital's role as a showcase city, where the Soviet state would seek to impress its Afro-Asian guests with displays of Central Asian modernity.[4] From the late 1950s until the collapse of the Soviet Union, Tashkent and Alma-Ata, Samarkand and Bukhara, and to a lesser extent, Yerevan, Baku, and Tbilisi disproportionately figured on many itineraries of African, Asian, and Latin American cultural delegations to the Soviet Union.

Indeed, Tashkent synthesized the dual, if contradictory, role the Soviet state sought to play, "a superpower offering a successful model of development and also the greatest Third-World country of all time," in Christine Evans's apt formulation.[5] Like few other Soviet cities, Tashkent captured both roles. On the one hand, the Afro-Asian visitors were hosted in the giant and ultramodern Hotel Tashkent, completed a few months before their arrival. In the opening speeches, the Uzbek hosts sought to emphasize their republic's success in overcoming the problems familiar to their African and Asian guests: poverty, mass illiteracy, the difficulties of creating a multinational state. They also extolled Soviet achievements in the cultural realm: the creation of Central Asian literatures and the elevation of the figure of the writer under Soviet rule. On the other hand, the cultural program the Soviet hosts ran specifically highlighted local Central Asian culture and performance. In this spirit, a number of visitors would be taken to the ancient cities of Samarkand or Bukhara (each several hours away from Tashkent).

Shridharani's interest in the Central Asian culture on display and praise for Soviet achievements did not keep him from complaining about the

monotony of the speeches, not all of which had much to do with literature, or the hosts' insistence on passing political resolutions written well
before the arrival of the delegates. Thus, for him and for many others,
the conference's real achievement lay not in the resolutions and planned
organizational growth of the emerging writers' movement but in the
person-to-person contacts it enabled between Asian and African writers, who had so far lacked basic familiarity with each other despite their
common schooling in the nuances of European literature. These encounters, he goes on to assert, "took place on the periphery rather than the main
conference auditorium."[6] While we should not take Shridharani's report as
representative of the experience of the Afro-Asian writers at the Tashkent
conference – for every critical newspaper article like his the archival folder
contains a dozen glowing accounts by other participants – it sheds light
on one of the most enduring and paradigmatic conflicts in the history of
the Afro-Asian Writers Association: between those writers who favoured
strong connections between literature and politics and a minority who
sought to maintain literature's independence; between the top-down official
program, drawn up by the Soviet hosts, and the unplanned encounters in
the corridors, the streets, and other spaces.

This chapter reconstructs the history of the Afro-Asian Writers
Association, which served not only as the central platform for Soviet
cultural bureaucracies' encounters with the literatures of the two continents and but also as one of the main Third-Worldist literary formations
of the Cold War era. It sought to be the literary equivalent of the newly
founded Non-Aligned Movement, except that it was aligned: the Soviet
Central Asian writers participating in it were supposed to offer a bridge
between emerging (post)colonial literatures and a post-Stalin-era iteration
of the Soviet Republic of Letters. Its vision placed it in competition with
other literary internationalisms of the decolonizing era: the postcolonial
initiatives of the CIA-sponsored Congress for Cultural Freedom (CCF),
negritude, and other Third-Worldist cultural movements, as well as the
major Maoist challenge that split the Association in the mid-1960s, resulting
in the first of its several crises. In designing the Association's structures
such as its international congresses, permanent bureau, literary prize, and
multilingual literary magazine (*Lotus*), the Soviet cultural bureaucracies
drew on their experience of earlier interwar literary internationalism. The
field of the association extended beyond these supranational structures, to
include numerous translation initiatives on the national level. This chapter

will examine only one: Progress Publishers, the largest Soviet translator, of and into, the languages of Africa and Asia. Though it had some spectacular successes with foreign readers, its efforts were not supported by Soviet ones, especially the elite Western-centric intelligentsia, who showed little interest in the vast range of Russian translations of Afro-Asian literatures that Progress and other Soviet presses and magazines made available. While it never managed to attract such readers or achieve its stated aim of breaking off from Western-dominated world literature, by the time it disappeared in 1991, the Association did forge "links that bind us," as one of its participants, Ngũgĩ wa Thiong'o, called the living connections between Afro-Asian literatures.

The Soviet (Re)discovery of Africa and Asia

Before the Thaw-era Soviet cultural bureaucracies could launch their project for Third-World literature, the two parties had to renew their acquaintance. As Chapter 1 showed, the efforts to expand the Soviet literary footprint in the colonial world came to an end in the second half of the 1930s, together with the Litintern itself and Comintern-affiliated institutions such as KUTV. And while Mulk Raj Anand, Nâzım Hikmet, and Emi Siao – participants in that earlier effort and members of the Popular-Front-era International Association of Writers for the Defence of Culture – did survive the turbulent decades in between to appear in Tashkent, many of their Soviet counterparts occupying the interface with foreign literary cultures did not. Foreign connections could prove dangerous during the purges of the late 1930s and the anti-cosmopolitan campaign of the late 1940s, both of which were tinged with spy-mania. Besides, for almost two decades between the mid-1930s and mid-1950s, the (post)colonial world had faded from the geopolitical and literary engagements of the Soviet state, leaving the latter with less expertise on and fewer links to the three continents than it had in the mid-1930s.

That was to change drastically after the 1955 Conference in Bandung, Indonesia, which inaugurated the political emergence of the Third World. Surprised by the emergence of a powerful Afro-Asian bloc, the Soviet state began to invest heavily in political, economic, and cultural connections with the newly decolonized states. In an interview tellingly entitled "What Is Mauritania? Toward the 50th Anniversary of the Soviet Committee for Afro-Asian Solidarity," the doyen of Soviet African Studies, Apollon

Davidson, tells the story of the campaign-style creation of Soviet area-studies institutions and expertise in the second half of the 1950s.[7] Academic and cultural institutions were founded, practically from scratch, scholars trained, languages learned, and exchanges established. At the same time, a similar, campaign-like expansion was taking place in Soviet cultural bureaucracies' contacts with post- or semi-colonial societies. Overall, the process paralleled the emergence of area studies in the United States.[8]

A number of characteristics distinguish this second, post-1955, edition of Soviet cultural engagement with the (post)colonial world from past initiatives. For one, the sheer scale was different: instead of clandestine support for underground movements, the USSR was now dealing with states, some very new, some very poor, but still much larger, complex entities and independent in a way that no interwar-era Communist Party from the USSR could be. The geography of those engagements was also new. Though Asian, African, and African-American cultural figures still visited Moscow, which now boasted the Patrice Lumumba People's Friendship University, the Institute of Africa, and numerous other such centres, Soviet Central Asia's cultural and economic development made it an increasingly popular destination for visiting delegations from Africa and Asia.[9] By the same token, Soviet ambassadors – actual or symbolic – to many Middle Eastern countries were heavily drawn from the Caucasus and the Central Asian republics. While such a division of labour was, in a sense, perfectly natural and aimed at showcasing the Soviet state's non-whiteness, it also left some Afro-Asian cultural producers wondering why the most famous Russian writers would never show up at their events and thus whether the Soviet Union was treating the Afro-Asian events as second-rate.[10]

The dynamic of the Cold War cultural engagements between the Soviet Union and Africa, Asia, and Latin America was quite different from those between the USSR and the Western Left. To a greater extent than was the case with Western leftists, some Afro-Asian cultural producers participated in those exchanges as representatives of their state rather than its opponents. Literary exchanges, therefore, more directly reflected the international relations between the USSR and the particular Afro-Asian state and were susceptible to a different set of geopolitical pressures. For example, if the Soviet intervention in Hungary in 1956, the Warsaw Pact crushing of the Prague Spring in 1968, the Sinyavsky and Brodsky trials, and the fate of Pasternak and Solzhenitsyn would temporarily freeze or at least immensely complicate Soviet literary relations with sympathetic Western cultural producers, their Third-Worldist peers were more sensitive to principled anti-imperialist positions and solidarity as well as the developmentalist model they saw in Soviet Central Asia. For them, far more important than the Solzhenitsyn and the Brodsky affairs were other events: the Sino-Soviet split in the 1960s, policy shifts such as Egypt's signing of the Camp David Accords in 1978, coups, and IMF agreements. The subsequent decline of the literary exchanges between the USSR and the three continents in the late 1970s and '80s was primarily a function of the state-centric nature of those exchanges as well as the Soviet state's dimming revolutionary flame rather than any imminent literary developments.[11]

The Soviet reopening to the colonial world in the mid-to-late 1950s coincided with a vast expansion in its general literary traffic vis-à-vis the West as well, achieved by relaxing censorship standards and by major investments in the translation and publication apparati and expertise in foreign literatures.[12] The re-founding of the interwar-era *International Literature* magazine under the more neutral title *Foreign Literature* [*Inostrannaia literatura*] in 1955 became one of the symbolic moments of the Soviet literary opening to world literature, after two decades of war and late-Stalinist retrenchment.[13]

It would be a mistake, however, to attribute the intensification of Soviet engagements with Africa, Asia, and Latin America in the second half of the 1950s to a purely intra-Soviet dynamic. Taking place concurrently with this new Soviet cultural opening to the world were the sweeping process of decolonization and the emergence of the Third-World as a political project of the formerly (semi-)colonial societies. Writers were quick to follow the politicians. The original Delhi Conference of Asian Writers in December 1956 explicitly modelled itself on the 1955 Bandung conference of the heads of states.[14] But there was one crucial difference: Soviet delegates, representing Soviet Central Asian literatures, were invited to Delhi whereas they had not been to Bandung. Such a reconfiguration was instigated by the Conference's official organizer, the great Indian novelist Mulk Raj Anand, whom we met in Chapter 1 in his capacity as one of the founding figures of the All-India Progressive Writers Association and Soviet cultural bureaucracies' chief Indian liaison.[15] Following Bandung's success, he had convinced Prime Minister Jawaharlal Nehru to sponsor an international writers' gathering "in the spirit of Bandung."

That first meeting anticipated many of the association's future problems. It took all of Mulk Raj Anand's diplomatic skills to navigate the writers and cultural bureaucrats from dozens of Asian states as well as India's own, highly pluralistic delegation around the more contentious issues at the Delhi conference. Prefiguring debates that would recur at every subsequent meeting, writers could never reach an agreement on the relationship between art and politics. "Writers [in China] are absolutely free to write what they feel. They generally support the Government because they believe whatever the Government does is for the good of the people," insisted Li Yang-Shao of China, echoing Anatoly Sofronov's point that "[w]e, Russian writers, enjoy the freedom to serve our people."[16] By contrast, a number of Indian writers demanded that politics be kept out of the Conference, identifying it as a divisive issue for such a politically diverse, multinational gathering. The question as to which of the delegates were bona fide writers and which just cultural emissaries of their governments also hung over the Delhi conference. The sheer lack of familiarity with each other's national literatures made the question impossible to answer. The necessity of combatting that ignorance with the help of translation and cultural exchanges was the one item of the agenda that nobody contested. Toward the end of the conference, the Soviet delegation (the above-mentioned Sofronov, the head of the Uzbek Writers Union Mirzo Tursun-Zade, and the founding editor-in-chief of *Foreign Literature* Aleksandr Chakovsky) telegraphed the Central Committee in Moscow about whether they could issue an invitation to the Asian writers gathered in Delhi to another meeting in Tashkent, with approximately 200 to 250 participants, two years later. The International Department of the Central Committee telegraphed its approval of the initiative.[17]

The Competition

Giving urgency to the Soviet literary outreach to writers from the decolonizing world were the numerous forms of internationalism in which those writers were beginning to participate: Maoism and Guevarism, *negritude* and pan-Arabism, *francophonie*, Commonwealth literature, and US literary outreach. The competitive dynamic among them opened up a multitude of venues for Cold War–era Africa, Asian, and Latin American writers in ways unimaginable before. As the classic Cold War adversary and by far the most ambitious and best funded one, the US, in particular the CIA-sponsored Congress for Cultural Freedom (CCF), founded in 1950 to combat what many at Langley saw as global Soviet cultural hegemony in the first place, elicited the most attention among Soviet cultural bureau-cracies.[18] Whether genuinely alarmed or – as often happened – seeking to justify their requests for resources, countless reports generated by Soviet embassies, Soviet writers' delegations sent abroad, pro-Soviet visitors, or the Foreign Commission of the Soviet Writers Union describe Western efforts to "manipulate" Afro-Asian writers, such as the long-term visits Nigeria's major writer Cyprian Ekwensi paid to the US and Canada[19]

> where almost all of his works have come out. The same could be said of the Nigerian writers [Onuora] Nzekwu, [Chinua] Achebe, and [J.P.] Clarke. Over the course of a number of years Englishmen and Americans have been courting the leading Sri Lankan writer Martin Wickramasinghe, offering him money to organize a literary journal and a publishing house. By contrast, in many cases, Soviet publishing houses and journals do not pay foreign authors royalties, which causes them serious offense and inflicts us serious political damage. (It is typical, for example, that no royalties have been paid to the above-mentioned Nigerian writers Ekwensi, Nzekwu, and Achebe.)[20]

Over the course of this competition, between the mid-1950s and mid-1960s, the CCF built a veritable literary empire of magazines, many of them situated in Africa, Asia, and Latin America: *Quest* (India), *Hiwar* (Lebanon), *Black Orpheus* (Nigeria), *Transition* (Uganda), *Horison* (Indonesia), *Cuardenoros* (Latin America). While the CCF's goals were constant everywhere – using the keywords of "freedom" and "democracy" to unite intellectuals worldwide against communism – in practice, the funding came with few strings attached because the Congress feared being seen as overly ideological and many of the fiercely independent non-Western writers and literary venues would simply not have agreed to collaborate if the material help came with greater requirements.[21] Thus, modernism, neutrality, and separation of politics from literature became more realistic criteria to maintain than an explicitly pro-Western, "anti-totalitarian" stance.

In addition to such magazines, the CCF's network organized numerous gatherings – from universal ones, such as its Second Congress for Cultural Freedom in Bombay (1951), to smaller, more specifically literary ones, such as the Makerere African Writers Conference, in June 1962, probably the seminal gathering of English-language writers. Whether through the

CCF or other vehicles, the US government also funded much translation, publication, and book distribution activity throughout Africa, Asia, and Latin America. The cumulative effect of these efforts was not only a massive amount of pro-Western and anti-Soviet propaganda to readers of the three continents but also a massive subsidy for local literary institutions.[22]

Much more complex and ambivalent was the Soviet position vis-à-vis the different Third-Worldisms. This chapter will be most concerned with Maoism, which for over a decade posed the most determined challenge to Soviet literary internationalism, splitting or duplicating Soviet-aligned platforms. Third-Worldist movements particularly concerned with racial justice were much more inconvenient to post-Second World War Soviet cultural bureaucracies than they had been to their predecessors in the interwar era, when, of all the great powers, the Soviet state enjoyed a near-monopoly on determined anti-racist and anti-colonial rhetoric and policies. The first time the Soviet literary bureaucracies were forced to clarify their relationship with *negritude* was the decision as to whether to invite Alioune Diop, the editor of *Présence Africaine* and the main organizer of the 1956 Congress of Black Writers and Artists, to the upcoming 1958 Tashkent Congress. On the one hand, they reasoned, his presence would help legitimize the event in the eyes of a number of African writers; on the other hand, it would introduce an agenda and an interest group that they were keen to avoid. As the question regarding his invitation was deemed broadly political and thus beyond the competence of the Writers Union, it was addressed to CPSU's Central Committee's Foreign and Cultural sections, where it was decided not to invite Diop.[23] At the same time, another of *negritude*'s leading figures, Leopold Senghor, was published and translated in Russian. (It helped that he was a head of state, that is, a serious person.)

The Soviet bureaucracies' mixture of intense interest and alarm about such Third-Worldist movements is easy to explain. On the one hand, the latter seemed progressive, if not always socialist, and shared the same opponent: Western hegemony. On the other hand, even (or especially) the more Marxist-inflected movements refused to acknowledge the leading role of the Soviet state and the Party, and their radicalism and espousal of revolution went against the more conservative orientation of the Soviet state and its commitment to peaceful co-existence. In this sense, Maoism's challenge of the 1960s and '70s was the sharpest. As we will see later on in the chapter, it produced a major schism in the movement. The question of race – or more precisely, the struggle for racial justice at the core of movements such as pan-Africanism – further alarmed Soviet cultural bureaucracies. While Cold War Soviet propaganda lambasted institutionalized US racism, thus facilitating the success of the civil rights movement, it rarely evoked the category of race domestically or in its African, Asian, or Latin American outreach, thus erecting a major barrier to its interactions with Third-Worldist forces.[24] Despite the division of Soviet cultural labour in which a disproportionate number of Central Asians and Caucasians (in the sense of people from the Caucasus) were positioned at the interface of Soviet engagements with Africa and Asia, Russian cultural bureaucrats would take a West African critic's comment that "[i]n white countries they do not know or publish the literatures of Africa and Asia" as a reference to themselves.[25] This dynamic is even clearer in the discussion among literary scholars held at the Soviet Union of Writers in preparation for the 1968 anniversary conference of the Afro-Asian Writers Association, also held in Tashkent:

> *Semyon Breitburg (an Orthodox Marxist literary critic):*
> We should take note of the popularity of the ideas voiced by Herbert
> Marcuse, a philosopher and sociologist, and more of an office
> academic, who unexpectedly – probably for himself, too – became
> one of the foremost intellectual figures of the world.
>
> One of my acquaintances likened Marcuse's views to a
> cigarette stub thrown into an oil barrel. There is some truth to
> this comparison. We should expose his mistaken views, but do
> so knowing a little bit about his writings so that we wouldn't find
> ourselves in the embarrassing situation when our accusations against
> him seem very superficial.[26]
>
> Marcuse proposes the following perspective: the working class
> in Western industrialized countries has been integrated, that is,
> incorporated into developed consumer society and has thus lost its
> revolutionary potential. In the same way, the revolutionary parties of
> this class, that is, the Western communist parties, have ceased to be
> revolutionary.
>
> In that case, what is the revolutionary force capable of destroying
> contemporary capitalist society? In Marcuse's opinion, the only such
> force are the oppressed races thrown overboard in this individualist

consumer society, who on account of their moral and intellectual strength, are not subject to incorporation. If from the national plane we switch to the international, it follows that the only real revolutionary agent today are Third-World countries.

The problem is that this view has spread well beyond the readers of Marcuse's philosophical tracts and can reach anybody who bothers to pick up a newspaper, where it is presented in the most vulgarized form. And at gatherings such as Tashkent, we should be prepared to counter such assertions that the only real revolutionary force in the world are former colonial countries.

Alexey Zverev (an Americanist, and subsequently a renowned Nabokov specialist):
We have to take into consideration that we have treated the negro movement and the literature about it in a somewhat simplified way. We have treated it as something unquestionably positively, without seeing its complexity.

At the same time, in the United States, black racism [*chernyi rasizm*], that is, the problem that will inevitably emerge in Tashkent, has taken some extreme expression. A project of a negro culture has emerged, based on a view that world culture was originally black, that Christ was a negro, that the New Testament was written by black prophets. Therefore, a negro culture must be built, thoroughly separate from human culture, which has been dictated by whites. What is interesting is that they do not recognize Chinese or Japanese cultures. The whole world, in their opinion, is divided into black and white. Japanese and Chinese are white, Arabs and Indians are black, and the most radical part of this movement calls for abandoning white Christian culture and returning to Islam, for allegedly they were once Muslims who had been forced to convert.

This new culture must be built in the United States, not Africa, and they must have their own state, where it could thrive based on Islamic teachings. At the head of this negro party is [Elijah] Muhammad [the head of the relatively small Nation of Islam, which had entered a crisis after Malcolm X's departure in 1964] and this wing is no less influential than [Martin Luther] King's wing, which we of course should in all ways support.

Evgeny Chelyshev (a leading Soviet scholar of Hindi):
Then we have the so-called idea of "the Asian spirit." This is very
dangerous as Eastern writers and critics say that we have more
in common among ourselves than with Europeans in a way that
resonates with Maoism.

   Even such an innocent topic as the classical tradition and
contemporary literature could be transformed into a question of
"the Asian spirit." That is, they could say that the classical tradition
is nothing but chains for us, that we must follow Elliot and bring the
experience of modernism to Indian literature. It could be a purely
literary or an ideological intervention. I am certain that this problem
of "the Asian spirit" will be present in a number of speeches [at the
conference] since it is becoming ever more widespread.

*Miriam Salganik (the senior consultant on Afro-Asian literatures from
the Foreign Section of the Soviet Writers Union):*
Of course, the writers who come from Latin America will be of a
Guevarist disposition. They suffer from a sense of shame for what's
going on in their countries. Mao and Guevara appeal mostly to those
who are far away from them, and less to those who are closer. ... If
they run into the Vietnamese delegates, we should not interfere, but
just sit back and watch.[27]

   And while Soviet organizers jealously watched over the loyalties
of African, Asian, and Latin American writers, as far as the latter were
concerned, participation in Soviet literary internationalism rarely precluded
a search for pan-Africanist audiences or acceptance of Western prizes, or an
appearance in a Maoist publication. While the organizers and ideologues
of those different networks saw themselves as competitors and jealously
guarded "their" writers, the vast majority of the latter participated – though
not indiscriminately – in multiple internationalisms.

The Afro-Asian Writers Association as a Field

The Afro-Asian Writers' movement founded in Tashkent (the Afro-Asian
Writers Association would be formally inaugurated at the Second Congress
in Cairo in February 1962) was thus part of a larger ecology of competing
internationalisms in which the literatures of these continents were becoming

integrated. But what was that Association itself? Shridharani's article points to the two very different perspectives from which it could be studied. On the one hand, it functioned as a site of South-South solidarities, of forging unpredictable but fruitful connections among writers and readers otherwise separated by geography, language, and national culture. Any examination of the literary texts published in the Association magazine, *Lotus*, or of the writers' accounts of meeting at the Association's congresses lends itself to frameworks such as imagined community or transnational public sphere. On the other hand, the Association, like previous Soviet-affiliated literary formations, could be viewed as a Cold War front structure meant to give Soviet cultural bureaucracies a measure of influence over Afro-Asian letters. Indeed, should a researcher limit her study of the Afro-Asian Writers Association to the transcripts of the Soviet Preparatory Committee or the Association's official resolutions, she would only confirm her suspicion of the Association as a propaganda vehicle for Soviet, Chinese, Egyptian, and even Indian foreign policy.

Referenced earlier, Bourdieu's notion of a field productively synthesizes these two divergent perspectives and avoids their attendant normativities.[28] Like any field, Afro-Asian literature operated as an arena of struggle for authority by its most powerful member-states (the USSR, China until the mid-1960s, Egypt until 1978, India). However, its existence cannot be reduced to the quest for domination. To exist as a field in the first place, it had to achieve a degree of internal cohesion and boundedness with respect to the outside. The outside, in this case, was Western literature, which dominated the bookshelves of African and Asian bookstores and libraries. The diverse agents of the Afro-Asian literary field – writers, cultural bureaucrats, publishers, critics, and readers – intuitively shared with contemporary dependency theorists such as Samir Amin, Raul Prebisch, and Walter Rodney an understanding of how they could escape their peripheral position within world literature: by delinking from the larger (literary) world-system, which kept them in a subordinate position; by developing their (literary) resources through interconnections; and by setting the terms of their own presence on the world (literary) stage. The Afro-Asian Writers Association represented just such an attempt to gain some autonomy from Paris and London and their interpretative authority.

For these reasons, what distinguishes the Afro-Asian Writers Association from previous Soviet-affiliated writers' associations is its geographical boundedness. The internationalism of those formations such as MORP, the

Writers for the Defence of Culture, or the Intellectuals for the Defence of Peace was, technically at least, a worldwide internationalism. By contrast, Afro-Asia was explicitly inscribed into the title of this writers' formation. The inclusion of the Soviet Union – a state straddling Europe and Asia, but with a mostly white population and an uncomfortable imperial history – posed particular challenges: while most of the Soviet writers who participated in the Association came from Central Asia, two of the chief Soviet representatives at the Association – Anatoly Sofronov and Aleksei Chugunov – were decidedly European.

Occasionally, the question of including Latin America would be raised at some of the meetings of the Association.[29] That never happened, most likely because of Latin America's combination of right-wing pro-American governments and radical (but not Moscow-oriented communist) writers, which was deemed potentially too disruptive for the fragile equilibrium that held the Association together. As a result, the enormously popular Latin American boom remained decoupled from the Afro-Asian Writers movement. The Soviet participation opened the door to other delegates from Eastern Europe – as observers, to be sure – further stretching the definition of the Afro-Asian writer.[30] At the same time, because of the Israeli occupation of Palestine, the Egyptian delegation made sure that Israel would never be invited. Similarly, at the insistence of the Chinese writers, their Taiwanese colleagues could not qualify for Afro-Asian status. As long as China remained part of the movement, the latter never received an invitation to any of the Congresses. In the aftermath of the Sino-Soviet split in the early 1960s, the China Writers' Association, one of the founding and most authoritative participants, boycotted the Afro-Asian Writers movement (or more precisely, as we shall see, founded its own, parallel one), creating a major white spot on its bicontinental map.

That the Association was organized in a national framework and many countries' delegates acted as state representatives tied its fortunes to the vicissitudes of interstate relations. Every international political conflict was reflected in the works of the Afro-Asian Writers Association and its definition of Afro-Asian literature. Even the Soviet side, notorious for making its own local agenda part of the general discussion, would often complain about local squabbles, such as the Arab writers' conflict with their Egyptian counterparts in the aftermath of the Camp David Accords, which threatened to derail any other agenda.[31] Indeed, a significant portion of every official statement at the conference addressed the struggles of the Palestinian people. Reflecting the political make-up of the Association's organizing committees, a lengthy list of concrete political causes defines the Afro-Asian writer in most of its declarations such as the following one from 1976:

> We, the writers of Africa and Asia ... represent 23 Afro-Asian countries, *10 East European countries* [italics are mine – RLD] and cultural, regional and international organization ...
> We now witness in Asia the prominent historical victory of the peoples of Indo-China over the aggression of American imperialism ...
> We, the writers of Asia and Africa, greet our militant brethren in the People's Republic of Angola, under the leadership of our great poet, President Neto, and his comrades in the Popular Movement for the Liberation of Angola ...
> We, the Afro-Asian writers, declare our unreserved support for the movement of the valiant Palestinian Resistance ...
> We, the writers of Asia and Africa, join our voice to the voice of the whole civilized world, which has condemned Zionism as a racist theory and movement.
> We, the Afro-Asian Writers, hail the prominent role played by socialist countries, foremost among which is the Soviet Union, in consolidating the national liberation movement in Africa and Asia. We affirm the necessity of strengthening the strategic alliances between socialist forces, world national liberation forces as well as democratic forces in the capitalist world with a view to reshaping the face of the world for liberation, independence, democracy, and social progress.[32]

Thus defined, via concrete geopolitical struggles, the Afro-Asian literary field became a function of the Third-Worldist political project and largely reflected the latter's fortunes. Moreover, while the above quotation does not reproduce the 1976 Declaration in its entirety, there is no particular item from that lengthy list that references any particular aesthetic the Association championed. A broadly defined realism, nevertheless, remained the most likely candidate for the Association's common aesthetic horizon, as Soviet delegates would occasionally assert.[33]

At its purest, the Soviet effort to gain political influence among foreign writers comes out in the transcripts of the Foreign Section of the Soviet

Writers Union and the Soviet Committee for Solidarity with Africa and Asia. With the Afro-Asian Writers Association, the Soviet side, in particular, lacked the kind of unquestionable authority – moral and organizational – it had enjoyed over previous associations, especially the World Peace Council. At a time when the self-confidence of the writers of these two continents as a new and emerging formation ran so high, the Soviet side took care not to appear as if it were co-opting the Association. Indeed, throughout the existence of the Association, Soviet representatives faced complex and constant choices whether to co-opt or confront, to humbly swallow speeches against white domination or challenge them. As a successor of an empire and as a mostly white society, the Soviet side continually needed to justify its place at the table.

The writers from the other three founding member-states, China, Egypt, and to a lesser extent, India, also acted as extensions of their national diplomacies. As a result, every political tension or crisis in Third Word geopolitics was replicated in the history of the Association. Heterogeneous though they were in their views, Indian writers for the most part observed the Indian Congress Party's reserved stance in geopolitical matters, thus at various congresses proving the greatest obstacle to the efforts of the Soviet, Chinese, and Egyptian delegations to politicize the Association's initiatives and vision of literature.

A much more severe, in fact, near-fatal crisis, in the life of the Association was caused by the Sino-Soviet split of 1960, which initially blocked its activity and eventually resulted in two competing organizations – a pro-Chinese Afro-Asian Writers Bureau and a pro-Soviet Afro-Asian Writers Association. Beyond fiery denunciatory speeches and conspiratorial committee meetings, the struggle between them took multiple forms such as the Chinese writers furtively waiting in the corridors of the 1967 Beirut Afro-Asian Writers Congress, handing out their anti-Soviet leaflets and inviting a bemused Ngũgĩ wa Thiong'o for a conversation.[34]

The Egyptian centrality to the Association, at least in the decade-long period when Cairo hosted both the Permanent Bureau and *Lotus*'s editorial offices, occasionally aggravated Soviet cultural bureaucrats. Expressing a common sentiment, the Chukchi writer and member of the Preparatory Committee for 1973 Alma-Ata Congress Yuri Rytkheu stated: "*Lotus* is situated outside of our influence – this is perfectly clear. Maybe we should pose the question of the physical presence of one of our representatives [in the Cairo editorial offices] so that we could steer it our way." The Moscow-Cairo axis continued to be central to the Association's work until the late 1970s, when Egypt's President Sadat, who succeeded General Nasser in 1970, practically switched his country's allegiance from the USSR to its Cold War adversary and made peace with Israel, angering most Arab intellectuals and writers.[35] If the Association managed to recover from its first major crisis (the Sino-Soviet split), Egypt's withdrawal plunged it into a state of permanent instability.

And while Arab writers (especially those united around the cause of Palestinian liberation) remained central to the Association even after the Camp David Accords, sub-Saharan Africa's role grew increasingly prominent, as reflected by the election of its new general secretary, the South African writer Alex La Guma, and, in 1979, the setting of its Sixth Congress in Luanda, the capital of the newly liberated Angola. The president of that country, the Lotus-prize recipient Agostinho Neto, played the role of the Congress's symbolic host. The Soviet Preparatory Committee's discussion of La Guma's choice on the eve of that Congress speaks volumes about the Soviet organizers' patronizing perspective on the Association:

> [Sofronov:] I remember La Guma. I had to meet him on quite a few occasions. He gets carried away sometimes and says that he hates it when other people dictate to him what to do ... But La Guma is our kid [*nashe ditia*]. We proposed him at the Alma-Ata Conference against al-Sibai's and Mukherjee's wishes. Mukherjee [the other candidate for the position] – is a wild man while he [La Guma] grew up in the communist underground, 11 years in prison and house arrest, and so on. And by the way, he is a good writer. That's nice.[36]

Secondarily, the by-the-way quality with which Sofronov brings up La Guma's literary talent is revealing of the role aesthetics played in the eyes of the Soviet organizers. The language of control and "usefulness," combined with some apprehension of La Guma's independence emerges in E.A. Kryvitsky's response to Sofronov:

> We knew that La Guma would be no sugar. We were not confused in this respect. But at the same time we knew that there are particular ways of approaching him, which would make him very useful for us. This is obvious. Considering his weaknesses, let us use his strongest side.[37]

Whatever measure of influence Soviet cultural bureaucracies sought and obtained in supporting the work of the Association, it certainly did not translate into literary practice. The mechanisms of control they had over Soviet writers – censorship, membership into the Writers Union, with all its available carrots and sticks – were poorly applicable abroad. Even such African and Asian graduates of Moscow's Gorky Literary Institute (the leading creative writing program in the USSR) as Maithripala Sirisena (future president of Sri Lanka), the above-mentioned Atukwei (John) Okai, and scores of Arab writers could hardly be thought of as orthodox socialist realists and conduits of Soviet influence abroad. By contrast, attraction from afar – the circulation of Russian or Soviet literary texts and their novel interpretations – among Afro-Asian audiences proved much more influential, and not in a way the Soviet state could have controlled.[38]

The Structures of the Afro-Asian Literary Field

Arguably, the main form that Soviet influence took was not in the struggles over geopolitical orientation but in the structures of the Afro-Asian literary field, which derived from earlier iterations of Soviet literary international-ism, such as the International Union of Revolutionary Writers (MORP) of the early 1930s, the Popular-Front-era Association of Writers for the Defence of Culture, and the early Cold War World Peace Council. The following section will identify and reconstruct the lineage of the four major structures around which the Afro-Asian Writers Association constituted itself: inter-national writers' congresses, a permanent bureau, a multilingual literary magazine, and an international literary prize.

The most visible of these were the Afro-Asian Writers congresses at which writers from the two continents would descend upon a city for a week, providing what we would nowadays call a media event as well as an opportunity for them to announce themselves as a movement and deter-mine its direction. In practice, congresses would be divided into official proceedings, a cultural program organized by the hosts in the city and beyond, and a less structured time for informal get-togethers with other writers or sightseeing, which of course could always be expanded at the expense of the official proceedings. The official proceedings were usually the least memorable part, but sometimes they would feature heated debates such as those that occurred during the Second Congress, held in Cairo, when the Sino-Soviet rivalry was played out in the open. As a whole, the congresses gave visibility to what were largely two imagined communities of Afro-Asian writers, on the one hand, and their readerships, on the other. Indeed, the local organizers of those congresses emphasized their guests' relations with reading publics from their country by facilitating formal and informal meetings between the two and showcasing local translations of the visitors' works. Illustrating the writers' commitment to progressive causes, at the end of each Congress, resolutions were passed on political issues such as ongoing independence struggles, military invasions, and disarmament.

Not unlike the gatherings of previous, Soviet-affiliated international writers' formations – MORP's Moscow (1927) and Kharkov (1930) conferences, the Association of Writers for the Defence of Culture Paris (1935) and Valencia-Madrid-Barcelona-Paris (1937) congresses, and the World Peace Council's Wroclaw (1947), Paris/Prague (1949), Sheffield/Warsaw (1950) assemblies – writers' congresses would be the main feature of the Afro-Asian Writers Association. Starting with the 1958 Tashkent Congress, Afro-Asian writers would similarly come together at seven other congresses: held in Cairo (1962), Beirut (1967), Delhi (1970), Alma-Ata (1973), Luanda (1979), again in Tashkent (1983), and finally in Tunis (1988). In between the larger congresses, the Association would hold regular meetings of the *Lotus* editorial board, and conferences, such as a poet's gathering in September 1973 in Yerevan, a young writers' meeting in Tashkent in the fall of 1976, and smaller anniversary conferences, also in Tashkent, held in 1968 and 1978.

The Soviet organizers published (in Russian) the transcripts of the first five congresses. It is difficult to evaluate the overall significance of the official proceedings, between the excerpting of the speeches, which smoothed conflicts or rough edges, and the nature of such formal events. For many participants, as Shridharani's coverage of the Tashkent Congress makes abundantly clear, it was not the formal resolutions passed by the congress or the individual speeches that left the most powerful impressions but rather the encounters and conversations outside of the conference hall, with locals or fellow visiting writers, some of which, as Shridharani's, were recorded in articles or other autobiographical writing.[39] Each of these tells us as much about its author's perspective as it does about the congress. Nevertheless, many of the motifs of Shridharani's article recur twenty years later, in the travel notes of the radical feminist Afro-American poet Audre Lorde, an invited American observer to the 1976 Young Writers Conference in Tashkent.[40] A not unsympathetic commentator, she is less taken by Soviet modernity (unlike the other delegates, she is, after all, visiting from New York) but does admire the bread, the free healthcare, and education, which the Soviet state – unlike the United States – guaranteed for its citizens. Reading her notes, one can sense the difference between her more distanced interactions with Russians in Moscow, where she visited the Soviet Writers Union, which had formally invited her, and the warmth and engagement she feels for the people of Uzbekistan:

> As we descended the plane in Tashkent, it was deliciously hot and smelled like Accra, Ghana ... I felt genuinely welcomed ... I had the distinct feeling here, that for the first time in Russia, I was meeting warm-blooded people; in the sense of contact unavoided, desires and emotions possible, the sense that there was something hauntingly, personally familiar – not in the way the town looks because it looked like nothing I'd ever seen before, night and the minarets – but the tempo of life felt quicker than Moscow; and in place of Moscow's determined pleasantness, the people displayed a kind of warmth that was very engaging. They are an Asian people in Tashkent. Uzbeki ...
>
> If Moscow is New York, Tashkent is Accra. It is African in so many ways – the stalls, the mix of the old and the new, the corrugated tin roofs on top of adobe houses. The corn smell in the plaza, although plazas were more modern than in West Africa ...
>
> And it's not that there are no individuals who are nationalists or racists, but that the taking of a state position against nationalism, against racism is what makes possible for a society like this to function. I remember the Moslem woman who came up to me in the market place, asking Fikre [a Patrice Lumumba University student from Ethiopia accompanying Lorde – RLD] if I had a boy also. She said that she had never seen a Black woman before, that she had seen black men, but she had never seen a Black woman, and that she so much liked the way I looked that she wanted to bring her little boy and find out if I had a little boy, too. Then we blessed each other and spoke good words and then she passed on.[41]

The actual Afro-Asian conference takes much less space in Lorde's travel notes. She is disappointed to find "only four sisters in this whole conference," unclear about her "observer" status as an African-American, and unhappy about the absence of a meeting for oppressed peoples of Black

America given the abundance of "meeting[s] of solidarity for the oppressed people of Somewhere."[42] The strict geographical demarcations of Afro-Asian solidarity left little space for her.

In between congresses – periods that could last a long time because of the Afro-Asian Writers Association's multiple crises and the inertia of its last decade – day-to-day decisions about the Association's running were made by a headquarters, an international bureau not unlike those previously coordinating the national sections of MORP and the Association of Writers for the Defence of Culture. Initially located in Colombo, Sri Lanka, as a neutral location equidistant between the great powers of the Association, it was presided over by the chairman of the Sri Lankan Union of Writers, Ratne D. Senanayake. The latter's decision to side with China during the Sino-Soviet split caused the first and nearly fatal crisis in the life of the Association.[43] That period of internal strife was reflected in the five-year gap between the 1962 Cairo and the 1967 Beirut Congresses during which much of the Association's activity was paralyzed. As the Bureau was the main decision-making organ of the Association between congresses and those were not taking place, the Soviet side even contemplated abandoning the Afro-Asian format and devoting their energies to a new, African Writers Association, which would be free of Chinese influence.[44] Eventually, the Soviet and the Egyptian sides organized an emergency meeting in 1965 at which it was decided to move the Permanent Bureau to Cairo and replace Senanayake with the Egyptian novelist Yusuf al-Sibai (1917–1978), the general secretary of the Afro-Asian Solidarity Organization.[45]

In the face of this decision, the Colombo-based Afro-Asian Writers Bureau did not back down and fold but continued to function as the focal point of Maoist literary internationalism, publishing a number of volumes of Afro-Asian poetry, model Peking operas, Maoist propaganda, and even a short-lived and nearly unfindable English-language literary journal, *The Call*. This effort to compete internationally with the pro-Soviet Association came to an end with the purges of the Cultural Revolution and the general solipsism into which the Chinese cultural policy of the late 1960s collapsed. While, as Duncan Yoon has shown, literary Maoism may have commanded the sympathies of individual Afro-Asian writers, it was a brief phenomenon and hardly a match for the cultural capital and material investments of the Soviet-Egyptian-Indian literary alliance.[46]

The decade during which Cairo hosted the Permanent Bureau of Afro-Asian Writers was a period of stability and growth. It ended abruptly in

1978 with the Camp David Accords, and al-Sibai's assassination earlier
that year by Palestinian militants upset with his personal support for the
peace treaty with Israel. This dual loss – both of a founding member-state
of the Association (Egypt) and of somebody who had been by all accounts
a capable, committed, and well-connected organizer (al-Sibai) – initiated a
period of uncertainty and homelessness, which was never fully resolved
until the very end of the Association ca. 1991.[47] In this last decade or so,
the Bureau's fortunes became intimately tied with those of the Palestinian
Liberation Organization (PLO), which first hosted it in Beirut until 1982,
when the start of the Lebanese Civil War and Israeli bombing drove the PLO
out of town, and then in Tunis. At the same time, al-Sibai's successor as the
Association's general secretary for most of this period, the South African
writer Alex La Guma (1925–1985), lived in Cuba, as a representative of the
African National Congress, and could not follow the day-to-day running
of the Permanent Bureau.

The Bureau (at least during its Cairo phase) hosted the Association's
literary quarterly, *Lotus* (1967–91), which offered the most tangible proof
of the existence of an Afro-Asian literary field.[48] While the idea of a journal
was broached as early as the 1958 Tashkent Congress, a detailed plan for
a magazine with a circulation of about 5,000 copies and length of about
150 pages (*Lotus*'s eventual parameters) had to wait until 1963, when Faiz
Ahmad Faiz submitted his proposal to the Soviet Writers Union.[49] It was
based on multiple conversations with writers, editors, and politicians in
Beirut, Cairo, Paris, and Geneva, and was made weightier by Faiz's recent
receipt of a Lenin Peace Prize. In a lengthy preamble, he explains the
need to counter several already existing hostile publications: on the one
hand, the jewel in the crown of the CIA-sponsored Congress for Cultural
Freedom, the Anglo-American *Encounter*, which, over the course of the
1960s, under the editorship of Stephen Spender and Melvin Lasky, had
increasingly turned its sights to (formerly) colonial literatures, and its allied
publications in Asia; on the other, against two English-language Maoist
magazines, the Hong-Kong-based *Eastern Horizons* and the Geneva-based
Revolutions in Africa, Asia, and Latin America.[50] As the ideal location for
such a magazine, Faiz proposes Beirut: in his view, the city combines
an excellent geographical location with an abundance of local writers
and politicians supporting the cause, good publishing and distribution
facilities, and a relative paucity of censorship restrictions, which he feared

might cripple the magazine if it were to be founded in Cairo.[51] Faiz's initial project was not realized until 1967, when *Afro-Asian Writings* began publishing prose and poetry, literary criticism, and book reviews by writers from all over the two continents. (At Mulk Raj Anand's instigation, the international editorial board decided to change the title to *Lotus* during a 1969 meeting in Moscow.)[52]

Faiz, however, had proposed an English-language magazine explicitly modelled after *Encounter*. Just like *Encounter*, he insisted, it should be prepared to publish major writers without "clear political views" and even material hostile to its agenda (as long as it is effectively countered).[53] His efforts to broaden the ideological parameters of the magazine ran against the model Soviet cultural bureaucracies had in mind: *International Literature*, the Moscow-based literary organ of the worldwide Popular Front. Indeed, as Faiz would discover later, during his five years at the helm of *Lotus*, it resembled *International Literature* in its unswerving loyalty to its hosts and sponsors – the USSR, Egypt, the PLO.[54] Another – more striking – commonality of the two magazines was that they simultaneously published issues in several languages: French, English, and Arabic in the case of *Lotus*; Russian, German, French, English, and, occasionally, Spanish and Chinese, in the case of *International Literature*.[55] Through translation, they sought to overcome the national and regional boundaries dividing their intended readership and to forge a truly international reading public, spanning Africa and Asia.

With only 5,000 of each issue printed in each language, *Lotus* could hardly reach numerically significant readerships in Africa or Asia, but a consistent effort was made to send it to libraries and writers' organizations in the two continents and beyond. For its distribution, it relied on its own transnational networks as well as on foreign publishing companies such as the French Maspero or the British London Publishers.[56] Practically, every aspect of the journal was international: not only the contributors and the readers but also its peripatetic editorial offices (Cairo, and after the Egyptian "defection," Beirut, and Tunis) and the location of its printing press (Egypt, for the Arab version; East Berlin for the English and French ones). The international editorial committee was spread among Algeria (Malek Haddad), Angola (Fernando da Costa Andrade), Iraq (Fouad al-Takerly), Japan (Hiroshi Noma), Lebanon (Michel Soleiman), Mongolia (Sonomyn Udval), the USSR (Anatoly Sofronov), India (Mulk Raj Anand),

Pakistan (Faiz Ahmad Faiz) and Senegal (Doudou Gueye). After al-Sibai's assassination, *Lotus*'s helm passed on to Faiz, who edited it out of Beirut until 1982. In the last and probably least documented part of its history, when publication and distribution grew increasingly irregular, *Lotus* was first briefly run by Faiz's deputy, the Palestinian poet Muin Bseiso, and later, after his death, by the PLO's chief press officer, Ziad Abdel Fattah.

Lotus's pages also reflected this imperative to cover as many national literatures in as many different genres as possible. The limited number of pages available meant that, unlike *International Literature*, it could not easily lend them to novels, so the main genres represented were short stories and selections of poetry. The magazine did not limit itself to literature but included neighbouring arts as well. In addition to the occasional play or folklore, most issues included several pages of images, whether of paintings or art objects, accompanied by a detailed explanation. The articles in the Studies section, prepared especially for the magazine, exhibited a certain regional or (bi)continental focus: "The Role of Translation for Rapprochement between the Afro-Asian Peoples," "The Popular Hero in the Arabic Play," "Where does African Literature go from here?" Occasionally a single author or national literature would be showcased, for example, "Ghalib and Progressive Urdu Literature."[57] Rounding out each issue were book reviews as well as a chronicle of current events of Afro-Asian literature. Such chronicles helped foster a sense of simultaneity and coherence of the whole among the bicontinental readers. Not unlike Benedict Anderson's newspaper, which helped its readers imagine the nation by placing next to each other articles on a natural disaster in province X and on a major cultural event in the capital, such chronicles or book reviews constructed the category of an Afro-Asian literature by placing its geographically dispersed manifestations alongside each other.[58]

The fourth and last structure through which the Afro-Asian Writers Association sought to consolidate Afro-Asian literature as a coherent field was the Lotus Prize. Awarded between 1969 to 1988 to leading Afro-Asian writers, it was modelled after the World Peace Council's Stalin Peace Prize given to writers, artists, and scientists who had contributed to the cause of world peace. (For a full list of recipients, see Appendix.) The World Peace Council established its award at the hottest moment of the Cold War, as a more political and less Western alternative to the Nobel Prizes for Literature and Peace. By the same token, the Lotus Prize acquired the reputation of an Afro-Asian Nobel for literature, at a time when very few

African and Asian writers were awarded an actual Nobel. In the process, it contributed to the production of an Afro-Asian literary canon. The success of this prize is reflected in the continued fame of its recipients: the Palestinian poet Mahmoud Darwish and the South African prose writer Alex La Guma (the 1969 awards); the Angolan poet-president Agostinho Neto (1970) and the Senegalese novelist Sembène Ousmane; the Algerian Kateb Yasin and Ngũgĩ wa Thiong'o (both in 1972); Chinua Achebe and Faiz Ahmad Faiz (the 1975 awards) are still among the best-known Afro-Asian writers. Some of them, like Mahmoud Darwish and Alex La Guma, received the award well before they reached the peak of their fame in the West.[59] There is no uniform aesthetic unifying the diverse writing of its recipients: the modernism of the older Egyptian novelist Taha Hussein, the militant anti-colonial verse of the Mozambican militant poet-independence-fighter Marcelino dos Santos, Aziz Nesin's biting satire of Turkish state and society, and Chinghiz Aitmatov's unique synthesis of socialist and magical realism.

Judging by the transcript of the discussion of the first batch of Lotus awards, its principles were not particularly well-codified, giving the prize committee a good deal of flexibility.[60] The award could be given not only for individual work but also for overall contributions to the Afro-Asian Writers Association; it would be desirable if at least one award (out of the six awarded for 1969–70) would go to a writer from a country fighting for independence. Palestinian literature was the major beneficiary of this last principle: in the first ten years of the award's existence, Palestinian writers won five Lotuses, making them the absolute leader in this regard. (By the time the last Lotus was given in 1988, Soviet prize-winners had overtaken them.) By the same token, as literatures fighting a foreign occupation, Vietnam and Lusophone Africa (Angola and Mozambique) were given four prizes each, making them a joint third. The Lotus Prize was only one of the ways through which the Association facilitated the Palestinian and other anti-colonial struggles for international cultural recognition. Otherwise, the Lotus Prize committees sought the widest geographical representation of its awards. The non-inclusion of a francophone African writer among the first six recipients became the main source of contention during the inaugural meeting of the Lotus Prize Committee in 1970, when the Senegalese representative Doudou Gueye asked that his protest be officially registered in the proceedings.[61]

While geography seems to have been a major consideration in selecting Lotus Prize winners, gender balance does not seem to have been a factor.

Figure 2.8   In the main auditorium of the 1973 Alma-Ata Congress.

In fact, of the fifty-nine awards that were given, only two went to women: the Uzbek poet Zul'fia and the Mongolian prose writer Sonomyn Udval. This poor representation of women was hardly limited to Lotus Prizes but extended to all other aspects of the Afro-Asian Writers Association: the awards were made by the nearly all-male *Lotus* editorial board, which in turn published mostly male writers.

Gradually, the award experienced a Brezhnevization of sorts. In a discussion of its workings in the Soviet Writers Union following the Association's last conference in Tunis (December 1988), one perestroika-minded Writers Union official, Yevgeny Sidorov, revealed what the main criterion for the Lotus awards over the previous decade had become: if you were a literary official heading your national section of the Afro-Asian Writers Association, sooner or later you would receive your Lotus.[62]

The congresses, the permanent bureau, the literary quarterly, and the Lotus Prize were only the most visible structures of the Afro-Asian Writers Association. Underneath them lay a whole network of nation-based committees, publishing houses, magazines, and translators located within different African and Asian countries, who were performing the much less

Figure 2.9   Yusuf al-Sibai presents the Lotus Award to Sembène Ousmane at the 1973 Alma-Ata Congress. The chairman of the Kazakh Union of Writers, Anuar Alimzhanov, is in the background.

Figure 2.10   Lotus Prize recipient Ngũgĩ wa Thiong'o shakes hands with Anatoly Sofronov, deputy head of the Soviet Committee for Solidarity with Africa and Asia, editor of the *Lotus* quarterly, and leader of the late-Stalin-era anti-Semitic campaign in the Soviet Writers Union. Alma-Ata, 1973.

Figure 2.11   The South African writer Alex La Guma, the poets Anatoly Sofronov and Rasul Gamzatov, and the Kyrgyz writer Chinghiz Aitmatov (from left to right) at the Fifth Congress of Afro-Asian Writers in Alma-Ata. 1 September 1973.

visible work of bringing foreign literature produced within the two continents to their national readerships. Lydia Liu has called this engagement the Great Translation Movement.[63]

Progress: Publishing Afro-Asian Literature in the USSR

Probably none of the presses connecting the literatures of Africa and Asia achieved the magnitude of the Moscow-based Progress Publishers. Though established in the interwar era and not even specifically targeted at Afro-Asian writers and readers, it became the main translator, publisher, and distributor of Russo-Soviet literature into the languages of the two continents and the main source of their literatures for Soviet readers. In this sense, Progress was the eventual realization of Maxim Gorky's project of a World Literature Publishing House (Izdatel'stvo Vsemirnaia literatura), which would translate all foreign literatures into Russian, Russian literature into all the major languages of the world, and finally, all of the above into the languages of the Soviet Union. As Maria Khotimsky and Sergey Tyulenev have shown, the World Literature Publishing House that appeared in 1919

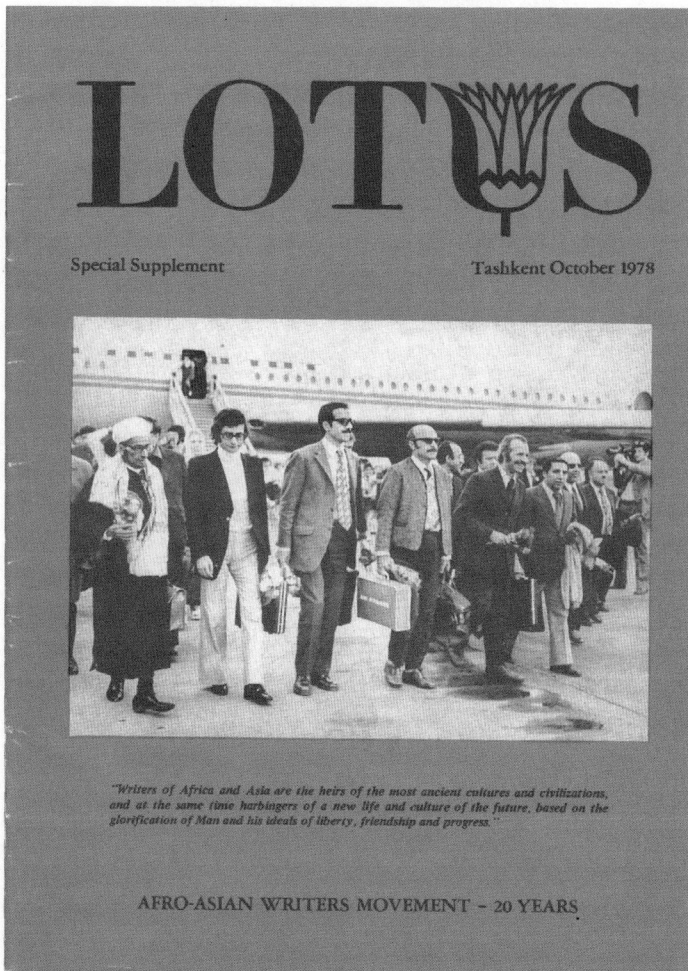

LOTUS

Special Supplement   Tashkent October 1978

"Writers of Africa and Asia are the heirs of the most ancient cultures and civilizations, and at the same time harbingers of a new life and culture of the future, based on the glorification of Man and his ideals of liberty, friendship and progress."

AFRO-ASIAN WRITERS MOVEMENT – 20 YEARS

Figure 2.12   Cover page of the September 1978 special issue of *Lotus* in English, published immediately after the murder of Yusuf al-Sibai and the loss of the Egyptian headquarters.

under Gorky's general editorship never quite lived up to this vision. While it offered much-needed employment to Petersburg writers as translators and editors, paper shortages, organizational difficulties, and lack of funding ultimately meant that that the press ceased to exist in 1924 and most of their translations remained unpublished.[64] The uniqueness of this press lies not only in Gorky's lofty vision of a world literature taken away from the market and put in the service of humanistic values – arguably, some of its premises were shared among the more radical sections of the international literary community – but in the extensive support the Soviet state extended to it at a time of destructive civil war. Khotimsky traces the afterlife of the project to two other presses – the Leningrad branch of the State Publishing house (Lengiz) and Academia, which inherited some of World Literature's unpublished manuscripts – as well as to the later book series, Library of World Literature (*Biblioteka vsemirnoi literatury*), which published 200 well-annotated volumes of the world literature canon, from ancient Indian poetry to the contemporary novelistic canon between 1967 and 1977.[65]

Though of very different institutional origins, Progress gradually evolved into the true successor of Gorky's project, capturing its ambitiousness, if not its lofty, humanistic pathos. Founded in Moscow in 1931, under the name of the Publishing Co-operative of Foreign Workers (ITIR), it entered the Soviet publishing landscape as a press devoted to the translation of Marxist political literature into foreign languages.[66] By that time, there were already several other foreign-language newspapers publishing out of Moscow: the Polish *Tribuna Radzecka*, the French *Journal de Moscou*, the English *Moscow News*, the multilingual *The Communist International*, not to mention its literary equivalent – *Literature of the World Revolution*, soon to be renamed *International Literature*. Besides, the Executive Committee of the Communist International (ECCI) was already translating and printing the works of Lenin and other political literature into different languages. ITIR drew its translators and editors from both polyglot Soviet citizens with foreign experience and the growing number of the city's foreigners, often political refugees with Comintern connections.[67] Indeed, ITIR's staff reflected the composition of Moscow's foreign community and its multiple shifts: from the influx of Spanish refugees in the late 1930s to their retirement or departures for Mexico, Cuba, or Spain in the 1960s and '70s, from the return of the Moscow-based East European exiles to their countries in the mid-1940s to the increasing numbers of Africans, Asians, and Latin Americans staying in Moscow in the post-Stalin era. A number of (foreign) faculty also helped with the selection, edition, and translation of texts: at the interwar-era KUTV and the post-Stalin-era Moscow State University's Institute of African and Asian Countries, People's Friendship University Patrice Lumumba (founded in 1960), and the various Institutes of the Soviet Academy of Sciences (of Oriental Studies, Africa, Latin America, and so on). Over the course of the 1970s and '80s, the publishing house increasingly came to rely on contracts with foreign translators located worldwide.[68]

Indeed, throughout its existence, it boasted relationships with counterparts such as the New York–based International Publishers, Lawrence & Wishart in London, and New Delhi's People's Publishing House (PPH), which would often reprint, commission, and help with the distribution of the texts. It also maintained a network of specialized bookstores in a number of major cities worldwide.

The institutional history of ITIR is a story of constant internal reorganizations and the accompanying renamings. In 1938, it became Publishing House of Literature in Foreign Languages, a name later taken by most of the publishing houses in the Soviet bloc modelled after it.[69] It lasted in that format until 1963, when it was renamed Progress Publishers following its merger with the major Soviet press dedicated to Russian translations *from* foreign languages (Publishing House of Foreign Literature). Thus, unlike its earlier iterations, Progress enjoyed a significant domestic readership. One constant factor in its history was the steady rise in the number of languages and volumes it published. Indeed, in the history of publishing, there has probably never been a press so linguistically ambitious. In its first year (1931), it published in ten Western European (English, German, French, Italian, Dutch, Swedish, Norwegian, Danish, Spanish, and Portuguese), seven East European (Serbo-Croatian, Czech, Bulgarian, Romanian, Hungarian, Polish, and Lithuanian), and five Asian languages (Japanese, Chinese, Korean, Persian, and Turkish). And while the first post-Second World War decade saw the emergence of an Afro-Arab (Arabic, Ahmara, Yoruba, Hausa, Swahili) and Indian (Hindi, Urdu, Bengali, Tamil, and Telog) sections, it was in the post-Stalin era that non-Western languages came to dominate the overall publishing plans. Over the course of the 1960s alone, the number of "Eastern" languages doubled, from fifteen to twenty-eight. By 1980, the Indian section was producing more titles than the English one, which had led the publishing house since its foundation. (Throughout this period, books in the colonial languages, English, French, Spanish, and Portuguese, were also being sent to Africa, Asia, and Latin America by ITIR's main distributor, *Mezhkniga*.) At its peak during the 1980s, Progress was a behemoth, publishing close to 2,000 new titles yearly, with a print run approaching 30 million copies and employing close to 1,000 full-time staff, in addition to hundreds of out-of-house translators[70] Moreover, its role was not limited to passive selection and translation of pre-existing texts. It actively commissioned books and supported whole subfields, such as foreign travelogues dedicated to the USSR (a genre that had needed much support after its peak in the interwar era) and aimed at foreign audiences as well as critical studies of Western social science theories (a genre jocularly known in the USSR as "critique of bourgeois perversities") targeting Soviet readers.[71]

It is not possible to have a single, coherent history of the reception of Progress's foreign volumes over the course of several decades, dozens of languages, and even more geographies.[72] In addition to the classics of Marxism and Leninism, which had initially been the main focus of ITIR's work, Progress published in three other areas: contemporary scholarship, textbooks and illustrated materials, and literature. In contrast to contemporary Russian scholarship, certain fields of post-Stalin-era Soviet scholarship, not only the hard sciences but also humanities and social sciences, were seen as world-leading and elicited much interest, in both the Western and non-Western world. The textbooks and illustrated materials were meant primarily for non-Western readers. The final area, literature, emerged only gradually as a distinct field of the publishing house. Over the course of the 1930s, however, some of ITIR's more distinguished translators, such as Alice Oran, George Rui, Maximilian Schick, Hilda Angarova, José Vento, Angel Errais, Margaret Amrome, and Aiwa Litvinova (Soviet foreign minister Mikhail Litvinov's wife), began to translate the classics of Russian and early Soviet literature into foreign languages. In 1982, when the literature sector's yearly output had surpassed 400 titles of Russian and Soviet fiction, making it the largest of the four foreign-language sectors, it evolved into a separate publishing house, Raduga (Rainbow). By that point, the editorial choices for texts to be translated could easily veer away from the safe classics to include more debatable contemporary Soviet literature such as Valentin Rasputin's and Chinghiz Aitmatov's novels. Some of Progress's translations reached their audiences not only in the more traditional book format but also via Radio Moscow, which was similarly broadcasting in several dozen languages (seventy-five at its peak in the 1980s) and included abundant literary programming, which was especially popular with non-Western audiences.

As a whole, the sheer volume of translation taking place in Progress and its predecessors made it a unique site for translation studies. Indeed, over the course of trying to standardize their practice, translators working within ITIR, the Publishing House of Foreign Literature, and the *International Literature* magazine pioneered the whole field of translation theory, eventually settling on a method called "adequate" or "realist" translation, which favoured free over literal translation. In its various iterations, the publishing house hosted multiple translation seminars and offered other opportunities for advancing the translation abilities of its employees and other Moscow residents. However, the much more challenging work of translating Russian literature into foreign languages, especially into non-European ones, remained rather uneven in quality. Readers' letters to the publishing house – never published but carefully archived – ranged between high praise and severe criticism. In one such letter, written in 1961 and from New Delhi, Hussein Joshi Iqbal writes:

> I have read all your books in Urdu, except for those that were impossible to find. I really like it that on the final page of almost all of your books there is an address to the reader [Iqbal is referring to the request to the reader that Progress books carried on their last page: "Progress Publishers would be glad to have your opinion of this book, its translation and design and any suggestions you may have for future publications. Please send all your comments to 21, Zubovsky Boulevard, Moscow, U.S.S.R." – author's note]. Responding to it, I would like to share some of my thoughts about the books I read. As a whole, they create a good impression, especially those translated by Anwar Zasim and Zoe Ansari. Other translations suffer from excessive literalness. Often, the Urdu sentences preserve English and Russian constructions to an unacceptable degree. In those translations, it is difficult to capture the individual style of the writer. For example, Maxim Gorky's *Mother*, Leo Tolstoy's *Cossacks*, Gogol's *Taras Bulba*, Ivan Turgenev's *Rudin* and *Fathers and Sons*, Nikolai Ostrovsky's *How the Steel Was Tempered*, and Pushkin's *Belkin Tales* and *Dubrovsky* read as if written by the same author, employing the same style.[73]

Such an observation was confirmed to me by one of the leading Russian scholars of Indian literature, Liudmila Vasilieva. She contrasted the quality of the Lotus Prize recipient Bhisham Sahni's translations of Russian literature into Hindi, which, in addition to carrying the imprimatur of a major writer, were very sensitive to the original's style, with the poor prose of the other major translator of Russian literature into Hindi, Madan Lal Madhu. Like other aspects of Soviet literary internationalism, there were hits and misses in the selection of translators. Vasilieva also singled out the Hindi translations of Manavendra Gupta, an engineering graduate from People's Friendship University, whose excellent Russian allowed him to bypass the English translations on which the other two had heavily relied.[74]

Starting from 1963, when it came about after the merger between Publishing House of Foreign Languages and Foreign Literature Publishing House, Progress also became the main vehicle through which African and Asian literatures would reach Soviet audiences. (Other Soviet presses, such as Vostochnaia literatura, Khudozhestvennaia literatura, and Molodaya Gvardiya also published Afro-Asian literature, if in significantly smaller volumes.) Well plugged into the two main Soviet cultural bureaucracies liaising with the Afro-Asian Writers Association (the Foreign Commission of the Writers Union and the Committee for Afro-Asian Solidarity), Progress offered the Soviet readers of the 1960s to the 1980s access to contemporary writings from these continents as wide as and sometimes greater than what their British, American, and French peers enjoyed. Other non-Russian Soviet presses, such as Gafur Guliam and Fan in Tashkent; Mektep and Zhazushi in Alma-Ata; Ifron and Adib in Dushanbe; Mektep in Frunze (today's Bishkek); Khordukhain grokh in Yerevan; Sabchota Skartvelo and Nakaduli in Tbilisi; and Yazici and Giandzhlik in Baku would then secondarily translate Progress's volumes into the languages of their republic. As far as Afro-Asian writers were concerned, in particular, the participants in the Afro-Asian Writers Association, who were particularly well-represented in Progress' publishing lists, a Soviet publication meant not only royalties but also cultural recognition.[75] In addition, Progress could and did extend invitations to foreign writers, whether to work in Moscow as translators (as was the case with the above-mentioned Lotus Prize winner Bhisham Sahni) or for an author's visit (typically arranged in co-ordination with the Writers Union). Either way, it became one of the main vehicles whereby the USSR extended symbolic and monetary capital to African and Asian writers.

The Soviet Readers of Afro-Asian Literature

What did Soviet readers make of this volume of Afro-Asian literature coming to them? The remainder of this chapter will offer a schematic history of post-Stalin-era Soviet readers' reception of Afro-Asian literature and thus expose one of the limiting factors of Soviet internationalism.

Soviet readers, especially the more elite ones, only poorly reciprocated the Afro-Asian interest in Russian literature. At first glance, this indifference may seem puzzling. If we judge by the contents of *Foreign Literature* magazine, the Soviet window on contemporary world literature, a significant portion of Soviet readers' attention should have gone to African and Asian literature. After all, approximately 460 of 2,270 (or over 20 per cent) reviews, general articles, and introductions published by the magazine between 1955 and 1974 were dedicated to the literatures of Africa and Asia.[76] Of course, on a per-country basis, the number of articles ranged from eighty-four texts about Chinese literature to a single text about a Malawi writer, but the encyclopedic coverage of non-Western literary geographies is impressive nonetheless.

The problem was precisely that the contents of *Foreign Literature* inadequately reflected the interests of the Soviet reader, especially those in the intelligentsia, who comprised most of its audience. According to Aleksandr Yakovlevich Livergandt, the editor of the contemporary version of the magazine, his Soviet-era predecessors would publish Afro-Asian literature just "to balance the issue."[77] That is, if the editorial board were to print a short story by Ernest Hemingway or some other "daring" text, they faced the pressure to include in the same issue more "politically progressive" material, for example, a selection of militantly anti-American Vietnamese poetry.

Though only approximate, and, we will see later, highly unnuanced, Livergandt's account offers a good start into the reception of Afro-Asian literature in the USSR. While *Foreign Literature* and Progress meticulously mapped the literary globe, Soviet reader interest in non-Western literatures could never approach the insatiable curiosity about texts coming from Western Europe and the United States. The latter dominate the comments and recommendations thousands of Soviet readers sent the magazine in the form of "letters to the editor," which the editors meticulously responded to and archived. This genre, the subject of an excellent study by Denis Kozlov, offers unrivalled material for reception studies.[78] As private letters (only a tiny fraction of them were published on the pages of the magazine), these often contain critical comments that would not have been possible in public utterances. If Kozlov's "readers of *Novyi Mir*" roughly represent the reformist, anti-Stalinist party in post-Stalin-era USSR, the political and social identity of "the readers of *Foreign Literature*" is not as clear-cut. Judging by the addresses and professions they occasionally left, they seem a fairly diverse group geographically and socially. However, a subscription to or active purchasing of *Foreign Literature* indicates a desire to be one of the "first" readers of foreign literature, a belonging, or at least an ambition to belong to, the Soviet intelligentsia, especially the more outward-oriented one.

It would be untrue to claim that the magazine's readership exhibited no interest whatsoever in non-Western literatures. There were certainly a number of readers personally or professionally interested in the literatures and societies of Africa, Asia, and Latin America. Especially in the magazine's first decade, when curiosity about the emerging nations might have been more general, we find positive mentions in readers' private letters, such as a 1962 letter from Mikhail Trofimovich, which praised an African work published in the magazine and asked for more. In his reply (also unpublished), the general editor, Aleksandr Chakovsky himself (or, more likely, a *Foreign Literature* employee who signed his name), explained the editorial position:

> You are of course very right to point out the heroic struggle of
> the peoples of Africa's colonial countries. However, you imagine
> somewhat primitively the development of literature there. Judging by
> your letter, if in real life there was such a progressive political leader
> as Lumumba ... and such instances of heroic struggle of the peoples,
> then there must be simultaneously literary works on such topics.
> Unfortunately, this is far from the truth. As a result of the colonizers'
> rule, millions of people in these countries remain illiterate, and are
> not able to read their national writers, who, in turn, are all too often
> educated abroad and thus do not always reflect the events and lives
> of their people. Contemporary African literature is a literature being
> born. It reflects the cultural and political development of African
> peoples. At the same time, if you read our journal regularly, you
> will not fail to see that *The Mission* hardly exhausts our African
> publications. For example, we recently published the novella
> *Tokolosh* by the progressive South African writer [Ronald] Segal,
> *The Old Man and the Medal* by the progressive Cameroonian writer
> [Ferdinand] Oyono, the Algerian Communist writer Mohammed
> Dib. Right now we are printing *The Musician Trees* by the
> imprisoned (possibly killed) [Stephen] Alexis, a Haitian, who always
> considered himself African by virtue of connections and traditions.

I am not even talking about the poetry and the material about Africa that we publish in the Literary Criticism section. Finally, the forthcoming fifth, May issue of our magazine would be exclusively devoted to Africa.[79]

Alongside statements of interest in African literature such as Mikhail Trofimovich's, however, from fairly early on in the history of *Foreign Literature* we find readers' letters expressing active indifference, if not hostility, to non-Western literature. Thus, in one such letter written in 1956, V. Radugin from Kharkov admonishes the editors:

[Jean-Paul] Sartre's *Lizzie* [a 1948 play better known as *The Respectful Prostitute*] repeats for a hundredth time the exhausted plot about an African-American man and a white woman. We of course sympathize with African-Americans and condemn racism, but you cannot write about that to exhaustion ... In India, in addition to poor peasants, there is also life and we'd like to read about it. We should not be agitated to sympathize with poor Indians – we are of course for them and against their oppressors but would also like to learn more about the Indian intelligentsia ... There is no reason to describe medieval Chinese theatre as some kind of accomplishment. For the European, this is a wild sight, playing on the nerves of the normal person.[80]

In the same spirit, in 1963, another reader, N.V. Firsov, is unhappy that

[t]here is nothing to read in the latest issues (8, 9, 10, 11). They lie on the kiosk shelves and nobody is buying them. And not so long ago the journal was read to tatters. One would only hear "Have you read the latest *Foreign Literature* issue?" These were times when it published such works as [John Steinbeck's] *Winter of Our Discontent* (1961), [Kingsley Amis's] *Lucky Jim* (1954), [Dieter Noll's] *The Adventures of Werner Holt* (1960), [Mitchell Wilson's] *Meeting at a Far Meridian* (1960). Of course, you can publish African poetry, Chinese prose, and some didactic short stories by Romanian, Hungarian, Bulgarian writers without worrying too much about the consequences. Why don't you publish Remarque's *Spark of Life* (1952)? According to the reviews in *The Literary Gazette*, that's a worthy novel.[81]

Such sentiments grow, in tone and frequency, from the second half of the 1960s onward. Two distinct explanations can account for such unsympathetic views of non-Western literatures: first, the novels of which Firsov speaks approvingly come from the US, UK, and Germany, the traditional sources of culture for a Western-centric member of the Soviet intelligentsia. Since an increasingly elitist conception of culture as an exclusive and elevated tradition accessible only to a chosen few (themselves) came to displace the intelligentsia's earlier Enlightenment impulse to make culture accessible to all, many of its late-Soviet representatives openly expressed doubts as to whether "real literature" could come out of Africa (or Bulgaria or Romania, which stood at the bottom of this Western-centric hierarchy, when applied to the Soviet bloc). Indeed, this Western-centric hierarchy also featured important gradations: despite its geographical position, Japanese literature and film were treated as nearly Western. Largely thanks to the magic realist novel, Latin American literature achieved wide regard among Soviet audiences over the course of the 1970s. In the eyes of this audience, literatures with longer traditions, such as India's or China's or the Arab world's, enjoyed greater cultural capital than newer and smaller ones such as those of sub-Saharan Africa.

Related to such geocultural assumptions is another, more purely political explanation, more applicable to the non-conformist, dissident-minded section of the readership: from the point of view of Soviet foreign policy, the countries or continents mentioned fell into the category of "politically progressive": Bulgaria, Romania, and China were all socialist countries. Though much of Africa had yet to achieve independence at the time Firsov wrote his letter (1963), in the eyes of the Soviet reader, the anti-colonial orientation of the new countries made them natural allies of the USSR. Moreover, outright support for revolutions in Africa, Asia, and Latin America – in which the USSR engaged rarely and reluctantly – in practice meant straining relations with the United States and the West more broadly, the cultural side of which the Soviet intelligentsia so treasured.[82] For considerations that rarely had anything to do with aesthetics, readers generally hostile to the Soviet state, whose number would grow in time, were taking an increasingly dim view of foreign writers who could somehow be construed as pro-Soviet (either because of their country of origin or left-wing sympathies). In this logic, the novels of Sembène Ousmane were "tainted" by his "socialist realist" style, Communist Party membership, and participation in official Soviet initiatives such as Afro-Asian Writers congresses. While only a minority among the dissident intelligentsia took the logic of mechanically inverting Soviet values to its extreme ("The Soviet Union is for Vietnam. We, therefore, are against it"), a milder, less articulated displeasure with official Soviet anti-racist and anti-colonialist campaigns persists among certain sections of erstwhile non-conformists in the post-Soviet era.

This phenomenon was to a large extent fuelled by Soviet cultural bureaucracies, whose instrumentalist treatment of (semi-)colonial cultures, translation, and publication choices, prioritized Cold War cultural politics at the expense of reader interest. Despite an impressive translation coverage in the post-Stalin era, nearly rivalling that available in English and French, a number of contemporary writers from these continents, such as the Nobel Prize winners J.M. Coetzee, Derek Walcott, Gao Xingian, V.S. Naipaul, and the perennial Nobel Prize hopeful Jorge Luis Borges, were denied access to the Soviet reader for various political transgressions they had committed until censorship was relaxed during perestroika. Conversely, there were numerous Afro-Asian writers poorly known in their own countries, but translated into Russian and other Soviet languages.[83]

Such political tests in choosing whom to translate and publish were not the only problems that Cold War literary diplomacy put in the way of Soviet readers' reception of Afro-Asian literature. After all, Soviet readers were not the only audience for those publications. Thus, ahead of every Afro-Asian Writers Congress, Soviet publishers, and Progress in particular, were instructed to print translations of many of the writers attending the event so that those writers could feel they had an audience in the USSR. The preparatory committee for the 1973 Alma-Ata Congress, for example, planned an exhibit of Soviet translations of 400 African and Asian works published on the eve of the conference.[84] These 400 volumes, the transcript makes quite explicit, were meant to prove the popularity enjoyed by the literature of the two continents in the USSR as well as the imagined community of those writers. In this spirit, in anticipation of the Sixth Congress of the Afro-Asian Writers Association in Nairobi, one of the leaders of the Soviet Writers Union instructed the director of a Kazakh publishing house as follows:

To the Director of the Zhazushi Publishing House Dzhumbaev
Dear Comrade Dzhumbaev!
The Sixth Congress of the Afro-Asian Writers Association will take place in 1977 in Kenya's capital Nairobi. In light of this circumstance,

it would be expedient to publish several works of Kenyan and East African Writers.

The leadership of the Soviet Writers Union and the Foreign Commission in particular would also like to ask you to look favourably upon E.Ya. Surovtsev's submission of a collected volume *We Are from East Africa*, and if possible, include the volume in the publishing plan for 1977.

Respectfully, N. Fedorenko, Secretary of the Soviet Writers Union[85]

The plans for the Nairobi Congress fell through, but Surovtsev's volume, and many others, nevertheless reached Soviet bookstores and libraries. Such campaign-style practices, which accompanied every congress or anniversary, were not only expensive, but as far as the elite Russian reader was concerned, they also amounted to literary dumping and reduced the value of the newly released books. They must have further reinforced the intelligentsia's tendency to look upon Afro-Asian literature as another propagandistic initiative of the Soviet government rather than art deserving of their attention.

Indeed, the very interface with which Soviet cultural bureaucracy engaged Afro-Asian literatures repelled elite, intelligentsia readers. Among such circles, Anatoly Sofronov, the deputy head of the Soviet Afro-Asian Solidarity Committee and leader of most Soviet delegations to the Afro-Asian Writers Congresses, was an odious figure best remembered for leading the late-Stalin-era anti-Semitic campaign within the Soviet Writers Union.[86] The other major Soviet bureaucrat curating the Afro-Asian Writers Association, Konstantin Chugunov, the deputy head of the Foreign Commission of the Writers Union, was only nominally a writer: he had come to the Union after a long and successful career in the NKVD. Both of these officials represented the Association not only in the eyes of foreign writers but to domestic audiences as well. The one Russian writer who specialized in Africa in a more literary capacity was Yevgeniy Dolmatovsky, though his involvement could hardly have allayed the intelligentsia's suspicions: by the time he completed his book of poems *Africa Has the Shape of a Heart* (1961), Dolmatovsky had acquired the reputation of a conformist hack, who could versify on any politically expedient topic. Regardless of any literary merits his Africa-themed poems may or may not have had, his literary reputation could only damage the literary reception of Africa among elite Russian readers, especially more non-conformist ones.

This reception history of Afro-Asian literatures in the post-Soviet USSR has been mostly focused on Western-centric intelligentsia readers based in Moscow and Leningrad, the so-called "first" readers. While they did enjoy significant cultural authority in shaping the preferences of wider sections of the reading public, their tastes were far from the sole determining factor. Certainly, they failed to explain the immense popularity of the Turkish author Aziz Nesin's satirical vignettes, which was most likely due to Soviet readers' love for this genre and the scant competition Nesin faced in it.[87] In addition, the sheer fact that an African or Asian text would appear on the pages of *Foreign Literature* or would be reviewed in *Literary Gazette* and other such epitextual sources meant that readers were more likely to pick up a library or bookstore volume written by its author.[88] As literature was one of the major ways of learning about other countries, the cheap and beautifully printed editions of Indian short stories or Arab novels would serve as such vehicles. Poetry of course was more demanding and thus, an even harder sell than prose texts. Yet in the translation of well-known Soviet poets such as Nikolai Tikhonov, Mikhail Isakovsky, Aleksandr Surkov, and Rimma Kazakova, the works of first-rate poets such as Faiz Ahmad Faiz would still reach their Soviet reader.[89]

Finally, in addition to readers with a professional and personal interest in African and Asian culture, there was one other type of audience among whom Afro-Asian literature enjoyed a much greater popularity: readers in Central Asia and the Caucasus, who shared a similar geography, culture, and literary traditions with many of their Asian peers.[90] There were specific correspondences: Tajik readers saw literature in Iranian and Dari (both Persian languages, like their own) as branches of their own national literature. By the same token, the main Soviet Buryat press specialized in Mongolian literature. Azeri publishing houses published a disproportionate number of Turkish texts, and so on.

Conclusion

The Afro-Asian Writers Association's life was very uneven: a spectacular birth in 1958, a schism and near-standstill in the first half of the 1960s occasioned by the Sino-Soviet split, followed by a decade of organizational growth. Then it became a dual casualty of Brezhnev-era stagnation and what Vijay Prashad has called "the assassinations" of the Third World. After the loss of its Cairo base in 1978, the Association entered a period of homelessness from which it never fully recovered. Over the course of the 1980s, *Lotus* was becoming a largely Arabic and increasingly irregular publication, compiled and edited within the PLO, using this underground organization's meagre resources, and supported by a Soviet subsidy and free printing in East Germany rather than subscriptions, as was the original hope. But what worried the Soviet delegation at the last, Eighth, Congress of the Association held in Tunis in December 1988 was the disappearance of major and young writers from the movement. Bemoaning the recent death of Alex La Guma, Faiz Ahmad Faiz, and Mirzo Tursun-Zade, and the non-attendance of others, their report described the measures taken by the Congress to bring fresh blood into the Association's bloodstream.[91] Heralded as "a perestroika," these included stabilizing its headquarters (a return to Cairo), electing a new general secretary (the Egyptian novelist Lutfi al-Khuli), entering into partnerships with other international organizations (UNESCO, PEN International), and even yet another proposal to publish *Lotus* in Russian first, thus helping the magazine break even. (Thanks to Soviet efforts to showcase the enormous quantities of Afro-Asian literature published in the USSR in various languages, many Afro-Asian writers must have placed their hopes in the Soviet reader as the most reliable supporter of the movement.) According to the last written trace I found of the Association's life in the Soviet archives, some of these proposals were followed up on. Despite its economic difficulties, the Egyptian government had given the Association a villa, and agreements were reached with PEN. There were plans to expand the Association to Latin America and to re-invite Chinese writers, absent since the 1961 Cairo Congress.[92] But such plans, whether realistic or not, were running up against time and geopolitical tides.[93] Already at the Tunis Congress, the East German Afro-Asian Solidarity Committee served notice that it was giving up publishing *Lotus* and in 1989, the last issue of the English edition, the 61st, came out. The Arabic issue lasted for two more years. Over these years the Soviet Writers Union's budget was being cut, and finally, in 1991, the Soviet Union itself, the state most invested – symbolically and materially – in the Afro-Asian Writers Association, ceased to exist.[94]

"The Links That Bind Us":
Solidarity Narratives in Third-Worldist Fiction

If the previous chapter reconstructed the now forgotten attempt to create a Soviet-aligned Third-World literary field, this one is concerned with its effects on writing. The difficulty of generalizing about "Third-World" literature as a whole has been well illustrated by the polemics around Fredric Jameson's "Third-World Literature in the Age of Multinational Capitalism" (1986) and especially its deliberatively provocative passages:

> The third-world novel will not offer the satisfactions of Proust or Joyce; what is more damaging than that, perhaps, is its tendency to remind us of outmoded stages of our own first-world cultural development and to cause us to conclude that "they are still writing novels like Dreiser or Sherwood Anderson" ... let me now, by way of a sweeping hypothesis, try to say what all third-world cultural productions seem to have in common and what distinguishes them radically from analogous cultural forms in the first world. All third-world texts are necessarily, I want to argue, allegorical, and in a very specific way: they are to be read as what I will call national allegories.[1]

Critics have read Jameson's text as an act of Orientalist lumping together of very different literary traditions and cultures and, as Imre Szeman points out, the whole episode has been treated as "a cautionary tale about the extent and depth of Eurocentrism in the Western academy."[2] Vijay Prashad's redefinition of the "Third World," which this book has adopted – "not a place ... [but] a project" – offers a simple and elegant way of resolving the whole affair.[3] Thus understood, the much smaller body of "Third-World texts," that is, the writings associated with an emancipatory, anti-colonial Third-World project rather than the mechanical sum of all literatures written in Africa, Asia, and Latin America, not only softens the brunt of the accusations against Jameson but also allows the kind of analysis the larger, geographical category does not.

Of greater concern from the point of view of this book, however, is that like most postcolonialists, Jameson chooses to compare "Third-World" literature with "ours," the literature of the First World (again understood not as the entirety of literature produced in the Western bloc but, specifically, as modernism). The Second World could have provided the mediating term between the First and the Third, removing – or at least, casting in a different light – the radical distinction that Jameson insists on. It is a missed opportunity, but one taken seriously a decade later by Dubravka Juraga and Keith Booker. Focusing on the genre of the historical novel, Juraga and Booker offer a polemical account of the parallels between socialist realism as practised in the Soviet Union and postcolonial literature.[4] Their largely theoretical argument is then confirmed in practice by Gesine Drews-Sylla, who takes Soviet socialist realism as a productive perspective through which to analyze Sembène Ousmane's novels *Oh Country, My Beautiful People!* (1957) and *God's Bits of Wood* (1960).[5] In carrying out this comparison, Drews-Sylla largely relies on Katerina Clark's by now canonical categories defining the socialist-realist novel: a positive hero, the narrative stages he or she undergoes, and, in the process, his or her acquisition of political consciousness.[6] There is, however, another aspect to socialist realism, which is decidedly missing from Senegal and France, where Sembène wrote his novels, and which limits its applicability outside of the Soviet bloc: namely, institutions such as the Soviet Writers Union and Soviet-type censorship.[7] (Not that there were no writers' associations or censorship in France and Senegal, but they operated entirely differently and could not produce the same textual effects.) Through the category of "the global proletarian novel," which in addition to Soviet socialist realism conveniently includes pre-Soviet and non-Soviet (Western European, Asian, and American) texts and extends to the postcolonial 1960s, Michael Denning helps us cut through the limitations of socialist realism as a category (though probably at the expense of losing the analytically useful "realism," which, through its different inflections, was the aesthetic horizon common to his authors).[8] Inspired by Denning's telegraphic history of magic realism as the heir to the tradition of the proletarian novel of the first half of the twentieth century as well as by Juraga and Booker, Drews-Sylla, and Popescu's comparative work, this chapter will seek to extend it by examining the migration and adaptation of certain topoi and narrative structures from proletarian to postcolonial texts.

More precisely, it will be interested in the ways a number of third-worldist texts, many of which were written by participants in the Afro-Asian Writers Association, attempted to situate their post- or semi- or still-colonial nation in a wider world. While Jameson's "national allegory" is still central to the world-making of these novels, it needs to be pollinated by a global imaginary. After all, these narratives symbolically resolved the tension between the competing imperatives of constructing national communities out of formerly colonial populations, on the one hand, and situating those emerging communities in a wider world vis-à-vis the West, the USSR, and other colonizing nations, on the other. The multiple idioms spoken by the progressive nationalisms united in the Third World project, to say nothing of the charged field of the Global Cold War, made aligning them internationally a particularly tricky affair. Cultural production was central to coalescing these emancipatory struggles within the broader internationalism of the Third World, muting their differences and giving the project, for a time at least, the appearance of a common front. Some of these narrative strategies, this chapter will show, were drawn from the internationalism of an early twentieth-century proletarian fiction.

The most common device Third-Worldist novelists resorted to in synthesizing these contradictions is the international solidarity/foreign-utopia topos, the evocation of foreign revolutions as an inspiration for the emancipatory struggles at home. Some of these evocations are more vertical (novelistic references to the USSR, the land of the victorious Revolution) while others are more horizontal (appealing to other Third-Worldist struggles taking place concurrently, or, most basically, to the solidarity of oppressed peoples everywhere). In addition, many Third-Worldist novels achieve the synthesis of those two imperatives through *chain narratives*. I have been able to identify two types of chain narratives, each with different mental geographies and political valences. The first is the supply-chain narrative, which serves as the structuring principle behind a whole subgenre of the Latin American political novel. This narrative allows the reader to follow the circulation of money and goods from the South American mines and banana plantations, where resources are extracted in a most brutally exploitative way, to the corporate boardrooms of New York and Chicago, where the desire for profit and power drive that exploitation. While lacking in the supply-chain narrative's geographical scope, the railway narrative, with its plotting of the action among capitals, provincial towns, and remote railway junctions as well as political struggles over control of the train and the railway, allows a much greater scope for class struggle and nation-building. It is this last trope that returned to Soviet Central Asian fiction as a form of critique of Soviet rule, questioning the unevenness of the much-touted Soviet modernization, its ecological consequences, and the meaning of local self-rule.

Third-Worldist Internationalism

The tension between nationalism and internationalism is as old as the leftist movement itself. In his essay "Internationalism: A Breviary" (2007), Perry Anderson contextualizes the emancipatory movements of the Third World in the left's *longue-durée* dialectic between nationalism and internationalism.[9] Anderson starts from the observation that if for most of the nineteenth century, the forces of labour (his term for the left) held a monopoly on internationalism – famously institutionalized by Marx's International Workingmen's Association – the late twentieth century finds capitalist globalization as the main idiom of transnational connectivity. To explain this shift in the political valences of internationalism, Anderson first examines the post-Second World War establishment of global commercial and ideological institutions, such as the monetary accords of Bretton Woods, continued with the Marshall and Dodge plans for the reconstruction of Europe and Japan, and culminating in the creation of free-trade zones and the rise of transnational corporations. If in the late nineteenth and early twentieth centuries, the property-owning classes had aligned themselves with their nations, often helping bring those nations into conflicts such as the two world wars, "[t]he existence of a single hegemonic power [the US] made possible an international coordination of their [capitalist states'] interests" after 1945.[10]

At the same time as capital was discovering its own internationalism, the forces of labour were increasingly aligning themselves with their own nation-state. Mid-twentieth-century "[n]ationalism," in Anderson's words, "becomes predominantly a popular cause, of exploited and destitute masses."[11] Unlike the highly centralized Comintern or Cominform Bureau, the social democratic Socialist International, the smaller Trotskyist and the more ephemeral anarchist ones, the Third-World project of the post–Second World War era comprised extremely heterogeneous national liberation movements, speaking in the diverse idioms of Kemalism in Turkey, Sukarnoism in Indonesia, Peronism in Argentine, Gandhism, pan-Africanism and *negritude,* and pan-Arabic nationalism. The mass basis of those anti-colonial movements was equally varied, but, numerically, its most important component was peasantry, a social group without much lived experience of cosmopolitanism. Anderson's sketch of the Non-Aligned Movement as a conglomeration of heterogeneous nationalisms explains its failure to maintain any semblance of unity in the 1970s and 1980s, a process described in greater detail in Parts II and III of Vijay Prashad's magisterial *Darker Nations: A People's History of the Third World.* What it cannot account for is the advent and initial success of the movement in the late 1950s and the 1960s, when it managed to speak in a unified voice.

During that brief window, I would argue, culture played a major role in sustaining an image (if not quite a reality) of a united Third World. The figure of Ernesto "Che" Guevara, the revolutionary icon of the 1960s, whose personal involvement in numerous local struggles helped interlink them emblematically in a global movement, was one important symbolic site for the internationalist nationalism of the 1960s. In this role, Che corresponds to Giuseppe Garibaldi, whom Perry Anderson posits as the embodiment of the symbiosis of the mid-nineteenth century's national-ist and internationalist struggles. If the Italian national hero Garibaldi fought for progressive causes throughout Europe and Latin America, the Argentinean Che deployed himself in Guatemala, Cuba, and Angola, before he met his death in the Bolivian mountains.[12] Not unlike the bearded Garibaldi, who received thousands of admiring letters from different parts of the world, the bearded Che captured the imagination of progressive publics worldwide.[13]

International Solidarity/Foreign-Utopia Topos

Novels were thus not the first texts to articulate international solidarities. Ever since Marx and Engels' *Communist Manifesto* (1848), for example, the common condition and collective task of "proletarians all over the world" became a staple of socialist journalism. Only with the rise of the proletar-ian novel in the first half of the twentieth century does this journalistic trope migrate to literature, in the form of a politically advanced character's declarations of workers' international brotherhood, like the following one from Maxim Gorky's 1906 *Mother*:

"What queer people you are!" said the mother to the Little Russian one day. "All are your comrades – the Armenians and the Jews and the Austrians. You speak about all as of your friends; you grieve for all, and you rejoice for all!"

"For all, mother dear, for all! The world is ours! The world is for the workers! For us there is no nation, no race. For us there are only comrades and foes."[14]

Most proletarian novelists' (and their characters') absence of lived experience or concrete knowledge of foreign cultures made their reliance on such formulaic representations of internationalism inevitable. The power of such lists, which came in a number of different varieties, lies in their equal, or horizontal, relations and simultaneous inclusion into an imagined community.[15]

With the revolutions at the end of the First World War, variations of this solidarity topos emerged. There were now states the communists and fellow travellers worldwide could declare their own. More hierarchical than the older solidarity topos, the "foreign utopia" topos took the form of references to revolutionary struggles abroad as an inspiration for the one at home. "Utopia" may not be the most precise term, for those places that the topos evoked actually existed, in some other part of the world, sometimes in a different era. But those "real utopias" did fire the imaginations of whole societies no less than Thomas More's once did. For a few decades after 1917, the Bolshevik Revolution held a certain monopoly on that utopia, at least in the pens of many leftist writers.

While the Soviet topos – a reference to the Russian Revolution or the Soviet state as a final political horizon for liberation struggles – first appeared in novels written by revolutionary writers in Western Europe and North America, it enjoyed a particular longevity in African, Asian, and Latin American novels, appearing throughout the 1970s. César Vallejo's *Tungsten* (1931), one of the first proletarian novels in Latin America, ends with an episode in which the political organizer Servando Huanca, having failed to persuade the geologist and intellectual Benito Leonidas of the viability of profound social change in Peru through other arguments, offers the Russian Revolution, which had taken place just before their conversation, as his ultimate argument:

"Have you read what they're saying in the newspapers that the workers and peasants have risen up in Russia? They've risen up against the bosses and the rich, against the great landlords, and against the government, and overthrown them, and now there's another government."

"Yes. Yes, I've read about it in *El Comercio*," said Benites.[16]

The "Russian topos" is a recurrent motif in Ngũgĩ wa Thiong'o's 1967 *A Grain of Wheat* and is typically evoked by the politically advanced members of the community ("General R. never forgot a friend or an enemy. R. stood for Russia"),[17] often serving to inspire wavering comrades into action:

> They [the prisoners] discussed education, agriculture, government, and Gatu had elaborate stories for all these subjects. For instance, he told them a wonderful story of what once happened in Russia where the ordinary man, even without a knowledge of how to read, write or speak a word of English was actually running the government. And now all nations on earth feared Russia.[18]

The deliberate naiveté of those references to "Russia" reflects the real-life dearth of information about the Soviet state and allows for the projection of the local community's desires and values. Usually, "the Russian topos" figures as a mere mention of a distant site of revolution. However, Mulk Raj Anand's *The Sword and the Sickle* (written in 1940, published in 1942) offers an extended account of indigenous peasants' efforts to adapt the Russian Revolution to local conditions. Understanding of the historical circumstances of the Russian Revolution decreases sharply with the political consciousness of the characters: from the experienced Communist functionary, the mysterious, deus-ex-machina-like comrade Sarshar; to the Count, head of the group of merry rebels, who offers an extended historical exposition of the three different Russian revolutions (1905, February 1917, and October 1917), but is a little mystified by the workings of the Revolution he is witnessing; to the protagonist Lalu Singh, who, though of peasant origins, has seen a good deal of Europe as a soldier during the First World War; and finally, to the Indian villagers who first hear of the Bolshevik Revolution from Lalu's mouth:

> For, in the land called Roos, too, the peasants once suffered as you do, and they set up their own Raj ... And the peasants and workers are ruling there, and all men there live like brothers ... So give a shout: "All men are brothers."[19]

The Russian topos reaches its crescendo in Nâzım Hikmet's novel-in-verse *Human Landscapes from My Country* (1938–50) and Pablo Neruda's epic poem *Canto General* (written approximately over the same period). Among the multiple parallels that could be found between the two national epics, each contains a section that places those nations in the global context of their historical moment: the Second World War in Hikmet's and the early Cold War in Neruda's.[20] While the political geography drawn in both cases is truly planetary, opening with a German and a British seaman in the Second World War sending each other off to the bottom of the Atlantic, in Hikmet's case, and with McCarthy-era United States and postwar Europe in Neruda's, it eventually comes to focus on the Soviet state, the source of hope for the whole globe. The poetic space continues to shrink, from the Second World War front, where, in Hikmet's epic poem, Soviet soldiers are fighting off the German invasion, or the industrial front in Neruda's, where the country is being reconstructed after the war, to "three rooms of the old Kremlin" (Neruda, 264) where "the man of steel ... with his cool, imperturbable, unflinching eyes / and bushy moustache, covering one of the wisest mouths in the century" (Hikmet, 391) "helped to conceive his [nation] as well, to build it, and defend it" (Neruda, 264).[21] Neruda's absence of lived experience in the USSR – he did not start regularly visiting Moscow on his annual (but in practice biennial) duty as a permanent member of the Peace Prize committee until after the completion of the poem – renders his Soviet imagery second-hand in sources and epically collectivist in scope:[22]

> Molotov and Voroshilov
> are there, I see them
> with the others, the high generals,
> The indomitable.
> Firm as snowy oak groves.[23]

While Hikmet did not have any direct knowledge of the Second World War except for the meagre dispatches he could receive in the Turkish prison, where he wrote the poem, the half-decade he spent in the USSR in the 1920s still shows through in lyrical moments such as the following in which he humanizes the iconic story of Zoya Kosmodemyanskaya, the eighteen-year-old Soviet guerrilla fighter, brutally executed by the Germans. His letter to Kosmodemyanskaya (here called Tanya) takes the form of a confession of love:

Tanya,
I love my country
          as much as you loved yours.
You were a Young Communist;
I am 42, an old Communist.
          You a Russian, me a Turk,
          but both Communists.
They hanged you for loving your country,
I'm in prison for loving mine.
But I'm alive,
and you are dead.
You left the world long ago,
And your time here was brief –
                    just eighteen years.
You never got your share of the sun's warmth.
You're the hanged partisan,
Tanya,
and I am the poet in prison.
My daughter, my comrade,
I bend over your picture:
Your eyebrows are thin,
Your eyes almond-shaped.
I can't tell their colour from the picture.
But it says here
                    They were dark chestnut.
That colour is seen a lot in my country, too.
Tanya,
Your hair is cut so short,
almost like my son Mehmet's.
Your forehead is so high,
like moonlight
bringing peace and dreams.
Your face is long and thin,
your ears a little big.
Your neck is still a girl's –
I can tell it hasn't felt a man's touch.
And something with a tassel dangles from your collar,
                    A decoration for the young lady ...
I called in my friends to look at your picture:

"Tanya,
I've got a daughter your age."
"Tanya,
my sister's your age."
"Tanya,
She's your age, the girl I love.
We live in a warm country:
        Girls become women overnight."
"Tanya –
I have friends your age in schools, factories, and fields."
"Tanya,
You died –
So many good people have been and are being killed.
But I
– I'm ashamed to say it –
I've never once
Put my life on the line
In seven years of war and live perfectly fine, even in prison."[24]

Hikmet's poetics of international solidarity, of course, far exceeds poetic evocations of the Soviet state, "the fatherland of the world proletariat," and include a number of more horizontal dedications to revolutions elsewhere. In the years immediately following his studies at KUTV, Hikmet penned two narrative poems, *Gioconda and Si-Ya-U* (1929) and *Why Did Bannerjee Kill Himself?* (1932), which imagine two of his classmates as martyrs for anti-colonial revolutions in China and India. Hikmet's horizontalist internationalism did not come to an end with Stalinism or the end of the Comintern era, however. An active participant in the Afro-Asian Writers Association, Hikmet devoted a number of poems as well as a whole poetry cycle, *Tanganyika Reportage* (1961), written after his visit to the newly independent country (renamed Tanzania three years later, upon the addition of Zanzibar). In her study of that hybrid, semi-poetic, semi-documentary text, Gül Bilge Han offers a rich account of the formal strategies Hikmet employs to find the poetic form for the solidarity slogans of the Afro-Asian Writers Association.[25]

Indeed, the solidarity and utopia topoi were profoundly geographically reconfigured during the post-Second World War decades of decolonization and iconic national independence struggles. Topoi were no longer confined to "the land called Roos" but also came to include "the land called Chin" (as Russia and China are called in Mulk Raj Anand's *Big Heart* [1945]), Gandhi's India, and other iconic, liberated spaces. By the time Ngũgĩ wa Thiong'o wrote *Petals of Blood* (1977) for example, his protagonists could inspire their interlocutors with multiple examples. So, in addition to "Russia [where] the working people and the peasant farmers had arisen against their foreign and native overlords,"[26] his protagonist speaks "about the people's revolutions in China, Cuba, Vietnam, Cambodia, Laos, Angola, Guinea, Mozambique ... Oh yes, and the works of Lenin and Mao."[27]

The sheer number of mentions (over a dozen) of China in *Petals of Blood* makes the country the primary instantiation of the foreign-utopia topos. What Duncan Yoon calls the "symbolic Maoism" of this novel perfectly amiably co-exists with the text's appreciation of the USSR, demonstrated both in the passage quoted above and in the acknowledgements section: "Thanks to ... the Soviet Writers Union for giving me the use of their house in Yalta in order to finish the writing of this novel."[28]

Ngũgĩ's abundant reliance on the vertical foreign utopia topos, however, is atypical. By the late 1970s, this topos had begun withering from the Third-Worldist novel. Even in the works of such a writer as Alex La Guma, a member of the South African Communist Party, who didn't shy away from associating his public persona with Soviet initiatives, the mention of "Russia" no longer stands for a distant and inspirational utopia but rather for the evocation of some anti-communist idiocy. Drunken speeches such as "You buggers should be in Russia, not here" originate from the most retrograde members of the community.[29] Another unrepentant communist, Sembène Ousmane, who had spent even more time in the USSR, as we will learn later on in this book, would assert the geopolitical independence of his revolutionary protagonists by having them explicitly reject the distant utopia:

"Joom Galle, Europe no longer has the power to attract us. Nor does any other country."

The father lifted his spectacles toward his son and asked: "Not even the Soviet Union?"

"No, Joom Galle."[30]

The Supply-Chain Narrative

A much more complex trope – an actual plot-structuring device that weaves together the national and the international – is the supply-chain narrative. Linking production in a (semi-)colonial country with consumption (or more importantly, ownership) in the West, the supply-chain narrative offers its readers not so much a call for solidarity with other oppressed people worldwide as a map of transnational economy and their place within it. It is most typical of neocolonial settings where foreign capital has taken hold of agriculture or resource extraction. These narratives are thus most common in the Latin American novel.

The very titles of many mid-twentieth-century novels foreground the extraction of local raw materials and their export abroad: Ramon Dias Sanchez's *Oil* (1936), Leonel Lopez Nussa's *Tobacco* (1963), a novel about the virtual enslavement of Cuban tobacco farmers to US commercial interests during the Machado dictatorship, and Miguel Asturias's *Green Pope* (1954), the green in its title referring to the colour of unripe bananas foreign companies harvested from Central America.[31] Indeed, the practices of United Fruit Company (present-day Chiquita) in particular gave birth not only to the very term "banana republic" but also to a whole subgenre of the Caribbean novel: most famously, Garcia Marquez's *One Hundred Years of Solitude* (1967) and Jorge Gaitan's *Banana Plantation Massacre* (1928), also devoted to the infamous 1928 massacre of striking banana workers by the Colombian army; Carlos Fallas's *Mamita Yunai* (1941), probably the best known Costa Rican novel; Joaquin Gutierrez's *Port Lemon* (1950) about United Fruit's rule of Panama; and Miguel Asturias's above-mentioned banana trilogy (*Strong Wind, Green Pope*, and *The Eye of the Interred*, all published in the 1950s).[32]

An archetypical extractive industry, mining in the Andes – or the practices associated with it – gave birth to another novelistic subgenre exemplified by Augusto Cespedes's *Devil's Metal* (1946), Nestor Teran's *The Price of Tin* (1960), and Fernando Soto Aparicio's *Rebellion of the Rats* (1962).[33] The plot of César Vallejo's *Tungsten*, one of the first such novels, offered a model for many subsequent representatives of the subgenre: once tungsten ore is discovered in a provincial Peruvian region, a US company appears, dispossessing previous owners and destroying the fabric of the traditional Indian society. Over the course of a few short years, the Indian peasants find themselves proletarianized miners. The company effectively runs the region, undisturbed by representatives of the state, who have grown dependent on its bribes and influence. The local community's attempt to protest the forcible "enlistment" of some of its members into the army is bloodily suppressed by the national police. Those arrested are turned over as indentured workers for the company, ever hungry for more bodies in their mines.

Like the dictator novel, the supply-chain novel flourished in Latin America.[34] Its narrative typically flashes from the dire consequences of resource extraction for the local population to the root of the problem in the workings and logic of the transnational company. Such a perspective requires an omniscient narrator, one capable of inhabiting the minds of miners, their foreign supervisors, and sometimes even distant company presidents for whom the daily reality of their company's day-to-day operations in the field is reduced to abstract profits. Asturias's banana trilogy, for example, makes Geo Maker Thompson (aka the Green Pope), the Chicago-based director of the whole company, and Lester Mead, its major investor-turned-investigator, protagonists of the novels, alongside their American and Guatemalan subordinates. The omniscience of these narratives, which allows them to contextualize the local story of resource extraction into the broader transnational story of capitalism, has received its fair share of critical dismissal, even from otherwise sympathetic observers, such as the literary critic Gene Bell-Villada:

> a serious flaw in Asturias's banana trilogy is that the Guatemalan
> author made the mistake of inventing protagonists who are Yankees,
> even going so far as to portray them from within. The artistic result
> is terribly defective and false: from the outset readers are aware that
> Asturias lacks thorough knowledge of his materials inasmuch as his
> Americans simply don't sound or feel like Americans. For example,
> we are informed that the Banana adventurer Lester Mead speaks
> English with an Oxford accent. And in an episode in *Strong Wind*,
> the Banana Company executives take to quoting, from memory, long
> passages from Shakespeare's *Othello* – all this without the slightest
> hint of parody (no post-Modernist harbinger of Barthelme here).
> Anyone minimally acquainted with the subculture of United States
> entrepreneurialism know full well that Asturias's portraits are, to

say the least, improbable. Similarly the gringos of Asturias's trilogy as well as those of Vallejo's *Tungsten*, speak a perfect un-accented Spanish, with no syntactic or phonetic peculiarities of their own.[35]

Such omniscience does entail some aesthetic risks, but the verisimilitude requirements Bell-Villada imposes on those texts sound somewhat arbitrary. Instead of serving as a ground for critical hostility, this novelistic reconstruction of multiple social strata connected via a transnational supply chain can help us reconstruct their lineage. On the one hand, it reminds one of Georg Lukács's totality – the hallmark of his ideal of a realist novel from Balzac to Gorky.[36] That a literary text could capture not only the cultural expression of class conflict but also its underlying economic basis must be a particularly remarkable achievement from the point of view of the author of "Realism in the Balance."[37] On the other hand, Asturias draws this socially and economically comprehensive world via a distinctly modernist technique, montage, which not only represents class conflict through abrupt and jarring switches of scenes featuring different social milieus but in the process also reconstructs political-economic hierarchies. The reader is reminded of the chain of command in Sergei Eisenstein's *Strike* (1924) represented by a series of phone calls from managers to industrial capitalists to higher-up police officials in anticipation of the factory strike. Montage was not only a cinematic technique but a trope in German and Russian reportage fiction in the 1920s and '30s, recently identified by Devin Fore as the industrial/corporate novel. Not unlike Asturias, leading practitioners of this genre, such as Ilya Ehrenburg and Erik Reger, reconstruct the vertical integration of national industry.[38]

While recalling to active duty that tradition of the interwar leftist novel from both sides of the realist-modernist divide, Third-Worldist novelists also extended the chain transnationally in a way that Gorky, Ehrenburg, Reger, or Eisenstein, whose accounts were limited to nationally-owned industries, could not. Foreign capital, especially North American capital, dominated production in Latin America in the way it never did in Germany or pre-Revolutionary Russia. The supply-chain narratives thus gave the local readership, for whom they were intended (indeed, the vast majority of those novels remain untranslated) a sense of place within the economic world-system. By showing subordination to transnational capital to be the defining characteristic of their nations, they negotiated the dual tasks of the literary construction of their nation and its placement in an unjust world economy.

The Railway Narrative

A special case of the supply-chain narrative is the railway narrative, which structures a number of African and Asian novels such as Mulk Raj Anand's Punjab trilogy (*The Village* [1939], *Across the Black Waters* [1940], and *The Sword and the Sickle* [1942]), Nâzım Hikmet's novel-in-verse *Human Landscapes* (1938–50), and Sembène Ousmane's *God's Bits of Wood* (1961). In none of these novels does the railway line extend beyond the boundaries of the nation(-in-construction), and in this way, the railway narrative has a shorter reach than the foreign utopia topos or the supply-chain narrative. Nevertheless, the novelistic trains and railroads still play a major role in placing characters in a broader world, by connecting them to distant and invisible countrymen in the imagined community of the literary nation or by serving as contested sites between the colonizers and the colonized.

As with the supply-chain narrative, the railway came to Third-Worldist literature from the Western novel. The symbolic valences of the railway in nineteenth-century fiction have been well established: the advent of modernity, man's conquest of nature, danger and catastrophe (iconically represented in *Anna Karenina*). The train first made an appearance in British literature, where the technology was first introduced. The landscapes the moving trains offered as well as the possibilities for social encounters across gender, social class, and politics in the enclosed space of the compartment, the corridor, or the dining car have served novelists ever since the mid-nineteenth century, when the train ride became a sufficiently common experience across most of Europe and North America.[39]

With the emergence of the proletarian novel in the first half of the twentieth century, a new type of railway narrative emerged, one focused not so much on the passengers inside the train, but on the labour, lives, and struggles around the railroad. Construction workers laying tracks, engine drivers, or African-American Pullman attendants and their families all had stories, lives, and grievances, which provided a basis to many a narrative, especially in North American fiction. Some of the most powerful American unions were in the railway industries, and railway strikes such as the Great Railroad Strike (1874), the Pullman Strike (1894), the Illinois Central Strike (1911) and the Harriman Strike (1915) are thematized in Alexander Saxton's *The Great Midlands* (1944) and Howard Fast's *The American: A Midwestern Legend* (1946).[40] To that North American proletarian novelistic appropriation of the initially bourgeois train narrative, we can add a particular Soviet variant, the armoured train (*bronepoezd*) narrative. A feature of the Russian Civil War and an effective technology for moving troops and spreading propaganda, the *bronepoezd*'s journey structures several Civil War novels, most famously Vsevolod Ivanov's *Armored Train 14-67* (1922), but we can see echoes of it as late as Boris Pasternak's *Dr. Zhivago* (1957). It is this more militant North American and Soviet proletarian tradition, focused on struggle and appropriation, that Third-Worldist novelists such as Mulk Raj Anand and Sembène Ousmane drew on.

When the railway came to the colonial world, it added new functions such as the maintenance of control over the colonized populations.[41] The train's arrival in the Third-Worldist novel also resulted in a functional repurposing of its symbolic valences. Indeed, its centrality to literary nation-building in African and Asian fiction was far greater than anything possible in the First or Second Worlds. From Mulk Raj Anand's *Coolie* (1936) to Ngũgĩ wa Thiong'o's *A Grain of Wheat* (1967), railway lines physically integrate the territory of the colonial or postcolonial nations, connecting remote provincial towns with the big administrative centres and enabling the novel's characters and concerns to move from the remote and provincial to the national. In the case of Nâzım Hikmet's epic poem *Human Landscapes*, a somewhat different, but equally symbolic geography, structures the narrative: that of the railway line running from the old capital of Istanbul to Ankara, the new one. The periodic stops along the way and the passengers' remarks about the surrounding landscape enrich this symbolic geography.

Between the third-class occupants of carriage number 510 of the regular Ankara train and the upper- and middle-class passengers of the express leaving a little later, Hikmet captures a veritable microcosm of Turkish society on the eve of the Second World War. This classifying mechanism structures the poet's obsessive attention to the train riders' biographies, and through them, to Turkey's post-independence history. Yet this overpopulation with characters serves another purpose as well. As a foundational narrative devoted to an emerging nation, *Human Landscapes* is consumed with the overwhelming ambition to represent *the people* of the new Republican Turkey, in both the social and national sense of that term. The poem's insatiable populism becomes evident in the alphabetical ordering of characters and the title it originally bore, "Encyclopaedia of Famous People" (the "great men" being housewives, soldiers, and thirteen-year-old girls working in textile factories):

Cloaked,
fat.
ADVIYE Hanum.
Originally from the Caucasus
She got measles in 1895
And married in 1902.
She washed clothes.
She cooked.
She bore children.
And when she dies, she knows
     Her coffin will be covered with a shawl
        From one of the sultan's mosques:
One of her sons-in-law is an imam.

On the steps, sunlight
    a stalk of green onion
    and a man:
    Corporal AHMET.
He fought in the Balkan war.
He fought in the Great war.
He fought in the Greek war.
"Hang in there, brother, the end's in sight!"
    He is famous for saying.

A girl goes up the steps.
She works at the stocking factory
In Galata – Tophane Street
ATIFET is thirteen.[42]

The figure of the train is not only a site of nation-building and imagining solidarities. In a way not dissimilar to the supply chain, in a number of Third-Worldist novels it also functions as contested terrain between the colonial power and the colonized people. It offers space for both oppression and of liberation struggle, in either capacity serving as a site of consciousness formation. The ambivalence of the railway is fully realized in Mulk Raj Anand's Punjab trilogy (1939–42), a *Bildungsroman* that follows Lalu Singh's journey from his native village in India, through the trenches of the First World War and German captivity, and, finally, back to India.[43] The opening sentence of the first volume, *The Village* (1939) anticipates the centrality of the train for the trilogy: "Nihal Singh walked out of the hall of Nandpur Station on a pair of sturdy legs, which had grown cramped during the ten-mile journey from the district town of Manabad in a crowded third-class carriage."[44]

Nihal Singh is then met by the trilogy's protagonist, his son Lalu Singh, and the two promptly proceed to argue over the merits of the train, which serves here as a proxy for modernity. As a member of a deeply patriarchal and superstitious society, Nihal Singh thinks of the train as a devil incarnate, an English-made device to destroy tradition and everything that is holy. His son, whose non-conformism soon gets him expelled from his native village, proves more inclined to admire technology. This debate sets the initial symbolism of the train: a technology of capitalist colonialism that destroys traditional society, it can also liberate more rebellious members of that society, such as Lalu Singh, from its omnipresent constrictions.

Though most of the action of the second book of the trilogy, *Across the Black Waters* (1940), takes place outside of India, making it one of the few literary representations of the First World War through the eyes of the many British colonial subjects serving in the army, the railway motif is anything but abandoned. Much of the protagonist Lalu Singh's journey to the Western front takes place inside a train car. As the train moves across the French and Belgian countryside, passes through towns, and stops on platforms, the sepoys, freshly shipped from India, are offered their first and somewhat peculiar glimpse of European realities, from the windows of their compartments. At the same time, lodged in an extremely overcrowded space, sometimes hungry, and without any possibility of getting out or communicating with anybody other than themselves, the Indian soldiers are stuck as if in a prison. Such circumstances prove highly conducive for irreverent commentary on what they see and a highly critical attitude toward the British authorities, who are shipping them to the slaughter. As Lalu, a naive country boy, listens to such conversations, he grows in political consciousness, as befitting the positive hero of any socialist-realist novel.

The third volume of the trilogy, *The Sword and the Sickle* (1942), brings Lalu back to India, where he – already a mature revolutionary – and fellow hotheads end up instigating a local revolution, which unfolds at a provincial train station. The uprising is a somewhat humorous one. Inspired by Lalu's merry band of revolutionaries, and the tales of what workers and peasants did in the land of Roos, local peasants take matters into their own hands, capture a train and improvise a demonstration at the train station:

"As Mithu [the peasant leader of the uprising] says, they are our trains." Yet another peasant echoed the gospel of Revolution.

"Kanwar Sahib," began the Stationmaster, lifting his joined hands, "I implore you ..."

But Mithu shut him up by saying:

"The old days of Sarkari Raj [the British empire] are gone, now it is peasant Raj, exactly as it is in Roos."[45]

The suppression of the railway revolution is a less humorous affair. The imperial British administration comes down with all its punitive might on the revolutionaries and the peasants who have joined them. Arrest orders quickly deprive the peasantry of its leaders. British soldiers brought by another train shoot a volley of bullets to disperse the crowd of remaining protesters.

Much more successful is the railway revolution in Sembène Ousmane's *God's Bits of Wood* (1961), a novel chronicling a train workers' strike in French Senegal in the late 1940s. The railway's salience is suggested to the reader by the very cover of the book, which features a railway map of central Africa. The map lends itself to two kinds of readings: as a representation of French colonial possessions in Equatorial Africa and as the contours of the new and independent nations, such as Senegal, Gambia, Guinea, and Sudan, not yet divided by national boundaries, but already named and connected by a common railway line. This ambiguity between colonial and national runs throughout Sembène's richly symbolic railway.[46]

As in Mulk Raj Anand's fiction, the train in the novel functions as both a vehicle for European power and as a site for an uprising against it. On the one hand, the railway line consolidates French colonial rule by connecting the colonial capital Dakar with the regional capital Thies and the smaller town of Bamako, the three settings of the novel. In fact, the main colonial administrator in the Thies region, Monsieur Dejean, happens to be the head of the railway company. His office and the train stations in Thies and Bamako are the nodes of power guarded by cordons of French soldiers. The actual trains, too, function as sites of colonial control as the French administrators and their local collaborators, like Diara, refuse to let the wives of the striking workers aboard. On the other, it is precisely the strike of African railway workers that anticipates and creates the possibility for the subsequent national independence struggle. The railway, with its trains, stations, station squares, and offices becomes the contested terrain of struggle. In the process, the Senegalese are shown transforming, abandoning an earlier fear and veneration for the French, learning how to self-organize in the face of the colonial power's superior forces. Because of the total mobilization required by the strike, women, younger men, and children challenge the patriarchal order of their society, which has held them back from participating. In the culmination of the novel, the women – the wives, daughters, and neighbours of the strikers – decide independently to march from Bamako to Dakar, placing themselves on the front lines of the strike. This march, alongside the railway line, becomes a symbolic reclamation of Senegalese geography by and for the people of Senegal.

The extended metaphors with which the spiritual leader of the strike, the engine-driver Bakayoko, seeks repeatedly to inspire his wavering comrades to equate the social movement with the moving train he is driving:

> Let us look at it in another way. We are driving a train down the track and ahead of us we think we see an obstacle, which makes us afraid. Are we going to stop the train and say to the passengers, "I can't go any farther; I think there is something ahead that frightens me?" No – we are responsible for the train, and we must go forward and find out if the obstacle really exists.[47]

Bakayoko also evokes the image of a moving train in his response to his friend and fellow strike leader, Alioune's, reproach that he, Bakayoko, shows little sympathy for the strikers' difficulties in following his uncompromising and demanding leadership:

> I wish I could make you understand something, too. When I am in the cabin of my engine, I take on a sense of absolute identity with everything that is in the train, no matter whether it is passengers or just freight. I experience everything that happens along the whole length. In the stations I observe the people, but once the engine is on its way, I forget everything else. My role then is nothing except to guide the machine to the spot where it is supposed to go. I don't know any longer whether it is my heart that is beating to the rhythm of the engine, or the engine to the rhythm of my heart. And for me,

that is the way it has to be with this strike – we must all take on a
sense of identity with it ...'[48]

As Roxanna Curto has shown in her study of *God's Bits of Wood*,
attitudes within the colonized society toward Western technology vary
widely – from admitting European superiority to condemning it as utterly
alien to local culture.[49] The position Sembène's "positive heroes" – and
presumably, the author himself – take is that such technologies – and I am
deliberately extending the list to include not only trains and the French
language but also the representational machinery of the novel – can only
be made useful for the colonized and thus appropriated after a prolonged
political struggle. Such is also the position taken by Mulk Raj Anand as
well as by scores of European and North American proletarian novelists
of the first half of the twentieth century, who fought to take ownership of
this quintessentially bourgeois genre.

Let us now return to the sentence of Jameson's "Third-World Literature
in the Age of Multinational Capitalism" with which we started and add to
it the hitherto omitted second part, which has usually been overshadowed
by the more provocative first:

> All third-world texts are necessarily, I want to argue, allegorical, and
> in a very specific way: they are to be read as what I will call national
> allegories, even when, or perhaps I should say, particularly when
> their forms develop out of predominantly western machineries of
> representation, such as the novel.[50]

Our analysis of railway narratives and supply chains supports Jameson's
assertion about the transformation resulting from "western machineries of
representation," but with an important qualification. The process is not one
of pouring local material into those "western machineries" to automatically
produce "national allegory," but rather, of constant struggle – by the author,
by his or her characters, to repurpose and appropriate that machinery. It
is this struggle – as much as the workings of narrative technologies – that
gives birth to "national allegories."

This chapter has examined only one type of those allegories – those that
place the emerging nation in relation to the rest of the world. In contrast
to the Company, an unredeemable vehicle for foreign exploitation, the
railway in Third-Worldist fiction is a profoundly ambivalent symbol, at

once a vehicle of colonial power but also a carrier of the anti-colonial revolution and a nation-building device. As structuring principles of the novel, however, both offered their readerships imaginative ways of relating themselves to the world. The omniscient eye of the Third-Worldist narrator constructs linkages few readers could actually have witnessed: from emancipatory struggles elsewhere to the faraway sources of oppression in Chicago boardrooms or inaccessible colonial administrators.

With the decline of the Third-World project in the 1970s and '80s, those narrative structures, which had once been at the centre of a number of African, Asian, and Latin American novels, began to move to the periphery. The Third World's real-life contradiction between nationalism and internationalism that the chain narrative symbolically resolved was no longer essential once the transnational movements connecting it had ebbed. The economic dependencies the supply chain narratives articulated gave way to different forms of transnational narrative connectivity, such as migration or memory, that operate in the plots of Nadine Gordimer, Orhan Pamuk, Salman Rushdie, and other representatives of the contemporary world/ postcolonial novel. Railways, too, wherever they have not given way to cars, buses, or planes, have lost their nation-building significance. As the Cold War wore on, foreign utopias lost their lustre, in life as well as in literature. The Red Stars over the Third World – first the Soviet one, subsequently also China's and Cuba's – had begun to dim.

Postcolonial Critique in Central Asia

As these narrative devices were disappearing from Third-Worldist fiction, some of them emerged – or perhaps re-emerged – in Soviet Central Asia. The November 1980 issue of *Novyi Mir* opened with Chinghiz Aitmatov's novel *The Day Lasts More than a Hundred Years*. (Its later Soviet reprintings would appear under a different title, *The Buranny Railway Stop*.) For the next five years, before perestroika, it remained the most widely debated officially published Soviet text, both in and out of the country. While some observers justly pointed to the novel's (mutated) socialist-realist topoi and successful fate – a State Award for Literature, translations into multiple languages, film adaptations, – others insisted on its critique of Stalin-era repressions – of which, as we saw in Chapter 1, Aitmatov's father was a victim himself – and the adverse environmental consequences of (Soviet) modernization.[51] Maybe more relevantly for us, in the eyes of many contemporary Kyrgyz, and indeed Central Asian readers, the novel read as a critique of the Soviet Union from a nationalist perspective.[52] Most observers have looked for this criticism in the *mankurt* (man without memory) motif and the larger question of remembrance, of Stalin-era purges, of suppressed cultural traditions. There is, however, another way in which the novel critiques Soviet authority, a more properly postcolonial one: through the railway narrative it deploys. No longer a carrier of progress and modernity, let alone revolution, the railway in Aitmatov's late-Soviet text becomes emblematic of the power relations between centre and periphery.

Most of the story is set in Boranly-Buranny – an isolated railway junction in the Kazakh desert, where a handful of railway workers live with their families. Little changes in Boranly in the over thirty years (mid-1940s to late 1970s) the protagonist Yedigei spends there, raising questions about any material progress Soviet rule has brought. An hour and a half away along the line lies Kumbel, a proper railway station, where the characters obtain food and news, take their children to school, and otherwise connect to the external world. Further still is Alma-Ata, Soviet Kazakhstan's capital, which Yedigei visits only once, reinforcing the sense of distance between his life and the seats of power from which it is ruled. The inevitability with which trains pass Boranly-Buranny, in accordance with the timetable, is emphasized through the novel's poetic refrain ("The trains in these parts went from East to West and from West to East") and serves to deprive the characters of any agency. Only once, in an extraordinary moment in his life, does Yedigei dare to disturb the progression of these external forces of inevitability by pulling the emergency brake. Whether this act amounts to a Benjaminian revolution is hard to say; it certainly represents an assertion of Yedigei's capacity to act. The railway/train complex also serves as the main source of tragedy in the novel as it brings from Alma-Ata to Boranly the KGB investigator Tansykbaev, who arrests Yedigei's friend Abutalip on charges of writing anti-Soviet memoirs. Unable to withstand Tansykbaev's harsh interrogations, carried out in the specialized KGB carriage, Abutalip jumps under the wheels of the engine car and is crushed. After Abutalip's death, Yedigei's white lies make the passing trains a source of false hopes for Abutalip's children, who live with the expectation that their father will one day descend from one of them.[53]

It is hard to say whether Aitmatov's critical use of the railway narrative in *The Day Lasts More than a Hundred Years* derives from an engagement with non-Western literatures and represents the coming home of world revolution. From the 1930s onward, official Soviet literature became rather resistant to foreign influences, let alone non-Western ones. Nevertheless, if there was a single Soviet writer open to them, it was Aitmatov. A regular participant in Afro-Asian Writers Association events, the deputy head of the Soviet Committee for Solidarity with Africa and Asia in the 1970s, and the last recipient of a Lotus Prize (1988), he was highly knowledgeable about African and Asian literatures. Literary critics and scholars, in the USSR and the West, have already singled him out as the most prominent practitioner of Latin American magic realism among Soviet writers.[54]

The literary engagement of other Central Asian writers with mid-twentieth-century decolonization is just as explicit. Mirzo Tursun-Zade, the head of the Tajik Writers Union, not only served as the head of the Soviet Committee for Solidarity with Africa and Asia until his death in 1961 but also thematized the independence struggles of the two continents in three poetic cycles: *Indian Ballad* (1948), *I Am from the Free East* (1950), and *The Voice of Asia* (1957). Directed at the newly decolonized peoples, his rhetoric of friendship, as Lisa Yountchi has shown, posits the Soviet East as a model for them.[55] His Uzbek counterpart, Kamil Yashen, who also headed his republic's Writers Union and the above-mentioned committee after Tursun-Zade's death, also reiterated official Soviet talking points vis-á-vis the decolonizing world in travelogues based on trips to Africa and Asia.[56] This position at the interface of Soviet cultural engagements with the Third World empowered those occupying it. Not unlike the political leaders of the Central Asian republics, who in the post-Stalin era began to demand greater resources from the Moscow centre so that their republics could indeed look like genuine models of development in the eyes of visiting African and Asian delegations, so, too, Central Asian and Caucasian writers and cultural bureaucrats used the international relations function with which they had been tasked to secure greater investments from Moscow in the republican cultural institutions they represented (and in themselves, too).[57]

But a younger and bolder generation of Russophone Central Asian writers such as the Kazakhs Anuar Alimzhanov and Olzhas Suleimenov, who, like Aitmatov, had started their literary careers after the Stalin era, ended up using their solidarity writing about the colonial world more critically, as a palimpsest for Russian and Soviet rule over Central Asia. Thus, for example, as Diana Kudaibergenova has shown in her study of twentieth-century literary nation-building in Kazakhstan, whole passages of Alimzhanov's fictional biography of Jomo Kenyatta, *The Flaming Spear*

(1965), which narrates British colonialism's efforts to represent Kenya's indigenous history as barbaric, lacking any culture, and thus a major beneficiary of Britain's civilizing mission, could be read as a reference to the excesses of Soviet propaganda of the modernity it brought to Central Asia without acknowledgement of its cost:[58] "To reassert their moral right to rule, the conquerors destroyed what was most precious: art and culture. African cities, palaces, and temples were burnt, trampled upon, and derided."[59] Similarly, Jomo's counter-task of "reconstructing the cultural history of his people ... and the lost connection of time," his writing about a marvellous African empire situated in today's Kenya, which was visited by Arab, Indian, and Phoenician pilgrims and whose statues amaze people even today with their perfection, could be compared to the idealized role Central Asian writers sought for themselves.[60] Indeed, in his next major work, the historical novel *Makhambet's Arrow* (1967), about the exploitation of Kazakh people by Khan Zhangir and the Russian tsar and the independence struggle waged by a Jomo-like nineteenth-century steppe poet and political leader, Makhambet, Alimzhanov himself takes on a similar task.[61]

But the most explicitly critical project of historical reconstruction came from another Kazakh writer, Olzhas Suleimenov, who moved from early celebration of the fruits of Soviet modernization in the 1960s to a polemic with official Soviet representation of Kazakh history in the 1970s and '80s. According to Kudaibergenova and Naomi Caffee, Suleimenov 's growing interest in Kazakh history as colonial was in part enabled by his engagement with the Afro-Asian Writers Association, of which he was an active participant, including as a co-organizer of the 1973 Alma-Ata Afro-Asian Writers Congress.[62] In addition to his best known (and much-debated) historical work *Az i Ya* (1975), which sought to demonstrate the abundance of Turkisms (and by implication, Turkic cultural influence) in the first text of Russian literature, the late-twelfth-century *Tale of Igor's Campaign*, he issued a number of poetic and public celebrations of Kazakh history, explicitly equating its denigration to a colonial act:[63] "I am not satisfied with claims about the dark past of my peoples. This is the kind of statement that colonial ideologues use."[64]

While Aitmatov, Alimzhanov, and Suleimenov all had their run-ins with Soviet censorship, they all served at different points in their literary careers as First Secretaries of their republican writers union, as deputies of the Supreme Soviet of the USSR (members of the Soviet parliament), and as heads or deputy heads of the Soviet Committee for Solidarity with

Africa and Asia, not to mention the dozens of important committees they chaired, the Lenin prizes and other awards they won, and the millions of copies their books sold in the different languages of the USSR. Even if at times their nationalism exceeded that allowed by official Soviet nationalities policy, it is difficult in any meaningful way to think of these cultural elites as dissident or oppressed writers. They certainly lacked the militancy of their African and Asian counterparts, limiting their critique to allusions. Judging by their conduct in the run-up to the dissolution of the USSR, they ·probably never even wanted their republics to be independent, unlike their peers from the Baltics and the Caucasus. Nevertheless, they were no mere tools of some monolithic Soviet regime. Their literary engagement with Africa and Asia gave them space not only to accumulate additional cultural and political capital but also to stake political claims, whether in the realm of preserving national culture (which the Soviet state allowed, but in highly constrained form) or in opposing the environmental destruction caused by Soviet modernization (an opposition few personified as well as Olzhas Suleimenov, who became the public face of the Nevada-Semipalatinsk anti-nuclear campaign). Thus, the impulse that the Bolshevik Revolution and the new Soviet literature had once given to anti-colonial movements and cultures worldwide came back as a form of critique of late-Soviet practices in the country's periphery.

The Tashkent Film Festival
(1968–1988) as a Contact Zone

Abortive Beginnings

Over a month before the inaugural Afro-Asian Writers Congress in Tashkent, the city hosted another event, the First International Festival of African and Asian Film. It turned out to be something of a false start, as testified by its erasure through another, much bigger and better-known festival with the same name inaugurated ten years later, to which this chapter will be devoted. Masha Kirasirova, the only scholar to have written about this one-off 1958 Tashkent festival, rightly focuses on the event's host, the Uzbek filmmaker and head of the Uzbek Cinematographers Union, Kamil Yarmatov, as a mediator between the Second and the Third World and the festival's role in showcasing Soviet Asian cinemas and Uzbek political leadership's entry onto the international stage.[1] An impressive twenty-two countries sent film delegations, and, judging by the Soviet documentary short, thousands of Tashkent viewers must have seen the films and the foreign delegations. Nevertheless, this was a much smaller and less distinguished group than the ones that arrived in Tashkent ten years later. The national cinemas in attendance were largely drawn from East and South Asia (Japan, China, North Korea, Indonesia, and India) and in most cases were represented by state officials rather than actual filmmakers. Tellingly, with the single exception of Paul Robeson, official Soviet statements about the event do not mention the names of the visiting filmmakers, suggesting the absence of distinguished figures. The October 1958 issue of *Iskusstvo kino* and the official photographic archive of the event are more generous in providing names, but few of them are recognizable.[2] A number of the delegates' statements, such as the Sudanese actor Sayed Khalifi's, explicitly stated that their country had no studios or film industry, just a few portable cameras and enthusiasts who had produced a few shorts, thus putting in question the claim of twenty-two national cinemas being represented in Tashkent.[3] Ten years later, the number of postcolonial countries with film-production capacity would be much higher. In the 1960s, the main commercial cinemas of the two continents – Japanese, Indian, and Egyptian – would reach record output (before stagnating in the 1970s, for different reasons) and international repu-tation. Moreover, Third Cinema, the Third-Worldist movement for radical anti-colonialist and socially emancipatory film, which would constitute another important cinematic stream in the post-1968 version of the Tashkent Film Festival, had not yet emerged in 1958. Cuba, too, had yet to have its 1 January 1959 revolution, which would propel it to the status of a cinematic powerhouse for the Third World.

Like the inaugural Tashkent Congress of Afro-Asian Writers, the 1958 Tashkent Film Festival was followed by others hosted by different Afro-Asian cities: there was a Second Afro-Asian Film Festival held in March 1960 in Cairo, and a Third (and last) in April 1964 in Jakarta. Unlike the Writers Association, however, the festivals did not result in permanent structures and wider networks being formed (each festival was run by a different country and bore little resemblance to the previous one, as testified by the different system of prizes: the Big Vase in Tashkent; the Golden Eagle in Cairo; Bandung, Patrice Lumumba, and other awards in Jakarta) and eventually fell victim to both Sino-Soviet rivalry and the CIA-backed coup that toppled one of the main sponsors of the event, the Indonesian government. Our main source for the final Indonesian festival is a plain-tive report by the Soviet delegation, which describes their extended, and, ultimately, unsuccessful struggle against their Chinese counterparts, who "accomplished their plan" for the jury's awards. And while the Chinese ultimately did not succeed in establishing a permanent committee for the film festival, which would have excluded Soviet participation, the alarmed authors of the report related how President Sukarno, the event's host, repeated some Chinese talking points such as "uniting on the basis of race" – a call that the Soviet delegation, made up of three Central Asians and two Russians, felt was aimed against it.[4]

The difficulties experienced by Soviet cultural bureaucracies in this early effort to organize Afro-Asian cinema were not only due to powerful

Chinese opposition or the early stage of national cinema in many African and Asian countries at the time. As the next several pages will illustrate, in cinema, unlike literature, Soviet bureaucracies had much less experience in organizing international networks and were in a clearly subordinate position. The first International Moscow Film Festival did not take place until 1959, by which time Venice (1932), Cannes (1946), Karlovy Vary (1946), Locarno (1946), Edinburgh (1947), Berlin (1951), Columbus (1953), and even the International Film Festival of India (1952) and Mar de la Plata (1954) had already developed their reputations and networks.[5] A Soviet Union of Cinematographers, which had an international committee with expertise in and relations with foreign cinemas, was only established in 1965, thirty years after the Writers Union had been formed. Its founding allowed actual Soviet filmmakers and film professionals to play a much greater role in Soviet cinema's foreign engagements, which until then had been the exclusive domain of government officials from the State Committee for Cinematography (Goskino) and its predecessors, on the one hand, and the traders from Sovexportfilm, on the other.[6]

Moreover, there was no interwar Soviet Republic of Cinema to build on. Until the emergence of the Soviet bloc in late 1940s, Soviet cultural bureaucracies could not offer alternatives to the reigning global commercial system of production, distribution, and circulation. The low starting point of the Soviet film industries in the global, post-First World War cinematic market, the capital-intensive nature of the film industry, the paucity of partners outside the Soviet bloc, and the stricter state censorship and control with which film was treated practically everywhere further disadvantaged it when compared to literature. If *Clarte*, MBRL, MORP, and the Association of Writers for the Defence of Culture, the subject of Chapter 1, had sought to nurture into existence and interconnect national proletarian, leftist, or just anti-fascist writers' organizations through a global network of publishing houses, magazines, writers' visits, and congresses, no comparable attempt was launched for a Soviet project for world cinema in the interwar era. While the Soviet state viewed literary internationalism as an ideological force with which to win foreign hearts and minds, its import and export of films and maintenance of cinematic relations with foreign countries and organizations followed to a much larger extent the existing commercial practices and motivations that were driving transnational cinema circulation elsewhere.[7] Testament to such a profit-oriented modus operandi is the kind of foreign films purchased for domestic audiences from the early 1920s onwards: one struggles to find anything explicitly political among the standard American, German, French, and British entertainment fare that dominated Soviet screens until the late 1920s, when it was reduced to a mere trickle, a casualty of the import-substitution logic of the First Five-Year Plan.[8] Similarly, even if the signature Soviet cinematic exports of the 1920s and '30s – the films of Sergei Eisenstein, Vsevolod Pudovkin, and Alexander Dovzhenko – were the face of Soviet political propaganda film, the Soviet companies charged with their sales rarely, if ever, departed from their commercial mandate.[9] To be sure, the propaganda value of film – at home or abroad – was also appreciated and ritually paid homage to with Lenin's oft-repeated dictum "For us, the most important of all arts is cinema." Yet comparing the growing pace of translation of non-Western writers in Soviet publishing houses with the total absence of non-Western film on interwar-era Soviet screens, or the active correspondence the Soviet Writers Union's Foreign Commission or the *International Literature* magazine maintained with left-wing writers' groups in Latin America and East and South Asia with the paucity of any similar activity in the realm of film, Soviet cultural bureaucracies did not initially extend to cinema the belief they had in Soviet literature's capacity to win foreign hearts and minds.[10]

There were, however, exceptions to the commercialism that dominated Soviet cinema's foreign engagements in the interwar era. In the first place, the All-Union Society for Cultural Relations with Foreign Countries (VOKS) on a number of occasions facilitated the travel of Soviet filmmakers abroad and the visits of foreign filmmakers to the USSR. Just as important, VOKS would occasionally send canisters of Soviet films to Soviet consulates abroad, friendship societies, and foreign workers clubs, letting them circulate outside commercial distribution (a practice that Soviet film trade organizations traditionally resented). Another important, though short-lived, source of non-commercial distribution of Soviet and other politically engaged film was Weltfilm, a Comintern-affiliated (rather than Soviet) company founded in Berlin in 1927, which operated under a mandate to foster revolutionary culture, and rented films, many of them produced by its sister studios, Moscow's Mezhrabpomfilm and Berlin's Prometheusfilm, to cinema societies, workers' groups, and clubs in Germany and abroad.[11] Between the Nazi takeover in 1933 and the gradual monopolization of the Soviet film industry by Sovkino/Soyuzkino/the Chief Directorate of Film and Photo-Industry, which eventually absorbed Mezhrabpom in 1936, Weltfilm remained a short-lived venture whose clients, that is, audiences, were limited to a small number of Western European and North American cities.

This relative paucity of interwar cinematic networks emanating from and directed by Moscow – at least when compared with those constituting the interwar Soviet Republic of Letters – should by no means minimize the reach of Soviet cinema among non-Western filmmakers, film critics, and viewers. Not unlike the spread of the nineteenth-century Russian novels in East Asia, however, that reach was largely a product of local initiative, rather than Moscow directives. Also, like Russo-Soviet texts arriving out of sequence and without proper contextualization, they were understood rather idiosyncratically. Thus, as film historians Masha Salazkina and Sarah Ann Wells have shown, between the precariousness of the channels by which canisters of Soviet film could reach the major cities of Latin America and the severity of local censorship, the dissemination of Soviet films and film theories on that continent was extremely haphazard and resulted in interpretations that had as much to do with the local conditions and struggles of Latin American cultural producers as with Soviet film thought and practice.[12] Writers and filmmakers on opposite sides of the ideological spectrum saw (or sometimes, as Wells has shown, did not see but only read about and imagined) in those films an "alternative to the cinematic models they encountered in western Europe and the United States."[13] In the realm of film theory, Salazkina has demonstrated the scale of translation and publication of some of the main Soviet texts in Rome and Paris, from whether they could travel via translation or cosmopolitan intermediaries to Latin America.[14]

As Soviet films were thus reaching audiences in Asia and Latin America, left-wing film clubs and even whole groups of filmmakers affiliated with unions or political parties, were similarly cropping up without instructions from Moscow. Probably the best-documented cases of such politically engaged formations are the Japanese and Chinese cinematic lefts, which went the furthest toward producing their own films and forming their own institutions: the Japanese Prokino (1927–34) and the Chinese Communist Party-linked Film Group (1932–36), which was succeeded by the Popular-Front-era National Salvation Association of Shanghai Cinema (1936–37).[15] Both were influenced by the Soviet example, but in their own, creative way and hardly as a matter of Soviet cultural policy. According to the historian of interwar Chinese film, Pang Laikwan, though accessible, the iconic films of Eisenstein, Vsevolod Pudovkin, and Dziga Vertov, which were

Soviet cinema's calling card as far as Western audiences were concerned, left Chinese filmmakers and audiences cold. Laikwan attributes Soviet avant-garde's failure with them to different cultural codes and the absence of a documentary tradition in Chinese film. Chinese left-wing fiction film – a powerful but short-lived phenomenon limited to the half-decade between 1932 and the Japanese invasion of 1937 – relied heavily on the kind of dramatization that avant-garde Soviet filmmakers had eschewed.[16] It is no surprise, therefore, that the socialist realist Soviet films of the 1930s tended to be much more popular among Chinese filmmakers than the better-known earlier avant-garde ones.

Conversely, it was in the sphere of the documentary that Soviet film theory and practice made a greater impact in Japan, according to Anastasia Fedorova's study of the Soviet-Japanese cinematic dialogue.[17] This is not to say, however, that Japanese political filmgoers saw Soviet documentary film with the same eyes as Soviet audiences. Vertov's *Man with a Movie Camera*, which was first screened and discussed in the charged context of Japan's initial 1931 invasion of China, was condemned by left-wing Japanese film critics as apolitical whereas the whole genre of Soviet *kulturfilm* – with its orientalizing representations of underdevelopment – enjoyed much greater popularity, informing the stream of Japanese documentaries (most of them by formerly left-wing filmmakers, who were now working in the Japanese Army's film unit) depicting the new territories Japan conquered in East and Southeast Asia during Japan's 1937–45 imperialist campaign.[18]

Like film circulation between the USSR and non-Western societies, filmmakers' travels before the Second World War were also strictly one-way. The *kulturfilm* genre in particular took many Soviet filmmakers to non-Western spaces such as China (Yakov Bliokh 1927 and Roman Karmen 1938–39), Japan (Vladimir Shneiderov 1933), and Iran (Vladimir Erofeev 1929). Most of these expeditions, as Chapter 5 will show, did not involve local partners, and left little trace on local filmmaking. The only spectacular exception was Eisenstein's fourteen-month-long sojourn in Mexico in 1931, the subject of Masha Salazkina's pioneering *In Excess: Eisenstein in Mexico* (2009). While Eisenstein never finished the film he was shooting there, *Viva Mexico!*, his work with local filmmakers had a lasting influence on the emerging Mexican filmmaking community, which until then had largely taken Spanish melodramas as its model.

Thus, unlike the Afro-Asian Writers Association, which had been formed by reanimating and rearticulating interwar literary networks, the post-Second World War Soviet project for Third-World cinema lacked a clear precursor. And when, in the last ten days of October 1968, 240 film-makers, actors, critics, film traders, and government figures from 49 African and Asian countries, as well as a few Eastern and Western European observers and hundreds of film canisters, descended upon Tashkent for the second attempt at a First Festival of African and Asian Cinema (Latin American participation was formally added in 1976), neither the participants nor the organizers could draw upon the longer history of engagements with Soviet literary bureaucracies available to the Afro-Asian writers who had gathered in the same city a decade earlier to inaugurate their Association. Among the participants at the 1968 festival were the major figures of Bollywood's Golden Age: Raj Kapoor and K.A. Abbas; the African filmmakers Sembène Ousmane and Souleymane Cisse, the latter still a student in Moscow; and Central Asian directors such as Malik Kaiumov and Tolomush Okeev. To the best of my knowledge, the Japanese documentarian Fumio Kamei and the doyen of Soviet film studies in the West, Jay Leyda, who attended the festival as an accredited journalist, were the only ones to provide some continuity with pre-war Soviet cinematic internationalism: both had studied film in the USSR in the 1930s.[19]

In addition to actual filmmakers, there were film trade representatives, several ministers, and dozens of embassy officials from Afro-Asian countries allied with, hostile to, or indifferent toward the Soviet state. Upon the invitation of the organizers, at that and subsequent festivals, students and alumni of the Moscow-based All-Soviet State Institute of Cinematography (VGIK) had a reunion and were showcased as a major Soviet contribution to African and Asian cinema. None of the participants was deterred by the Warsaw Pact invasion of Czechoslovakia just over a month earlier, which temporarily froze and permanently debilitated Soviet engagement with Western cultural producers. Second-to-Third-World relations had a logic and fault lines that were distinct from those between Soviet and Western cultural producers.[20]

Every even year from 1968 until 1988 – with the exception of 1970, when a cholera epidemic broke out in Asia and the festival had to be cancelled – hundreds of cinematic guests would repeat the journey to hospitable Tashkent. Just like their literary counterparts but with much greater regu-larity, they would get to know each other, interact with Uzbek audiences in the movie halls designed specifically for the festival, and explore Tashkent's Central Asian modernity and the narrow streets of the Old City.

Figure 4.1   Reception of vGik alumni by the Soviet minister of education Vyacheslav Petrovich Eliutin of guests of the IX Moscow International Film Festival in 1975. From left to right, starting from the third figure on the left: vGik rector Vitalii Zhadan, Minister of Education Vyacheslav Eliutin; sixth from left: Hassan Akhmed Mohammed (Palestine), then Ursan Fatih (Syria), Konrad Wolf (GDR), Wali Latifi (Afghanistan), Nedelcho Iliev (Bulgaria), Sebastián Alarcón (Chile), and Gonzalo Martinez (Mexico).

The festival's combination of geopolitical ambition (capturing all of non-Western cinema) and its peculiar format (explicit embrace of politics as well as refusal of competitiveness and stardom) makes it a unique event in the history of Cold War film festivals in need of historical reconstruction. This chapter posits the festival as the most visible platform of Soviet cinematic internationalism vis-á-vis Africa, Asia, and Latin America. The broader ambition of the Soviet organizers and participants from the three continents was to make Tashkent a launching pad for a Third-World cinema that would hold its own against Hollywood or Western European cinema's global domination in the realm of both aesthetics and distribution, an ambition shared with the Third-World Filmmakers Committee, which was active in the early 1970s. In constructing that platform, the Soviet cultural bureaucracies incorporated other post-Second World War institutions that had been connecting Soviet cinema to Africa, Asia, and Latin America, such as the scholarships at vGik; the major Soviet film trade organization (Sovexportfilm), which saw in Tashkent a market through which to centralize its non-Western film trade; and Soviet material help to countries only beginning to establish their cinemas. Though no such

Figure 4.2   Official opening of the I International Festival of African and Asian Film at the Palace of the Arts in Tashkent, 1968.

field characterized by strong South-to-South or South-to-East relations, lasting internal structure, and principles of operation actually emerged, the Tashkent Film Festival succeeded in establishing an important contact zone where its participants – Soviet cultural bureaucracies, non-Western filmmakers, and Tashkent audiences – got to know each other and to see each other's films. In the contact zone of Tashkent a number of national cinemas made their international debut. It also helped make Third Cinema the original Latin American movement for the political film of the late 1960s and '70s, a truly Third World one despite the near-complete absence of Soviet journalism and scholarship. As a whole, especially from the 1960s onwards, when Soviet institutions dealing with non-Western

Figure 4.3   III Tashkent Film Festival. Seminar on the role of cinema in the struggle for peace, social progress, and freedom of the peoples.

Figure 4.4   III Tashkent Film Festival, 1974. The Kyrgyz writer and chair of the Kyrgyz Cinematographers Union Chinghiz Aitmatov (centre) speaking to Indian filmmakers Mrinal Sen (left) and Ramu Kariat (right).

Figure 4.5   Tashkent was not without glamour. The People's Artist of the USSR, the Hero of Socialist Labour, Uzbek director Kamil Yarmatov, with the Mexican actresses Alicia Encinas (to the left) and Susana Dosamantes. III Festival, 1974.

cinemas became fully developed, their archives offer an almost completely unexplored perspective on Asian, African, and Latin American film.

This chapter concludes by expanding the notion of this contact zone to include Soviet viewers' encounter with Afro-Asian film. Two films shown at the 1968 Tashkent Film Festival – the Indian *Motherly Love* (1966) and the Senegalese political satire *The Money Order* (1968) – will serve to illustrate the vastly different functions of Indian, Egyptian, and Mexican melodrama, on the one hand, and political Third Cinema, on the other, performed in the Soviet sphere. The immense popularity of the former made it an enduring source of images of Indian, Egyptian, Mexican, and Argentinian societies among Soviet publics; by contrast, the empty halls that greeted the latter became a limiting factor for Soviet cinematic internationalism vis-á-vis Third-Worldist movements on the three continents.

The Road to Tashkent

In the two decades before the Tashkent Film Festival launched the Soviet cinematic engagements with the non-Western world into a new orbit, these relationships had been invisibly growing in number and institutional complexity. The late-Stalin-era Soviet Union was nobody's idea of a cinematic powerhouse. The severity of the censorship practices of late Stalinism reduced the once vibrant Soviet film industry to a fraction of its interwar output.[21] Nevertheless, it was precisely then that films from Asia, Africa, and Latin America began to find their way to Soviet viewers. The paucity of contemporary Western films on Soviet screens in the late 1940s and early '50s, only partially compensated by the gigantic collection of trophy film taken from the Reichsfilmarchiv in Babelsberg, may have actually facilitated this debut.[22] Thus, in 1949, Soviet viewers saw an Indian film for the first time: K.A. Abbas's *Children of the Earth* (1946). The following year, the *Daughters of China* (Zifeng Lin 1949) inaugurated Chinese films' decade-long presence on Soviet screens, and in 1951, *The Village Girl* (Emilio Fernandez 1948), did the same for Mexico. Japanese cinema premiered in 1952 with Tadashi Imai's *And Yet We Live* (1951), Argentina's in 1955 with *The Age of Love* (Julio Saraceni 1954), and in early 1956 Soviet viewers saw their first Arab film, thanks to Yussef Chahine's *Struggle in the Valley* (1954). Each of these cinemas, with the exception of Chinese films, which predictably disappeared in the early 1960s, massively expanded its footprint on Soviet screens over the course of the Thaw period and kept it until 1991.[23]

Although foreign consulates and friendship societies in Moscow and other big cities also organized film weeks, and professional cinematic organizations would ensure that the Soviet film community had a much wider access to foreign film, as far as the mass viewer was concerned the main organization in charge of bringing foreign film to the USSR was Sovexportfilm (SEF).[24] Ever since the downsizing and subsequent closure of Mezhrabpomfilm, SEF (or more precisely, its predecessor, Soyuzintorgkino) also enjoyed a monopoly on the sales of Soviet films abroad. Initially, its trading partners were exclusively Western, but over the course of the 1930s and especially during the Second World War and the late-Stalin-era – not periods we associate with Soviet cultural expansion abroad – they began to extend toward Africa, Asia, and Latin America.[25] Thus, by the time of Stalin's death, New Delhi, Jakarta, Tokyo, Montevideo, Buenos Aires, to say nothing of Peking, Hanoi, and Pyongyang all hosted Sovexportfilm offices, which were responsible for selling Soviet films in neighbouring countries as well. The films that sold best in the three continents were hardly titles we would remember today. The success of Leonid Varlamov's concert-film *The Circus Arena* (1951) was repeated by Sergei Gurov's and Yurii Ozerov's *The Arena of the Bold* (1953), which also featured live performances by Soviet circus artists. Together with the epic *Great Warrior Scanderbeg* (1953), a Soviet-Albanian biopic directed by Sergei Yutkevich, and Alexander Ptushko's 1952 fantasy film *Sadko*, they continued to be the main Soviet bestsellers in Asian, African, and Latin American countries through the 1950s, testifying to non-Western audiences' interest in visual spectacle over politics and local censorship's ability to exclude films it deemed too political.[26] As we shall see later on in this chapter, similar forces shaped the reception of non-Western films on Soviet screens.

While Soviet efforts to promote and sell domestically-made films abroad were centralized through a single organization, they were otherwise not radically different from the practices of other states. A more specifically Soviet network was instantiated by the scholarships that sent Asian, African, and Latin American students to the Moscow-based All-Soviet State Institute of Cinematography (VGIK). The sheer number of directors and camera operators who were VGIK-trained constitutes one of the main, if neglected, Soviet contributions to African and Asian cinema. While VGIK was indeed an All-Soviet institution before the Second World War, with only the occasional foreigner studying there, after the war it began to enrol large numbers of students from a number of East European countries, especially those like Bulgaria, Romania, Hungary, and Albania, which had no film schools of their own.[27] Eventually, as such film schools began to appear over the course of the late 1950s and early '60s, the number of East Europeans fell, freeing up space for scholarship students from Africa and Asia. Among the graduates we find the major figures in sub-Saharan African cinema, such as the Malian Souleymane Cisse and the Mauritanian Abderrahmane Sissako. Two other black Africans, Sembène Ousmane, and the pioneer of Mozambican film and one of the first female African directors, Sarah Maldoror, learned the basics of filmmaking by attending a shortened, year-long course for mature students, during which they also worked as Mark Donskoy's interns at the Gorky Film Studio. The Syrian auteurs Mohammad Malas, Samir Zikra, Abdellatif Abdelhamid, and Ossama Mohammed were all trained at VGIK, as were the leading figure of Indonesian film of the 1970s and '80s, Sjumandjaja, and the prolific Mexican director Sergio Olhovich. Their very first films – their diploma shorts, some of which can still be found in VGIK's archives – were shot in the USSR.[28]

As a whole, it is difficult to evaluate the comparative significance of VGIK's contribution to training African, Asian, and Latin American cinemas. Existing as they did in the overall field of the global cultural

Cold War, however, Soviet VGIK scholarships initiated a dynamic of their own, much like the Cold War literary competition for writers and readers from the three continents. They were undoubtedly one of the reasons why the French Ministry of Cooperation (charged with relations to France's former colonies) established its own Film Bureau, which extended similar resources to francophone countries.[29]

VGIK's success in training directors varied widely from country to country, depending heavily on the state of each country's film industry, on the availability of institutions of cinematic training there, and of course, on its relationship with the USSR. Upon their return from Moscow to a less-than-friendly regime, many budding directors were viewed as "Moscow agents," never to be trusted with making a film.[30] The fifteen or so North Yemeni VGIK graduates, for example, could not produce a single feature film upon their return simply because their country never developed a film industry. Cinematographic powers such as Japan, India, and Egypt could provide film education opportunities at home and thus were unlikely to send students to the USSR to study filmmaking. And the Parisian La Fémis and École nationale supérieure Louis-Lumière might have been a more obvious training ground for francophone African film students even if Soviet scholarships managed to bring a few of them to Moscow. Illustrating the extent to which student enrolments were shaped by geopolitics, Chinese students disappeared from VGIK rolls soon after the Sino-Soviet split in 1960 and Nicaraguans began matriculating only after the 1984 electoral victory of the Sandinistas under General Ortega. The total number of students from each country could range from 143 (Vietnam) to 1 (Burkina Faso). Not all of them studied directing (other disciplines included camerawork, economics, film studies, or stage-work) and certainly not all directing graduates became filmmakers, let alone successful ones.

Nevertheless, entire national cinemas, such as Vietnamese, Mongolian, and Afghan cinemas (before the 1990s, after which the Taliban forbade cinema), and to a lesser extent, Syrian and Algerian, were dominated by VGIK graduates. Operating under a similar mandate of solidarity with the non-Western world, other Soviet-bloc film schools such as the Film Faculty of the Czechoslovak Academy of Performing Arts (FAMU) in Prague trained such well-known filmmakers as the Syrian Nabil Maleh, the Algerian Mohammed Lakhdar-Hamina, and the Cuban Octavio Cortazar while the

Polish National Film School at Łódź educated the Moroccans Mohamed Abdelkarim Derkaoui and Abdekader Lagtaa and the Algerian Mohammed Meziane Yala.[31] Under Joris Ivens's influence, the East German Academy for Film Art and Television initially offered specialized short courses for Latin American cameramen, subsequently discarding this format in favour of fully integrated education in which foreigners (the non-East European section was dominated by Latin Americans but also included a few Palestinians) studied alongside East German students.[32]

There was, of course, no uniform Soviet "stamp" that VGIK's international graduates could take away with them as there was no house style of Soviet filmmaking. They came to Moscow from vastly different ideological and aesthetic backgrounds and returned to societies where they were subject to very different political and professional pressures. Their stay in Moscow coincided with different periods in Soviet history and involved different degrees of engagement with Soviet society. It is difficult, for example, to compare the year Sembène spent in Thaw-era Moscow (1961–62) with the decade Sissako lived in the USSR, first as a Russian-language student in Rostov and subsequently in Moscow (1983–93), hardly a time of great enthusiasm about the Soviet project. Without much Russian and on a mission to learn as much directing and camerawork technique as he could for a year, Sembène did not have the time and leisure to immerse himself in Soviet life.[33] By contrast, Sissako's films, about African students in the USSR (the semi-autobiographical *October* [1993] and *Rostov-Luanda* [1997]), testify to his extended engagement with Soviet realities.[34] Additionally, for the practical (and most influential) part of their directing education, students interned with different Soviet filmmakers (*mastera*), each of whom offered very different pedagogical training and cinematic styles. For their 2016 exhibit at the Garage Art Gallery in Moscow, Rasha Salti, Koyo Kouo, and the gallery's Russian curators identified the following Soviet fiction-filmmakers with whom the majority of foreign students at VGIK interned: Igor Talankin, Mark Donskoy, Marlen Khutsiev, Alexander Zigurdi, and Alexander Stolper.[35] Between the 1950s and mid-1970s, non-fiction film training was dominated by the figures of Ilya Kopalin and Roman Karmen. Yet for all the differences in their education, the VGIK alumni had much in common, from the Russian language and life in Moscow to belonging to an alumni network that included such benefits as periodic invitations to the Tashkent Film Festival.

Seeing Afro-Asian Cinema
like a post-Stalin-era Soviet State

Indeed, Tashkent was meant as a nodal point where the disparate networks – educational or trade – connecting Soviet and non-Western cinemas could be brought together and showcased and where Soviet film directors, bureaucrats, traders, and critics met their peers from Africa, Asia, and Latin America. In addition to the commercial and scholarly goals, the festival also pursued a political agenda: organizing the more politically outspoken among the visiting filmmakers around a common project for Third-World cinema. Before these goals could be acted upon and even before the First Tashkent Festival could take place, the Soviet festival organizers needed to gain some basic familiarity with non-Western cinemas.

While SEF offices in different countries regularly sent reports to Moscow outlining the state of the cinema markets in the countries they were responsible for, these were mostly concerned with the possibilities of selling Soviet film abroad rather than forging relationships with local filmmakers. For this reason, in the months before the First Tashkent Film Festival in 1968, the Soviet Union of Filmmakers sent out small delegations made up of filmmakers, film critics, and film officials to produce snapshots of the state of cinema in most of the countries participating in the Festival and to identify films, actors, and directors to represent that country. Depending on the degree of government involvement in filmmaking, the Soviet delegation often had to negotiate the country's participation at the festival with local officials. While in India and Japan, for example, the delegation would approach commercial studios and directly invite films and participants. In countries such as Pakistan and Iran the cultural ministries reserved those choices for themselves, allowing little input from the festival organizers. Either way, the detailed reports the Soviet delegations wrote upon their return constitute a unique snapshot of Afro-Asian cinema, ca 1968, as well as of Soviet thinking about it.

The basic question these delegations had to answer was whom to invite. Officially, the film festival was dedicated to Afro-Asian (adding Latin American later) cinema since this formula (and more specifically, its Asian part) allowed for the participation of Soviet Central Asian and Caucasian cinemas. However, the continental designation came with its own problems, which the organizers debated at great length: much to the chagrin of Soviet organizers, it included China, Israel, and the Republic of South

Africa, whose exclusion they had to somehow justify. The exclusions did not stretch much further and they did invite Indonesian films and filmmakers, even though the regime ruling their state had killed over 500,000 real and suspected communists just three years earlier. But the major problem of defining the festival on the basis of geography – a problem that the festival struggled with for the rest of its existence – was the immense heterogeneity of the cinemas represented. Along with the cinematic powerhouse of India (by 1968, it was producing over 300 feature films per year), the festival included countries without a single feature-length film to their name. The geographical designator made films with vastly different styles eligible for participation as long as they did not contradict the motto of the festival: "For peace, social progress, and freedom of the peoples." Indeed, that motto not only distinguished this festival from most Western ones but also suggested a certain tension that never left the festival – between fully representing the cinemas of the three continents in their diversity and privileging political (progressive, anti-colonial, pro-Soviet) film. These two criteria competed with another, central to any film festival: the aesthetic quality of the films.

To illustrate how the Soviet organizers resolved these tensions in practice, let us accompany them to a few countries they visited. In Japan, they had to select delegates and films from three different and competing film consortia: the Japanese Film Association, which included the major studios and distribution channels; the Association for the Renewal of Japanese Film, which was affiliated with the Japanese Communist Party (JCP); and the Filmmakers' Guild, which had ties to a breakaway current within JCP. The politics that the Soviet representatives G.B. Mariamov and S. Shermukhamedova had to navigate were quite complex: the Association for the Renewal of Japanese film used its proximity to JCP to claim that it alone should represent Japanese cinema in the Soviet Union while the other two groups did not want to participate in the same delegation with it. As the maximally broad representation of Japanese cinema – the leading Afro-Asian cinema, in terms of international recognition at least[36] – was a priority for the Soviet delegates, they concluded their report by highlighting their success in bringing to Tashkent films and representatives from all three film consortia.[37]

India was an even more familiar terrain for Soviet film officials as there was already a good deal of cinematic traffic between the two countries. The task the committee set itself was to represent Indian cinema in all its variety. As the director of the most popular film to be screened in the USSR in the 1950s, practically a household name in the USSR, and a frequent visitor there, Raj Kapoor was the most obvious Indian invitee. To represent Calcutta's more intellectual cinema, the festival organizers invited Satyajit Ray, whose reputation as India's main auteur must have been more in line with Soviet organizers' understanding of "serious" cinema. (He declined, citing unavailability.)[38] Despite barely concealed contempt for the mass Hindi cinema of Madras, the delegation consisting of N.Ia. Volchenko (the chair of the International Relations Commission of the Soviet Cinematographers Union), S.M. Mukhamedov (the chair of the Uzbek Union of Cinematographers), and A.P. Kaiumov (the overall head of the Tashkent Festival) invited filmmakers from that centre as well:

> In Madras, inside a spacious, well-designed studio, we watched a number of films, which were united in their absence of taste. Their audience cannot have been a particularly demanding one: the unmotivated tricks and fistfights in which those films abounded were mixed with equally unmotivated singing and dancing. The one conceivable motivation for the making of those films is the desire to make money ... On 7 Aug. 1968 we met the prominent artist and film producer Randy. Then we saw a film of his about the noble actions of a young man, who stood up to the evil deeds of his father. At Randy's recommendation we also saw the film *Love and Money* about the triumph of good over greed and social prejudices. We had to invite both films.[39]

In countries where cinema was a matter of state interest, the negotiations were with state officials, which did not make them any simpler. The Soviet film archives include a diplomatic correspondence regarding Iranian participation in the Tashkent Festival.[40] Upon learning about the Festival from a Soviet diplomat, Iranian officials coolly agreed to consider the invitation but declined to host a Soviet film delegation and rejected any form of Soviet participation in the selection of Iranian delegates or films to be screened. As an effort to entice Iranian diplomats, the Soviet Union then organized Iranian evenings at which it had screened a short Iranian documentary film about the coronation of the Iranian king and queen. Gratefully noting this and other Soviet efforts, the Iranian cultural bureaucracy agreed to participate, and in addition to sending a fiction film, hastily produced a documentary entitled *Soviet Prime Minister A.N. Kosygin's Visit*, which it sent to the shorts section of the festival.

In fact, most countries' selections took the short film and documentary program as an opportunity to exhibit films about the new nation. Just a quick look at some of the titles at the first edition of the Festival reveal the prominence of this mode of filmmaking: Morocco, for example, was represented by *The Country of Civilization*; Liberia by *The Country of the Future*; Uganda by *Our National Monuments*; Pakistan by *Panorama of Pakistan*; and Uzbekistan by *8 Minutes According to Uzbekistan*. The Democratic Republic of Vietnam called attention to its plight with *One Day in Hanoi*. The documentary programs also tended to be the site for the most explicit political messages.

Whenever festival organizers were not able to send delegations, the task of extending invitations fell to Soviet embassy officials, who left their own stamp on the process. In arranging Cambodia's participation in the festival (Prince Norodom Sihanouk's film *Shadow of Angkor*), for example, Soviet Ambassador Kudriavtsev advised the festival organizing committee:

> It would be desirable to if the relevant authorities ensured that the reception and the whole visit of the Cambodian delegation went well and also awarded the film *The Shadow over Angkor* with one of the festival prizes. [To support the latter suggestion, meant to warm Sihanouk to the USSR, Kudriavtsev attaches a local review of the film, where we read: "From among the films of the Head of State this (*The Shadow over Angkor*) is the deepest and most interesting one, testifying to the talent of the author. This, however, does not mean that all previous films of the Head of State are less interesting."][41]

Such a letter is typical of the efforts by Soviet embassies to use the cultural recognition extended by the festival as an instrument of Soviet soft power. Upon learning that a Lebanese film, *Mobilization*, was on the festival program, the Turkish embassy remonstrated with the Soviet authorities, branding it "anti-Turkish."[42] What happened in the aftermath of this diplomatic démarche is unclear, but no such film was shown in Tashkent.

In addition to ensuring the broadest festival participation, selecting a repertoire that fit, or more precisely, did not conflict with, the anti-colonialist mission statement of the festival, and to generating the currency of diplomatic good will, the Soviet delegations operated under a more traditionally commercial mandate. Although film trade was deliberately kept less conspicuous than at other class A festivals such as Cannes, Venice, or Berlin, an important part of the Soviet organizers' calculus was to establish direct commercial relations with and among Afro-Asian nations, and even more importantly, to create a market for Soviet cinematic exports. Wherever they went, Soviet delegations duplicated the work of monitoring the presence (or absence) of Soviet cinema on local screens typically done by Sovexportfilm. In this spirit, the author of the report about Sri Lanka, V.A. Volkov, complains about the difficulty of entering the Sri Lankan film market, which was dominated by Hollywood and Bollywood films. (Indeed, the motif of US monopoly over film distribution in African and Asian countries emerges in a number of these reports.) Instead of trying to break into the existing film distribution systems, Volkov suggested renting cinema halls to exhibit Soviet films and otherwise expanding the non-commercial efforts of the Soviet embassy, the Soviet Society for Friendship, and the Colombo Film Society. He also informed his superiors of the preliminary negotiations he conducted with the senator (and film producer) Regi Pereira and sent the script Pereira proposed for a possible Soviet-Sri Lankan co-production.[43] In their role as commercial representatives of Soviet cinema, the Soviet delegates themselves had to field uncomfortable queries by cultural bureaucrats or film studio representatives of foreign countries about the Soviet Union's own trade imbalance vis-á-vis African and Asian countries. A Japanese official, for example, pointed out that over the last three years $1,947,000 worth of Soviet films had been bought by Japanese film companies whereas only $222,000 worth of Japanese films was procured by the Soviet side.[44]

All these complex considerations had to be negotiated in Tashkent itself, where SEF purchased approximately ten fiction films and made over forty-five sales of twelve Soviet films, numbers that were nearly tripled at the Second Festival. Eventually, most African and Asian films purchased for Soviet distribution came through the Tashkent Festival.[45] The lists of Soviet films purchased at the first festival contain Mosfilm and Lenfilm productions, but approximately half of the films come from Central Asian and Caucasian film studios, especially Uzbekfilm.[46] The Tashkent market was thus disproportionately important for the international distribution of films made in Soviet Asia. The festival organizers also emphasized its importance for non-Western and East European distribution companies, who – as different reports repeatedly point out – had fewer direct contacts with each other.[47] Indeed, the Indian films that went on to become sensations on Bulgarian, Romanian, Yugoslav, and other Soviet-bloc screens usually reached their destinations via Tashkent.[48]

Tashkent as a Contact Zone for the Cinemas of the Three Continents

Tashkent was not the only place that opened its doors to African, Asian, and Latin American filmmakers. The oldest and most prestigious film festivals in Venice, Cannes, and Berlin, and especially Rotterdam, welcomed new geographic discoveries. The stiffness of the competition, the conservative aesthetic criteria, and the European focus of those festivals, however, proved to be significant barriers for African, Asian, and Latin American entries. Even the Rotterdam festival, which distinguished itself by snubbing the others' preoccupation with commerce and stars and making a much greater investment in new forms and geographies, could mainly only accommodate African and Asian films in its "special programs," that is, films screened outside of the main competition. The signature Soviet-bloc film festivals – the Czechoslovak Karlovy Vary, the East German Leipzig Documentary Film Festival, and the Moscow International Film Festival – also recruited a number of non-Western films and filmmakers in their selections, sharing many of them with Tashkent but also maintaining a certain division of labour. Especially in the 1960s and early 1970s, Leipzig became the preferred European destination for militant Cuban and Latin American filmmakers, who were among the festival's most feted guests and regular recipients of the *Kämpfende Kamera* (The Fighting Camera) prize.[49] Similarly, Karlovy Vary was particularly hospitable to Brazilian cinema novo, films that were rarely invited to the USSR.[50] Eager to maintain their reputation for "high art," none of these three festivals would invite either the melodrama or "one of the nation's first films" that would constitute a significant component of Tashkent's program.

By the end of the 1960s, by which time most newly decolonized countries had made their first attempts at cinematic production (sometimes documentaries or shorts), the case for a non-Western film festival was growing stronger. Several international film festivals had already emerged on the cinematic periphery: Carthage in Tunisia, New Delhi in India, and Cartagena in Colombia. In practice, however, those festivals were only regional. Founded in 1966, Carthage became the obligatory stop for Arab and North African films. Since its establishment in 1960, Cartagena had been the festival for Latin American film, and New Delhi rarely managed to attract films made outside of India.[51]

Although they were trying to establish a unique event, the Tashkent organizers were perfectly aware that the festival also took place within the context of the international film festival circuit, as testified by the abundant information they assembled on the other festivals.[52] With the proliferation of festivals in the post-Second World War-era, the organizers were competing for the attention and the limited availability of leading filmmakers. The issue was not only the time of the year the festival would take place or the travel subsidies the Soviet organizers were able to offer to entice some participants.[53] By the rules of most festivals, for example, films that compete for the prize of one cannot do so at another. They can participate only in auxiliary film programs, if the festival had any. Partly to circumvent this rule, which would have barred the more ambitious African and Asian filmmakers, and partly to avoid scandals, which inevitably accompany the choice of winners, the Tashkent Festival was non-competitive and without a jury. Instead, Soviet public organizations such as labour unions, creative artists' organizations, women's committees, newspapers, and magazines awarded dozens of prizes each year.

Despite such egalitarian strategies, there was no way to smooth over the cinematic inequalities evident at the festival. As already mentioned, the countries represented ranged from cinematic heavyweights such as India and Japan to newer African and Asian cinemas, represented at Tashkent only by documentary shorts, often unaccompanied by translation.[54] The Soviet state, as the organizer of the event, was over-represented in the form of nine different cinemas, from its eight Asian republics (Azerbaijan, Armenia, Georgia, Kazakhstan, Kyrgyzstan, Tajikistan, Turkmenistan, Uzbekistan) and of course Russia. At the same time, according to Elena Razlogova, the Tashkent Festival offered a more relaxed and less controlled space than its Moscow counterpart and the proverbial Tashkent hospitality diluted the official speeches and ceremonies.[55]

What united most of the participants, Soviet cultural bureaucracies, and the Afro-Asian filmmakers, even the less political among them, and consistently provided an agenda for the festival, was these cinemas' shared peripheral status vis-à-vis Western (Hollywood, but also Western European) cinema. It is this aspect that Soviet coverage of the first festival singles out:

We must push out of our cinemas [Western] B-movies. But all the movie-theatres belong to Italians and the choice of films to screen depends on them," says the Somalian [delegate Hadj Mohamed] Giumale. [The African-American actor, filmmaker, and African solidarity activist] Osei Davis could not exhibit in Nigeria his film *Congi's Harvest* because, in his words, the film distribution system is controlled by Lebanese and Indian businessmen, who doubt the economic potential of Nigerian films and don't give us a chance.[56]

The insurmountable difficulty for film produced in Africa, Asia, and Latin America, to break through the foreign (mostly American, but not only) monopoly of domestic and international film distribution, became the main refrain of the filmmakers' seminar held at all festivals. Indeed, while informal encounters and film screenings were the most important ways for filmmakers, actors, and other kinds of participants from different countries to meet each other at the festival, the seminar – another unusual feature of the festival – was the only venue where their visions of an alternative cinematic world were transcribed and subsequently published. Entitled "On the Role of Art in the Struggle for Peace, Social Progress and Freedom of the Peoples," these seminars brought together the leading political directors, along with government bureaucrats responsible for the film industry of their country, and foreign film critics.[57]

Partly as an expression of the filmmakers' gratitude to their hosts but also reflecting a genuine sentiment, the participants in those seminars would return again and again to the point of Tashkent's importance as a meeting place for the cinemas of the three continents. In an interview conducted at the First Festival, the Guinean minister of information and Soviet-educated film director Costa N'Diane remarked that a Senegalese filmmaker had to go to Tashkent to be able to see a Guinean film.[58] Echoing him, the Senegalese filmmaker Blaise Senghor confessed to seeing a Somali film for the first time in the Soviet Union.[59] In fact, the sub-Saharan African program of the First Tashkent Festival was quite remarkable, including short films from Chad (Edouard Sailly's *Le Troisième Jour*, 1967), Sierra Leone, Guinea, Uganda, Mali, Cameroon, and, of course, Senegal. While some of these films were also being screened at Rotterdam and Leipzig, it was the critical mass of works and directors that rendered the Tashkent Film Festival such a productive site of exchange. In this context, Tashkent emerged not only as a space where African, Asian, and Latin American filmmakers could be guaranteed a spot to screen their films, but also to meet each other, see each other's work, and set up networks for further collaboration.

Judging by the participant lists in its ten editions, the filmmakers' seminar was attended by some of the leading Third-Worldist filmmakers of the period: the Sub-Saharan Africans: Sembène Ousmane, Paulin Vieyra, Sarah Maldoror, and Med Hondo; the Arabs: Youssef Chahine, Mohamad Slim Riad, and Souheil Ben-Barka; the leaders of Indian parallel cinema: Mrinal Sen, K.A. Abbas, Basu Bhattacharya, Goutam Ghose, Tapan Sinha, and Adoor Gopalkrishnan; and the exiled Chileans: Miguel Littin, Patricio Guzmán, and Sebastián Alarcón, most of whom came to Tashkent multiple times. Throughout its history, the festival secured the participation of filmmakers from societies in the throes of liberation struggles: first, Vietnam and Palestine, but also Mozambique, Angola, and Nicaragua. Even before Latin America was formally included at Tashkent, Cuban cinema was there, starting from the First Festival, represented in different years by Jose Massip, Enrique Pineda Barnet, and Pastor Vega Torres, the future head of the Havana Film Festival. While the theoreticians of guerrilla filmmaking, Octavio Getino and Fernando Solanas, and a number of other Latin American political filmmakers are missing from this list, for reasons that will become clearer in the next chapter, many of the key names of Third Cinema, especially beyond its Latin American core, showed up at every festival.

Though it was the biggest forum for filmmakers from the three continents, Tashkent was not the only one. Filmmakers from the three continents had other opportunities to meet, not only at other festivals, but, more significantly for our purposes, at the 1973 Algiers and 1974 Buenos Aires gatherings of the short-lived Third World Filmmakers Committee, which were followed up by a 1974 Montreal meeting in the case of the Latin American filmmakers and the slightly more regular encounters of the Pan-African Federation of Filmmakers (FEPACI).[60] The early Tashkent festivals should thus be considered alongside these gatherings as a major platform that facilitated Third Cinema's spread beyond its Latin American core. While the statements at the Tashkent filmmakers' seminar do not by themselves constitute a coherent program, certain recurring proposals mirror the manifestos issued in Algiers and Niamey: combatting Hollywood's global monopoly and Western economic and ideological control over cinema; nationalizing existing structures for film production and distribution, and in general, transforming them in non-capitalist ways; securing state support for local filmmakers; representing progressive struggles and national culture and history; and facilitating distribution, co-productions, film markets, film festivals, and information exchanges among the national cinemas of the three continents.[61] Though similar in substance and featuring many of the same filmmakers, the gatherings differed in tone: in contrast to the heated debates in Buenos Aires and Montreal, the filmmakers' seminar in Tashkent was moderated by the Soviet hosts and consisted of prepared speeches emphasizing unity.[62] What has made it difficult to compare these gatherings and connect them in a common history is their lack of reference to each other. Reflecting the Third World project's division over the Soviet Union, in the resolutions of the Third-World Filmmakers Committee produced in Algiers in 1973, Tashkent and Soviet cinema in general remain unmentioned, either as a potential ally or as an adversary (a status reserved for the "imperialist system dominated by the United States of America"), leaving an opportunity for different factions of Third-Worldist filmmakers to have their own position on the Soviet Union.[63] The suspicion was mutual: neither the Tashkent filmmakers seminar nor Soviet cinematic journalism makes any mention of such parallel, Third-Worldist initiatives.

While African, Asian, and Latin American participants constituted the majority at the filmmakers' seminars, these were also attended by Soviet directors, drawn largely from Central Asia. Besides the directors in charge of Uzbekfilm at the time of each festival – Sabir Mukhamedov, Malik Kaiumov, Shukhrat Abbasov, and Anatoly Kabulov – who traditionally chaired the meeting together with Vladimir Baskakov, the head of All-Soviet Research Institute of the History and Theory of Cinema, we also see in the booklets extended statements by Grigory Chukhray, Sergei Gerasimov, Elyer Ishmukhamedov, and Chinghiz Aitmatov, and numerous references to other Soviet filmmakers in attendance who do not speak out. They speak about socialist art, the dangers of Western commercial culture, assert that the struggles Third-Worldist filmmakers are waging are their struggles, too, and sometimes posit their national Soviet cinema as an example of what the cinemas of their countries could aspire for.[64]

In addition to other filmmakers, the foreign participants at the Tashkent Festival were also able to interact with local audiences, leaving both parties with deep impressions of each other. Indeed, the articles published about Tashkent in the foreign, especially the Western, press frequently mention the highly impulsive reaction of local audiences to foreign films, contrasting it with the much more disciplined Moscow viewers. In a piece entitled

"The Second World Organizes a Festival for the Third," describing the 1974 edition of the festival, Father Ambros Eichenberger, president of the International Catholic Organization for Cinema, wrote: "Uzbeks, if they don't like a film, react thoroughly "normally": they whistle and leave the hall. This happened particularly frequently during the screenings of political films: sometimes the whole of the 2,300-seat Palace of Culture would get emptied out."[65] The reverse side of this reaction, Eichenberger argues, is the audience's enthusiasm for popular genre films. The average Tashkent filmgoer, he concludes, is not that much different from her Swiss counterpart and seems similarly averse to experimental film.[66]

That same discovery caused much greater distress to politically outspoken visitors such as Mrinal Sen, whose own films brought together avant-garde technique and radical social and political consciousness. In his remarks at the filmmakers' roundtable of the third Tashkent Festival, Sen expressed his great discomfort with the applause the Tashkent audience gave to the Pakistani film *Clay Doll*, which he labelled "anti-worker." The viewers' reaction, he claimed, testified to the fact that the broad masses remained the same as they were fifty years ago despite officially proclaimed socialism.[67]

Afro-Asian Film as a Lens on Soviet Audiences

Two films that were shown to Tashkent audiences and then purchased by SEF at the First Festival – Asit Sen's *Motherly Love* (India 1966) and Sembène Ousmane's *The Money Order* (Senegal 1968) – can help us expand upon Father Eichenberger's and Mrinal Sen's observations of the Soviet mass audience and thus offer a peek into the range of receptions enjoyed by the non-Western films among Soviet audiences. Understanding this reception, in turn, provides an empirical way to study the internationalism of those audiences.

Motherly Love is a typical Indian popular production from the 1960s, by which time the early wave of popular and socially critical films that dealt with burning questions of the new nation, such as caste and social injustice, had begun giving way to lavish spectacles of song and dance.[68] Not that the film is thoroughly shorn of "social issues": the plot revolves around the fate of Deviyani, a young and beautiful, but poor, woman. Her marriage to her fiancé Monish is postponed by his departure to England to study law. While he is away, financial difficulties force her father to marry her off to one of his creditors. Disgusted by the abusive and dissolute ways of her husband, the pregnant Deviyani escapes, finding refuge in a house of ill repute. There she not only becomes the star dancer but also raises her daughter, Suparna, the one joy in her otherwise difficult life. Her reprieve, however, proves short-lived as her husband – now thoroughly degenerate – reappears, threatening to reassert his rights over her daughter unless she pays him off. To protect her seven-year-old daughter, Deviyani sends her to a Catholic boarding school in a different town, vowing never to visit her again so that Suparna would never have to live under the cloud of her mother's reputation. Many years later Deviyani meets her former fiancé, Monish – now a successful lawyer – who happily takes over the role of her daughter's benefactor. As Suparna is about to become a lawyer in her own right under Monish's tutelage and marry a dashing young man, her degenerate father learns of her true identity (a secret kept between Monish and Deviyani) and threatens to make it public unless her mother gives him even more money. Temporarily driven out of her mind by this threat to her daughter's well-being, Deviyani shoots her estranged husband. At the ensuing trial, Monish takes on her defence, but she pleads with him not to reveal the one circumstance that would mitigate her guilt – the existence of her daughter for whose sake she killed her husband. At the end of this three-hour-long film, Suparna learns whose daughter she really is, appears in court, and gives a most passionate trial speech – her first as a lawyer – in defence of her mother. Overwhelmed by love at seeing her daughter for the first time in many years, the mother's heart stops beating.

Popular in India and outside of it, *Motherly Love* went on to become something of a sensation among Soviet viewers when it entered commercial distribution in December 1969. According to the official statistics, the 52 million movie-goers who saw it make it the seventeenth most-watched foreign film ever shown on Soviet screens and fiftieth overall if we include Soviet films in that ranking.[69] Sudha Rajagopalan's excellent book *Indian Films in Soviet Cinemas* (2008) offers a convincing explanation of the extreme popularity of Indian melodrama among Soviet audiences. The centrepiece of Rajagopalan's book is her reconstruction of those films' reception based on an extended questionnaire surveying a number of Russians from different social groups who remember seeing popular Indian films in the 1950s and '60s. Most of them speak about the entertainment qualities of those films – the glamour of Indian actors and actresses, the unusual singing and dancing scenes, the spectacular dresses worn by the actresses, and the colourful scenery. The melodramatic form of popular Indian films appealed to Soviet mass audiences unused to watching Cinderella stories and family tragedies without a heavy political subtext. Most interviewees readily acknowledged the escapist qualities of those films, which took them away from the drab Soviet realities they lived through or saw in Soviet films and offered them access to a new, exciting, and exotic world.[70] Responses, of course, varied based on the interviewee's social and even ethnic backgrounds: by all accounts, elite viewers tended to be much less enamoured of the genre conventions on which melodrama relied. Most such audiences were highly critical of the mass fascination with this "low" form while others were politely disengaged.[71]

What we can add to Rajagopalan's explanation of the popularity of these films is a broader consideration of the dynamics of the genre deficits under which Soviet culture operated and their international implications. Melodrama was a genre that Soviet cultural bureaucracies treated as suspect and that most Soviet film directors regarded as low. The combination of these factors accounts for the difficulty of domestically producing cinematic spectacles with few social issues but with exaggerated plot and characters that appeal to viewers' emotions. And yet foreign melodramas – and other genre films – tended to be more successful than their "serious" counterparts in filling movie theatres and producing immense profits, which, as Kristin Roth-Ey has demonstrated, allowed the commercially-minded SEF officials to override repeated complaints by the Communist Party's Central Committee about the questionable political content of these films.[72] It was not until the mid- and late 1970s that the restrictions on this genre were somewhat relaxed and Soviet screens were hit by a wave of domestically-produced films such as *The Red Snowball Tree* (Vasily Shukshin 1974), *Queen of the Gypsies* (Emil Loteanu 1976), *Office Romance* (El'dar Riazanov 1977), *Moscow Does Not Believe in Tears* (Vladimir Men'shov 1980), which all earned a place in the top twenty most popular Soviet films ever. Importing melodramas from the West would have been a trickier option because of the stiffer ideological requirements Western European and Hollywood films had to meet before they could reach the Soviet public. The ideological unsoundness of the melodrama and its regular displays of luxurious lifestyles made such films coming from the wrong side of the Iron Curtain nearly doubly problematic.[73] By contrast, non-aligned countries with a good relationship to the USSR, such as India and Egypt, were a much better source of melodrama, assuring SEF of excellent box office at a much lower political cost. Commercial parity considerations also required screening many Indian films domestically if as many Soviet films were to be sold in India. Thus, between the early 1950s, when Indian films began their triumphant march through Soviet screens, and the mid-1970s, melodrama imports, primarily from India but also from Egypt, Mexico, and Argentina, enjoyed privileged access to Soviet viewers.[74] While facilitating the circulation of non-Western film, this cultural division of labour helped affix exotic stereotypes of dancing and singing Indians, fiery Latin Americans, and vengeful Arabs, which diminished the political content of Soviet internationalism or at least tinged it with some orientalizing affect.

The enormous success of these films during the late-Soviet period is captured by various statistics. By far the most-watched film ever shown on Soviet screens was an unpretentious Mexican melodrama, *Yesenia* (1971), directed by Alfredo Crevenna, which was seen by 91 million viewers.[75] Among the 50 most-watched films on Soviet screens – again including both Soviet and foreign ones – there are also seven Indian ones, including *Motherly Love* (#50 with 52 million viewers), and the Egyptian *White Dress* (#23 with 61 million), all of them varieties of melodrama. For purposes of comparison, the number of Western-made films in this list is roughly similar: four American adventure films (Westerns or action films), three Italian and French comedies, and a Western from West Germany. The longer list of the top 1,000 films screened in the USSR (nearly three quarters of which are Soviet) also features 47 films from India, 12 from Egypt, 10 from Mexico, 5 from Argentina, and 2 Pakistani ones.[76]

Not unexpectedly, Sembène Ousmane's political satire of postcolonial Senegal, *The Money Order* (1968), experienced a very different journey through the USSR, which exemplifies Third Cinema's trajectory at the hands of Soviet cultural bureaucracies and audiences. In this film, Sembène transitions from a critique of Western colonialism, the main subject of his previous film *Black Girl* (1966: the first full-length feature film shot by an African director) to an examination of class relations in post-independence Senegal, which is ruled by an alliance of exploitative bourgeoisie and corrupt bureaucracy. The protagonist, Ibrahim, receives a money order from a nephew working as a street-sweeper in France and embarks on a quest to cash it. He cannot, however, cash the cheque without an ID card. To obtain the latter, he would need a birth certificate. Even that turns out to be impossible to obtain without being literate. Cheated at every step of this ever more absurd bureaucratic process, this otherwise honest and gentle person often takes out his frustration on his two wives and big flock of kids. When another nephew enters the scene, promising to cut through this nightmare, Ibrahim entrusts the cheque to him only to realize in the end that his money has been stolen. The movie ends with Ibrahim's despairing cry. In the process of reconstructing Ibrahim's tale of woe, the all-seeing camera uncovers the corrupt nature of the post-independence regime, from top to bottom, as well as the backwardness of traditional religious society.

Based on Sembène's own novel by the same name, this film remains much better known internationally than *Motherly Love*. A month before the Tashkent Festival, it had been awarded the 1968 Special Jury Prize at the Venice Film Festival. While the Tashkent Film Festival had no jury or winners, Sembène's was one of the names with which the main Soviet cinema journal *Iskusstvo Kino* (Cinema Art) opened its review article on the festival.[77] After the Tashkent Festival, this film was purchased by Sovexportfilm, dubbed by Lenfilm Studios in Leningrad in 1969 and distributed to Soviet cinemas in 1971.[78] Its further journey to Soviet audiences is something of a mystery, as testified by the absence of any reviews. Most likely, it was indeed screened, but, expecting little audience interest, only at a very small number of theatres in major cities (possibly, only in Moscow). With hindsight, it is hard to imagine the didactic, Brechtian quality of the film appealing to Brezhnev-era audiences. The schematism of the plot – in which one misfortune follows another, inexorably leading Ibrahim's family to poverty – and the uncomfortable, claustrophobic camerawork – serving to highlight the absence of any escape from the bureaucratic absurdity and dishonesty that Ibrahim runs into every time he attempts a new solution – could not bring either elite Soviet viewers interested in poetic expression, or a mass audience searching for more escapist fare. The former, like their literary counterparts, strongly doubted that the peaks of cinematic achievement could be found in Africa; the latter could not find the familiar genre formulas they were looking for.

Thus, if *Motherly Love* and other Indian, Egyptian, Mexican, and Argentinian melodrama populated the lists of most-watched films in the USSR, the opposite is true of politically engaged cinema from Africa, Asia, and Latin America. A number of films by canonical Third Cinema directors were indeed commercially distributed in the USSR: Sembène Ousmane's *Borom Sarret* (1963), *Money Order* (1968), *Emitai* (1972), *Xala* (1974), *Ceddo* (1972); Miguel Littín's *The Jackal of Nahueltoro* (1969), *Letters from Marusia* (1975), *The Widow of Montiel* (1979), *Alsino and the Condor* (1982); Mrinal Sen's *Interview* (1971), *Chorus* (1975), *The Man with the Axe* (1979),

Genesis (1986); Mohammad Lakhdar-Hamina's *Chronicle of the Years of Fire* (1975); Humberto Solas's *Manuela* (1966), *Lucia* (1968), *Cecilia* (1979, 1981), *Amada* (1984); Tomás Gutiérrez Alea's *History of the Revolution* (1960), *The Death of the Bureaucrat* (1966), *The Survivors* (1979). None of these films appear in the available Soviet viewership statistics. That is, their attendance rates were not large enough to register. SEF purchased such films largely as a form of symbolic and material support for progressive Third-Worldist filmmakers despite Soviet viewers' lack of interest in most of them. Sometimes the purchase was largely a diplomatic gesture to the filmmaker – a "we appreciate you" message – with no effort to promote the film to Soviet audiences. This was the case with an unnamed Mrinal Sen film (most likely, *Parashuram* [1979]), which became yet another occasion for officials of the Cultural Section of the Soviet Communist Party to scold SEF's preoccupation with profit over ideology. Noting that SEF's purchases of the early 1980s came almost exclusively from the commercial Bombay film studios and largely avoided South India's and Calcutta's intellectual and political filmmakers (Satyajit Ray and Mrinal Sen), a report by a Soviet delegation visiting India in 1983 focused in particular on the slight inflicted upon Mrinal Sen, whose film SEF considered for purchase for five months and then returned damaged and without a response. After describing the details of the case, the report recommends that such films, which may not necessarily be commercially viable for Soviet distribution, could still be purchased in a very small number of copies (two or three) as a matter of cultural diplomacy with foreign friends of the USSR, such as Mrinal Sen.[79] On occasion, however, the Soviet side did attempt wide distribution of Third-Worldist film, such as Sembène Ousmane's *Emitai* (1972), 339 copies of which were released in 1974. The small audience it brought (800,000 viewers), or more precisely, the very low viewers-to-copies ratio (2,400 viewers per copy, or a quarter of the average of a Soviet film and one sixth of the average of a Western film) meant that it was being played to largely empty halls, practically at a loss in the calculations of the commercially minded SEF.[80] In this sense, Brezhnev-era Soviet audiences' tastes served as the main limiting factor of Soviet cinematic internationalism.

Though a secondary factor, SEF itself could have been the obstacle on the path of a Third-Worldist film toward Soviet audiences. Like any bureaucracy, it was constrained by budgets and quotas, its personnel made occasional misjudgments, and the great difficulty of negotiating with multiple other bureaucracies – Soviet and foreign, state and private – in changing and often precarious political climates meant that many great films never reached Soviet audiences.[81] And even though the censorship standards and practices to which "films from capitalist countries" were held were much more demanding than what "films from developing countries" experienced, censorship still accounts for some significant exclusions.[82] It is hard to imagine other reasons why no film of the most-acclaimed Turkish filmmaker and outspoken leftist Yılmaz Güney was ever purchased by Sovexportfilm while other, lesser-known, and, importantly, less popular Turkish films were screened in the USSR. The (melo)dramatic and suspenseful plot of Güney's Palm d'Or-winning *The Road* (1980), about five prisoners in post-1980-coup Turkey who are given a week to visit their villages and families, would not have wanted for a Soviet audience and neither would many of Güney's other films. While the film critic Sergei Kudriavtsev attributes this absence to Soviet diplomacy's unwillingness to upset its Turkish counterparts by showing the persecuted director's film, the German cultural historian Karl Lebt suspects that Güney's unorthodox communism – both personal and cinematic – was the main reason.[83] SEF oversight, quotas, or problems with negotiations over the purchase of the film (usually, what they deemed an excessive price) could also have been a possible reason.

Similarly, Gillo Pontecorvo's celebrated *The Battle of Algiers* (1966) was even purchased by SEF and dubbed in Russian in 1968, but never shown on mass Soviet screens. While a French diplomatic démarche to block it might have proved successful, an equally plausible explanation for its non-distribution would be the representations of revolutionary movements uncontrollable by the USSR, or even more likely, statements Pontecorvo might have made about the 1968 Soviet-bloc invasion of Czechoslovakia.[84] Another battle, *The Battle of Chile* (Patricio Guzmán 1975–79), occasionally ranked as the greatest documentary film in the history of the genre, never entered Soviet distribution.[85] Indeed, the absence of the major Latin American Third Cinema practitioners from both Soviet commercial distribution and the lists of Tashkent invitees suggests that this continent was the greatest casualty of Soviet political censorship.[86] Chapter 5 will explore at greater length the ideological obstacles standing in the way between Latin American filmmakers and Soviet screens. For now, it suffices to say that Soviet cultural bureaucracies such as SEF, multiple film selection committees, and the Central Committee of the Party, ultimately overseeing the process of foreign film purchases, simultaneously sought to facilitate the journey of certain Third Cinema films and directors to Soviet screens while erecting barriers to others. The main limiting factor for that journey was the late-Soviet mass audience, which, as Fr. Eichenberger pointed out, differed little from its Western counterpart, being averse to aesthetic experimentalism and political engagement. The small viewership such films attracted not only negatively reflects on the Soviet audience's international solidarity vis-á-vis anti- or postcolonial struggles in Africa and Asia but also became a limiting factor of the Soviet state's cinematic support for the political cinemas of those continents. As the immense popularity of Indian, Egyptian, Mexican, and Argentinian exotic melodramas showed, it is not as if Soviet viewers stayed clear of African and Asian films. Rather, their strong preference was for a "global popular" aesthetic that was embodied by those melodramas rather than the aesthetics of solidarity Third Cinema called for.

The End of the Affair

After the First Tashkent Festival, its coverage in the Soviet press became increasingly routine. Reports by special correspondents of Soviet newspapers listed the number of attendees and countries represented – with each festival exceeding the previous record – named the distinguished filmmakers in attendance, and interviewed some of them. The same motifs – the interconnections the festival enabled, the hospitality of the Uzbek people, the inspiration and help Soviet cinema provided to its non-Western peers – run through these interviews. The booklets produced after each festival on the basis of its filmmakers' seminar are, too, barely distinguishable from each other. The same problems – of commercial forces blocking the pathway of political film, of Western monopolies, of the need to nationalize production and distribution, and collaborate internationally – absorb the bulk of the discussion in each of them.

On the basis of these materials, it is very difficult to write the twenty-year history of the festival: it would take a very astute observer not to see its editions as interchangeable, except maybe for the increasingly less familiar names at the last festivals. At the same time, despite the foundation of the Havana Latin American Film Festival in 1978, which attracted radical filmmakers from beyond the Americas, and the continued (if declining) work of the Pan-African Federation of Filmmakers (FEPACI), who issued their last major manifesto in Niamey in 1982, the Third-Worldist moment in world cinema and the networks and initiatives that sustained it were coming to an end.

And then came the Tenth, the 1988 Tashkent Festival, which was also the last. Its format was significantly redesigned, more conservative, both formally and ideologically: a competitive program was introduced, and with it, prizes: the Golden Simorgh[87] for the best film, a prize for the preservation of national traditions in cinema, another one for the best debut, and two more for the best male and female roles. Unlike previous festivals, which lasted ten days, this one was kept to a week. Novel forms such as a beauty contest were introduced. The festival took place without its signature motto "For peace, social progress, and freedom of the peoples" and the filmmakers' seminar was renamed "Socialism and Democracy." But more significant than these reforms was the scathing tone with which participants, domestic and foreign, spoke about it. That tone ran through the different Soviet publications that covered the festival, from *Pravda*, where the first three quotations are taken, to *Iskusstvo kino*, where the second three are taken:

Luis Alberto Garcia, Cuban actor:
In Uzbekistan I discovered a continent of which I had previously no experience. But the films that I liked were mainly in the retrospective and informational screenings. As for the main competition, out of the eleven films only a couple could be said to correspond to the requirements of contemporary art. For an international festival of this scale and status, this situation is not normal.

Souheil Ben-Barka, director, general director of the Moroccan Cinematographic Centre:
In Tashkent they spoke a lot about the changes in the status and the format of the festival, but I don't think this should be exaggerated. The festival has yet to acquire its proper image. In the present version, there is too much that is formulaic, borrowed from more prestigious festivals – beginning from the Miss Festival competition and ending with the introduction of competitive prizes. The timing of the festival was also unfortunate: immediately after Cannes and just before Karlovy Vary. It is natural that the best of films will go to these better-known festivals.

Tamara Shakirova, distinguished artist of Uzbek SSR:
The Tashkent festival has been in decline for many years already.
There was hope that this spring will see a turning of the tide. Alas,
we were in for a disappointment. I am sad that no first-rate stars
came here. It's not the same without them. It is not realistic to have
a serious conversation without the participation of major actors and
directors who determine the face of contemporary art. We were all
expecting memorable films – this is what a festival is for – but they
were too few. Even if there were some excellent films among the
stream of average ones, it would have been very hard to find them as
program information was scarce. The poor organization, the frequent
mess-ups, and bureaucratic inflexibility – all these cast a shadow
on the whole festival. It was upsetting to see too many officials'
relatives and friends rather than filmmakers at the closed events of
the festival.[88]

*R. Batyrov, head of the selection committee of the Tenth Tashkent
Festival, film director:*
I myself am unhappy about the competitive program. This is our
tenth festival, an anniversary, so to say. But it's also a moment of
crisis. We have had our triumphs in the past. But now we are getting
extinguished. It was decided to tinker a little bit with the format: they
moved it in time, created a competition. Our work is quite specific:
what is good for Mozambique can be bad for India. Each film was
treated differently. This is how this gigantic unevenness of the
competitive program came about. From my point of view, only five
or six films really deserved to be there. Maybe we should have limited
ourselves to them rather than inflate the competition with a dozen
patently weak films?

Kirill Razlogov, film critic:
No festival is ever perfectly organized. The main shortcoming of
this one is that it is not focused on the films themselves. First and
foremost, the festival should be about films, their screenings, and
their reception by audiences. In Tashkent many interesting events
and entertainment coincided with competitive screenings, which
seems to me thoroughly unacceptable.

Sebastián Alarcón, director (Patriotic Forces of Chile):
I would like to ask the organizers how they imagine the future existence of the Tashkent Film Festival. I have been attending it since 1974 and with every year, its degradation becomes more visible. There is a feeling that no one needs it, or rather that it's only necessary to the Uzbek authorities and numerous organizations – Sovexportfilm, Soyuzinfilm, Sovinterfest. Don't you think the festival has exhausted itself?[89]

The Soviet journalists sent to Tashkent – especially from *Iskusstvo kino*, which devoted over twenty pages to the tenth festival – added their own stories of organizers' incompetence, which had left some participants without hotel rooms or waiting in the scorching heat of the Tashkent airport for three hours and kept pretty much everybody very poorly informed of the program of events and locations. They were not kind to the films themselves either, describing scenes in the Tashkent movie theatres resembling airport arrival halls at the entrance of the Palace of the Arts: every ten to fifteen minutes, groups of passengers would leave the building.[90] While these assessments do reveal the particularly bad organization of the Tenth Tashkent Festival, it is doubtful that it was so much worse than the previous ones. Rather, the festival coverage reflected the period in which it was written: just as Brezhnev-era reports convey the pacifying tenor of that age, so do perestroika-era journalism and public commentary reflect their period's preference for devastatingly critical statements. Perestroika suddenly revealed – sometimes in exaggerated form – the problems that had been accumulating during the Brezhnev era. As Sebastián Alarcón told me in an interview, many Soviet participants were beginning to look upon the last editions of the festival as ten-day getaways, when they could drink for free and without limit, which must have become even more appealing as an opportunity during the anti-alcohol campaign of the 1980s.[91] As for non-Western filmmakers, the dimming appeal of the Soviet Union and the growing number of festival opportunities elsewhere had been taking their toll on the stellar power of the foreign attendees. Exactly what perestroika meant for Third-Worldist intellectuals and cultural producers we will see in the epilogue to this book. For now, suffice it to say that no Tashkent Festival took place in 1990.

"Brothers!": Solidarity Documentary Film

"I didn't see [*Battleship*] *Potemkin* when it first came out. I was too young. I remember the shot of the meat. Definitely. With the maggots. And the little tent where the dead man was laid out and when the first person stops in front of it. And the bit where the other sailors take aim on the bridge of the battleship. And just when the officer gives the order to fire, a huge sailor with a big moustache shouts out a word which spreads itself all over the screen: 'Brothers!'"

Some readers might remember these as the opening words of Chris Marker's magisterial account of the global left's turbulent 1960s and '70s, the four-hour-long essay film *A Grin without a Cat* (1977). Produced as a summation of a whole cycle of leftist struggle, this film, like no other cinematic text, captures the structures of feelings of the New Left in the West and the emancipatory forces of the Third World. Unlike those movements, however, which were animated by generational as well as political struggles, Marker is also preoccupied – as he usually is, in his subtle, non-dogmatic way, often through the vehicle of his highly idiosyncratic memory – with recovering genealogies.[1] Hence Marker's reminiscence of *The Battleship Potemkin* (1927), narrated against the visual background of Eisenstein's film and followed by Luciano Berio's triumphant music. Later in Marker's film, the moustached Potemkin sailor, Vakulenchuk, and the Russian intertitle, *Brat'ia!* (Brothers!) make one more appearance on the screen, montaged into footage of Czechoslovak citizens vehemently gesticulating before an embarrassed Soviet tank-driver on the streets of Prague in August 1968. In that sequence, the state born out of one democratic revolution half a century earlier, the state that twenty-three years earlier had liberated those same streets from the occupying German Army (Marker prefaces the whole episode with newsreel footage from May 1945 of Czechs enthusiastically greeting similar Soviet tanks) is shown crushing another democratic revolution, the Prague Spring. To multiply the contradictions of the historical moment, Marker then cuts to Fidel Castro, a bona fide Third-Worldist revolutionary if ever there was one, and, at the same time head of a state very dependent on Soviet support against an imminent US invasion, giving a speech in defence of the Warsaw Pact invasion of Czechoslovakia.

Following Marker's effort of recovering the history of the left in all its contradictions, this chapter seeks to map the global contours of a contradictory "Soviet trace" in Third Cinema, above all in its Latin American documentary core. While a significant number of African and Asian political filmmakers of the period, from Sembène Ousmane to Mrinal Sen, either extensively acknowledged their engagement with early Soviet cinema or even received their cinematic training in the USSR, Latin American documentarians actively resisted such appropriation into a Soviet lineage. Determined to decolonize themselves from European models (and Soviet culture was, in their eyes, decidedly European, and, in its contemporary version, not all that appealing), these New Leftists and cinematic avant-gardists sought to establish a new and authentic Latin American art.[2] Nevertheless, a "Soviet trace" connecting Soviet avant-garde film of the 1920s to Latin American documentary film of the 1960s and '70s could be found by following the evolution of a genre identified by Thomas Waugh as solidarity film.[3]

While Waugh discusses solidarity film solely in relation to Joris Ivens's work of the late 1930s, this chapter will offer a historically and geographically expanded overview of the genre, first as it emerged in the films of early Soviet documentarians of the late 1920s and early '30s, such as Dziga Vertov, and then in the long, intertwined filmmaking trajectories of Ivens and his Soviet doppelgänger Roman Karmen, which took them to Civil War Spain, Popular-Front China resisting the Japanese invasion, and Vietnam resisting French and American occupiers. By the 1960s, when Ivens and Karmen trained their cameras on Latin America, they were joined by a new cohort of solidarity documentarians led by Chris Marker and the Cuban, Santiago Álvarez. Through the contact zones of Vietnam, Cuba, and Chile, their solidarity films of this period and their engagements with Latin American documentarians became important contributions to

Third Cinema. As film histories already place Vertov among the founding fathers of documentary film, treat Joris Ivens and Chris Marker as established twentieth-century auteurs, and elevate Álvarez, Getino, Solanas, and Guzmán to the status of major representatives of Latin American documentary film, the main beneficiary of this line of inquiry is Roman Karmen, whose globe-roving oeuvre spanning the period from the early 1930s to the mid-1970s – like the whole tradition of post-Vertov Soviet documentary itself – has received relatively little scholarly attention.[4] The other contribution this chapter will make is toward a genealogy of the solidarity documentary itself, a genre – as it will show – rooted in the early Soviet articulation of cinema's potential for internationalist struggles, capable of placing some of the best-known political documentaries and documentarians of the short twentieth century within a very different, longitudinal context. It will do so through tracing the evolution of the three engagements that, according to Waugh, defined the genre: 1) with the Other/cultural difference, even conflict; 2) with a domestic constituency; and 3) with the documentary form, craft, and language.[5]

The Third Cinema Question

What makes Third Cinema a difficult object to study or make claims about is its vagueness as a category. Its lack of membership rolls or authoritative definition (except maybe for an emphasis on anti-colonialism, militancy, and democratic praxis) renders any claims about it questionable.[6] While the term originated in Latin America, where its key manifestoes were written, it has been claimed by or applied to a number of political filmmakers from Africa and Asia, and even, more debatably, from Europe and the United States.[7] In writing their histories of Third Cinema, Paul Willemen ("The Third Cinema Question" [1987]) and Mike Wayne (*Dialectics of Third Cinema* [2001]) have sought to locate its origins in early Soviet cinematic thought and practice of the 1920s and the kindred European avant-garde of the 1930s.[8] In both cases, however, as well as in Joshua Malitsky's later and much more comprehensive account of post-revolutionary nonfiction film in the USSR and Cuba, the line of argument rests on parallels between the pre-Second World War European and Soviet avant-garde and the Latin American cinematic uprisings of the late 1960s and '70s.[9] Indeed, these films' reactivation of the manifesto as a form and aesthetic experimentalism reinforces such parallels. What is missing from these accounts of structural affinities, however, and what this chapter seeks to produce, is a materialist *genealogy* underlying the similarities, that is focused through the transnational history of the solidarity documentary genre. With this more specific goal in mind, this chapter does not aim to produce a full-fledged account of the interaction of Soviet and Latin American cinemas, or the reception of one on the territory of the other but will limit itself to the minimum context necessary for establishing the Soviet trace in Latin American Third Cinema.[10]

The case for such a trace in African and Asian fiction film is much easier to make. First, as Chapter 4 demonstrated, VGIK trained a much larger number of African and Asian filmmakers than it did Latin American ones.[11] Second, a number of prominent leftist filmmakers from these two continents have explicitly and copiously acknowledged the inspiration that early Soviet film and theory had given them. Third, less glamorous but no less important, as part of Soviet developmental aid, cameras and studio equipment were sent to various African and Asian countries.[12] In Latin America, such exchanges were largely confined to post-1959 Cuba, Allende-era Chile (1970–73), and the similarly brief government of the Sandinistas in Nicaragua (1984–90). And even when Latin Americans were officially included in the Tashkent Film Festival (starting from the Fourth Festival in 1976), the weaker links between Soviet and Latin American cinema meant that filmmakers from that continent were usually present in the single digits, thus constituting only a small fraction of the overall number of festival visitors.

Soviet film and theory of the late 1920s and early 1930s influenced politically and aesthetically radical filmmakers worldwide. What distinguishes its reception in Africa, Asia, and Latin America from that in Western Europe and North America is a certain time lag. While the 1960s saw a renewal of European interest in Soviet film theory and practice, as we can see from the names of Jean-Luc Godard's Dziga Vertov group; Chris Marker's *Groupe Medvedkine/Iskra*; or cinéma vérité, the French translation of Dziga Vertov's *kino-pravda*, most of the major Soviet films had made their way to the major Western European and US cities and the theories had already been familiar to Western avant-garde cinematic circles in the 1930s.[13] Because of much weaker cultural links with the USSR, Soviet films and theories did not start reaching filmmakers and theoreticians in Africa and South Asia until after the Second World War. According to the leading Indian political filmmaker Mrinal Sen, who entered cinema via film criticism, the first book about film aesthetics he read in the late 1940s was Vladimir Nilsen's *Cinema as a Graphic Art (On a Theory of Representation in Cinema)*, translated from the Russian in London in 1937 with an introduction by Sergei Eisenstein.[14] Soon afterwards, Sen found and drew from the lecture course on acting delivered by Vsevolod Pudovkin at VGIK and translated into English by Ivor Montagu, along with other Pudovkin essays, as well as Jay Leyda's first translations of Eisenstein's theories.[15] It was only later, at the Calcutta branch of the Indian Film Society, of which Sen was one of the organizers, that he got to see the actual films of Eisenstein and Vsevolod Pudovkin, Dovzhenko, Abram Room, and Mark Donskoy, which he would cite as inspirations.[16] In fact, that branch's opening screening in 1947 was *The Battleship Potemkin*. Thus, when Pudovkin actually visited Calcutta as part of an official Soviet delegation in 1951–52, he was met by a group of Indian cinephiles (among them Sen, Ritwik Ghatak, and Utpal Dutt) who were familiar with his films and theoretical texts, and eager to discuss them.[17]

The Recalcitrant Latin Americans

By contrast, the number of acknowledgements Latin American filmmakers of the 1960s and '70s extended to the early Soviet avant-garde is probably exceeded by their disavowals. The most significant of these occurs in Third Cinema's founding manifesto, Fernando Solanas and Octavio Getino's "Towards a Third Cinema" (1969). Although a few Western filmmakers were embraced as representatives of this category, the only Soviet-bloc film mentioned in the text, Sergei Bondarchuk's epic *War and Peace* (1966–67), is classified as First (that is, Hollywood-like, studio-based commercial) cinema.[18] This mention spurred a whole tradition in Third Cinema scholarship of grouping post-Stalin-era Soviet cinema either with Hollywood or with the auteur (Second) cinema of Western Europe, but almost never aligned with Third Cinema. Elaborating on his original manifesto in a subsequent interview, Solanas polemicized with the Italian critic Guido Aristarco, who situated Third Cinema beside the early Soviet cinema of Eisenstein or Vertov:

> The analysis certainly could be correct on the plane of experiment and form, but is nevertheless wrong in isolating it from its historical context, as the large part of European critics do. Which is to say that we thought that what was really new in the majority of the Latin

American countries – and not only in our film – ... is a cinema on the margins of the system, a cinema radicalized ideologically, a cinema of combat, of essay and of reflection born of some very precise circumstances which were occurring in unliberated countries where the mechanisms of oppression are powerful. Eisenstein and Vertov had the Soviet power behind them; the Latin American filmmaker has the police behind him. That is the difference.[19]

Fervent believers in Peron's *socialismo national* (a concept hardly compatible with the Soviet version of international socialism), Solanas and Getino were also inspired by Mao's radicalism, as testified by his quotations (3 out of 17 citations) in their Third Cinema manifesto. An acknowledgement of any Soviet lineage would have been out of place in this text.

Even earlier, Glauber Rocha, the pioneer of the Brazilian Cinema Novo, one of the rich streams that flowed into Third Cinema, had issued a much more militant call to distance Latin American cinema from Soviet and European avant-gardes: "We do not want Eisenstein, Rossellini, Bergman, Fellini, Ford, or anybody else ... our cinema is new because the Brazilian man is new and Brazilian problems are new, and our light is new, and that is why our films are born different from European film."[20] Needless to say, the key figures in Latin American cinema, Solanas, Getino, or Rocha, never had a film commercially screened in the USSR before perestroika or were extended an invitation to the Tashkent or Moscow festivals.

A slightly more discreet form of disavowal of the connections to Soviet cinema could be found in the leading Cuban documentarian Santiago Álvarez's refusal to acknowledge Dziga Vertov's influence on his films on the basis that he "did not know Vertov's works until the early 1970s." His reply to the obvious similarity between their films referred to "the similarity of the situations" in which they were operating.[21] This refusal of identification was mutual. I had never encountered Soviet scholarship, despite its standard trope of how the flame of October lit up other societies and cultures, claiming Third Cinema as its own progeny, or even using that category.

There are many reasons for this disconnect, some of them already suggested in the Solanas quote. By 1969, when he and Getino published their manifesto, the Soviet state had long ceased to be a revolutionary formation. Cold War Western propaganda, which tended to see "Moscow's hand" behind every anti-colonial movement, as well as official Soviet self-representation, with its emphasis on the Revolution, only obscured the fact that the post-Stalin-era Soviet leadership was for the most part committed to the doctrine of peaceful co-existence and looked dimly upon foreign "adventures." As the member of the International Section of the Central Committee, Karen Brutents, amply demonstrates in his memoir *Thirty Years on the Old Square* (1998), nowhere was this cautiousness more visible than vis-á-vis African, Asian, and Latin American societies, where Moscow instructed the communist parties loyal to it to maintain their legality and stick to electoral struggles in almost all circumstances.[22] With few exceptions and even then reluctantly, only after having its hand forced into supporting revolutions already underway, the Soviet state preferred to maintain relations with other states, no matter how anti-communist, rather than with organized leftist undergrounds. Such conduct stood in stark contrast to pro-Chinese Marxist-Leninist parties, Guevarist, and other anti-colonialist movements, which were all too happy to claim the mantle of revolutionary struggle. Even leaving aside their discomfort with the concept of "guerrilla filmmaking," Soviet film officials could not possibly have celebrated Third Cinema's fiercely independent, grassroots model of production that denounced the very kind of centralized industry that Soviet cinema represented.

While rarely indicting specific films or directors, but, rather, adopting a strategy of omission, official Soviet film criticism, too, had developed formulas for dismissing Third Cinema's radical politics and aesthetics: "This is the position adopted by filmmakers from Latin America under the influence of radical-left [*sic*] theory of deconstruction. They create films far removed from real life, considering that the most important thing in art is the revolution in the realm of form."[23] The spectre of deconstruction occurs elsewhere in Soviet scholarship dealing with Latin American film.

The Early Soviet Solidarity Genre

Solidarity had been a watchword of the Soviet state, and as we saw from Chris Marker's appreciation of the *Potemkin* sequence, early Soviet filmmakers were seen by their leftist foreign colleagues to have found a powerful cinematic language to convey it on screen. Despite Vakulenchuk's Ukrainian surname, his call – "Brothers!" – was issued in Russian. Its diegetic addressees were other Russian-speaking sailors, and beyond them, an implied Russian-speaking audience. And while this powerful word resonated with Marker, and with the millions of Western Europeans, North and South Americans, Caribbeans, Asians, and Africans who saw it, full-fledged cinematic tropes meant to represent solidarity across different languages and cultures took some time to develop.[24] Finding a cinematic language to express specifically *international* solidarity was no trivial matter. Yet the generic elements of the international solidarity film began to appear even before Karmen and Ivens developed it – both in conversation with each other as well as independently – into a distinct genre. Soviet fiction films of the late 1920s and early 1930s, especially those made by the Moscow-based, Comintern-affiliated Mezhrabpomfilm, such as Vsevolod Pudovkin's *Deserter* (1933), attempted to emplot international solidarity. But the increasingly Stalinized version of international solidarity they had to reproduce – namely, loyalty to the USSR, the only proletarian state – rendered these films unwatchable in the post-Stalin era.[25]

Another, also problematic, source for the international solidarity documentaries came from the ethnographic *kulturfilms* about the non-Russian Far North, the Caucasus, and Central Asia, many of which were made at the Vostokkino studio.[26] One of the studio's leading directors – Vladimir Erofeev – made several films that dealt not only with Soviet Central Asia (*The Roof of the World: Pamir* [1928] and *Far in Asia* [1931], on which a young VGIK camerawork major, Roman Karmen, interned) but also with the neighbouring Asian countries (*The Heart of Asia: Afghanistan* [1929] and *The Land of the Lion and the Sun: Iran* [1935]).[27]

These are now only available in the archives; by contrast, the politically engaged ethnographies of Erofeev's main opponent during the charged documentary debates of the 1920s, Dziga Vertov, still offer the iconic vision of an organically interconnected multinational Soviet mosaic. Set in the "inner East," Vertov's *Sixth Part of the World* (1926) and *Three Songs about Lenin* (1934) adapt the socialism-in-construction genre, which by the early 1930s had become one of the staples of Soviet documentary filmmaking, to the social and economic periphery of the Soviet state. Both films make gestures to the "outer" East, either through the use of found footage, as in *Sixth Part of the World*, in which British archival film from the African colonies illustrates the workings of global capitalism, or through intertitles, as in *Three Songs about Lenin*, in which the songs of the peoples of the Soviet East represent the worldwide lament for the leader of the Bolshevik Revolution. So necessary to demonstrating the progress made by the "inner East," the contrast between "past" and "present" in films dedicated to socialist construction on the periphery sometimes led to patronizing images of backwardness and accompanying exoticism. Indeed, exoticizing temptation and the struggle against it would be a constant feature in the history of solidarity film shot by Soviet or Western filmmakers in non-Western locations.

A full-fledged application of the socialism-in-construction genre to solidarity with the "outer East" had to wait until Sergei Yutkevich and Leon Arnshtam's 1934 *Ankara – The Heart of Turkey*, the first Soviet documentary film shot abroad to be dedicated to a foreign society building, if not quite socialism, then at least some form of statism diplomatically congenial to the USSR.[28] Because they lacked the time or the necessary (cultural) access, the Soviet filmmakers visiting Turkey were unable to capture the process of labour, limiting themselves to its product: newly built and statically shot Ankara buildings and neighbouring dams. As it was produced at a time when sound was still being experimented with, it does not incorporate one of the defining features of the Stalinist documentary form: the ubiquitous voiceover narration providing the ideologically correct evaluation. The sound of the film is reserved for the triumphant music of Claude Debussy and Maurice Ravel, meant to highlight the achievements of the Kemalist Republic while the commentary takes the form of rare intertitles. The film, a cinematic celebration of the ten-year-old republic and its new capital lends itself easily to another of the defining features of the Stalinist documentary form – staging, if not outright re-enacting, as in the demonstration scenes in which the film culminates.[29]

The second main subgenre of the international solidarity documentary film – solidarity-in-armed-struggle – was initiated by Yakov Bliokh in *The Shanghai Document* (1928), which begins with a detailed class analysis of Shanghai society and ends with sequences of the massacre of the Chinese Communist Party by the Guomindang in April 1927. But the first Soviet documentary film solely devoted to a foreign conflict, *Abyssinia* (1936), was made when two cameramen, Vladimir Yeshurin and Boris Zeitlin, were commissioned by the Central Committee to film the Italian invasion of Ethiopia.[30] With footage from the Ethiopian point of view, the resulting film documented the destruction caused by Italian bombardments, bacteriological warfare, and civilians' corpses. Conservatively shot – with a largely static camera and in mid-shots – and even more conservatively edited in Moscow by Ilya Kopalin, the footage is accompanied by an uninterrupted voiceover narration meant to guide the Soviet viewer. At the 1937 London Film Society, double screening of this film and an Italian propaganda documentary glorifying the invading Italian troops (Corrado d'Errico's *The Path of the Heroes* [1937]), the juxtaposition of the pomp and spectacle of Mussolini's marching "heroes" or the spectacular bombings shot aboard an Italian plane and the devastation they produced among Ethiopian civilians, which the Soviet film recorded, produced a powerful effect on the audience.[31] Such a contrast between the two perspectives, the two sides of the war, would become a central trope of the solidarity-at-war documentary.

Spain

These diverse elements, constituting the two main subgenres of solidarity documentary, came together during the Spanish Civil War to produce two foundational films: *Spain* (1939), which is sometimes attributed to Roman Karmen, who shot the footage in Spain, with Boris Makaseev's help, and sometimes to Esfir Shub, who edited it in Moscow, following Vsevolod Vyshnevsky's narration; and Joris Ivens's *Spanish Earth* (1937), which likewise brought together a dream team of Popular-Front figures: Ernest Hemingway, who wrote the narration; Orson Welles, who read the text; Marc Blitzstein and Virgil Thomas, who compiled Spanish music for the score; and Ivens's partner, Helen von Dongen, one of the great female editors of her time, whose career, like Esfir Shub's, and Vertov's wife, Elizaveta Svilova's, remained in the shadow of men.

Karmen and Ivens, whose intertwining trajectories we will follow closely in the rest of the chapter, relate to the early Soviet cinematic avant-garde in different ways. In film histories, Karmen is often seen as a Stalinist responsible for introducing socialist realism to the mid-twentieth-century Soviet documentary.[32] Indeed, from the mid-1930s onward, Karmen did enjoy a vertiginous career, receiving the most prestigious shooting assignments and, especially after the Second World War, holding numerous key positions in the world of Soviet documentary (secretary of the Governing Body of the Union of Cinematographers, professor at VGIK, and so on). Although in his own cinematic practice he abandoned many of the earlier stylistic experiments of the 1920s in favour of a highly structured, realistic narrative, voiceover narration, and staging, he remained heir to the avant-gardist tradition of sharp montage, extending it, importantly, to the sonic realm. And it is through many of his iconic shots that we remember the wars of the mid-twentieth century: in Spain, China, the Second World War–era USSR, and Vietnam.

Figure 5.1   Awarding the Lenin Prize "For Strengthening the Friendship of the Peoples" to the Dutch filmmaker Joris Ivens (1898–1989), one of the greatest documentarians of all time. From left to right: Roman Karmen, Joris Ivens, and the Soviet filmmaker Sergei Gerasimov, 12 November 1968.

Joris Ivens's membership in an interwar leftist European avant-garde needs fewer qualifications than Karmen's. A founding father of documentary film, and an authority and inspiration to many over the course of his long career, he developed his practice both in parallel and in conversation with the Soviet giants of the 1920s. The record of his engagement with them is extensive: as the *spiritus movens* of the Dutch Film League in the late 1920s, Ivens was among the foreign filmmakers most knowledgeable about early Soviet film theory and practice. Upon receiving an invitation from Pudovkin to visit the USSR, he spent three months in 1930 touring the country, delivering lectures, screening his own films, and meeting Soviet directors and seeing theirs.[33] His next trip to the USSR would be longer: he would direct *Komsomol* (1931), a Mezhrabpomfilm production about the construction of the Magnitogorsk complex, with an illustrious avant-gardist team of collaborators: Sergei Tretiakov wrote the script and Hanns Eisler wrote the music. Following the Second World War, which Ivens spent as an exile in the United States, he worked for nearly a decade for the East German film studio (DEFA) after which he left for France, retaining his communist loyalties but gaining a greater agency over the topics and methods of his work. In the late 1960s, his disappointment with the political caution and pragmatism of the Soviet Union would lead him to side with China during the Sino-Soviet split and thus to exiting the Soviet orbit.[34]

While Ivens's *Spanish Earth* has received abundant critical attention and is today the best-known documentary about the Spanish Civil War, Karmen's Spanish film is now reduced to circulation in Russian and an occasional mention in studies of 1930s Soviet documentary filmmaking.[35] Aside from occasional mention of the two filmmakers' sharing the same hotel in Barcelona, the existing scholarship has not discussed the relationship between the two films, nor Ivens's abundant use of Karmen's footage from the University City battle, the air raid over Madrid, and a number of political speeches. And yet despite Karmen's relative youth and inexperience vis-à-vis Ivens – he had started making his own films only a few years earlier and had been an admirer of the already famous Ivens – his Spanish film turned out to be by far the more significant contribution to solidarity filmmaking.[36] Part of the reason is that Karmen had more time and material at his disposal to develop filmmaking techniques suited to this particular terrain than any other filmmaker on the Republican side. Footage from the twelve newsreels he shot during 1936–37 appears in most Spanish Civil War documentary films, made contemporaneously or later. (Just before embarking on *Spanish Earth*, Ivens and Helen von Dongen, for example, had made a compilation film, *Spain in Flames* [1937], drawing exclusively on Karmen's footage, but dubbing it for American audiences.)

It was in Spain that both filmmakers established the cinematic language of war-filmmaking – and its connection to socialist construction – that they would refine later on in their careers. The basic plot structures of the two films run parallel: after an opening set in a village, where we witness the beneficial effects of and the popular support for the Spanish republic's land reforms, we are gradually introduced to the bigger picture of the civil war, culminating in the battle of Madrid. It is also partly the chronological development of the war itself that accounts for the similarities between the films. But Ivens's film offers a much tighter plot structure than Karmen's. This effect is achieved by intermittently following a Republican volunteer, Private Juan, as he leaves the village as a volunteer for the Republican Army, fights, and eventually returns to the village, which in the meantime has resolved its irrigation problem. By contrast, Karmen's *Spain* keeps introducing us to new characters (International Brigades, Spanish villagers, political leaders, volunteers and supportive civilians) – only to let them go.

Addressed to the Soviet viewer, its sloganistic ending does not offer any sense of closure. It suggests that some temporary setbacks have occurred, but promises that the Spanish people will never fall to their knees. (The ambiguity is quite understandable: the film was completed at a time when Republican Spain was retreating but had not yet fully surrendered.)

Beyond the larger plot, their air raid sequences – something Ivens and Karmen must have filmed for the first time – appear closely matching: air alarm, followed by enemy bombers in the sky, followed by evidence of the destruction (cameras cannot capture the moment of bombardment at close range), followed by families crying over corpses. Possibly because he stayed longer in Madrid, Karmen developed particular vantage points for the air raids. He shot some of the scenes of the bombardment's aftermath from an elevated position, giving a better sense of the magnitude of the event as well as the vulnerability of the civilian population, while for others he positioned himself in the path of the crowd escaping the bombardment to capture the panicked human stream passing by him. And while we do not see those vantage points in Ivens's *Spanish Earth*, they are clearly used in Ivens's next solidarity film, *The 400 Million*, made shortly thereafter in China.

Another commonality between the two films, which became a trope in the solidarity film genre, is the deployment of music to emphasize the presence of different cultures. In addition to the more generic orchestral music (composed by Marc Blitzstein and Gavriil Popov, respectively), both Ivens and Karmen deploy a number of Spanish tunes to highlight the beauty and richness of Spanish culture and nature. Karmen, for example, contrasts a solemn Francoist march, against a funereal musical background, with a sequence of lively, smiling soldiers from the Comintern-organized International Brigades. The latter are themselves introduced with an abundance of revolutionary marches that range from the Russian Civil War-era "The March of the Far-Eastern Partisans" ("Po dolinam i po vzgoram") to Hanns Eisler songs, such as "Rot Front." As a whole, Karmen's *Spain* exhibits a much wider emotional range than Ivens's film, owing in part to its wider musical range and in part to its narration (Vyshnevsky's anger, satire, solemnity, and admiration all contrast with Hemingway's characteristic restraint and succinctness).

As a result of the dual censorship of American film industries, on the one hand, and Popular-Front willingness to downplay the role of the communist party for the sake of the broader anti-fascist alliance, on the other, the

International Brigades are missing from Ivens's film.[37] In the absence of detailed local politics or a closer study of domestic and foreign alliances, the main conflict in *Spanish Earth* becomes a more abstract and eternal struggle between freedom and oppression, self-determination and tyranny meant for as broad an American public as possible. As Waugh points out, however, communist audiences of the film should have been able to recognize in Jose Diaz (introduced as "a former carpenter, now a member of Parliament") and Dolores Ibarruri ("the wife of a poor miner in Asturias") the leaders of Spanish communism.[38]

Karmen's film was subject to a different, Soviet kind of censorship, which vilified Spanish anarchists and Trotskyists, the latter accused by the narrator of surrendering Madrid to the fascists.[39] Karmen's *Spain* is also more explicit about communist and Soviet participation on the Republican side, just as it is about denouncing the shameful role of the British and French in the Committee for Non-Intervention, which "doesn't intervene into the Franco-German aggression." The Soviet state figures only briefly in the film, though significantly: the narrator's emotional plea "Hold on, Spanish brothers, you are not alone!," against the musical background of the Internationale, are followed by the appearance of the first Soviet ship (*Zirianin*) in Barcelona's harbour. The lengthy shot-countershot sequence in which *Zirianin*'s appearance and triumphant progress through the harbour are greeted by jubilant Spanish crowds, aboard smaller boats, waiting on shore, and in the city itself, anticipates the interminably long rally sequences, which became a topos of Karmen's documentaries of the late-Stalin era. At the end of the film, the Soviets are once again shown as a benevolent force from across the sea: other Soviet ships are shown taking Spanish children to safety. In these sequences, the maternal bond and care, shown through tears and last-minute hugs, is transposed to the ships, standing for the Soviet state, which, as the narrator promises, "will accept them and warm them up with its care." Concrete, material objects sent as aid thus come to stand for the solidarity of the state – and hence, the people – who sent them.

China

While these two films established the canon of international solidarity film, it was Roman Karmen's and Joris Ivens's Chinese films that took this genre to non-Western culture. Both filmmakers made it to China driven by the parallel forces of Soviet foreign policy and Popular Front anti-fascism supporting Republican China's resistance against the 1937 Japanese invasion. Once again, Karmen had the advantage of spending a much longer time, producing over the course of a year almost thirty newsreels, which served as the basis of two longer films, edited, respectively, by Vladimir Erofeev (*Heroic China* [1938]) and Karmen himself (*China in Struggle* [1941]). Just as in Spain, Ivens would again borrow footage from Karmen (of the communist-led Eighth Route Army's ambush of a Japanese unit, which Ivens could not have shot because his Guomindang hosts did not allow him to proceed to the communist-controlled Yanyan province) for his own China solidarity film, *The 400 Million* (1939).

The narratives of Ivens's *400 Million* and Karmen's *China in Struggle* again exhibit a very similar structure: both pay homage to the great Chinese civilization and its contribution to world culture. Both tell – briefly – the story of European imperialism and the sorry state to which it has brought this great culture. After offering this historical background, the main focus of both films becomes the Japanese invasion and the Chinese resistance to it. At this point, however, they depart in their evaluation of Chinese society. In part in the name of the Popular-Front alliance with the Guomindang republican government, in part because of the restrictions that very same Guomindang imposed on Ivens during his stay in the areas they controlled, his film is much more hopeful about the Chinese state and society, inserting into the overall narrative sequences illustrating the country's social and economic development as well as its spiritual reawakening from semi-colonial status.[40] By contrast, as he edited his own footage after the dissolution of the Popular Front, Karmen treats the Guomindang-controlled Chinese society to the kind of rigorous class analysis that Bliokh had already applied to it in *The Shanghai Document*, stressing its extreme inequality. At the same time, his access to the communist-controlled Yanyan province allows him to offer viewers a glimpse of the birth of a new, classless China.

While the two films are lacking in any overtly internationalist motifs that the earlier Spanish films, especially Karmen's, engage in they find different ways to demand solidarity from their intended Soviet and American audiences. Aside from Karmen's comparisons between the contemporary China and pre-revolutionary Russia, between the rhetoric, rallies, and resistance of the Chinese Communist Party and that of the Bolsheviks, *China in Struggle* makes two explicit references to the USSR. The first – clearly staged by Karmen – is a shot of Mao reading from a

Chinese book with a portrait of Stalin on the cover, not so subtly suggesting what, or rather, who, is guiding Mao. The second is a sequence of a guerrilla unit fording a river with their mules. The commentary – "Travelling with the guerrillas along the mountainous paths was a Soviet film chronicle expedition" – forces us to look closer at the group and recognize the blond Karmen among them. Largely divorced from the rest of the narrative, this episode leaves us wondering whether to interpret it as a self-indulgent "selfie" that Karmen habitually inserted into his films or as a little Soviet flag planted in a faraway land.

Ivens's address to his American audiences includes three much more concrete calls for solidarity. The first of these sequences begins with a bank cheque that Madame Chiang Kai-shek authorizes. The commentary then proceeds to explain the origins of the cheque: "This bank draft has come six thousand miles." The omniscient camera then takes us to Manhattan, with a shot of its iconic skyscrapers, followed by a sequence of a China solidarity parade: "A foreign flag [a Chinese one, as we see] invades New York. But look! Money is thrown on this flag. Americans still believe in the rights of the people, in New York or in China. The flag comes home again, with money to buy rice for the orphans of this tragic war." To witness the full cycle of this international solidarity, we are transported back to Madame Chiang Kai-shek's desk, where the money is processed, and then to an orphanage, where a long shot establishes identically-clad Chinese children, eating from identical rice bowls the rice thus purchased. The second solidarity sequence suggests to American audiences a target they could conceivably take on, even if removed by thousands of kilometres from the Chinese battlefronts: the commercial shipments of metal from San Francisco to Japan, which end up sowing destruction in China. The third is the final speech of the narrator, which, while praising the commitment of the Chinese people, is in fact addressed to Ivens's American audiences:

Here is a great people – one fifth of the human race – fighting in defence of their freedom, their fine culture, their independence against an undeclared war. Will these people win? They believe they can. They say it may take them ten years or so and they fully realize the suffering they will have to endure. But they have weapons to fight with and they understand why they are fighting. In the end, those are the things that mean victory.

While both filmmakers perfected some of the war-filming techniques they employed in Spain (especially in the filming of aerial bombardment and its consequences), in certain ways their Chinese films represented a step back in comparison with their Spanish ones. Both had a much easier time achieving cultural proximity to their Spanish subjects than to their Chinese ones. The overall impression is that the former seem much more individuated whereas the latter appear as anonymous, undifferentiated crowds, as testified by the above quote where "they" appears twelve times! This lack of individuality comes across the strongest in the nearly identical scenes Karmen and Ivens shot of Chinese children (orphans, in Ivens's case). Examined in both cases predominantly through long shots, pre-teen boys with shaved heads wearing uniforms appear barely distinguishable from each other. In between the long shots, both directors insert a sequence of medium shots of individual kids' faces, but the sequence is so fast and the activity in which they are engaged (eating) so synchronously performed that the individuation effect the filmmakers undoubtedly sought is lost. The montage with which Ivens's scene ends, between the shot of these children streaming out of the gates of their orphanage in a very disciplined manner and the opening shot of the next scene of young men marching on the street, creates the impression that Chinese young people spend their youth moving collectively.

Although the avant-garde leftist cinematic tradition of the 1920s of which Ivens was a trailblazer and within which Karmen embarked on his cinematic career was, precisely, interested in the role of classes rather than individual heroes as agents of history, it always distinguished a few faces from the masses, whether by introducing them as episodic protagonists, like Vakulenchuk, or by following them over time, and lingering on and exploring their faces. While these are all quite common in Karmen's 1939 *Spain*, where we are introduced to a whole cast of characters (Dolores Ibarruri, General Lister, Andre Marty, Gustav Regler, and others) and the camera lingers on close-ups of the faces of the International Brigade soldiers, following them as they leave Spain, *China in Struggle* offers us an endless succession of people, most of whom are observed in medium or long shots, few of whom are given names. Indeed, the only characters to receive a name and more than two seconds of attention in *China in Struggle* are Chiang Kai-shek, Mao Zedong, and the "legendary" Communist general Zhu De. Except for Mao, shown addressing sympathizers, we do not hear any Chinese person. Strictly speaking, the words we hear are not even Mao's: solidarity documentary film of the late 1930s had yet to master synchronous sound, especially in a foreign language as distant from the Soviet viewer as Chinese, so the narrator ends up speaking for his characters in Russian. Indeed, the voice-of-god narration, which Karmen wrote himself, is the dominant force driving this film.

Somewhat more polyphonous, Ivens's film occasionally gives voice to ordinary Chinese people speaking out against the Japanese invasion (in short, sloganistic statements summarized by Ivens's narrator). Drawing on his experience with "Private Juan" as a framing device in *Spanish Earth*, Ivens deploys a "Sergeant Huang, a brave, courteous man" as the main narrator of the last episode of the film, a victorious military engagement with the Japanese. Another of Ivens's strategies to let the Chinese people speak for themselves is the introduction of Chinese music in interludes within Hanns Eisler's score. But probably the most successful use of sound is the voice recording from Radio Tokyo, over the course of which a Japanese general dwells on how "Chinese women met Japanese officers with flowers." While these words are spoken, we witness the effects of a Japanese air bombardment – eerily resembling flowers – on a Chinese port. This clash between the visual and the sonic (as well as the grotesquely high-pitched voice of the general) serve to discredit Japanese propaganda. For all these efforts to let the Chinese speak, *The 400 Million*, too, is dominated by Ivens's voiceover. Such a limitation was not a product of ill intent or even prejudice on the part of the filmmakers: linguistically and musically, Spain was a much easier terrain to operate on than the culturally unfamiliar China.[41]

Southeast Asia

If we count the vast number of state-commissioned newsreels produced to bolster public morale and support for allies, the Second World War saw the explosion of solidarity documentaries. Our protagonists were deeply involved in that effort. Joris Ivens, for example, made one of the best known such documentaries, *Our Russian Front* (1942), using exclusively Russian footage shot by Karmen and five other Russian cameramen (Arkadi Shaftan, Dmitry Rymarev, Ivan Belyakov, Mark Troyanovsky, and Vladimir Yeshurin). Karmen fought the war with a camera from beginning to end, capturing (or on occasion staging) some of its iconic moments: the surrender of General Paulus in Stalingrad, the planting of a Soviet flag on top of the Reichstag (a scene re-enacted several days after the actual event), and, ultimately, *The Nuremberg Trials* (1948). These were primarily solidarity-at-war films, informational, made quickly as part of the war effort. For this reason, technically or aesthetically, they hardly break new ground. Neither are they concerned with the colonial question as the Second World War had made the major imperial power (Great Britain) a Soviet ally.

After the war, Karmen was commissioned to shoot a series of films about socialist construction on the Soviet periphery: *Soviet Kazakhstan* (1949), *Soviet Turkmenistan* (1950), *Soviet Georgia* (1951), and probably the best-known of this series, which also exploded its underlying aesthetic framework: *The Tale about the Oil Workers of the Caspian Region* (1953). While this film continued the series' practice of turning into clichés what had once been legitimate cinematic tropes of collective labour, celebration, and rest, it has also come to be regarded as the first post-Stalinist documentary and praised for its shift toward "poetic" documentary.[42] In this film, Karmen solves the problem of conflictlessness that characterizes the other films as well as late-Stalinist narrative as a whole by centring the film around a massive fire on an oil platform in the Baku Bay, thus dramatizing nature's (oil's) resistance to being mastered (drilled). But outside of these tense sequences, the unstoppable succession of triumphs characteristic of late-Stalinist documentary can be exhausting.

In the Thaw era, with a new Soviet leadership much more internationally mobile than Stalin had ever been and much more generous in extending invitations to foreign political leaders, Karmen played a key role in the development of a new Soviet solidarity subgenre, the visitor film, which documents either the foreign trips of Soviet leaders (*Austria Greets Peace Visitors* [1960], about Khrushchev's charm offensive in that country) or the trips of foreign heads of state to the USSR (*Jawaharlal Nehru in the USSR* [1955] or *A Visitor from the Island of Freedom* [1963], about Fidel's Soviet tour). *A Visitor from the Island of Freedom* stands out from this otherwise drab genre, largely thanks to Fidel's immense charisma, emotional and improvised speeches, and the Soviet people's genuine curiosity and enthusiasm about him in 1963, which few other foreign leaders could replicate. As a whole, however, the "visitor film" is so instrumental, so leader- and state-centric, and so circumscribed (with a set of conventions consisting of background information on the state of the [newly decolonized] country, the leader's speeches before small and large audiences, visits to factories, farms, or prestige objects, to which the leader reacts appreciatively, and assertions of everlasting friendship between the USSR and the relevant country) that it is hard to think of it as a serious aesthetic contribution to the overall solidarity genre.[43]

From the United States, where he spent the Second World War, to the DEFA studio in East Germany, where he worked during the first postwar decade, Ivens was similarly institutionally constrained. While deeply internationalist, his projects of the DEFA era are inflected by the grammar of the Cold War. Shot with footage from East Germany, Poland, Czechoslovakia, and Bulgaria, *The First Years* (1948) shows the construction of the socialist bloc. The epic *The Song of the Rivers* (1954), compiled with footage by fifty-two cameramen located worldwide (including Karmen, who was filming in Vietnam at the time) is premised on the contrast of labour in capitalism and state socialism.[44]

Another DEFA film made by Ivens, *The Compass Rose* (1958), employs a similar frame to address the position of women.[45] The one Ivens film of that period that escapes both Second World War exigencies and Cold War framing is, predictably, the twenty-two-minute long *Indonesia Calling* (1946), which he filmed after leaving the US and before arriving in East Berlin, as an expression of support for Indonesia's struggle for independence against the Dutch. Overcoming the enormous challenge of being stranded in Sydney and prevented from visiting Indonesia by the Dutch authorities, Ivens structured his solidarity film around the Australian dockworkers' boycott of the Dutch ships loaded with soldiers and munitions needed to crush the Indonesian independence struggle. Like his films of the preceding American period, this one is very strongly addressed to and meant to elicit solidarity from a local (Australian) audience. The voiceover in the opening sequence asks the audience to remember how during the war Indonesian servicemen fought the Japanese alongside "our boys" (Australian soldiers), how Indonesian men labour alongside "our (white, Australian) men," how Indonesian women learned the English names of groceries in Australian markets, and how their children walk "our streets" and are fawned over by nice Australian women. And while, rhetorically, the appeal to the audience is premised on basic human decency, the solidarity we witness on the screen is directed by the dockworkers' union. The boycott itself is a multi-ethnic effort, with white Australian, Chinese, Indian sailors willing to sacrifice their own time, energy, salaries, and jobs to support the dignity of their Indonesian colleagues and the independence of a faraway republic. Combining the genres of an international solidarity documentary with a union documentary (the film was sponsored by Australia's Waterside Workers' Federation), it features interracial pickets, speeches in different languages, and other labour union rituals, over the course of which the racial and national differences become central and unimportant at the same time: central because their presence and multiplicity are highlighted in every way possible; unimportant because they are ultimately subordinated to the common struggle.

Southeast Asia, and particularly Vietnam, would gradually become, together with Cuba and Chile, the central site for anti-colonial solidarity filmmaking, partly because of the sheer length and bloodiness of the three Indochina Wars (1945–89).[46] The history of the multiple solidarity films devoted to it starts with Karmen's *Vietnam* (1954), which inaugurated the post-Stalin-era Soviet cinematic offensive to the decolonizing world. Ironically, however, the documentary would also represent the peak of Karmen's aesthetic Stalinism. It employs a characteristically dominant voiceover narration, which leaves the Vietnamese subjects voiceless, and re-enacts whole historical episodes, the march of hundreds of French POWs, for example, and, most spectacularly, the Battle of Dien Bien Phu, to which Karmen arrived too late to witness.[47] Neither of these strategies is in itself a sufficient condition to call a documentary film Stalinist. Ivens himself practised and theoretically defended staging. And the all-knowing, and at the same time, emotional commentary that ranges from triumph to bitter satire, from warmth to admiration, is hardly unique to Soviet documentary: we hear it also in later Latin American documentaries such as Getino and Solanas's *Hour of the Furnaces* (1968). Rather, more than anything else, what defines the Stalinist documentary is its exultation of the socialist state. While *Spain* and *China in Struggle*, too, were meant to support Republican countries fighting for their very survival, the focus in both is the struggle of ordinary people. In neither of these two films is the state as central a character as it is in *Vietnam*. The very opening of that film, with an interminably long victory parade in Hanoi's centre, constructed out of dialectical shots of the leader(ship) waving from a podium, against a red fortress, and the Vietnamese people, civilians and military, clapping and hooraying, saluting and marching, and sometimes carrying a gigantic poster of Ho Chi Minh, must have been very familiar to Soviet viewers. The triumphalist spectacles, rhetoric, and music constitute the least likeable characteristics of the film. Otherwise, it follows the typical expository narrative arch Karmen developed in his China film, of telling the history of a great culture, European (in this case, French) colonialism, and the contemporary struggle for national liberation. *Vietnam* also offers the Soviet viewer a travelogue of Vietnamese landscapes, jungles, and villages, as well as Hanoi. As for its representation of Vietnamese society, the prevalence of highly synchronized collective labour, and the absence of any individual characters (except for Ho Chi Minh) creates the impression of a human beehive. In its preoccupation with mapping the country, demonstrating the transformation of nature and the achievement of socialist welfare, the documentary also seems heavily stamped with what Raisa Sidenova has called "the topographical aesthetic," the dominant modality of late-Stalin-era Soviet documentary.[48]

Its Stalinism notwithstanding, *Vietnam* is a historically significant film. As most likely the only documentary to tell the events of the First Indochina War from the Vietnamese side, it has served as a source of footage for many subsequent documentaries. The seven months Karmen spent in Vietnam, as well as his easy access to the Vietnamese state (as testified both by his autobiography and the shot of himself interviewing Ho Chi Minh) allowed him to work with a number of Vietnamese, whom the titles prominently acknowledge as co-authors of the film.[49] At the same time, it nearly became a casualty of the new, post-Stalin-era drive toward "a peaceful co-existence." Shortly after its release, it was withdrawn from domestic distribution and in Karmen's absence (he was abroad, shooting *Our Friend India*) was subjected to a peculiar censorship. In his letter to the Cultural Sector of the Central Committee of the Communist Party upon his return, Karmen lists the references to French colonialism and American military support for it that had been excised from the film without his knowledge or permission. Whole sequences such as the march of French POWs had been removed. As a result, he complains, the Vietnamese people appear to be struggling against an anonymous enemy, rendering their anti-colonial struggle nonsensical. Thanks to the investigation conducted by somewhat puzzled Central Committee officials, we discover that this censorship was ordered by a representative of the Soviet Ministry of Foreign Affairs. Testifying to the relation of forces between different Soviet institutions and ideological wings, the outcome was a compromise: while most revisions were reversed, references to American support to the French were kept out of copies meant for screening in cities with foreign consulates.[50]

When he went to Vietnam during the hottest phase of the Second Indochina war, Ivens may have operated under a number of limitations, but "peaceful co-existence" was not one of them. Comparing Ivens's *The 17th Parallel* (1968) with Karmen's film reveals the diverging paths of the solidarity genre. Such a comparison may at first sight appear grossly unfair: not only was a vastly different war and enemy being represented, but new cinematographic possibilities had become available to Ivens that did not yet exist in 1954, most important, portable cameras with synchronized sound. Ivens's film thus features an abundance of Vietnamese voices that earlier technologies could not have captured so comfortably. Largely made possible by Marceline Loridan, a sound specialist and Ivens's partner in his last decades, this partial adoption of the precepts of cinéma vérité made the film much less reliant on the narrator, giving instead voice to Vietnamese people (their synced speech is then dubbed). Nor is the Vietnamese state as present in this film as it is in Karmen's. While *The 17th Parallel* opens with a map of Vietnam and on two brief occasions the camera does enter a Viet Cong military headquarters (where we hear a more strategic, long-term perspective on the war), unlike most of Ivens's earlier solidarity documentaries, this one largely assumes the viewer's familiarity with the Vietnam War and deliberately limits itself to how the inhabitants of one village organize themselves. For this reason, maybe for the first time in his career as a solidarity filmmaker, Ivens organizes the entire film around two female figures – Mien, the leader of the local militia, and Thu, the village president – and follows them as they go about their work: leading other women to work in the fields, chairing committee meetings, attending self-defence classes. Neither they nor the other villagers speak much of the larger Viet Cong structures, ideologies, or even Vietnam itself; rather, they are concerned with everyday matters, the digging of a trench here, supplying provisions there, helping a villager whose house and belongings have been destroyed by a US air raid, and, of course, keeping safe from the constant bombardment to which they are subjected. The camera's following of these characters' performance of routine tasks is occasionally interrupted by scenes of US bombings and the workings of Viet Cong air defence. But even there, Ivens avoids shots of corpses or bleeding children – a staple of the solidarity-at-war subgenre – emphasizing not the victimhood but the resilience and ingenuity of the people, not only in self-defence but also, for example, in taking apart a downed US plane (to the last bolt) to meet their needs. Indeed, ordinary people's capacity to self-organize has been put at the centre of the film, deepening an element that has always been present in Ivens's oeuvre. Such an emphasis, away from the state and toward self-organization, anticipates Patricio Guzmán's *Battle of Chile*, especially Part III (1979), which we will discuss later on in this chapter. As a whole, however, *The 17th Parallel* marks a significant reworking of the solidarity genre from its pre-Second World War foundation. This ultimately allowed contemporary New Left filmmakers in Latin America to recognize Ivens as one of their own.

Indeed, despite the immense evolution in Ivens's aesthetics through the 1960s, his movement from the Old to the New Left style, apparent in *The 17th Parallel*, it was another filmmaker who was leading the solidarity filmmaking genre and mining its possibilities. Chris Marker had cut his teeth in the solidarity genre with two films: *Sunday in Peking* (1956), shot in China, and *Letter from Siberia* (1957), shot in the USSR, developing a new subgenre – the solidarity travelogue. While it bears some similarity to the visitor film practised by Soviet filmmakers, it focuses on ordinary citizens and spaces rather than government leaders and the achievements of the state. While we could trace the travelogue's origins to Ivens's *Song of Rivers* (1954), Marker added to it a playfulness and humour missing in Ivens. But he truly exploded the possibilities of the genre in *Far from Vietnam* (1968), which he edited based on footage shot by himself, Jean-Luc Godard, Agnès Varda, Alain Resnais, Claude Lelouch, William Klein, and Ivens. Watching this omnibus film may not be the most comfortable of activities, but comfort was not the aim of a collective of filmmakers determined to bring the Vietnam War to the Western public. The radical heterogeneity of the filmmakers' styles – from cinéma vérité reportage of street protests to first-person essays – is multiplied by the highly heterogeneous materials that went into it: Tom Paxton's satirical 1960s anti–Vietnam War song "Lyndon Johnson Told the Nation"; Hanns Eisler's repurposed soundtrack from the concentration-camp-themed *Night and Fog* (Resnais 1956); a lengthy interview with Fidel Castro; found footage (including some of Karmen's *Vietnam*); a traditional Vietnamese street performance adapted to the US occupation; news clippings; and visually distorted television broadcasts.

Other than Ivens, who contributed original footage from the Vietnamese side, the filmmakers involved in *Far from Vietnam* had a much more complex task to solve, not unlike the one Ivens faced in Indonesia twenty years earlier: how to shoot a solidarity film without being in the country fighting for independence. A variety of solutions are offered, which result in an unusually self-reflexive documentary more focused on what the Vietnam War has done to France and the United States rather than vice versa. Thus

William Klein's hectic and unsteady exploration of an anti–Vietnam War protest in New York verbally and physically confronted by both police and "patriotic" citizens shows American society split down the middle. Godard and Resnais's contribution revolves around lengthy monologues of anguished Western intellectuals unable to find an adequate response to the war. Varda and Lelouch used footage from the French and the American side to offer a multi-sided history of Vietnam's colonial occupation. Perhaps most striking is Marker's construction of a dialogue between two women, Ann Uyen, a Vietnamese woman living in France, and the widow (also named Anne) of a Baltimore Quaker, Norman Morrison, who had doused his body in kerosene and set fire to himself in front of the Pentagon on 2 November 1965 to protest the US bombing of Indochina. While the two women are separated by an ocean, language, and skin colour, they are brought together by the filmmaker's questions about Morrison's self-immolation. Ann Uyen speaks of the meaning of this sacrifice to the people of Vietnam; Anne Morrison voices approval of her husband's actions. Segments of their interviews are interspersed with each other, creating an imaginary conversation between the two women.[51]

Latin American Solidarity Acts

Vietnam was not the only site to which international solidarity filmmakers flocked in the 1960s. Indeed, the Island of Freedom – Cuba – became to international leftist filmmaking what Civil War Spain had been for the Soviet Republic of Letters. In the early years of that decade, Cuba attracted a whole procession of Western and Soviet filmmakers. Along with the familiar trio of Ivens, Marker, and Karmen, came Albert Maysles, Mikhail Kalatozov, Armand Gatti, Richard Leacock, D.A. Pennebaker, Agnès Varda, Cesare Zavattini, and Theodor Christensen. Of all the films they made about the Revolution and the construction of a new society, Cuban filmmakers have tended to regard Chris Marker's *Cuba Si!* (1961) as the best.[52] This acknowledgement as well as the popularity it enjoyed on Cuban screens suggests that unlike most solidarity documentaries, this one proved successful in addressing not only Western but also local audiences. While offering a highly compressed, five-minute summary of Cuba's colonial and neocolonial history, Marker's film aims not so much to construct a historical narrative about the Cuban Revolution as much as to capture the everyday experience of it. The multiplicity of characters Marker introduces (no longer anonymous masses, but different people all swept up in different ways by the revolution); his refusal to dub them, letting them speak for themselves and subtitling their words; the different documentary modalities between which he switches (from expository voiceover narration to much more whimsical essay mode) all allow us to see the everyday of the revolution from multiple, though always sympathetic, perspectives. Sonically, the film offers a very intense experience, thanks to the *nueva trova* songs by Cuban musicians, popular songs such as "The March of the Revolutionaries" and "Gracias, Fidel," as well as intense drumming and ubiquitous street sounds. But as Nora Alter notes, it is the use of synchronized sound – Chris Marker's and solidarity documentary's first – that not only provides rhythm to the film and a fuller access to its subjects but also allows political messages to come from filmed sequences and not only from the voiceover.[53] Visually, too, the sheer speed with which one shot, one type of material gives way to another – from archival footage to photographs, newspaper clippings, cartoons, political posters, and commercials to a non-diegetic sequence of a racing car crash – cannot but remind us of Dziga Vertov's earlier and Santiago Álvarez's later documentaries. Even the usually staid talking-head mode occasionally employed is animated by the magnetism of Marker's recurrent interviewee – Fidel Castro. One particular sequence of fast-moving iconic images of anti-colonial struggles – from Algeria, Congo, Laos, Africa, and the US South – shows the Cuban Revolution to be a link on a global anti-colonial chain, thus prefiguring Marker's later efforts in *Far from Vietnam* and *A Grin without a Cat*.

The New Left reconfiguration of the solidarity genre affected Karmen, although not as powerfully as it did Ivens. While its strict expository mode renders it dated in comparison with Marker's film, Karmen's Cuban film, *Island in Flames* (1961), appears as a major advance on his *Vietnam*. Sonically, it is much richer, incorporating the songs of Carlos Puebla and other Cuban music that came out of the struggle against the Batista regime and US imperialism. While it abounds in images of collective labour and similarly collective defence preparations against a possible US invasion, the Cuban society that emerges out of this film is much more personalized than the silent human hive we witness in Karmen's China and Vietnam films. This greater personalization is due in part to Karmen's knowledge of the Spanish language and greater comfort with Hispanic culture than he ever enjoyed with his Chinese or Vietnamese films, in part to his evolving out of the aesthetic Stalinism that we witnessed in *Vietnam*, and his growing acceptance of new technological advances and aesthetic sensibilities. At the same time, the framing device of the little boy Buenaventura (good fortune), who is being told at the beginning and the end of the film what the Revolution did for him, seems – in retrospect at least – a little patronizing. The largely chronologically sequenced sections into which the film is divided – the hard, exploitative, and semi-colonial life before the Revolution, the history of that Revolution, the present-day building of socialism (featuring the tired trope of the contrast between before and after), and the defence of Cuba from US invasion – appear rather static when compared with Marker's film. Although occasionally interrupted by speeches and street sounds, the voiceover narration addressed to the Soviet viewer still dominates the interpretative plane of the film.

Ivens, too, shot not one but two shorts on the Cuban Revolution: *Travel Notebook* (1960) and *A People in Arms* (1960).[54] The main effect of his Cuban trip, however, lay elsewhere. If the Cuban film community had distinguished Marker's film as the best foreign solidarity documentary about their revolution, it was ultimately Ivens whose contribution they valued more than any other foreign solidarity filmmaker's. If Karmen (whom Ivens must have met in Havana, judging by his brief appearance in *Island in Flames*), Marker, and other Western solidarity filmmakers had come to Cuba to shoot their own films, Ivens seemed more interested in training the eight Cuban cameramen who accompanied him and otherwise imparting his experience to the emerging Cuban film community.[55] José Massip – one of those eight cameramen and subsequently one of Cuba's leading documentarians – recollected some of those lessons in a special Ivens issue of *Cine Cubano*.[56] In 1962, Ivens returned for a visit, during which he would not only lecture at the newly founded Cuban Institute of Cinematographic Art and Industry (ICAIC) but would also lead a two-month crash-course in camerawork for forty to sixty soldiers, a number of whom would subsequently populate the film unit of the Cuban Revolutionary Armed Forces and send reportages from Angola to Ethiopia. For now, however, his film "school" had one 16 mm Polaroid camera and a number of wooden imitation cameras.[57]

Ivens's interests and ambitions in Latin America extended beyond the Island of Freedom, as testified by another teaching stint in Santiago, Chile, where he flew upon the completion of his second Cuban visit.[58] His course at the Centre for Experimental Cinema of the University of Chile would culminate in the shooting of three travelogue documentaries meant in large part as training opportunities for the Chilean students: *In*

Valparaiso (1963), and the shorts *Little Circus* (1963) and *The Victory Train* (1964). These travels through Latin America (as well as his visits in the early 1960s to East Berlin and Moscow) were part of a larger project, an account of which is absent in Waugh's authoritative biography and garners a mere mention in Hans Schoots's, which is much more interested in "the Moscow gold." The project, which we can now reconstruct on the basis of a number of letters Ivens sent that year to officials in the Soviet Union of Filmmakers, was to establish a pan-Latin American organization aimed at making films devoted to the life and struggles of peasants and workers, the social contrasts in urban life, and the semi-colonial work conditions, as well as mass movements, protests, and strikes. Ivens's proposal also insisted that these films should represent national cultures, but cautioned against indulging in exoticism (*ekzoticheskogo naleta* – all such correspondences were translated into Russian).[59] In effect, his plan was to create indigenous, pan–Latin American cinematic production based on the solidarity film genre that Western leftist/Soviet documentarians like him had produced:

> For the realization of this project, we need to create a centre in Havana with the help of the USSR, GDR, and Cuba and communist party organizations from Latin America. We have already begun planning production, distribution, and financing. The first films are already in the making. If a few years ago, such a project would have been impossible, in the new political situation that came after the Cuban Revolution, the realization of such a plan is a necessity. The screening of these films in Latin American countries will stimulate anti-imperialist struggle ... We've seen the enthusiasm with which the workers of Venezuela watched [probably Ivens's own] Cuban films showing Cuba's peasant militia, new houses for workers. Such films will be widely screened in socialist countries, and whenever possible, in a few capitalist countries and on television, and will tell the truth about Latin America ... Young cameramen, who have dedicated themselves to the service of liberating their countries, will take in their hands the film industries, when the countries become independent. (Today's Latin American cinema is thoroughly subservient to US film companies.)[60]

It is with the training of these "young cameramen" that the rest of the proposal is mostly concerned:

From the above-mentioned, it follows that we have to train for a short period of time a new type of film-makers: militant cameramen. We need young filmmakers, dedicated to the revolutionary and emancipatory movement of their country, filmmakers, who relate to cinema not as a lucrative career, but as a means of fulfilling their duty to their party and their commitments; people who are ready to operate in difficult economic and technical conditions. In the studios of the USSR and other socialist countries, as well as in Rome and Paris, there is a number of Latin American students, but usually their degree takes four to five years and upon their return home, they can start making socially-conscious films only after many years (if that's at all possible). Under the aegis of the DEFA, six stipends have been established to prepare such filmmakers, emphasizing the difficult conditions they will encounter at home. The cadres must be selected among politically conscious people with a prior general and cinematic background.[61]

As part of this initiative, Ivens lists his pedagogical work with Cuban cameramen during the shooting of his Cuban films as well as the three-month-long teaching stint he had accepted at the Centre for Experimental Cinema at the University of Chile in Santiago. Ivens ends the proposal with an urgent, short-term request from the Soviet authorities for a substantial amount of film stock, cameras, and internships at Soviet studios for the students and a long-term budget for establishing such a centre.

As costly as it was, Ivens's proposal was not unreasonable. As a renowned documentary filmmaker, a recipient of the 1954 Stalin Peace Prize, and somebody who had proven his loyalties to the USSR for over three decades, he was perfectly positioned to make such a request. In fact, other requests he made to Soviet Minister of Culture Ekaterina Furtseva as part of the same correspondence (such as the establishment of a Sergei Eisenstein museum) were granted.[62] In the resolution that ends the folder, Sergei Drobashenko was commissioned to write a biography of Ivens, the first of many to come.[63] However, the main request that Ivens kept repeating in new letters with increasing urgency (as the DEFA-trained students from Argentina, Brazil, and Peru were waiting in vain for their Soviet visas, internships, cameras, and film stock) was not granted. Judging from the multiple inquiries with which he bombarded his Soviet acquaintances, he never received a proper response. According to Hans Schoots, the whole project eventually folded when the Soviet Union pressured Havana to end it.[64] Unlike Peking, with which Ivens would openly side, starting from the late 1960s, Moscow would not support guerrillas, even cinematic ones.

Still, his pedagogical initiatives were not without fruit. In addition to the first and only class of DEFA-trained militant camera operators, there were the Cuban and Chilean filmmakers he helped train. The most famous of these in the realm of documentary cinema is Patricio Guzmán, the cameraman of Ivens's last two Latin American films, the Little Circus (1963) and Victory Train (1964). Another one, Miguel Littin, who after the Pinochet coup went on to a successful cinematic career elsewhere in Latin America (his Mexican film Letters from Marusia [1976] and his Nicaraguan Alsino and the Condor [1982] were both nominated for Best Foreign Film Academy Awards), put Ivens's contribution to Chilean cinema in the following terms: "[T]he presence of Joris Ivens in Chile, when he came to make his film Valparaiso, was fundamental for the whole young Chilean cinema. Our whole experience is marked by Ivens' trip in 1962."[65]

Ivens's contribution to Latin American filmmaking did not limit itself to pedagogical work but included active promotion and advocacy while in Europe. It went far beyond Cuba and Chile. The Argentinian filmmakers Octavio Getino and Fernando Solanas, for example, not only borrowed a number of sequences from Ivens's La Ciel y la Tierra (1965, about Vietnamese struggle against US occupation) in their epic Hour of the Furnaces (1968) but also place his work at the origins of Third Cinema in their "Towards a Third Cinema" manifesto.[66]

Chris Marker's solidarity work in Latin America followed a similar pattern. After his Cuba Si! (1961) and The Battle of the Ten Million (1970), a film he made about the Cuban sugar harvest, he turned his gaze to Allende-era Chile with the intention of making his own film on the social transformations there. Discovering a number of Chilean filmmakers already working on the topic, he, like Ivens, decided that a more useful form of solidarity would be helping them make their own films. In this spirit, having watched Patricio Guzmán's First Year (1971), which documented the achievements of the Popular Front in its first year in power, Marker showed up at Guzmán's doorstep, and offered to purchase it for distribution in France. With Guzmán's permission, Marker re-edited it, furnished it with his own eight-minute introduction to familiarize the French viewer with Chilean politics, and organized his friends to do the dubbing, resulting, according to Guzmán, in a much superior version, which went on to win prizes at the Nantes and Mannheim festivals.[67] Beyond the festival circuit, Marker set about organizing its publicity and distribution in France and elsewhere in Europe.

A year later, in 1972, Guzmán and his Chilean crew were working on another film, which over the next few years would take shape as *The Battle of Chile*. Desperate about the absence of film stock (a casualty of the US economic embargo against Chile), Guzmán once again turned to Marker. The following week he received a telegram: "I'll do what I can. Best wishes, Chris Marker." A month later, at the Santiago airport, Guzmán and his team were unloading some 43,000 meters of 16-mm Kodak film stock and over a hundred Nagra sound tapes. That shipment did not exhaust Marker's role in the making of this film. After being briefly detained in the first days of the Pinochet coup, Guzmán was able to escape to France, where he was met by Marker, who put him up with a friend of his in Paris for several months while furiously fundraising for Guzmán's film.[68] Eventually, cashing in on the good will he had earned among the Cuban film community, Marker was able to send Guzmán to Havana for six months, which would turn into six years, to finish his film. Today *The Battle of Chile* is not only considered among the pinnacles of Third Cinema but also tops various lists for the best documentary film of all time.

As all these examples illustrate, in encountering Latin America, some leading Western solidarity filmmakers began to turn away from making their own documentaries and toward helping the explosively growing radical Latin American film community make its own films. Cuba in particular no longer needed to be represented cinematically: it could represent itself. Within three months of the overthrow of the Batista regime, the Cuban Institute of Cinematographic Art and Industry (ICAIC) was established with a mandate to produce, distribute, and screen films as well as train filmmakers. It is telling that its foundations represented the first cultural initiative of the Revolutionary government. If the Bolsheviks had prioritized literature above all other arts, the Cuban Revolution made film its signature and arguably most successful art form. And even though Cuba was under a US embargo, its films began reaching interested Western and Soviet audiences.

Cuban filmmakers did not limit themselves to commemorating their own revolution or documenting the social transformation of their country. Thanks to Cuba's internationalism, institutionalized around the Organization for Solidarity with the People of Africa, Asia, and Latin

America (OSPAAAL), and the talents of the country's leading documentarian, Santiago Álvarez, ICAIC itself became a major producer of solidarity
films devoted to foreign societies: *Now!* (1965, about racial struggles in the
US), *79 Springs* (1969, about Vietnam), *The Tiger Jumped and Killed, but It
Will Die, It Will Die* (1973, about Chile), *Maputo: the Ninth Meridian* (1976,
about Mozambique), *And the Night Became a Desert* (1979, about Ethiopia),
and *The Forgotten War* (1967, about Laos).[69] All of these films build upon
and radicalize the hitherto existing solidarity documentary conventions,
giving them a distinct Third-Worldist tinge. Dedicated to the American
bombardment and military operations in Laos, for example, *The Forgotten
War* not only borrows iconic footage from Roman Karmen's *Vietnam* but
also contains all of that film's generic components: a history of Laos's great
culture, an account of European imperialism, a travelogue of Laotian landscapes, as well as stories of American bombardment and Laosian resistance.
The abundant use of animation and maps in Álvarez's documentary may
be largely missing in Karmen's Vietnam film, but not in Marker's. But
judging by the brevity of the shots, the sharpness of the montage, and
the heterogeneous nature of the material, the main influence on Álvarez's
best known, avant-gardist films such as *Now!* is the late-1920s montage of
Dziga Vertov.

Memorializing the Revolution

While Roman Karmen's role in developing the solidarity documentary
as a genre is unquestionable, his engagement with Latin American documentary filmmakers in particular seems less visible than Joris Ivens's and
Chris Marker's. Following the three months he spent in Cuba, his trips
to Latin America and the length of his cinematic expeditions seemed to
have been severely constrained by his deteriorating health. Nor did Latin
American filmmakers acknowledge his contribution as profusely as they
did Marker's and Ivens's. Such coolness was probably the combined result
of his direct association with Stalinism and socialist realism, both of which
were explicitly rejected by Latin American directors, and by the short
length of his trips (unlike his extended stays in Spain, China, and especially Vietnam, where he trained local cameramen, his three trips to Latin
America were short and featured more meetings with politicians than with
fellow filmmakers). In fact, he seems to have been more inspired by Latin
America, than Latin Americans were by him. Cuba and the continent as a

whole became the main objects of Karmen's revolutionary romanticism, a sentiment he shared with many Soviet citizens.[70] In addition to his Cuban films, this engagement resulted in the panoramic *Continent in Flames* (1972) and three compilation films about the coup in Chile and its consequences: *Chile: Time of Struggle, Time of Discontent* (1973), *Camarados-Comrades* (1974, dedicated to Salvador Allende, Pablo Neruda, and Victor Jara), and *Corvalan's Heart* (1975). Using the first of these, the magisterial but forgotten *Continent in Flames*, I will argue for a different relationship Roman Karmen had with Latin American documentary film: he anticipated its memory turn, which took the place of the more militant Third Cinema.

Such a claim may seem farfetched at first glance. Even if we acknowledge – as we have to – that Karmen's films of the 1960s and '70s look back nostalgically onto the history of recent heroic struggles, whether in Spain, the Second World War, or Cuba, and attempt to relate the present moment to them through the filmmaker's memories, the cinematic contexts between the USSR of the 1970s and Latin America and its diasporas are so radically different that any comparison between the two would seem historically ungrounded. And not all films shot in the continent before the 1980s that deal with memory could be said to anticipate the Latin American cinematic turn toward memory.

There is, however, an underlying subject that unites Soviet and later Latin American filmmakers: the fate of the revolution. In both cases, the memory turn is a response to the end of a revolutionary cycle. In Karmen's case, that cycle was the Russian Revolution. The last decade of his life (he died in 1978) would see the proliferation of anniversaries, monuments, commemorative medals, and stamps devoted to the Revolution, its heroes, and its culture. In different ways, but mostly through their backward gaze on past glories, these forms of memorialization would all confirm what was not allowed to be spoken: that the Revolution that once gave birth to the Soviet state had lost its momentum. While looking back, however, Karmen also looked sideways, to other revolutions occurring contemporaneously. Such a compensatory strategy – most memorably performed by Karmen but also practised by other Stagnation-era Soviet filmmakers who filmed national liberation struggles raging in Africa, Asia, and Latin America during the Cold War – creates in their work a continuous lineage between the Bolshevik Revolution and the emancipatory uprisings of the Third World.[71] Our revolution is very much alive, these films seem to argue, if not quite at home.

Now largely forgotten, Karmen's panoramic *Continent in Flames* weaves a single narrative of the red wave that seemed to sweep over the whole continent. The scope of the film – Karmen had focused his previous documentaries on emancipatory struggles in a single country – necessitated not only the unusual running time of over two hours but also establishing relationships as well as differences between the societies making up the continent. As with previous films, much of this demarcation of territories and periods is accomplished through music. While it is all in Spanish (except for Hanns Eisler's Spanish Civil War march that accompanies footage of the US Abraham Lincoln Brigade), the upbeat and forward "Himno del 26 de Julio" ("Anthem of the 26 of July"), the March of the Cuban Revolutionaries, for example, contrasts with the slower, haunting, and funereal "Viva la Revolucion!" by the Chilean band Tiempo Nuovo. And while the expository mode, characterized by an authoritative voiceover narration, articulates official Soviet positions ("Left extremists are muddying the water, helping the enemy"), it quickly gives way to a more poetic and essayistic style. The narrator's opening is a case in point:

> We crossed the Atlantic Ocean at night and when the sun came
> up, we saw the Cordeliers. Flying over the land of South America,
> I couldn't cease to think of our future film. It will be clearly a
> continuation of the one we shot twelve years ago in revolutionary
> Cuba. But even more likely, the Latin American film will continue
> what we shot on the barricades of Madrid, in the fight for Moscow,
> Stalingrad, Berlin, and then in Vietnam. People of our generations
> know what dear price, the price of millions of lives, had to be paid
> for the struggle for a just world, for dignity. The struggle continues
> in our day, in the jungles of Indochina, on the land of Ireland, on the
> hills of Africa. It continues here in Latin America, the place they call
> "the continent in flames."

Throughout the film, Karmen's memory serves as a time-travel vehicle between the images of the present and the heroic struggles of the past. Thus, one of the characters Karmen is filming in a factory, the president of the state company for the copper industry, Julio Sombrano, turns to him: "Do you recognize me?" Karmen does not. "You filmed me ten years ago with Comrade Che Guevara in the copper mines of Pinar de la Rio." Upon finishing the sentence, Sombrano looks away from the camera, wistfully.

Karmen finds – and shows – the ten-year-old, black-and-white footage with Sombrano and the by-now-dead Che, whose aura dominates the sequence. Karmen's personal experience of loss comes across in another memory spurred by the sight of a bullfight in Venezuela, which transports us to another, unforgettable bullring in August 1936 in Spain, where instead of bulls, Spanish volunteers with raised fists would circle around the arena before their dispatch to the Saragossa front.

Later on, images of far-right symbols and thugs in Chile are followed by black-and-white footage – German as well as Karmen's own – of Nazi crimes. In the same spirit, several shots of American soldiers from the Abraham Lincoln Brigade from Karmen's own cinematic archive take him to footage of other, perhaps less heroic, but still brave American veterans of the Vietnam War, who are demonstratively throwing away the medals they won in that criminal affair. Grainy historical footage from the Mexican Revolution and of Emiliano Zapata in particular, is followed by Karmen's essayistic reflection on Zapata's American friend Johnny, who lies buried near the Kremlin, the same John Reed who authored *Ten Days that Shook the World*. In each of these cases, Karmen's voiceover elucidates the temporal montage. Latin America in 1972 is full of psychological triggers that send Karmen's memory racing to the past and reconstructing revolutionary continuities over the course of the century. Indeed, in no other earlier film (except for *Grenada, My Grenada* [1966], which is specifically structured as an exploration of Karmen's memory of the Spanish Civil War) is he so heavily present. We can even see him conversing with the writer Francisco Coloane or asking President Allende for a few words that he would like to say to the Soviet audience.[72]

The experience of watching Karmen's *Continent in Flames* alongside Guzmán's later and better-known *The Battle of Chile* is an uncanny one. While they are addressed to two very different kinds of viewers (as Allende's message to the Soviet people and Karmen's abundant usage of "our," denoting Soviet, suggest), they are not only focused on the same process (the radical politics of Allende-era Chile) but also employ a similar repertoire of solidarity tropes (primarily drawn from the socialist construction subgenre) and documentary modes (expository, essayistic, poetic) developed over the long history of solidarity film. Like Karmen's film, Guzmán's *The Battle of Chile*, which viewers saw only after the Pinochet coup, is also a film about memory and the end of a revolution, this one brutally suppressed by outside forces rather than internally degenerating. These films are precursors to a whole memory turn, which crescendos in the following decades, when whole Latin American societies were re-examining their recent past, exhuming the literal and metaphoric corpses that years of military coups had buried on their soil. Guzmán's *Chile, Obstinate Memory* (1997), for example, follows the filmmaker's return to his country after more than two decades of exile. A highly personal essay film, it is as much about Chile around 1973 and 1997 as it is about the director's own experience of these historical moments. The exhumation takes a literal turn in Guzmán's more recent *Nostalgia for the Light* (2010), in which Chilean women have been digging the desert of Atacama for nearly three decades in vain hope of finding the remains of their loved ones, disappeared during the Pinochet dictatorship. Memory is also the main concern of Fernando Solanas's post-Third Cinema, *auteurist* fiction films *Tangos, Exile of Gardel* (1986), *Sur* (1988), *The Journey* (1992). Gone from these films are the radical hopes that once animated these filmmakers in the years of Third Cinema, when the cycle of uprisings was still at its peak. A product of a historical defeat, the memory turn took a much more sombre tone and more of an interest in human rights than in socialist transformation. Seen in light of these films, the hidden referent of Karmen's *Continent in Flames* is also a defeat: that of the Bolshevik Revolution, whose absence from the conservative Soviet society of the 1970s is compensated for not only by lavish anniversaries and commemorations at home but also by documentaries about contemporary revolutions elsewhere.

Born in the late 1920s, primarily to represent the Soviet periphery in Asia, the solidarity documentary developed its multiple subgenres – solidarity-at-war, solidarity-in-socialist-construction, solidarity-travelogue, solidarity-visits – through the interlocking careers of Joris Ivens, Roman Karmen, and Chris Marker, and the battlegrounds, hopes, and new societies of Civil War–era Spain, China, Indonesia, Vietnam, and post-Revolutionary Cuba. First the Cuban Revolution and then the electoral road to socialism embarked upon by President Salvador Allende (1970–73) brought these and other Western solidarity filmmakers to Latin America, thus connecting the Soviet cinema of the 1920s with the Latin America of the 1960s and '70s. The sheer vibrancy of the Cuban, and in a different way, Chilean filmmaker communities, meant that many of the Western or Soviet solidarity documentarians ended up not only shooting their films but also engaging in dialogue with their Latin American colleagues, who were in the process of articulating their own Third Cinema practice. This engagement allowed these two traditions to connect and accounts for much of their formal similarity. Indeed, it is worth emphasizing the dialogical nature of this engagement as far as Marker and Ivens were concerned. Between 1967 and 1974, Marker had entered his SLON/ISKRA/*Groupe Medvedkine* phase of intensely collaborative work, thus renouncing the auteurist model for which Getino and Solanas had criticized European cinema.[73] Himself a member of the Besançon branch of the *Groupe Medvedkine*, Ivens had been greatly concerned with pedagogical work ever since his first visit to the USSR in 1930, when he delivered over a hundred lectures to professional or general audiences. He continued to share his knowledge and engage in collaborative work with filmmakers from China, Vietnam, and other places his solidarity filmmaking took him to. But it was Latin America during the early 1960s that saw the culmination of his pedagogical efforts. In light of this engagement, it is easy to understand why out of all Western filmmakers, "Towards a Third Cinema" extends an acknowledgement to Ivens and Marker. By comparison, Roman Karmen's engagement seems relatively absent from Latin American film histories or the memoirs of filmmakers from that continent. Such an absence might have reflected the suspicion New Left filmmakers felt toward all things Soviet. But it could have also been a question of the different audiences Karmen's films were addressing: the Soviet state and Soviet viewers, Latin American political leaders, History.

And while Karmen (and Soviet film more generally) stood at the origins of the solidarity genre before it entered into a dialogue with Third Cinema documentary, the reflexive turn of his last films strangely prefigures the memory turn of Latin American film of the late 1970s and 1980s. Both deal with revolutions that had, for different reasons, come to a halt.

Epilogue

In October 1998, Olga made it to the United States for the first time in her life. The occasion was the annual conference of the African Literature Association, which took place in Austin, Texas. For Olga, that was a precious moment. Trained at Moscow State University's Institute of African and Asian Countries as a specialist in one of the autochthonous African languages, she had had an uneasy career, in no small part due to her Jewish ancestry, the status of her father – a major but dissident historian – and her own reputation as someone not on board with Soviet ideology (*inakomysliashchii*). It did not help that, like a number of her colleagues who did not want their knowledge to be instrumentalized by the Soviet state, she had deliberately chosen a philological track and an obscure language. But perestroika lifted some of the professional barriers that she had previously faced. Not only was she offered two proper academic positions after years of working as an assistant in her own department and then editor at the Vostochnaia Literatura Publishing House, but she could also go abroad: first, to London's School of African and Oriental Languages, and later, to the United States.

In Austin, however, she was in for a surprise. While she was excited to meet her African colleagues, she got into a number of heated political arguments with them. Much to her chagrin, they seemed unanimously opposed to perestroika and the subsequent transition, which they saw both as a victory of the right and a Soviet betrayal of the Third World. No matter how hard she tried to argue with them about the lack of democracy in the USSR, about the corrupt nature of Communist Party rule, she could not get through.

Though Olga and her interlocutors came to no agreement, with hindsight both parties were right. As the conduct of the late-Soviet Communist Party leadership in the 1980s and its successors in the 1990s, by this point the Soviet political elite had become so ideologically corrupt that not many of them believed in any meaningful version of communism. In the eyes of most ordinary Soviet citizens, the system over which they presided was restrictive and hypocritical. The African scholars were also right: perestroika and the subsequent dissolution of the USSR meant Soviet reneging on its political, military, economic, and cultural commitments to the Third World. They also turned out to be prescient in their suspicion that the democracy for which Olga and millions of Soviet people had been genuinely yearning turned out to be a pretext for incorporating the Soviet bloc into the capitalist world-system, a process resulting in the impoverishment and loss of socio-economic rights of hundreds of millions of people, and societies that are far from anybody's idea of democracy.

Collapse

These processes, however, did not become obvious until after the disappearance of the USSR. Since then, most of the area studies institutions around which Olga's academic life revolved – the Institute of African and Asian Countries, the Institute of Oriental Studies, the Institute of Africa, the Vostochnaia literatura publishing house – have experienced a decline even greater than what post-Soviet humanities and social sciences went through generally. The physical deterioration of their buildings testifies to the budgetary priorities of the contemporary Russian state. While political science expertise on regions neighbouring Russia – the Middle East or East Asia, for example – continues to be relatively strong, the same cannot be said of area studies humanities or scholarship on regions such as sub-Saharan Africa, Central and Latin America, and those parts of Asia that are less economically or politically entangled with contemporary Russia. The Soviet ambition to map the whole world and its belief in the power of culture, and especially literature, to reach out to other societies, has given way to contemporary Russia's shrunken geopolitical priorities. As a result, the once formidable area studies apparatus, which fully competed with and, in certain areas, bested that of the United States, is no more. Thus, when the author of these lines was invited to give a talk at the Institute of Oriental Studies – an institution with a glorious 150-year-old history, his hosts from the Department of the Literatures of the East found it necessary to apologize for the low attendance. If in 1990, they explained, the department had employed over forty researchers, that number was now fewer than ten, with the majority of them well into retirement age. Indeed, if this and other such institutes continue to function at all, it is because of these people's commitment to the languages, literatures, and cultures they study. But it is not the kind of employment that pays the bills.

Also gone, in any meaningful sense, is the Soviet Writers Union, with its Foreign Commission, which employed dozens of consultants in the 1980s, who served as Soviet experts and liaisons with national literatures worldwide.[1] While work there – being so close to Soviet foreign policy – was often more political than work at the research institutes, the Foreign Commission boasted many remarkable translators, scholars, and people genuinely committed to the cultures in which they specialized. The famous Progress publishing house – the flagship of Soviet translation efforts – too, has ceased to exist. What is left of it is a giant building on Zubovsky Boulevard, fading memories, and mouldering copies of neglected literature in public and private libraries throughout the former Soviet Union. Khudozhestvennaia literatura and Molodaya Gvardiya, which also published translations of Afro-Asian literature, are still around but without their African and Asian series. Outside of Moscow, non-Western literature was generously translated and printed in the capitals of Central Asian and Caucasian Soviet republics. As most of the Soviet presses outside of Russia relied on Moscow-produced Russian translations for secondary translations into the language of their republic, the disappearance of the former, along with the whole Soviet division of cultural labour, has meant the end of the flow of Afro-Asian translations into the Soviet republics. With it, the post-Soviet world lost the readers who were probably the most genuinely interested in other Asian literatures.

The result is that today the once rich ecology of non-Western literature in Soviet print culture, imbricated with ideology though it may have been, has been reduced, as in the late-Stalin era, to a tiny number of representative contemporary writers who can be found in Russian bookstores today: on the contemporary Russian publishing map, J.M. Coetzee stands for the whole of African literature, Orhan Pamuk for West Asia, Salman Rushdie for India, Haruki Murakami and Kazuo Ishiguro for Japan. Most non-Western national literatures are, however, left without a single representative. Relatively better off is the situation of Latin American literature: judging by their user cards in Moscow libraries, it remains popular among Russian readers. But the overall impression has been well-captured by the translator Elena Malykhina, who complained that "if you enter a [Russian] bookstore, you'd think that literature is being written only in English and German."[2]

Just as important as readership trends are the pathways by which foreign books reach and are selected by Russian publishing houses. In the absence of significant direct relations between contemporary Russian and non-Western literatures, the approbation of publishers, critics, and publics in the West (primarily, Paris, London, and New York) determines the selection available to Russian readers. In a sense, after several decades of trying to become the core of an independent literary world-system, Russian literature has returned to being in a dominated position in Casanova's version of the World Republic of Letters, just as the Russian economy has reintegrated into the global capitalist economy by deindustrializing and once again becoming a peripheral provider of raw materials.

Today's situation of Soviet cinematic exchanges with Africa, Asia, and Latin America mirrors that of literature, if only in more extreme form. In today's Russia, contemporary films from sub-Saharan Africa and the Arab world cannot be seen in cinemas; the only possibility of watching them would be at rare film festivals, or, more realistically, via pirated copies online. Even the mighty stream of Indian films, once massively popular with post-Stalin-era viewers, has been reduced to a trickle: twenty-five new releases, or less than half a percent of all new films shown on Soviet screens since 2004.[3] The majority of them, and certainly the most popular ones, are co-productions in which Western film companies play the dominant role. Older popular Indian films, enjoying a subculture of a largely older generation of viewers, can be found more easily outside official commercial distribution, in the form of pirated DVDs and online sites, and occasional showings on television channels catering to an elderly audience.[4] The handful of Latin American films that have appeared on Russian cinema screens in the last decade have done so after a significant time lag and usually after being nominated for an Academy Award for best foreign film or some other such prize: *Love's a Bitch* (Alejandro Inarritu, 2000), *City of God* (Fernando Meirelles, 2002), *Secret in Their Eyes* (Billy Ray, 2009), *Instructions Not Included* (Eugenio Derbez, 2013), and *Wild Tales* (Damián Szifron, 2014).[5] All in all, the ideological membrane through which Latin American films had to pass during the Cold War to reach Soviet screens seems to have been less of an impediment than Hollywood's domination today, which has accounted for 45 per cent of all new releases in Russia since 2004 and has an even greater share of overall viewership.[6]

While platforms exclusively devoted to non-Western film, such as the Tashkent Film Festival, have disappeared, just as significant is the transformation of other sites that in the past carried such films without being exclusively devoted to them. The Moscow Film Festival is a case in point. For the first quarter of a century of its existence, it regularly invited African, Asian, and Latin American filmmakers to its jury, featured films from the three continents in its competition, and regularly awarded prizes to them, starting with the Pakistani *The Day Shall Dawn*, the Golden Medal winner of the inaugural 1959 festival; and ending with the two winners of the 1983 film festival, the Senegalese-Moroccan co-production *Amok* by the Third Cinema veteran Souheil Ben-Barka, and Miguel Littin's *Alsino and the Condor*.[7] Over the first two post-Soviet decades, even though the festival switched from a biennial to an annual format, no non-Western film has appeared among the prize winners. Only since 2008, in part by following the prevailing trends at other international film festivals, and in part because of the difficulty of attracting well-known Western filmmakers, has the main St George Prize gone to an Iranian, Venezuelan, Turkish, and most recently, a Chinese film.

Concentrated largely in a single Research Institute of the Theory and History of Cinema (renamed Research Institute on Cinema, and integrated or, rather, downsized into VGIK in 2012, before being completely disbanded in 2018), Soviet academic expertise on African, Asian, and Latin American film was never as great as its expertise in the literatures of those continents. Now it has collapsed even more radically. In light of today's level of expertise, for example, it is nearly unimaginable to think that thirty years ago the same institute brought out numerous monographs and edited scholarly volumes on African, Indian, and Latin American cinemas.[8] Reflecting on the Institute's fortunes, Tatiana Vetrova, head of its non-European cinemas division and a scholar of Latin American cinema, kept referring to herself and her colleagues as the "last of the Mohicans." This reduction in geographical coverage – in area studies expertise and popular cultural access – should temper any enthusiasm about 1989–91 as signalling an "opening to the world" or "breaking down the wall" as far as Sovet(-bloc) people are concerned. While this may arguably have been true regarding the West, as far as their relationship with African and Asian culture is concerned the process has been one of closure.[9]

This post-Soviet thinning out of the literary and cinematic networks that once connected the socialist bloc with Africa, Asia, and Latin America sits uneasily with the optimistic Anglo-American discourses on world literature and world cinema, which are focused on the emergence of cultural formations, the travel of books, canisters, literary and cinematic models, and the expansion of cultural exchanges. And yet it cannot be regarded as an exception: rather, such declines, disappearances, and wanings are illustrative of the workings of world literary and cinematic systems.

Post-Soviet Racial Imaginary

Ruins, of course, are sad to witness, but not as much as the backlash against Soviet internationalism, and the resulting racism, especially widespread among elite cultural and formerly anti-Soviet publics. This is not the kind of racism that gets non-white bodies sent to hospitals and morgues, or generates Sova Centre's statistics for racially motivated crimes – there are other, more violent strains, with different social bases – but it is of particular interest to us because of its epistemological implications.[10] After all, this kind of geographical hierarchy determines which subjects, authors, and texts are worth studying, and just as important, which are not. As we saw from previous chapters, the Western-centrism of the Russian intelligentsia dates back to the very origins of this estate. And yet the kind of aggressive contempt for non-Western cultures that one can often hear from certain liberal sections of the late- and post-Soviet Russian and East European intelligentsias is a relatively recent phenomenon. As we saw from the declining Soviet audiences for African, Asian, and Latin American literature and film, Soviet internationalism lost a good deal of its substance and appeal to domestic and international publics over the course of the ideologically cynical Stagnation era. Resistance to the workings of the Soviet "affirmative action empire" with respect to the two "Easts" (an inner East of Central Asia and the Caucasus and an outer East of Africa and Asia) and to the way the Soviet state enforced this sympathy became commonplace, particularly among sections of the dissident intelligentsia. In their opposition to the Soviet state, the latter would often mechanically invert its values, following the logic "the USSR is for Vietnam, I am, therefore, against it." Moreover, these anti-Soviet publics saw that Soviet internationalism – maybe not entirely without reason – was part of a zero-sum game in which engagement with "the East" – whether via a publication, translation, or invitation – was

necessarily at the expense of the "convergence," or Westernization, they
desired. In political terms at least, Soviet support for a non-Western national
liberation movement or a Third-Worldist government in conflict with some
Western power often meant greater political tensions and reduced cultural
traffic with the West. Owing to official censorship, however, such statements
as the one about Vietnam rarely transcended the format of informal conversations. They could of course be found in texts written outside of Soviet
censorship, in *samizdat, tamizdat,* and emigration. Thus, for example,
speaking of Angela Davis before the AFL-CIO in New York City, Alexander
Solzhenitsyn described her imprisonment in the following terms:

> You have [in the states] a certain Angela Davis. I don't know whether
> people know her in this country. But in our country whole year
> round we hear nothing but Angela Davis. In the whole wide world,
> there is only her and she is suffering. Our ears are tired of hearing
> her name. Little kids in schools have been told to sign petitions in
> support of Angela Davis. Boys and girls of eight, nine, ten. Even
> though she didn't have it so bad in US prison, she came to the
> Soviet seaside to recover. And some Soviet dissidents, or rather
> Czechoslovak dissidents, turned to her: Comrade Angela, you've
> spent time in prison. You know how bad it is there, especially when
> you consider yourself innocent. You have such an authority, please,
> help our Czechoslovak prisoners, defend those who are persecuted
> in Czechoslovakia. Angela Davis said to them: they got what they
> deserved. Let them spend time in prison. Here is the face of the
> communist. Here is the heart of the communist.[11]

Setting aside the fact that this was not Davis's reply to Czechoslovak
dissidents and that she did plead on behalf of those in prison before the
state-socialist authorities (but, as usual for Western leftists, in private
rather than public statements), Solzhenitsyn's account shows very little
understanding of the American racial context of her imprisonment or the
significance of the global solidarity campaign for her release, in which she
stood for the victims of state-sponsored racism in the United States. Seen
through the perspective of Solzhenitsyn's monomaniacal struggle against
communism, however, the civil rights movement in the United States at
best did not exist and at worst amounted to communist propaganda.[12]
With the disappearance of censorship after 1990, what had previously
been the domain of private expression could become public statements.

In the post-Soviet era, the accumulated racial prejudice, whether against distant Africans or residents of the "inner East," could be expressed without inhibition.

In this spirit, the principled dissident Valeria Novodvorskaya, who had spent years in Soviet psychiatric incarceration for her human rights activism and become a major public figure of the democratic camp of the 1990s, responded to the enfranchisement of blacks in South Africa with the following observations: "Apartheid is a normal thing. South Africa will see what kind of political order will be established under the native majority, which takes pleasure in arson, murder, and violence."[13] More recently, a similar public role has been taken up by the writer, journalist, and prominent liberal intellectual Yulia Latynina, who too likes to reflect in a similar manner on the "barbarity" of Africans and the civilizational danger constituted by non-white labour migrants, whether Central Asians in Russia or Arabs and Africans in the European Union.[14] To be sure, few post-Soviet intellectuals express such views so publicly, but a strange preoccupation with EU and US immigration policies, often couched as a staunch defence of Western values, persists among many liberal sections of the Russian and East European intelligentsias. After the dissolution of the Soviet bloc, the mechanical negation of Soviet values, previously confined to a section of the dissident movement, became inflected by assertions of the privileges of whiteness, more neutrally masked as "returning to Europe." In an only half-ironic idiomatic expression that became popular in the late-Soviet period and the equivalents of which appeared in most East European languages, they wanted to live "kak belye liudi" (as befitting white people).[15]

Indeed, such cultural attitudes, as well as a pitiless struggle against "political correctness," align many self-professed Russian and East European liberals with figures such as Samuel Huntington, Allan Bloom, and David Horowitz, and many others firmly on the American and European right. Such positionality reminds one of the title of a recent interview with sociologist Gregory Yudin: "Scratch a Russian liberal and you'll find a well-educated conservative."[16] The epistemological implications of these dispositions for scholarship are as vast as they are underestimated. Today, for example, these cultural attitudes account for the overwhelming absence of interest in minority cultures in the Russian academy or in the active resistance to postcolonial studies. The examples could easily be multiplied. Such reduced sensitivities are not solely limited to questions of race, ethnicity, and more broadly to cultural geography, but to other hierarchies as well, whether based on gender or economic privilege.[17]

Consequences in the Non-Western World

In African, Asian, and Latin American societies, too, the once vibrant Soviet–Third World cultural engagements have become a fading generational phenomenon. As Olga's encounter with the African scholars suggests, the end of the Soviet Union was experienced as a heavy blow, often figured as betrayal or abandonment, by many politically engaged intellectuals and cultural producers in the three continents. The title of the Chilean Communist Luis Gostavino's memoir, *The Fall of the Cathedrals* (1990), written as the Soviet centre was crumbling, is telling.[18] But as many Cubans would testify, the sentiment extended well beyond communist party members.[19] In addition, outside of certain leftist communities in the non-Western world and their function as "classics," Russian and Soviet literature and film have ceased to be a major point of reference or source of inspiration for politically engaged artists and audiences from these continents. Radio Moscow, which used to broadcast in seventy-seven foreign languages, has similarly disappeared from local airwaves.[20] The regular literature programming made it probably the single most important pathway by which Russian literature, even in excerpted form, would reach broad audiences in Africa, Asia, and Latin America. The steady volume of letters and presents its Soviet radio hosts would receive from grateful Afro-Asian listeners testified to the strength of the latter's interest.[21] While this was no utopia – one Soviet scholar of Indian literature and part-time staff member of the Hindi section of Radio Moscow told me of the humiliating task of having to check the text of the Indian radio presenters so that no ideological mistake could creep its way to the listeners – among other things, these platforms brought to Moscow hundreds if not thousands of native speakers of African and Asian languages and employed an even greater number of Russians familiar with their languages.[22]

With a small number of exceptions, such as Syria, and to a lesser extent, China, Japan, and South Korea, contemporary Russian film has few commercial pathways to audiences in Africa, Asia, and Latin America. In transforming itself into Roskino, Sovexportfilm has sold the vast majority of the offices and cinemas it owned in almost seventy countries. Though the immense changes in the very infrastructure and mode of cinematic circulation introduced by internet and digital technologies complicate comparisons between now and then immensely, today's Russian cinema is a much less international phenomenon than post-Stalin Soviet cinema ever was.

What is left of the Soviet engagement in the non-Western world is an abundance of memories, plenty of Ivans and Vladimirs, Natalias and Nadezhdas in Latin America, and mixed marriages in the Middle East as well as a number of Russian speakers among the political, cultural, and economic elites of those African and Asian countries that had sent students to the USSR.[23] Even today, nearly three decades after the end of the USSR, some of Africa's and the Middle East's leading filmmakers, from Abderrahmane Sissako to Mohammad Malas, are VGIK graduates. Copies of old Progress books can still be found in private libraries and second-hand bookstores from India to Ethiopia.[24]

Yet even those afterlives cannot make up for the sense of loss, of lost possibilities. With the disappearance of the Soviet bloc, the political fields available to politicians, writers, filmmakers, and audiences from the three continents have become profoundly reconfigured. For one, the available room for manoeuvre has vastly shrunk: no longer is a prominent African writer simultaneously courted by two sets of cultural outreach bureaucracies, Soviet and Western, willing to outbid each other to secure that writer's manuscript, presence, and goodwill. In discussing these effects, however, one should be careful not to exaggerate Soviet agency at the expense of local Africa, Asian, or Latin America actors, or teleologically attribute any post-1991 development to the end of the Cold War. The Third World project, as Vijay Prashad has shown, had its own dynamics, sometimes quite independent from, at other times only indirectly related to, the policies of the Cold War's main antagonists.[25]

And while only a minority of Third-Worldist cultural networks passed through Moscow and Tashkent, those that did, such as the Afro-Asian Writers Association or the Tashkent Film Festival, were permanently disrupted. And with them, down went a whole set of interconnected literary subcapitals of the Third World Republic of Letters: Beirut and Cairo, New Delhi and Tunis, Algiers and Havana. Indeed, even those Third-Worldist cultural initiatives not directly sponsored by the USSR were affected by its fortunes. Though it survived the loss of the favourable trade terms with the Soviet bloc, and the latter's military assurances against the constant menace coming from the United States, after 1991 socialist Cuba entered "a special period" of austerity and was no longer able to sponsor the volume of cultural exchanges it had enjoyed before. Though it still exists, the Havana-based OSPAAAL has severely declined in its role as a meeting place for many radical artists and activists and a source of Third-Worldist aesthetics in the realm of documentary film and visual culture.[26] The same could be said of the Havana Film Festival, which was once the true home of Latin America's Third Cinema.[27]

Postcolonial Studies

In this hollowed-out One World, in the absence of a cultural Second and with a severely weakened, possibly extinguished, Third, the work of championing non-Western literary and cinematic production, introducing it to Western audiences, and, more generally, fighting for their place on the world literature and world cinema canons, has shifted to postcolonial scholars on Western campuses. After the publication of Edward Said's *Orientalism* in 1978 and the ensuing debates, scholarship on non-Western and even Western texts could not be the same. In many cases, it became possible to include art from Africa, Asia, and Latin America in syllabi and make it the subject of scholarship for the first time, that is, as far as Anglo-American literature departments were concerned. Indeed, placed in a longer history of Third-Worldist cultural movements and Marxist thought, even in its very problematic, Soviet instantiation, postcolonial studies' act of valorizing non-Western cultural production and exposing the mechanisms of Western cultural hegemony appears less novel. It suffices to reiterate Vera Tolz's discovery in *Russia's Own Orient* that Said's key definition of Orientalism as a European system of knowledge meant to control colonial populations was a commonplace in Soviet scholarship and features prominently in the "Vostokovedenie" ("Oriental Studies") entry of the late-Stalin-era authoritative encyclopedia:[28]

> Reflecting the racist worldview of the European and American
> bourgeoisie, Oriental studies from the very beginning opposed
> "the West" (European and later North American culture) to "the
> East," slanderously claiming Eastern peoples as racially deficient,
> inherently backward, unable to take control of their destiny, merely
> an object of history rather than its subject ... Even some of the best
> works of Western oriental studies were shaped by this corrupt,
> bourgeois ideology. Together with the idealism, metaphysics, class
> tendentiousness and lack of objectivity characteristic of bourgeois
> scholarship in general, Oriental studies more than any other field
> of knowledge exhibits a narrowly formal-philological character,

interest in the religious and mystical at the expense of the social and the economic while ignoring the role of small peoples, especially those that lost their state early on or lived nomadic lives ... The deeply corrupt nature of bourgeois Oriental studies and its anti-scientific methodology stems from its organic connection with the interests of imperial expansion. A number of Oriental scholars were in fact colonial agents and bureaucrats (St. John Philby, George Curzon, Percy Sykes and so on). Bourgeois Oriental studies failed to understand the history, the principles of social, political, economic and cultural development of the people it studied. Within it, Eduard Meyer's reactionary concept of the "cyclicity" of historical development has enjoyed particular prominence. Bourgeois Oriental scholars proposed reactionary theories about the alleged permanence of the East and the reign of some unchangeable "universal feudalism" there. They cultivated the myth of the inability of Eastern peoples to develop on their own ... Bourgeois Oriental scholars are responsible for the propagation of different racist "theories" for justifying the policies of imperialist expansion, plunder, and oppression of the peoples of the East. They are responsible for turning their discipline into a handmaiden of imperialism, preaching the "civilizational mission" of the West and systematizing data on different countries for the purposes of colonial conquest and rule.[29]

Tolz argues that this criticism of Western Oriental scholarship probably reached Said via a Soviet-trained Egyptian sociologist, Anouar-Abdel Malek, whom Said acknowledges in the preface to his book.[30] Her study, however, has remained unnoticed by postcolonial scholars.[31] By showing how canonically postcolonial twentieth-century writers and filmmakers passed through Soviet-aligned networks, *From Internationalism to Postcolonialism* has offered another argument for the continuity between earlier Soviet anti-colonialism and later postcolonial studies across 1990.

The trajectories of two writers whose texts we encountered earlier – Ngũgĩ wa Thiong'o and Sembène Ousmane – perfectly illustrate this continuity. In the late 1960s and early and mid-1970s, Ngũgĩ was an active participant in the Afro-Asian Writers Association. His personal meetings with Afro-Asian writers at the Beirut and Alma-Ata Congresses and encounters with their literature is reflected in his syllabi at the time, which included Vietnamese poetry.[32] As the preface to his 1976 novel *Petals of Blood* testifies, he finished it during a six-month-long stint at a dacha of the Soviet Writers' Union in Yalta.[33] Of course, his engagement with Soviet literary internationalism was never exclusive: he had started the novel while a visiting professor at Northwestern University and had completed an MA degree at the University of Leeds even earlier. Another literary internationalism in which Ngũgĩ participated is suggested by his studies at the Makerere University College, Uganda, where he participated in the famous 1962 Conference of African Writers of English Expression.[34] Sponsored by the Congress of Cultural Freedom, this conference brought together the leading English-language writers at the time: Wole Soyinka, John Pepper Clark, Lewis Nkosi, Dennis Brutus, Okot p'Bitek, Grace Ogot, Langston Hughes, and Chinua Achebe, to whom he managed to pass the manuscripts of his first two novels (*The River Between* and *Weep Not, Child*) and who would facilitate their publication in Heinemann's African Writers Series.[35] For reasons that he does not fully remember, over the course of the late 1970s and early 1980s, Ngũgĩ dropped out of the Afro-Asian Writers Association's orbit. The process coincided with his leaving Kenya, where he had been persecuted by Daniel arap Moi's seemingly eternal regime, first for England and eventually for the US as a professor of literature, and with his switch from fiction to essay-writing and postcolonial scholarship.[36] His transition from a Third-Worldist to a diasporic positionality was mirrored by other writers over this period.

Unlike Ngũgĩ, Sembène returned permanently to his native Senegal in the early 1960s, after many years in France and one in the USSR, during which he mastered the basics of filmmaking. Nevertheless, until the end of the Cold War, he remained connected to French, Soviet, and Third-World literatures and cinemas, and was a distinguished guest at film festivals in Europe and Moscow, Tashkent and Ouagadougou. Over the course of the 1980s, however, invitations from Moscow dried up, and so did Soviet translations of his books and Soviet purchases of his films. After the last festival, in 1988, Tashkent, too, disappeared from the map of Third-World filmmakers. Third-Worldist cinematic institutions with which Sembène was involved, such as the Committee of Third-World Filmmakers, had come to an end even earlier, in the 1970s, shortly after their birth. Thus, despite his stated goal and active efforts toward the creation of a Third-World literary and cinematic field independent from the West, by 1990 his main audiences, interpreters, and popularizers could mainly be found precisely in the colonial metropoles that he had sought to demote.

Though radically different, these trajectories in their own way illustrate the end of the anti-colonial, Third-Worldist moment and the inauguration of a new, Western-centred, postcolonial one. Other prominent participants in the Afro-Asian Writers Association and the Tashkent Film Festival, and many leading writers and filmmakers from the three continents have repeated this literal or textual westward journey over the course of the 1980s and '90s. At the same time as Third-Worldist networks and centres, Soviet-aligned or not, were disappearing, a whole cohort of diasporic scholars entered and eventually gained prominence in Anglo-American academia.[37] Initially located in (English) literature departments, they – and their concerns – have made themselves felt in most humanities fields. Though Said's *Orientalism* announced the emergence of the field in 1978, it was not until after the Cold War that postcolonial studies began to experience explosive institutional growth in positions, publication outlets, conferences, and grants. The relationship between the geopolitical context and this new field did not escape one of its pioneers, Robert J.C. Young, who stated in the inaugural issue of the flagship journal *Interventions: International Journal of Postcolonial Studies* (1998):

Does "postcolonialism" mark the end of the "Third World"? ... With the collapse of the Soviet bloc, and the conversion of China to a form of controlled capitalist economy, today there is effectively no longer any choice: de facto there is now only a single world economic system. One implication of this is that with the demise of the second world, a Third World no longer exists. Indeed, the emergence of postcolonial theory could be viewed as marking the moment in which the Third World moved from an affiliation with the second to the first. The rise of postcolonial studies coincided with the end of Marxism as the defining political, cultural, and economic objective of much of the third world.[38]

In many ways, postcolonial scholars have continued the work of earlier Third-Worldist critics and scholars. What has changed, however, was not only the location where that cultural and intellectual labour is performed (from the capitals of Africa, Asia, and Latin America or Moscow to Anglo-American literature departments) but also its substance. Partly in reflection of the historical period in which it was born (the retreat of the left globally, the rise of neoliberalism, the hegemony of poststructuralism in the humanities), partly as a critique of the limitations of earlier emancipatory projects (Soviet-aligned or not), mainstream postcolonial scholarship has struggled to take its progressive political aspirations beyond its writings and the classroom; and even there, revolutionary Third-Worldist rhetoric has given way to subtle French poststructuralism; the harsh (neo)colonized-colonizer binaries with which Third-Worldists and Soviets operated has been sidelined in favour of a (autobiographical and deconstructionist) celebration of hybridity; the embrace of progressive nationalisms, discursively compatible with Soviet internationalism, replaced by postcolonial interest in diasporas and transnationality. Following Homi Bhabha, mainstream postcolonial theorists have been suspicious of the nation, which had constituted one of the main political horizons of earlier national liberation struggles.[39] They have been even more critical of the (postcolonial) state, in which earlier Third-Worldist intellectuals and Soviet bureaucracies had placed so much hope: to reduce inequality, to industrialize the country, to raise national culture. In the theory of social change underlying the writings of the Subaltern Studies historians, one of the main intellectual streams within postcolonial studies, there has been a remarkable suspicion of, if not active hostility to, organizations, parties, and other representative political structures as vehicles of advancing the interests of "the subalterns." Whether implicitly or explicitly, this view represents a major challenge to Marxist political strategy. Instead, the subaltern scholars' main focus has lain on the spontaneous and unorganized resistance of "the subalterns" to impositions from above.[40]

Indeed, following Spivak's "Can the Subaltern Speak?," mainstream postcolonial scholars have questioned the very possibility of political or even aesthetic representation in which they see an elite act of assertion of power over the represented.[41] Like most poststructuralist interventions into politics, Spivak's warning that speaking for a subaltern can render them into an object makes for a brilliant intellectual critique, but offers little by way of alternative or political engagement. Soviet internationalists felt no such compunction when they issued their calls:

> People of the East! To you belong the richest, most fertile, most extensive lands of the whole world. Once the cradle of all humanity, these lands could feed not only their inhabitants but the population of the entire world. Yet now, every year, ten million Turkish, Persian, and Indian peasants and workers are unable to find a crust of bread

or employment in their wide and fertile homelands and are obliged to go abroad and seek a livelihood in alien lands. They have to do this because in their homeland everything – land, money, banks, factories, workshops – belongs to British capitalists ... Now we summon you to the first genuine holy war, under the red banner of *the Communist International.* We summon you to a holy war [*ghazavat*] for your own well-being, for your own freedom, for your life.[42]

Similarly, Dipesh Chakrabarty's critique in *Provincializing Europe* of the Enlightenment tradition and other Western conceptual categories as inapplicable to the East – a radicalization of Said's original questioning of the West's knowledge of the Orient – has marked another departure from Soviet internationalist and even most Third-Worldist thought.[43] Vis-á-vis Soviet Marxism, Chakrabarty's argument may sound more meaningful. Though born out of Lenin's famous revision of Second International thought to Russian conditions, Soviet Marxism grew increasingly rigid over the course of Stalin's three decades in power, subordinating itself to the interests of the Soviet state, positing that state as the final stage to which postcolonial societies should aspire. A critique of that rigidity, however, took the form of Mao's and Fanon's, Cabral's and Che Guevara's, and many other thinkers' and activists' creative adaptations of a Marxism born in Western Europe to the particular conditions of their own societies. The natural corollary to Chakrabarty's line of thought – the dismissal of any universalism and ideas, even values, applicable to both East and West – makes the very articulation of a global emancipatory agenda, of international solidarity well-nigh impossible.

In thus exposing the limitations of earlier emancipatory movements, Third-Worldist or Soviet, the mainstream postcolonial theory associated with Spivak, Bhabha, Chakrabarty, and the Subaltern Studies collective has offered the whole cohort of humanities students who took it as the most radical emancipatory thought of the present little by way of real political alternative to the prevailing neoliberalism. While it has produced scintillating analysis, its contribution to, or connections with, political practice has been scant.

Such a critique of postcolonial theory "from the left" is of course not new. In its best known, most aggressive version, it could be found in *Postcolonial Theory and the Specter of Capital* (2013) by the Marxist sociologist Vivek Chibber.[44] *From Internationalism to Postcolonialism* certainly does not share Chibber's crude dismissal of postcolonial studies as a reactionary phenomenon best left in the rubbish heap of academic fads. Rather, by reconstructing one of the possible genealogies of contemporary postcolonial studies, it has contributed to the historization of the field, which has traditionally preferred theorizing to historicizing. In this goal, it has much more in common with the work of Robert J.C. Young, the Postcolonial Print-Culture Network, and the Warwick school of Marxist postcolonial studies, which all along has challenged the mainstream post-colonial accommodation with capitalism and in much greater nuance than Chibber, and which has sought to reconstruct the historical continuity of anti-colonial, emancipatory thought and practice of the twentieth century.[45] The seven-decade-long Soviet cultural engagement with the Third World was a central part of this story.

In 2001, David Chioni Moore famously asked "Is the Post- in Post-colonial the Post- in Post-Soviet"? In the ensuing years, Slavists have offered a plethora of responses, adopting and adapting postcolonial methods in their efforts to pry into the complex dynamics between the Russian metro-pole and the societies and cultures on its periphery, be they Ukrainian, Polish, Baltic, Caucasian, Siberian, or Central Asian. Ironically, as *From Internationalism to Postcolonialism* has shown, this scholarly develop-ment represents only the latest stage of a cycle begun a century ago, when the former Russian empire (newly reconfigured as the USSR) emerged as a gigantic experiment in understanding and contesting the political, economic, and cultural hierarchies among societies, within the USSR as well as globally. Yet the other audience Moore addressed – postcolonial scholars – has been much slower to take up his challenge. Through its historical reconstruction of the cultural engagements between the two worlds, *From Internationalism to Postcolonialism* has sought to extend a bridge between the two fields. A comprehensive account of these engage-ments, involving many more countries, artists, and audiences, in all the different genres and cultural media, will take many more books and articles. This has just been the beginning.

APPENDIX

LOTUS PRIZE WINNERS, 1969–1988

1969	Alex La Guma (South Africa), Mahmoud Darwish (Palestine), Tô Hoài (Vietnam)
1970	Agostinho Neto (Angola), Zul'fia (Uzbek SSR), Harivansh Rai Bachchan (India)
1971	Sonomyn Udval (Mongolia), Sembène Ousmane (Senegal), Taha Hussein (Egypt)
1972	Hiroshi Noma (Japan), Mikhail Naimy (Lebanon), Marcelino dos Santos (Mozambique)
1973	Kateb Yacine (Algeria), Ngũgĩ wa Thiong'o (Kenya), Thu Bon (Vietnam)
1974	Aziz Nesin (Turkey), Yusuf al-Sibai (Egypt), Anatoly Sofronov (Russia), Kamal Nasser (Palestine), Ghassan Kanafani (Palestine)
1975	Chinua Achebe (Nigeria), Faiz Ahmad Faiz (Pakistan), Muhammad Mahdi al-Jawahiri (Iraq), Kim Chi-ha (South Korea)
1976	Subhas Mukherjee (India), Tawfiq al-Hakim (Egypt), Mikhail Sholokhov (Russia)
1977–78	Meja Mwangi (Kenya), Nguyên Ngoc (Vietnam), Yoshie Hotta (Japan); Kamil Yashen (Uzbek SSR), Abu Salma (Palestine), Sami al-Droubi (Syria)
1979–80	Muin Bseiso (Palestine), Antonio Jacinto (Angola), Bhisham Sahni (India), Husayn Muruwwa (Lebanon), Gunasena Vithana (Shri Lanka), Atukwei Okai (Ghana), Choizhilyn Chimid (Mongolia)

1981–82   Georgi Markov (Russia), Assefa Gebremariam (Ethiopia),
           Sulaiman al-Issa (Syria), Ataol Behramoğlu (Turkey)
1983   Sarvar Azimov (Uzbek SSR), Nguyen Dinh Thi (Vietnam),
           Jose Craveirinha (Mozambique), Kaifi Azmi (India),
           Mustapha Fersi (Tunis)
1984   Sulaiman Layeq (Afghanistan), Jeane-Fernand Brierre (Haiti-
           Senegal), Azraj Omar (Algiers), H. Karunatilake (Sri Lanka)
1985   Abdulaziz al-Maqaleh (Yemen), Rasul Gamzatov (Russia),
           Chon Se Bong (North Korea)
1986   Tahsin Saraç (Turkey)
1987   Makoto Oda (Japan)
1988   Chinghiz Aitmatov (Kyrgyz SSR)

Source: *Pisateli Azii i Afriki v bor'be za mir I sotsial'nyi progress
(K 30-letiu I Tashkentskoj konferencii pisatelei Azii i Afriki,* edited by
N. Ibragimov and U.M. Aripov (Tashkent: Izdatel'stvo Fan, 1990), 122–4.

Notes

Introduction

1 See the Slovak comparatist Dionýz Ďurišin's basic classification of relationships into typological affinities and genetic contacts. *Theory of Literary Comparatistics*, 108.

2 Sauvy, "Trois Mondes, Une Planète," 14.

3 Gordon, interview. For some of those debates, see Casula, "Two Soviet Responses to Franz Fanon."

4 Let us not forget that the conference held in Bandung in April 1955 was still called Afro-Asian and one of the first organizations to emerge from it was the Cairo-based Afro-Asian People's Solidarity Organization. It was only with the Cuban Revolution in 1959 that the Non-Aligned Movement gained a foothold in the Americas.

5 There is a growing body of literature about the inclusion of African-American writers in the Soviet Republic of Letters. Moore, "Local Color, 'Global Color'"; Moore, "Colored Dispatches from the Uzbek Border"; Baldwin, *Beyond the Color Line;* Steven Lee, *The Ethnic Avant-Garde;* Clark, "The Representation of the African American as Colonial Oppressed"; Mukherji, "'Like Another Planet to the Darker Americans."

6 Babiracki, *Soviet Soft Power in Poland;* Babiracki and Jersild, *Socialist Internationalism in the Cold War;* Applebaum, *Empire of Friends.*

7 For the appeal of Maoism in the US, see Kelley and Esche, "Black Like Mao." Specifically literary Maoism and its role in the Afro-Asian Writers movement is the subject of Yoon, "Cold War Africa and China."

8   For a detailed study of the process, see Friedman, *Shadow Cold War*.

9   Mahler, *From the Tricontinental to the Global South*.

10   For an account of how the Cultural Revolution cannibalized Chinese citizens located at the interface with other cultures and how its gradual reversal over the course of the 1970s diminished Maoism's foreign appeal (in a sense, repeating the Soviet scenario of the late 1930s), see McGuire, *Red at Heart*, 342–65. For a timeline of Cuba's years of Sovietization, see Loss, *Caviar with Rum*, 18–21.

11   Unkovski-Korica, *The Economic Struggle for Power in Tito's Yugoslavia*.

12   There is a growing scholarship on the cultural dimensions of the engagement between different East European countries and Third-World spaces. See Lovejoy, "The World Union of Documentary"; Zubel, "Toward a Second World Third World Cinema"; Stejskalova, ed., *Filmmakers of the World, Unite!*; Reilly, "Remains of Red Letters."

13   Under the Hallstein Doctrine (1955–69), West German governments refused to recognize any nation (aside from the USSR) that recognized their eastern counterpart. Diplomatically cut off from many western states, the GDR thus scrambled to establish relations with Asia and Africa before West Germany did. See Engerman, "The Second World's Third World," 197.

14   RGALI f. 5, op. 36, ex. 92, l. 76.

15   Popescu, *South African Literature beyond the Cold War*; Popescu, *African Literatures, Postcolonial Cultures and the Cold War*.

16   For Comintern scholarship, consult Pons and Smith, *The Cambridge History of Communism, Vol. 1*; Petersson, "We Are Neither Visionaries nor Utopian Dreamers; Brasken, *The International Workers' Relief*. For "Global Cold War" scholarship, see Westad, *Global Cold War*; Friedman, *Shadow Cold War* and other works from the Westad-edited New Cold War series at the University of North Carolina Press. Prashad's *Red Star over the Third World*, Hilger's edited volume *Die Sowijetunion and die Dritte Welt*, and Roth-Ey's forthcoming manuscript on Cold War communication are among the few culturally sensitive histories of Soviet engagements with the whole of the Third World.

17   On nation or region, or continent-based studies of Soviet–Third-World engagements, see Matusevich, *No Easy Row for Russian Hoe;* Matusevich, *Africa in Russia, Russia in Africa*; Rupprecht, *Soviet Internationalism after Stalin*; McGuire, *Red at Heart*; Engerman, *The Price of Aid*. The series of workshops Margaret Litvin has organized on Soviet-Arab exchanges and the forthcoming sourcebook on that subject that she, Masha Kirasirova, and Eileen Kane have edited make the Soviet-Arab cultural engagements a particularly well-studied phenomenon. However, other such initiatives are emerging, often in the form of

workshops: one, organized by Steven Lee, Leftist Aesthetics in North East Asia (Berkeley, January 2017) and another by Elizabeth Banks, Africa and the Soviet Union: Technology, Ideology, and Culture (New York University, October 2017).

18 Kirasirova, "The Eastern International."

19 These aspirations are captured in their raw and lyrical power in Prashad's *Red Star over the Third World*.

20 Denning, *Culture in the Age of Three Worlds*.

21 For the rise of the "Soviet superiority complex" over the course of the 1930s, see David-Fox, *Showcasing the Great Experiment*, 285–311.

22 Friedman, *The Shadow Cold War*, 1–24.

23 For a study of the somewhat turbulent relationship between the two, see the special issue of *Critical Sociology* entitled "Marxism and Postcolonial Theory?" and Sinha and Varma's introduction, "What's Left of the Debate." See also Lazarus and Varma, "Marxism and Postcolonial Studies."

24 See Rasberry, "The Right to Fail."

25 See Hakim, *Pan-Africanism and Communism*, 401–16.

26 Recent work on Soviet mass culture has also challenged this traditional Soviet cultural history timeline. See Roth-Ey, *Moscow Prime Time*; Evans, *Between Truth and Time*.

27 Fortunately, some of questions are already being addressed. For non-Western students' education in the USSR, see Katsakioris, "Burden or Allies?" For Soviet development aid, see Mëhilli, *From Stalin to Mao*; Engerman, *The Price of Aid*. For the emergence of regional varieties of socialism insistent on keeping a certain distance from the Soviet model, see Lal, *African Socialism in Postcolonial Tanzania*.

28 Pratt, "The Arts of the Contact Zone."

29 Despite this demotion of Central Asia's role, it still featured prominently in African-American itineraries to the USSR in the early 1930s, whether by high-profile visitors such as Langston Hughes or by lesser-known but longer-term visitors such as the colony of African-American collective farm workers Hughes encountered during his travels through Uzbekistan. See Hughes, *I Wonder as I Wander*, 191.

30 Khalid, "Introduction: Locating the Postcolonial in Soviet History"; Kirasirova, "Sons of Muslims in Moscow"; Kalinovsky, *Laboratory of Socialist Development*.

31 Djagalov, "Literary Monopolists."

32 The latter's tragic fate is the subject of Part V of McGuire's *Red at Heart*.

33 The major scholar of this phenomenon, Masha Salazkina, examines how a particular interpretation of Soviet film theory of the 1920s reached Cuban

filmmakers of the 1950s and '60s via Italian Marxists. See her "Moscow-Rome-Havana."

34   See Wolff's work on Western European images of Eastern Europe in *Inventing Eastern Europe*; Susan Layton's on nineteenth-century Russian literary Orientalism in the Caucasus in *Russian Literature and Empire*; Maria Todorova's on Balkanism as a counterpart to Orientalism in *Imagining the Balkans*; David Schimmelpenninck van der Oye on late-imperial Russian Oriental studies in *Russian Orientalism*; Harsha Ram on Russian poetry between the 1730s and 1840s and its relationship to empire in *The Imperial Sublime;* Alexander Etkind on nineteenth-century Russian peasantry in *Internal Colonization*.

35   Moore, "Is the Post- in Postcolonial the Post- in Postsoviet?"; Smola and Uffelmann, eds., *Postcolonial Slavic Literatures after Communism*; Chernetsky, *Mapping Postcommunist Cultures;* Tlostanova, *Postcolonialism and Postsocialism in Fiction and Art;* Tlostanova, *What Does It Mean to Be Post-Soviet?*; Condee, *The Imperial Trace on Recent Russian Cinema*; Platt, "Occupation versus Colonization"; Platt, ed., *Global Russian Cultures*; Platt, *Near Abroad: Russian Culture in Latvia*; Oushakine, "How to Grow out of Nothing."

36   Young, *Postcolonialism: An Historical Introduction.*

37   Brennan, "Postcolonial Studies Between the European Wars."

38   D'Haen, Damrosch, and Kadir, eds., *The Routledge Companion to World Literature.*

39   Tihanov, "The Location of World Literature"; *The Birth and Death of Literary Theory*, 175–85; "Ferrying a Thinker"; "Foreword."

40   Clark, *Moscow, the Fourth Rome*; Sherry, *Discourses of Regulation and Resistance;* Khotimsky, "World Literature, Soviet Style"; Ostrovskaya and Zemskova, "Between the Battlefield and the Marketplace'; Zemskova, "Istoria zhurnala Internatsional'naya literatura"; Ostrovskaya, "'Na puti k "'Writers' International'"; David-Fox, *Showcasing the Great Experiment.*

41   Dobrenko, "Naideno v perevode"; Frank, "The Impact of Multinational Soviet Literature on Post-Soviet Literary Develoments"; Ram, "City, Nation, Empire"; Kudaibergenova, *Rewriting the Nation in Modern Kzakh Literature;* Schild, "Between Moscow and Baku"; Yountchi, "Between Russia and Iran"; Erley, "Reclaiming Native Soil"; Feldman, *On the Threshold of Eurasia;* Caffee, "Between First, Second, and Third Worlds."

42   Andrew, "An Atlas of World Cinema"; Gabriel, *Third Cinema in the Third World.*

43   Salazkina, *In Excess;* Salazkina, "Soviet-Indian Co-Productions."

44   Malitsky, *Post-Revolution Non-Fiction Film;* Rajagopalan, *Indian Films in Soviet Cinemas*; Fedorova, "Formirovanie shkoly montazhnoi vyrazitel'nosti."

45   Litvin, *Hamlet's Arab Journey;* Litvin, "Fellow Travelers?"; Ertürk, "Marxism,
      Communism, and Translation"; Cho, *Translations Forgotten History;* Loss,
      Dreaming in Russian; Lee, *The Ethnic Avant-Garde;* Volland, *Socialist
      Cosmopolitanism*; Chan, *Chinese Revolutionary Cinema;* Qian, *Visionary
      Realities*; Humphreys, *Fidel between the Lines*; Dickinson, *Arab Cinema Travels;*
      Kouoh and Salti, *Saving Bruce Lee.*
46   Cheah, *What Is a World?.*
47   Damrosch, *How to Read World Literature,* 46–65.
48   Andrew, "An Atlas of World Cinema."
49   Anderson, *Imagined Communities.*
50   Few of the main theoreticians of Third-World socialism were even translated
      in the USSR. Michel Aflaq, Samir Amin, Aime Cesaire, Paolo Freire, C.L.R.
      James, George Padmore, Walter Rodney, and M.N. Roy still await their
      Russian publications. Relatively luckier were Third-World thinkers heading
      a government: Amilcar Cabral, Jomo Kenyatta, Ho Chi Minh, Gamal Abdel
      Nasser, Kwame Nkrumah, Leopold Senghor, Sekou Toure, and Mao Zedong
      (before 1960) were all published as a matter of diplomacy, in carefully curated
      selections. In general, Soviet Marxism did not like competitors, whether Western
      or Eastern.

Chapter One

1   "On pesenku etu/ Tverdil naizust' .../ Otkuda u khloptsa/ ispanskaia grust'?"
     translated by Margaret Wettlin.
2   Compare the celebratory tone with which Marx and Engels discuss the spread of
     capitalist technologies outside of Europe in their *Communist Manifesto* (1848)
     with Marx's condemnation of colonialism in his "The Future Results of the
     British Rule in India" in *Collected Works*, 217. For the most detailed treatment of
     Marx's position on the colonial question, see Anderson, *Marx on the Margins.*
3   Guettel, "The Myth of the Pro-Colonialist SPD."
4   Young, *Postcolonialism.*
5   Eby, "Global Tashkent."
6   See Kirasirova, "Soviet Central Asian Mediators to the Foreign East, 1955–
     1962"; Kalinovsky, *Laboratory of Socialist Development*; Clark, "Eurasia without
     Borders?"
7   Riddle, *To See the Dawn.*
8   See Riddle's Introduction and the Call to the Baku Congress in *To See the Dawn*,
     11–48.

9 Ertürk, "Baku, Literary Common."

10 Ertürk has further argued that the spirit of the Baku Congress was continued in the 1926 Baku Turcological Congress. See her "Towards a Literary Communism: The 1926 Baku Turcological Congress."

11 *The First Congress of the Toilers of the Far East (January-February 1922)*. More information on the Washington Conference could be found in Vinson, "The Drafting of the Four-Power Treaty of the Washington Conference," 40–7.

12 Ironically, prior to the massacre, the Comintern had been pressing the Chinese Communist Party for an alliance with the Guomindang against the better judgment of local cadres. For a longer account of this episode, see Pons, *The Global Revolution*, 56–60.

13 Panteleev, "Repressii v Kominterne (1937–1938gg.)."

14 For the precise contents of "the friendship of the peoples," see the last chapter of Terry Martin's *Affirmative Action Empire*, 432–61.

15 Erez Manela, *The Wilsonian Moment*.

16 Smith, "The Bolshevik Revolution from a Global Perspective."

17 Prashad, *Red Star over the Third World*.

18 See Petersson, "We Are Neither Visionaries Nor Utopian Dreamers." The Edwin Mellen book published on the basis of the dissertation is almost impossible to find.

19 Prashad, *The Darker Nations*, 16–30.

20 Petersson, "We Are Neither Visionaries nor Utopian Dreamers," 149–200.

21 Wright, *The Color Curtain*, 138. The League against Imperialism itself fell victim to both Third Period politics, which made the presence of non-communist participants untenable, and later, to the Nazis coming to power in Germany, where the organization had been primarily based. (On the League's demise, see Petersson, 510.)

22 In examining the reception of Russian literature in African and Asian countries, I have relied on the following studies: Cho, *Translations Forgotten History*; Gamsa, *The Chinese Translation of Russian Literature*; Gamsa, *The Reading of Russian Literature in China*; Gerasimova, *Russkaia klassika v Afganistane*; Margaret Litvin's forthcoming book on Soviet-Arab exchanges; ali-Zade, *Russkaia literatura i arabskii mir*.

23 Cho, "Rethinking World Literature," 10.

24 Ibid.

25 Gamsa, *The Reading of Russian Literature in China*.

26 Lu Xun [Lu Hsun], "China's Debt to Russian Literature," 181. Quoted in Cho, "Rethinking World Literature," 10.

27 See Chapter 3 of Cho, *Translation's Forgotten History*.

28 Litvin, *Hamlet's Arab Journey*, 115. Litvin's forthcoming work offers an even more extensive reception study of Russian culture in the Arab world in this period.

29 Booker and Juraga, "The Reds and the Blacks," 274 and 276.

30 Popescu, *South African Literature beyond the Cold War*, 2.

31 Ibid.

32 Malik, "The Marxist Literary Movement in India and Pakistan."

33 Balogun, "Russian and Nigerian Literatures," 483-96.

34 The only exceptions that come to mind are French: in the interwar period, the role of the main writer-politician in the West was played by Leon Blum of Popular-Front fame. André Malraux also served as the minister of culture for over ten years (1958-69) under General de Gaulle's presidency.

35 Joseph Stalin, after whom the university was named in 1923, articulated its role in an 18 May 1925 speech to KUTV students, more famous for the "proletarian in content, national in form" definition of Soviet culture it offered: "The Political Tasks of the University of the Peoples of the East." *Works*, vol. 7, 135-54.

36 Naumkin, *Mchashchiiskia skvoz' vremia*, 18.

37 Filatova, "Indoctrination or Scholarship?"; Kirasirova, "The 'East' as a Category of Bolshevik Ideology and Comintern Administration"; McGuire, *Red at Heart*, 67-154; Ravandi-Fadai, "'Red Mecca'"; Meyer, "Children of Trans-Empire"; Clark, "Eurasia without Borders?"; Usova, "Kommunisticheskii universitet trudiashchikhsia Vostoka," 1-3; Shashkova and Shpakovskaya, "KUTV: Its Establishment under the Comintern in 1920s and 30s."

38 The most detailed description of the KUTV and its research institute, through all the institutional transformation they underwent, could be found in Timofeeva's dissertation "Kommunisticheskii universitet trudiashchikhsia Vostoka, KUTV."

39 Davidson, Apollon, *Stanovlenie otechestvennoi Afrikanistiki*, 74-136. Maybe less dramatically, the much bigger Soviet Asian studies were also downsized in the late 1930s through a mixture of political repression and institutional reorganization.

40 RGASPI f. 495, op. 154, ex. 256, l. 28.

41 Adi, *Pan-Africanism and Communism*. Adi questions Padmore's charges against the USSR, pointing out the multiple ways in which Comintern's pan-Africanist position proved instrumental in the formation of trans-Atlantic networks among African, Afro-American, and Caribbean intellectuals and activists.

42 Sheng, *Sun-Yatsen University in Moscow*, 164-83.

43 Martin, *Affirmative Action Empire*, 132-45.

44 Tamari, "Najati Sidqi (1905–1979)," 86–7.

45 Hikmet, *Life's Good, My Brother*; Xiao (Siao), *Zhengui de jinian*; Haywood, *Black Bolshevik*; Malaka, *From Jail to Jail*; Qu, *Superfluous Words*.

46 Haywood, *Black Bolshevik*, 311–21.

47 Ibid., 315.

48 To the point that the largest, Chinese, section seceded into its own university: See Yu, "Sun Yatsen University in Moscow, 1925–1930."

49 Tamari, "Najati Sidqi (1905–1979)," 88.

50 For a cultural background on Hikmet and the other Turkish students at KUTV, see Clark, "European and Russian Cultural Interactions with Turkey"; Meyer, "Children of the Trans-Empire."

51 Khalid, *Making Uzbekistan*.

52 As literarily productive an institution as KUTV was, both for the multinational Soviet literature and for the literatures of the colonial world, I have found no mention in the available memoiristic literature of the two Easts converging, that is, students from the inner (Soviet Asian) encountering their peers from the outer (foreign) sections.

53 For an account of the congresses, Djagalov, "The Red Apostles," 400–6. Susanna Witt has characterized interwar-era Soviet translation "the largest, more or less coherent project of translating the world has seen to date." See Witt, "Between the Lines." For a history of the *International Literature* magazine, its precursors and successors, see the work of the InterLet group, and especially Elena Zemskova, Elena Ostrovskaya, and Natalia Kharitonova as well as Baer, "From International to Foreign: Packaging Translated Literature in Soviet Russia." For a history of ITIR and its successors, see Chapter 2.

54 A. Lunacharsky, "O Mezhdunarodnom B'iuro Proletarskoi Literatury," RGALI, f. 1698, op. 1, ex. 882, l. 2–11. One of its main champions was the black Guadeloupean writer and anti-colonial activist Joseph Gothon-Lunion. On his role, see Edwards, "The Shadow of Shadows," 27.

55 For a study of his pilgrimage to the USSR, see Baldwin, *Beyond the Color Line and the Iron Curtain*, 25–85.

56 McKay, "Soviet Russia and the Negro," 61–5, 114–18. See also McKay's autobiography *A Long Way from Home* and his autobiographical novel, which Jean-Cristophe Cloutier and Brent Edwards recently restored, *Amiable with Big Teeth*.

57 Lee, *The Ethnic Avant-Garde*.

58 Mally, *Culture of the Future*.

59 Sheshukov, *Neistosvye revniteli*.

60 Dubovikov and Lanskii, *Iz istorii* MORPa.

61 Illes, *Vestnik inostrannoi literatury*, 121.

62 Lunacharsky, "Mezhdunarodnaia konferentsiia proletariskikh i revoliutsionnykh pisatelei."

63 RGALI, f. 2876 (the papers of M. Ia. Apletin), op. 1, ex. 2, l. 2.

64 Li, *China und China-Erfahrung in Leben und Werk von Anna Seghers*, 71–2.

65 Wright, *The God that Failed*, 115–62.

66 Cho, *Translation's Forgotten History*.

67 Dubovikov and Lanskii, *Iz istorii* MORPa, 504.

68 Wang-Chi Wong, *Politics and Literature in Shanghai*.

69 Dubovikov and Lanskii, *Iz istorii* MORPa, 518–27. For a more detailed history of NAPF, see Shea, *Leftwing Literature in Japan*.

70 Djagalov, "The Red Apostles," 396–422.

71 Dubovikov and Lanskii, *Iz istorii* MORPa., 530–1.

72 Ibid., 533–4. For a more detailed study of Japanese-Korean literary solidarity over this period, see Floyd, "Bridging the Colonial Divide."

73 Dubovikov and Lanskii, *Iz istorii* MORPa, 539–42.

74 Kim, "KAPF Literature in Modern Korean Literary History."

75 Wright, "The Initiates."

76 For the list of participants and transcripts of their (somewhat edited) speeches, see *Mezhdunarodnyi kongress pisatelei v zashchitu kul'tury, Parizh, iun' 1935*. This congress has been extensively analyzed in the section "Mezhdunarodnoe pisatel'skoe antifashistkoe predstavlenie v 3-x aktakh" of Frezinskii, *Pisateli i sovetskie vozhdi* and Clark, *Moscow, the Fourth Rome*, 169–209.

77 Zaheer, *The Light*.

78 For Mulk Raj Anand's entry into the Soviet orbit via British mediation, see Clark "Indian Leftist Writers of the 1930s Maneuver among India, London, and Moscow."

79 Mukharjee, "Writing as Activism," 59.

80 Hart, *Cesar Vallejo: A Literary Biography*, 157–211.

81 For the full list of participants, see Soller and Schneider, *II Congresso Internacional de Escritores Para la Defensa la Cultura*.

82 Sibichus, "Kul'tura Meksiki," 372.

83 Neruda, *Ispania v serdtse*.

84 The first inquiry about a possible Russian translation of Amado was sent to him by David Vygotsky in 1934, but Amado's reply was firm: "A novel such as my *Cacao* cannot be of interest to a people who has [Fyodor Gladkov's] *Cement.*" In Belyakova, *Russkii Amadu*, 35.

85 Kharitonova, "K istorii zhurnala *Inostrannaia literatura* i ego ispanskogo izdaniia." For the post-Stalin-era expansion of Soviet–Latin American literary engagements, see Kuteishchikova's memoir *Moskva-Meksiko-Moskva: doroga dlinoiu v zhizn'*.

86 Djagalov, "Literary Monopolists and the Forging of the Post-WWII People's Republic of Letters."

87 Dobrenko, "Conspiracy of Peace."

88 The International Peace Prize, awarded by the World Peace Council, has been frequently confused with the Stalin (as of 1957, Lenin) Peace Prize awarded by the Soviet state.

Chapter Two

1 Mal'tsev, *Tashkentskie vstrechi*. All in all, in the archive of the Soviet Union of Writers, there are over eighty folders devoted to the Afro-Asian Writers Association. RGALI f. 631, op. 2, ex. 6100–80.

2 Shridharani, "Pisateli stran Azii i Afriki v Tashkente." Translations of archival passages, here and elsewhere, are mine – RLD.

3 Ibid., l. 1–2.

4 A more extended treatment of Tashkent as a showcase Soviet city for the Third World was offered in Stronski, "Exporting Modernity."

5 Evans and Djagalov, "Moskau, 1960," 90.

6 Shridharani, "Pisateli stran Azii i Afriki v Tashkente," 8.

7 Davidson "Chto takoe Mavritaniia?"

8 For a history of North American Soviet studies, see Engerman, *Know Your Enemy*.

9 Katsakioris, "The Lumumba University in Moscow."

10 RGALI f. 631 Writers Union, op. 2, ex. 6100, l. 1. Krishnalal Shridharani was not alone in wondering "where were the more famous names such as Sholokhov, Ehrenburg, Dudintsev, and Pasternak, who received a Nobel Prize for literature soon after the [Tashkent] Congress of Afro-Asian Writers." As early as 1956, in a discussion of the Soviet Committee for Solidarity with Africa and Asia, its deputy head and Tajik writer Mirzo Tursun-Zade expressed apprehension that the Defence of Peace initiatives are focused on Europe and attract the major Russian writers while delegations of the Soviet Committee for Solidarity with Africa and Asia seem exclusively Central Asian. GARF, f. 9540, op. 1, ex. 2, l. 15.

11 For the most compelling account of that decline, see Prashad, *The Darker Nations*, 119–275.

12 For the most comprehensive account of this literary opening to the West, see Gilburd, *To See Paris and Die*, 103–57.

13 For a comparison between the two and a history of *Foreign Literature*, see Baer, "From International to Foreign."

14 Prashad, *The Darker Nations*, 51–61.

15 Clark, "Indian Leftist Writers of the 1930s," 63–87.

16 Desai, "The Asian Writers' Conference December 1956."

17 RGANI f. 3, op. 34, ex. 205, l. 45.

18 For the classical history of CCF, see Saunders, *The Cultural Cold War*.

19 RGANI f. 5, op. 55, ex. 103, l. 169.

20 Ibid., l. 170–1.

21 A full-fledged account of these journals could be found in Scott-Smith and Lerg, *Campaigning Culture and the Cold War*. See also Kalliney, "Modernism, African Literature, and the CIA."

22 For a more detailed discussion of this subsidy, on the Soviet and American side, see the interview with Arun Som in Bachman, *Bollywood and Bolsheviks*.

23 For Soviet reports monitoring with apprehension the growth of the *negritude* movement in the mid-1950s, see RGALI f. 631, op. 26, ex. 4806. For the resolution not to invite Diop to Tashkent, see RGANI f. 5, op. 36, ex. 63, l. 1.

24 Dudziak, *Cold War Civil Rights*.

25 Stenogramma podgotovitel'nogo komiteta kongressa Afro-aziatskikh pisatelei, Alma-Ata (12.06.1973), Moscow. RGALI f. 631, op. 27, ex. 1365, l. 50.

26 Marcuse's "Essay on Liberation" was published, with an appropriate preface and for limited distribution, by Progress Publishers in 1970. The same year Batalov's critical volume *"Novye levye," and Herbert Marcuze* was published.

27 Transcript of literary scholar's discussion of the forthcoming symposium of the Afro-Asian Writers Association in Tashkent (18.06.1968). RGALI f. 631, op. 27, ex. 467, l. 19–51.

28 Bourdieu, *Distinction*, 97–256.

29 Shridharani, "Pisateli stran Azii i Afriki v Tashkente," 5, 8.

30 The Eastern European presence was occasionally questioned, for example, by Yoshie Hotta, the Japanese representative at the Association's Permanent Bureau, who expressed unhappiness at seeing a Yugoslav text in *Lotus*. RGALI f. 631, op. 27, ex. 767, l. 33.

31 RGALI f. 631, op. 30, ex. 1590, l. 25. Signed between the Egyptian president Anwar El Sadat and the Israeli prime minister Menachem Begin on 17 September 1978, the Camp David Accords paved the way for an Egypt-Israel Peace Treaty, which broke the hitherto united ranks of Arab countries opposed to Israel.

32   "General Declaration of the Fourth Meeting of the Executive Committee of the Afro-Asian Writers, 13–15 March, 1976. Baghdad-Iraq."

33   For example, at the 1973 Alma-Ata Congress, Chinghiz Aitmatov made realism the centrepiece of his speech and proposed to the rest of the Soviet delegation to follow suit. RGALI f. 631 op. 27, ex. 1365, l 60.

34   Ngũgĩ, interview.

35   Transcript of the Soviet Committee for Relations with the Writers of Africa and Asia and Soviet Preparatory Committee for the Alma-Ata Congress of Afro-Asian Writers, RGALI f. 631, op. 27, ex. 1365, l. 85.

36   RGALI f. 631, op. 30, ex. 1869, l. 65.

37   Ibid., l. 80. La Guma was of course a familiar quantity to the Soviet cultural bureaucracies, having previously visited the country multiple times and even written a loyal, though not thoroughly idealizing, book about it in a genre many writers sympathetic to the USSR were encouraged to practise. La Guma's *A Soviet Journey* (Moscow: Progress Publishers, 1978) largely draws on the six weeks he spent in the USSR in 1975. Recently, Christopher Lee has made this travelogue available in a new edition, with a sixty-page introduction.

38   Thanks to Jessica Bachman's ongoing work, the case of Progress Publishers books providing tens of millions of Indian readers with affordable access to Russian literature, popular science, and Marxist scholarship has been best understood. See Bachman's oral histories with Indian readers and translators at *Bollywood and Bolsheviks*.

39   See, for example, W.E.B. Du Bois's recollections of the inaugural Tashkent conference in his 1968 autobiography and the Japanese writer Kato Shuichi's account of the same event in his memoir *A Sheep's Song*. Both are more focused on their admiration of Tashkent's modernity (and the developmentalist model the USSR offered to the Third World) than on meeting other writers.

40   Lorde, "Notes from a Trip to Russia." I am grateful to Jennifer Wilson for pointing out this travelogue to me.

41   Ibid., 22–5.

42   Ibid., 22, 26–7.

43   Surkov, "O perspektivakh pisatel'skogo dvizheniia stran Azii i Afriki," RGANI f. 5, op. 36, ex. 149, l. 161–4.

44   RGALI 631, op. 26, ex. 6186, l. 1–4.

45   There is only one English-language study of the writings of this figure of the Afro-Asian Writers Association: Ramsay, *The Novels of an Egyptian Romanticist*.

46   The fate of the pro-Chinese Colombo-based bureau is the subject of Yoon, "Our Forces Have Redoubled."

47   RGANI f. 5, op. 55, ex. 46, l. 129.

48 For a more detailed, content-based study of the magazine, see Azab, "Dar el-Odaba"; Halim, "Lotus, the Afro-Asian Nexus, and Global South Comparatism." Other recent scholarship on Lotus include Kassamali, "'You Had No Address'"; Ghouse, "Lotus Notes" and Tariq Mehmood's Lotus Project, based at the American University in Beirut.

49 RGALI f. 631, op. 27, ex. 627, l. 20.

50 Faiz's proposal and the preliminary labour on which it is based, could be found here: RGALI f. 631, op. 26, ex. 6164.

51 Ironically, sixteen years after this proposal, in 1979, Faiz would become Lotus's editor after its offices were forced to migrate from Cairo to Beirut. See Kassamali, "'You Had no Address'."

52 RGALI F. 631, op. 27, d. 628, l. 9 (27 June 1969).

53 RGALI F. 631, op. 26, ex. 6164, l. 24.

54 Liudmila Vasilieva, Faiz's personal Russian translator during his regular visits to Moscow, describes his conflicts with Soviet cultural bureaucracies, who sought a clearer alignment between the magazine and the Association's geopolitical goals. Vasilieva, interview.

55 Anatoly Sofronov would periodically propose to the leadership of the Writers Union to publish the magazine in Russian, but apparently unsuccessfully. RGALI f. 631, op. 30, ex. 2337, l. 51.

56 RGALI F. 631, op. 27, d. 628, l. 10 (27 June 1969).

57 All article titles are drawn from Lotus's fifth issue published on April 1970.

58 Anderson, Imagined Communities, 33. A more detailed study of the contents of the magazine could be found in Halim's "Lotus, the Afro-Asian Nexus, and Global South Comparatism" and Duncan Yoon's forthcoming manuscript.

59 Of course, tribute was paid to the cultural bureaucrats running the Association: its head Yusuf al-Sibai and the head of the Soviet Committee for Solidarity with Africa and Asia Anatoly Sofronov received the two 1974 awards.

60 Stenogramma zasedaniia Postoiannogo Biuro APSAA o prisuzhdenii premii Lotos afro-aziatskim pisateliam (22.06.1970). RGALI f. 631, op. 27, ex. 767.

61 Ibid., 79–85.

62 RGALI f. 631, op. 30, ex. 2337, l. 45.

63 Lydia Liu, "After Tashkent."

64 Khotimsky, "World Literature, Soviet Style"; Tyulenev, "Vsemirnaia Literatura."

65 Khotimsky, "World Litrature, Soviet Style," 151.

66 Petrov, K istorii izdatel'stva Progress, 5.

67 For the cosmopolitanism of 1930s Moscow, see Clark, Moscow, the Fourth Rome, 79–104.

68 Petrov, K istorii izdatel'stva Progress, 80–1.

69   After the communist consolidation of power in East European countries,
      foreign language presses began to appear in Warsaw, Sofia, Bucharest, Budapest,
      Belgrade, Hanoi, and on a somewhat bigger scale, East Berlin, Tirana, and
      Beijing. Most of them (except for the GDR's Seven Seas Publishers, which was
      focused on translating its national literature into English) published texts about
      their country, its history, and contemporary achievements. The Chinese version
      (Foreign Languages Press), which still exists, was particularly active during
      the Sino-Soviet split and Cultural Revolution. From 1966, it began printing
      in multiple languages one of the world's absolute bestsellers, *Quotations from
      Chairman Mao* (aka the *Little Red Book*).

70   Ibid., 67, 108.

71   Progress ran several series on contemporary Western scholarship, such as
      *Critique of Bourgeois Ideology and Revisionism, Western Economic Thought,
      Social Sciences Abroad.* While outwardly critical of the Western theories and
      philosophies they were dedicated to, these series offered generous summaries of
      them, thus providing unique access to the adroit Soviet reader, who would easily
      skip the criticism. In addition, it published politically sensitive material such as
      the writings of Zigmund Brzezinski, Henry Kissinger, and Leonard Schapiro
      for pre-approved audiences or at least for research libraries. For more on these
      series, see Petrov, *K istorii izdatel'stva Progress*, 108.

72   The most sustained effort in that direction was conducted in a recent volume
      The East Was Read: Socialist Culture in the Third World, edited by Vijay
      Prashad, where a number of readers active in the 1960s–80s, primarily from
      India but also from China and Latin America, reflect on their relationship with
      Soviet books.

73   GARF f. 9590, op. 1, ex. 503, l. 1–2.

74   Vasilieva, interview.

75   The issue of royalties is a complex one. Generally, the Soviet Union joined
      the Geneva Copyright Convention in 1973, which obliged Soviet publishing
      houses to pay royalties to the foreign writers they published. But even prior to
      that, Soviet publishers would pay royalties to writers who were too important,
      too insistent, or badly in need of the money. Whether the money was paid in
      rubles (and thus could only be used in the USSR) or in foreign currency was
      another matter.

76   Calculations are based on the catalogue of the magazine for the first two decades
      of its existence: *Inostrannaia literatura: ukazatel' soderzhaniia, 1955–1974*.

77   Livergant, interview.

78   Kozlov, *The Readers of Novyi Mir*.

79 RGALI f. 1573, op. 3, ex. 188, l. 20–1

80 RGALI f. 1573 op. 1, ex. 22, l. 171.

81 Ibid., l. 125.

82 See the memoir by a member of the Central Committee's International section, Brutents, *Tridtsat' let na Staroi Ploshchadi*, 136, 245–7.

83 While it is nearly impossible for translations from one national literature into another to reflect fully the state of affairs in the former, over the course of the Stalin era, alternative canons of contemporary national literatures were created in the USSR, consisting of left-wing writers sympathetic to the Soviet state. (Something similar was done during the Cold War to Soviet-bloc literature in the West.) During the Thaw period, the bias remained in much more subdued form. See Friedberg, *A Decade of Euphoria*. This phenomenon is also discussed by visiting foreign writers such as Shridharani, "Pisateli stran Azii i Afriki v Tashkente," 3–4.

84 Protokol zasedania Sovetskogo komiteta solidarnosti stran Azii i Afriki po podgotovke k Almatinskomu kongressu afro-aziatskikh pisatelei (12-go iulia 1973, Moskva). RGALI f. 631, op. 27, ex. 1365, l. 50.

85 RGALI f. 631, op. 27, ex. 1795, l. 4.

86 RGANI f. 5, op. 11, ex. 437, l. 181.

87 Nearly forgotten in post-Soviet Russia, Nesin enjoyed immense popularity among Soviet readers, judging by my preliminary studies of a few Moscow libraries. Available in many editions, his collections of short stories were by far the most frequently checked-out items of contemporary African and Asian literature in the 1980s, easily besting in this respect many Soviet favourites of Western literature.

88 For this explanation of the educational function of the magazine, I am obliged to Bessmertnaya, interview.

89 While in the case of foreign prose published in the USSR the authorship of the introduction and translation would be important in determining whether the reader would pick it up in the first place, for poetry it was the single most decisive factor. Vasileva, Interview.

90 Ibid.

91 Such an account of the organization's gradual decline could be found in the report the leader of the Soviet delegation to the Tunis Congress, Yevgeny Sidorov, had to deliver to the Soviet Writers Union. RGALI f. 631, op. 30, ex. 2337, l. 42–56.

92 All these plans are recorded in the Arabic section of the internal Bulletin of the Soviet Writers Union, *Literaturnaia zhizn' za rubezhom*, 20–22.

93 The idea to establish a Russian version of *Lotus* or include Latin America had
    been floated for decades but had come to nothing.

94 The final international gathering of the Association took place in Istanbul,
    in December 1990, and was hosted by the Turkish writer Aziz Nesin.
    Vlasova, interview.

Chapter Three

1 Jameson, "Third-World Literature in the Age of Multinational Capitalism," 65, 69.

2 For one of the most famous and trenchant rejoinders, see Ahmad "Jameson's
   Rhetoric of Otherness and the 'National Allegory.'" This debate and the
   different position taken in it have been analyzed in Szeman, "Who's Afraid of
   National Allegory."

3 Prashad, *The Darker Nations,* xv.

4 Booker and Juraga, "The Reds and the Blacks."

5 Drews-Sylla, "Ousmane Sembène's Hybrid 'Truth.'"

6 Clark, *The Soviet Novel.*

7 This institutional aspect is best described in Dobrenko, *The Making of the
   State Writer.*

8 Denning, *Culture in the Age of Three Worlds,* 51–72.

9 Anderson, "Internationalism: a Breviary."

10 Ibid., 18.

11 Ibid., 16.

12 Remembered today as an Italian nationalist, Giuseppe Garibaldi was a
   profoundly internationalist figure. After the defeat of the Italian Republic, he
   fought for a decade as a soldier for progressive causes in Brazil and Uruguay,
   was offered a leadership position in the Union army during the Civil War (a
   proposition, as Anderson notes, that Garibaldi rejected, rightly suspecting
   Lincoln's attitude to slavery), and finally was elected a deputy of the French
   National Assembly for his services to the Third French Republic in the
   immediate aftermath of the Franco-Prussian War of 1870. See Anderson,
   "Internationalism: A Breviary," 10–11.

13 Gavin O'Toole and Georgina Jimenez's anthology *Che in Verse* with poetry by
   Allen Ginsberg, Yevgeny Yevtushenko, Derek Waltcott, and a number of Latin
   American writers testifies to Che's poetic resonance among the leading literary
   representatives of the 1960s generation.

14 Gorky, *Mother,* 47.

15   Anderson, *Imagined Communities*, 22–36.

16   Vallejo, *Tungsten*, 112.

17   Ngũgĩ, *A Grain of Wheat*, 156.

18   Ibid., 107–8.

19   Anand, *The Sword and the Sickle*, 133.

20   Hikmet, *Human Landscapes from My Country*, 362–403; Neruda, "Let the
     Woodcutter Awaken" from *Canto General*, 255–2.

21   Hikmet, *Human Landscapes*, 391.

22   Feinstein, *Pablo Neruda*, 323.

23   Neruda, *Canto General*, 264–5.

24   Hikmet, *Human Landscapes*, 396–8.

25   Han, "Nâzım Hikmet's Afro-Asian Solidarities."

26   Ngũgĩ, *Petals of Blood*, 137–8.

27   Ibid., 404.

28   Ibid., viii; Yoon, "Our Forces Have Redoubled," 239.

29   La Guma, *The Stone-Country*, 49.

30   Sembène, *The Last of the Empire*, 37.

31   Interestingly, *Tobacco* was also the title of Dimitar Talev's great 1951 novel. The
     pre-communist setting as well as the decisive role of foreign capital as a narrative
     agent of Talev's novel makes it closer to a third-worldist supply-chain narrative
     than a Soviet production novel like Fyodor Gladkov's *Cement* (1925) or Nikolai
     Ostrovsky's *How the Steel Was Tempered* (1936). Note, however, the common
     preoccupation with raw materials, their extraction and processing in leftist
     novels within and without state socialism.

32   The exploits of United Fruit will even be sung in poetry, as in Pablo Neruda's
     "La United Fruit Co.," a part of his epic poem *Canto General*.

33   Marquez, "The Andean Novel."

34   For a detailed account of the Latin American dictator novels, see Echevarria,
     The Voices of the Masters, 64–85.

35   Bell-Villada, *Garcia Marquez's One Hundred Years of Solitude*, 131.

36   Lukács proposed the concept of "totality" – as something lost in modernity –
     already in his early pre-Marxist essay *Theory of the Novel* (1916).

37   Written during his Soviet period as he was participating in polemics over
     socialist realism, Lukác's essays "Narrate and Describe" and "Realism in the
     Balance" (a polemic with modernism) capture a more mature and more clearly
     Soviet version of "totality."

38   Fore, *Realism After Modernism*, 75–132.

39 Extensive treatments of the valences of the train in British and North American fiction could be found in Daly, *Literature, Technology, and Modernity, 1860–2000* and Burns, *The Railroad in Modern American Fiction.*

40 It is telling that one of the chronologically last Western European railway narratives that has come to my attention is Raymond Williams' *Border Country* (1960), the story of a son, now a university lecturer in London, who visits his sick father, a once-militant railway union leader-turned-cynical-small-time contractor. If in Western Europe the waning of railway narratives, and more generally, of the proletarian novel, was largely due to class transformations, in the United States an added factor was the disappearance of the railways themselves.

41 See the collection of essays edited by Clarence Davis, Kenneth Wilburn, and Ronald Robinson entitled *Railway Imperialism* as well as Spiers, *Engines for Empire;* Earle, *Turkey, the Great Powers, and the Bagdad Railway.*

42 Hikmet, *Human Landscapes from my Country,* 25.

43 As early as his 1935 novel *Untouchable,* Anand employs the railway motif as a vehicle for exploring the profound ambivalence of modernity and representing the humanity of third-class carriages.

44 Anand, *The Village,* 9.

45 Anand, *The Sword and the Sickle,* 319.

46 Curto, "Technology Transfer, the Railway and Independence in Ousmane Sembène's Les bouts de bois de Dieu."

47 Sembène, *God's Bits of Wood,* 241.

48 Ibid., 210.

49 Curto, "Technology Transfer, Railway, and Independence."

50 Jameson, "Third-World Literature in the Age of Multinational Capitalism," 69.

51 These debates are captured in the opening of Katerina Clark's "The Mutability of the Canon: Socialist Realism and Chinghiz Aitmatov's *I dol'she veka dlitsia den'.*

52 Asanalieva, personal communication, 20 April 2017.

53 Testifying to the longevity of the railway narrative's critique in the post-Soviet era, the novella *The Dead Lake* (2011), written in Russian by the Uzbek Hamid Ismailov, radicalizes some of the critical motifs of *The Day Lasts More than a Hundred Years.* The setting of Ismailov's novella (the Kara Shagan way station of the East Kazakhstan Railway) is even more remote than Aitmatov's Buranly: "the way station (which everyone called a 'spot') ... consisted of two railway houses. ... And that was the entire population of Kara Shagan, if you didn't count the fifty or so sheep, three donkeys, two camels, and the horse, Aigyr" (15–16). Unlike Aitmatov, Ismailov pulls fewer punches in depicting the extreme unevenness of Soviet modernization, which ranges from Moscow's cultural richness –

Oistraikh and Dean Read – to the poverty of cultural opportunities in this desolate province. The fenced-off rocket-launching cosmodrome in Aitmatov's novel (an allusion to Baikonur), which physically stands in the way of the burial procession to the old Ana-Beyit cemetery, becomes the deadly Zone (a nuclear explosion site) with its Dead Lake, a dip into which renders our protagonist a dwarf, thus destroying his life. Ismailov, *The Dead Lake*.

54 Clark, "The Mutability of the Canon," 574–5.
55 Yountchi, "Between Russia and Iran."
56 Yashen, "Tashkent-Kair," 117–22.
57 This use of Soviet internationalism to extract resources from reluctant Moscow bureaucrats has been reconstructed by Artemy Kalinovsky in his study of Soviet Tajikistan, *Laboratory of Socialist Development*.
58 Kudaibergenova, *Rewriting the Nation in Modern Kazakh Literature*, 123–49.
59 Alimzhanov, "Pylaiushchee kop'e," 321.
60 Ibid.
61 Kudaibergenova, *Rewriting the Nation*, 131.
62 Ibid. 149–72; Naomi Caffee, "Between First, Second, and Third Worlds."
63 For a study of Suleimenov's *Azi i Ya* and a coverage of the scandal that followed its publication, see Ram, "Imagining Eurasia."
64 Suleimenov, *No liudiam ia ne lgal*, 22.

Chapter Four

1 Kirasirova, "The Eastern International," 360–7, 372–5.
2 O.A. Mertsedin's twenty-seven well-annotated photographs of the 1958 festival can be found in the Russian State Documentary Film and Photo Archive (RGAKFD), 1–117845 to 1–117873. Of the dozen or so foreign participants mentioned in the issue I was able to identify only the Egyptian actor-cum-director Hussein Sidki and his compatriot, the actress Madiha Yousri. See "Dukh Bandunga v zhizni i iskusstve."
3 Ibid., 77.
4 RGALI f. 2918, op. 4, ex. 106, l. 16–19.
5 There had been, of course, the one-off 1935 First International Film Festival in Moscow, but its proposed sequel in 1936 was cancelled and it was not until the Thaw era that another inaugural First International Film Festival in Moscow took place. See *Istoriia kinootrasli*, 570–84.
6 An organizing committee led by Ivan Pyr'ev had been in existence since 1957. See Fomin, *Isstoria kinootrasli v Rossii*, 1147–9.

7   This division of labour between Soviet literature and cinema could be traced back to their institutional locations. From its very beginning in 1934, the Soviet Writers Union in 1934, with its publishing houses, magazines, and Foreign Commission, was formally put under the charge of the Central Committee of the Communist Party. By contrast, most Soviet cinema institutions (Goskino and Sovexportfilm) belonged to the Soviet government apparatus and were thus much more concerned with making and meeting budgets.

8   Miller, *Kino*, 24.

9   The main state companies in charge of Soviet film trade in the 1920s were Kinoexportimport and Soyuzkinoexport, which merged in 1932 to form a single organization with a monopoly on foreign film trade, Soyuzintorgfilm. The latter was reorganized in 1945 into Sovexportfilm (SEF), which lost that monopoly only in November 1989.

10   For the most comprehensive list of foreign film on Soviet screens, see sujs, "Zarubezhnye fil'my v prokate SSSR i RF, 1933–1993."

11   Kepley, "The Workers' International Relief and the Cinema of the Left, 1921–1935," 16–17.

12   Salazkina, "Eisenstein in Latin America"; Wells, "Parallel Modernities?"; Chan, *Chinese Revolutionary Cinema*.

13   Wells, "Parallel Modernities," 160–9.

14   Salazkina, "Moscow-Rome-Havana."

15   Laikwan, *Building a New China in Cinema*.

16   Ibid., 144–7.

17   Fedorova, "Formirovanie shkoly montazhnoi vyrazitel'nosti v iaponskom dokumental'nom kino 1930x-50x godov," 32–46.

18   According to Fedorova, *Pamir* (Schneiderov, 1928), *Turksib* (Turin, 1929), *Oasis in the Sand* (Klado, 1931), *Great Tokyo* (Schneiderov, 1932), and *Cheliuskin* (Posel'skii, 1934) entered commercial distribution in Japan in the late 1920s and early 1930s. Ibid., 38–9.

19   See Leyda's article on the first Tashkent festival, "Filme aus Asien und Afrika," 1678–80.

20   RGALI f. 2944, op. 13, d. 1204, l. 155.

21   See the statistics in Appendix A of Belodubrovskaia, *Not According to Plan*, 227–8.

22   Of the gigantic trophy film collection, 86 were released between 1946 and 1953 – mostly American but also German, French, Italian, British, and Austrian ones, all made in the decade and a half before the end of the Second World War. By

comparison, during that period, 89 new Soviet films and 115 legally purchased foreign ones entered domestic distribution. For a more comprehensive study of the trophy film phenomenon and more detailed statistics, see Knight, "Stalin's Trophy Films (1946–1956)."

23 See the complete list of foreign films screened in the USSR, see sujs, "Zarubezhnye fil'my v prokate SSSR i RF, 1933–1993."

24 Rajagopalan, "Emblematic of the Thaw."

25 As early as 1936, Soyuzintorg was selling films to Cuba, Colombia, Puerto Rico, China, Japan, Iran, Turkey, Palestine, and Syria. At the very beginning of the Second World War, India, Egypt, and Iraq were added to this list. See *Istoriia kinootrasli v Rossii*, 556, 794.

26 For the production and reception history of this blockbuster, see Mëhilli, "Globalized Socialism, Nationalized Time," 620–5.

27 That particular generation of Bulgarian film directors, for example, largely comprises VGIK graduates. See "Bulgarski kinematografisti."

28 The complete lists of VGIK alumni from Africa, Asia, and Latin America were kindly provided to me by Tatiana Fazylovna Tursunova, head of the university's international department. For scholarship on VGIK's African graduates, see Chomentowski "L'expérience soviétique des cinémas africains au lendemain des indépendances," 11; Chomentowski, "Going Abroad to Study the Craft of Filmmaking," 27–31; and Woll, "The Russian Connection: Soviet Cinema and the Cinema of Francophone Africa."

29 Genova, *Cinema and Development in West Africa*, 131–2.

30 This suspicion many of his classmates faced was described to me by the Russo-Chilean filmmaker Sebastián Alarcón. He would have confronted it in extreme form had he returned to Pinochet-ruled Chile upon his graduation in 1974, but the Soviet authorities exempted him from the requirement to return to his country upon graduation, thus making him one of the very few foreign-trained VGIK graduate to have had his cinematic career in the USSR. Alarcón, Interview.

31 Czechoslovak cinema's Third World connections have recently become the subject of Tereza Stejskalova's excellent bilingual anthology: *Filmmakers of the World.*

32 Ebbrecht-Hartman, "Socialist Competition or Window to the West," 17–18.

33 The little that could be gleaned about his time there could be found in Josephine Woll's pioneering "The Russian Connection."

34 See Monica Popescu's elegant reading of the latter film, "On the Margins of the Black Atlantic," 91–109.

35   Kouoh and Salti, *Saving Bruce Lee*, 15.

36   Akira Kurosawa's *Rashomon* (1950) was the first non-Western film to win a major film festival prize (Venice's Golden Lion in 1951), symbolically marking Japanese film's breakthrough onto the world stage.

37   RGALI f. 2944, op. 13, e.x. 1200, l. 22–5.

38   RGALI f. 2936, op. 4, ex. 1841, l. 47.

39   RGALI f. 2944, op. 13, e.x. 1200, l. 48.

40   Ibid., e.x. 1202, l. 5–6.

41   Ibid., l. 118.

42   RGALI f. 2936, op. 4, ex. 1841, l. 41.

43   RGALI f. 2944, op. 13, e.x. 1200, l. 81–91.

44   Ibid., l. 27.

45   For the number of films and sales in 1968, see RGALI f. 2918, op. 6, ex. 28, l. 12. For the 1972 figures, see RGALI f. 2944, op. 26, d52, l. 19.

46   RGALI f. 2918, op. 6, ex. 28, l. 12

47   RGALI f 2936, op. 4, ex. 1835, l. 4–5.

48   For the international popularity of Indian film, see Iordanova, "Indian Cinema's Global Reach."

49   Moine, *Screened Encounters*, 157–86.

50   Camara, "From Karlovy Vary to Cannes," 63–76.

51   Since 1968, a few more were established: the Pan-African Film and Television Festival in Ougadougou (Burkina Fasso) in 1969, the short-lived Tehran International Film Festival (1972–79) under the patronage of the Shah, the Cairo Film Festival in 1976, and the openly political Havana Festival of New Latin American Cinema in 1978.

52   Numerous references to them could be found in RGALI f. 2944, op. 13.

53   To enable the participation of Arab filmmakers, the Tashkent organizers had to arrange for a special Aeroflot flight to transport the participants in the Carthage film festival, which was scheduled at the end of September 1968, days before the Tashkent festival.

54   In such cases, the improvisational capacity of Soviet interpreters often saved the day. See Razlogova, "Listening to the Inaudible Foreign."

55   Razlogova, "The Politics of Translation of Soviet Film Films during the Cold War," 66, 74.

56   "Pervyi somaliiskii." *Iskusstvo Kino* 1(January 1969): 134.

57   Except for the first, eighth, and tenth festivals, transcripts of all the seminars were published under the title *Kino v bor'be za mir, sotsial'nyi progress i svobodu*

narodov (tvorcheskaia diskussia na Mezhdunarodnom kinofestivale v Tashkente) a few months after each festival by the Research Institute for the History and Theory of Cinema in Moscow.

58 Chertok, "Kino chernoi Afriki."

59 Ibid.

60 See Mestman, "From Algiers to Buenos Aires" and "Algiers-Buenos Aires-Montreal." For more specifically African initiatives, see the "Niamey Manifesto of African Filmmakers," 111–16.

61 Compare this list, distilled from the filmmakers' seminar booklets, with the "Resolutions of Third-World Filmmakers in Algiers, December 1973," 155–65. While Soviet cinema was not represented at the Algiers gathering, some of the leading figures in attendance such as Sembène Ousmane and Med Hondo were also Tashkent regulars.

62 For the arguments, see Mestman, "Algiers-Buenos Aires-Montreal," 32–7.

63 See the "Resolutions of the Third-World Filmmakers Committee."

64 For an example of the last one, see Shukhrat Abbasov's long speech about the successes of Soviet Central Asian (and especially Uzbek) cinemas in *Kino v bor'be za mir* (1978), 12–15.

65 Eichenberger, "The Second World Organizes a Festival for the Third," 100.

66 Ibid.

67 Kumar, "Tashkent Promises a Cinematic Brotherhood," 85.

68 Rajagopalan, *Indian Films in Soviet Cinemas*, 5–8.

69 This and other viewership statistics used in this chapter are drawn from the list composed by film scholar Sergei Kudriavtsev, "Poseshchaemost' otechestvennykh i zarubezhnykh fil'mov v sovetskom prokate," which serves as the basis for the Kinopoisk.ru database "SSSR: Samye kassovye fil'my." The viewership numbers should not be thought of as absolute: they are based on the statistics of the first fifteen months after the film's release and do not reflect specialized screenings or TV audiences. The decision on the extent of the film's advertisement, number of copies that circulated, and the length and geography of the film screenings always retained an element of arbitrariness and sometimes reflected the relevant officials' desire to promote or restrict the film.

70 Rajagopalan, *Indian Films in Soviet Cinemas*, 29–65.

71 Ibid., 120, 127, 134, 143.

72 Roth-Ey, *Moscow Prime Time*, 43–5. In a subsequent paper delivered at the 2018 ASEEES convention, "We, as Commercial People, Understand," Roth-Ey has deepened her exploration of the profit-mindedness of SEF officials.

73   This said, SEF did purchase significant numbers of American action film and French and Italian comedies, which also filled Soviet film theatres. Oleg Sulkin (former vice-president of Sovexportfilm), personal communication, 22 July 2018.

74   It was not only Soviet audiences who flocked to Indian films in that period but also their peers from Eastern and Western Europe, Africa, Asia, Latin America. See Iordanova, "Indian Cinema's Global Reach."

75   Roth-Ey, *Moscow Prime Time*, 44.

76   For comparison purposes, the most watched film screened in post-Soviet Russia, *Avatar* (Cameron, 2009), was seen by 14 million viewers, significantly lower than the 1,000th most watched film in the USSR. For post-Soviet Russian statistics, since their resumption in 2004, see "Distributors' Database of New Film Releases."

77   M. Chernenko. "Pochtovoi perevod," 142–3.

78   For *Money Order*'s pathway to Soviet commercial distribution, see sujs, "Zarubezhnye fil'my v prokate SSSR i RF, 1933–1993."

79   RGANI f. 5, op. 90, ex. 223, l. 77–8.

80   According to Goskino data for domestic film distribution for the pre-perestroika era, each copy of a Soviet film was seen on average by 10,000 viewers while a foreign one would attract 15,000. Vorontsov, *Sotsiologicheskie problemy prokata*, 150.

81   According to Marina Ivanovna Kosinova, the plan for foreign films to be purchased and released in the USSR in the early 1960s, which more or less remained in place until perestroika, included seventy films from socialist countries, thirty films from developing countries, and twenty-five to thirty films from capitalist countries (including five to six American ones). See Kosinova, "Mezhdunarodnye otnosheniia sovetskoi kinematografii i epokhi 'ottepeli'," 638.

82   Ibid., 636. In the interest of fairness, Soviet films seeking foreign audiences were subjected to similar censorship. General Abdel Nasser famously banned Mark Donskoy's 1955 eponimous adaptation of Gorky's novel *Mother*.

83   Karlo Lebt and Sergei Kudriavtsev, personal communication, 22 July 2018. I am inclined to side with Karlo Lebt as Güney's name does not appear in any list of potential Tashkent invitees that I have seen. Most likely, he had made statements or sided with the wrong Turkish political groups, thus becoming uninvitable by Soviet authorities.

84   See the entry for *The Battle of Algiers* in sujs, "Zarubezhnye fil'my v prokate SSSR i RF, 1933–1993." I was not able to find such statements or signatures by Pontecorvo, but if they do exist, they would have also been a reason for his not coming to Tashkent. As an Italian filmmaker, who had once abandoned his

membership in CPI over its support for the Soviet invasion of Hungary in 1956, he would hardly have applauded the Warsaw Pact invasion of Czechoslovakia.

85 Part II of the film *The Coup d'Etat* was screened at the Fourth Tashkent Festival in 1976 and Guzmán himself attended it. According to Tatiana Vetrova, the leading Russian specialist in Latin American cinema, SEF almost never purchased documentary film. Personal communication, 7 September 2017.

86 When perestroika significantly reduced the censorship demands of foreign films and the revolutionary radicalism of Third Cinema had subsided, Fernando Solanas's *Tangos, Exile of Gardel* (1986) and Paul Leduc's *Frida, Still Life* (1983) were released in the USSR.

87 The Simorgh is a benevolent bird in Iranian literature and mythology.

88 Artemenko and Pavlyuchik, "Net prazdnika bez zvezd."

89 Brashinskii et al., "S militseiskoi migalki v poiskakh kino."

90 Ibid., 107.

91 Alarcón, interview.

Chapter Five

1 Other Marker films such as *The Train Rolls On* (1973) and *The Last Bolshevik* (1993), which deal with the legacy of early Soviet documentarian Alexander Medvedkin, testify to his enduring interest in the Soviet avant garde. In a recent lecture, "Medium of Intimacy," Robert Bird has sought to illuminate the engagement between the two filmmakers.

2 Of course, a complete emancipation from Western cinema was never achieved. The influence of Italian neorealism and French New Wave has been extensively documented. See, for example, the chapter "Neorealism and Art Cinema" in Schroeder, *Latin American Cinema* and the chapter "Latin America" in Nowell-Smith, *Making Waves*.

3 Waugh, "*The 400 Million* (1938)," 7–17.

4 Most of that attention has come from abroad. See Hicks, *Dziga Vertov* and more recently, Barabat, "Roman Karmen"; Sidenova, "From Pravda to Verite."

5 Waugh, *The Conscience of Cinema*, 526.

6 See Gabriel's seminal study *Third Cinema in the Third World*.

7 The main manifestoes of Third Cinema, such as Glauber Rocha's "Aesthetic of Hunger" (1965), Julio Garcia Espinosa's "For an Imperfect Cinema" (1969), "Problems of Form and Content in Revolutionary Cinema" (1976), and most importantly, Fernando Solanas and Octavio Getino, "Towards a Third Cinema" (1969) can be found in Martin, *New Latin American Cinema*, vol. 1, 1–134.

8   Willemen, "The Third Cinema Question"; Wayne, *Political Film,* 25–47.

9   Malitsky, *Post-Revolutionary Nonfiction Film.*

10 For much more comprehensive studies of the reception of Soviet film in Latin America, see Salazkina, *In Excess*; Salazkina, "Eisenstein in Latin America"; Salazkina, "Moscow-Rome-Havana," 97–116; Wells, "Parallel Modernities?" discussed in the previous chapter.

11 Of the latter, only the Mexican Sergio Olhovich and comes to mind. All of the films of another possible candidate, Sebastián Alarcón were shot in the USSR/Russia. A graduate of the Czechoslovak FAMU, Octavio Cortazar is the only Cuban director of note to have been trained in Eastern Europe.

12 Chomentowski, "State Modernization in the Time of Decolonization."

13 A second wave of translation and popularization of early Soviet film theory in the West took place in the 1960s.

14 Chertok, *Tashkentskii kinofestival',* 77.

15 Pudovkin, *On Film Technique;* Pudovkin, *Film Acting;* Eisenstein, *The Film Sense.*

16 Majumdar, "Debating Radical Cinema," 743.

17 Ibid.

18 Solasnas and Getino, "Towards a Third Cinema," 41. By including Joris Ivens and Chris Marker in their manifesto, Solanas and Getino initiated a tradition of extending Third Cinema to European and North American filmmakers outside of the mainstream (Ibid., 35).

19 Solanas, "Interview with Louis Marcorelles," 42.

20 Quoted in Viany, "The Old and the New in Brazilian Cinema," 142.

21 Channan, *Cuban Cinema,* 30. We need not take Álvarez at his word: he was one of the founders of the Cuban Film Society, which did screen Vertov in the late 1950s. Besides, Soyuzintorgkino had been selling Soviet films to Cuba since the 1930s. See Fomin, *Istoriia kinootrasli v Rossii,* 556.

22 Brutents, *Tridsat' let na Staroi ploshchadi*; Gonzales, "Communism in Latin America."

23 Baskakov, "Boriuhchiisia ekran," 14.

24 For the most detailed study of foreign reception of Eisenstein's Battleship Potemkin, see Taylor, *Battleship Potemkin,* 98–120.

25 For a history of Mezhrabpomfilm, see Jamie Miller's "Soviet Politics and the Mezhrabpom Studio in the Soviet Union during the 1920s and 1930s."

26 For a comprehensive account of those, see Sarkisova, *Screening Soviet Nationalities.* For a history of Vostokkino, see Chomentowski, *Cinema in Central Asia,* 33–44.

27 Sarkisova, *Screening Soviet Nationalities*, 165–72.

28 Hirst, "Soviet Orientalism Across Borders."

29 In fairness, it has to be acknowledged that staging and re-enactment were common in most documentary traditions, such as the British Documentary Film Movement and the New Deal documentary. The purist anti-staging, anti-reenactment argument came later in the late 1950s with cinéma vérité.

30 Tseitlin, *Puteshestvie v Abissiniiu*.

31 Ivens, *The Camera and I*, 137; Miller, "The Fog of War."

32 Graham, *Forward, Soviet!*, 141–2.

33 Schoots, *Living Dangerously*, 59–64; Waugh, *The Conscience of Cinema*, 145–63.

34 Waugh, *The Conscience of Cinema*, 560.

35 Recognizing the multiplicity of authorships of the film, I will still attribute it to him.

36 Karmen, *No Passaran!*, 132.

37 For instances of this self-censorship and Popular-Front framing see Waugh, *The Conscience of Cinema*, 215–16.

38 Schoots, *Living Dangerously*, 120.

39 Needless to say, we cannot expect any mention from Vsevolod Vyshnevsky's narration of the sheer destructiveness of the Soviet struggle against Spanish anarchists and (real or imagined) Trotskyists, which opened a major rift within the Republican coalition, or in general, a more objective evaluation of the ambivalent role played by the Soviet state. For an account of that, see the chapter "Love and Death in the Time of the Spanish Civil War" from Clark, *Moscow, the Fourth Rome*, 242–73.

40 Waugh, *The Conscience of Cinema*, 248–9.

41 Waugh, "*The 400 Million* (1938)," 3–6. Portable synchronous-sound equipment, which did not become common until the 1960s, might have eased the problem.

42 Raisa Sidenova, personal communication, 18 April 2019.

43 See Alexander Markov's film *Our Africa* (2015) specifically devoted to this genre.

44 Musser, "Utopian Visions in Cold War Documentary."

45 Bonfiglioli, "Cold War Gendered Imaginaries."

46 The outcome of the First Indochina War fought between 1945 and 1954 was Vietnam's achievement of independence from its previous colonial rulers, France. In the Second (and best-known) Indochina War (1954–75), the US took up where the French had left off, set up a proxy government in South Vietnam, and fought North Vietnam, the Vietcong, and their allies in Laos and Cambodia. The Third Indochina War (1975–90) is a loose name for several skirmishes/ border wars among China, Vietnam, and Cambodia.

47 Barberis and Chapuis, *Roman Karmen: Documentaire Arte.*

48 Sidenova, "The Topographical Aesthetic."

49 Karmen, *No Passaran,* 207–27.

50 RGANI f. 5, op. 36, ex. 29, 157–61.

51 Waugh, "*Loin du Vietnam* (1967), Joris Ivens, and Left Bank Documentary."

52 Chanan, *Cuban Cinema,* 193.

53 Alter, *Chris Marker,* 68–9.

54 I have seen neither as they seem to be available only at the Ivens Foundation in Nijmegen, the Netherlands.

55 See Waugh, "*Travel's Notebooks,*" 25–9.

56 Massip, "Una lección de cine," 24–8.

57 Shoots, *Living Dangerously,* 269–70. For a full account of ICAIC, Michael Chanan, *Cuban Cinema,* 1–20.

58 Panizza, *Joris Ivens en Chile.*

59 RGALI f. 2936, op. 1, ex. 1534, l. 70.

60 Ibid., l. 70–1.

61 Ibid., l. 23.

62 Ibid., l. 24.

63 Drobashenko, *Kinorezhiser Joris Ivens.*

64 Shoots, *Living Dangerously,* 273.

65 Interview with Miguel Littin from *Cahiers du Cinema* (July/August 1974): 251–2. Cited in Chanan, *Chilean Cinema,* 53.

66 See footnote 19 as well as Stam, "The Two Avant-Gardes," 271–86.

67 Guzmán, "What I Owe Chris Marker." As Guzmán remarks, the timing of ICAIC's invitation was fortuitous as a year later (he may have been wrong by three years), when Marker's magisterial *A Grin without a Cat* (1977) appeared, featuring the episode of Fidel Castro justifying the Soviet crushing of the Prague Spring, the warm relationship that had existed between ICAIC and Marker came to an end.

68 Ibid.

69 A detailed investigation of Álvarez's films is beyond the scope of this book and has been conducted in Chanan, *Cuba Cinema,* 184–246; Malitsky, *Post-Revolutionary Non-Fiction Film,* 189–216.

70 For Cuba's (and Latin America's) special place in Soviet internationalism see Gorsuch, "'Cuba, My Love.'"

71 See, for example, *The Hot Wind of Freedom* (V. Komarov 1971) about Oman's independence struggle.

72 The memorializing tone becomes even more dominant in the immediate years after the coup when Karmen would return to his (and others') Chilean archives

to compile three post-coup solidarity films: *Chile: A Time of Struggle, a Time of Alarm* (1974), *Camarados-Comrades* (1974), and *Corvalan's Heart* (1975).

73 Lupton, *Chris Marker,* 109–47.

Epilogue

1 At the break-up of the USSR, it too broke up into numerous writers' associations in the post-Soviet space with none of them possessing the symbolic or financial power of its Soviet predecessor. In Russia alone, there are at least three such associations. Tellingly, it is the nationalist Union of Writers of Russia (UWR) that maintains the most active engagement with respect to non-Western literatures beyond the former Soviet space. In fact, UWR has become a founding member of a renewed Afro-Asian Writers Association, which has had its revival congress in Cairo in 2012 and has re-established *Lotus* (in Arabic only). More of this second iteration of AAWA and *Lotus* could be found in Hala Halim, "Afro-Asian Third-Worldism into Global South."

2 Kalashnikova, *Po-russki s liubov'iu,* 256.

3 The statistics of Russian viewership of foreign films by country between 2004 and 2019 could be found on the Database of New Film Releases on Russian Screens.

4 Ibid. Since statistics became available in 2004, a total of 5,300 films, Russian and foreign, have been released, increasing from 120 per year in 2004 to over 500 in 2018.

5 For a more detailed account of the presence of Latin American film in post-Soviet Russia, see Vetrova "Territoria latinoamerikanskogo kino na rossiiskom ekrane."

6 According to the Distributors' Database of New Film Releases, out of the 5,300 new releases since 2004, 2,370 (45%) have been American. Russian cinema is a distant second with 1,150 (22%).

7 In constructing these lists of African, Asian, and Latin American films, I am excluding Japanese films, which had by that point secured a place in the Western cinematic canon.

8 Chinese, Japanese, and Korean film studies may be the sole exception to this development, in part owing to the vibrancy of these cinemas, in part owing to the greater support by East Asian cultural agencies for this kind of scholarship in Russia.

9 For the post-1991 disappointment of many Russians with their Soviet-era ideal of the West, see Gilburd, *To See Paris and Die,* 319–39.

10 The Sova Center is the main non-governmental organization tracking racially and ethnically motivated violence in Russia. For their statistics for the last ten years, see https://www.sova-center.ru/database.

11 Solzhenitsyn, "Plamennaya Andzhela."

12 It is of course undeniable that (pro-)Soviet media made a great deal of US Jim Crow throughout the Cold War. Whatever their motivation (genuine anti-racism or a simple desire to tarnish the enemy), according to Mary Dudziak, they greatly facilitated the domestic Civil Rights struggle. See Dudziak, *Cold War Civil Rights*.

13 Novodorskaya, "Ne otdadim nashe otechestvo na levo."

14 See Latynina's radio shows on "Kod dostupa: avtorskaya peredacha."

15 For a more detailed analysis of this phenomenon, especially in relation to Russian diaspora, see Matusevich, "The Red and the Black."

16 Yudin, "Scratch a Russian Liberal and You'll Find an Educated Conservative."

17 Djagalov, "Anti-populizm postsotsialisticheskoi intelligentsii."

18 Gostavino, *Caen las Catedrales.*

19 See, for example, Ferrer, "Around the Sun," 99.

20 Of the seventy-five languages Radio Moscow broadcast at its peak, its successor – a purely propagandist news outlet by the name of Radio Sputnik – has retained only English and hardly any literary content can be found. Radio Moscow was the first radio to broadcast abroad and yet, unlike Radio Free Europe, BBC, and VOX, has remained strangely without any scholarly coverage. For Alexander Zhokovsky's recollections of his time in the Ethiopian section of Radio Moscow, see his *Stories from Yesteryears.*

21 Vasilieva, interview.

22 After Vladimir Danchev, a Soviet newscaster from the English-language section of Radio Moscow, denounced the Soviet intervention into Afghanistan over the course of several broadcasts in 1983, policies were further tightened.

23 For Arab students' reflection on their time in the USSR, see Litvin, "Fellow Travelers?" For the historical background on educational opportunities for African, Asian, and Latin American students in the USSR, see Constantin Katsakioris's work as well as Djagalov and Evans, "Moscau, 1960."

24 For the trace left of those exchanges today, see the interviews conducted by Jessica Bachman with Indian readers and viewers on her *Bollywood and Bolsheviks* website.

25 Prashad, *The Darker Nations.*

26 Mahler, *From the Tricontinental to the Global South*, 210.

27 Razlogov, *Moi festivali*, 104–5.

28 Tolz, *Russia's Own Orient*, 100.

29 "Vostokovedenie." *Bolshaia Sovetskaya entskiklopedia.*

30 Tolz, *Russia's Own Orient*, 101.

31 Rather, it was picked up by more conservative members of the Russian academic establishment, who have taken this link to "expose" Said's *Orientalism* and the whole postcolonial endeavour as another Western leftist reiteration of ideologically-preoccupied Soviet literary studies. For such conservative criticism, see for example Sergei Serebriany's more measured "Comparative Literature and Post-colonial Studies," which does attempt an overview of the (small) impact of postcolonial studies on contemporary Russian scholarship. In a more bellicose version, Serebryany's argument was repeated in Evgeny Steiner's lecture "Orientalistkii mif ili mif ob orietalizme." See Schimmelpenninck van der Oye, "The Curious Fate of Edward Said in Russia" for a more detailed reception history.

32 Ngũgĩ, interview.

33 For Ngũgĩ's account of his time in Yalta, see *The East Was Read*, 31–8.

34 Gikandi, *Ngugi*, 39–71. Tellingly, Ngũgĩ's authoritative biography does not mention his participation in the Beirut and Alma-Ata congresses of the Afro-Asian Writers Association, the Lotus prize he received at the latter, or his six months in the Soviet Union.

35 Currey, "Ngugi, Leeds, and the Establishment of African Literature."

36 Ngũgĩ, interview.

37 In Arif Dirlik's somewhat provocative words, the postcolonial began when "Third-World intellectuals arrived in the First-World academy." See his "The Postcolonial Aura," 329.

38 Young, "Ideologies of the Postcolonial," 6–7.

39 Bhabha, "A Question of Survival," 102.

40 See the ten volumes of the Subaltern Studies collective printed between 1982 and 1999 by the New Delhi branch of Oxford University Press.

41 Spivak, "Can the Subaltern Speak?"

42 "Manifesto of the Peoples of the East." In Riddell, *To See the Dawn*, 227, 231.

43 Chakrabarty, *Provincializing Europe.*

44 Chibber, *Postcolonial Theory and the Specter of Capital.*

45 A more comprehensive critique of mainstream postcolonialism by its Marxist wing can be found in Brennan, "Postcolonial Studies Between the European Wars"; Lazarus and Varma, "Marxism and Postcolonial studies"; and Kaiwar, *The Postcolonial Orient.* See also the "Marxism and Postcolonial Theory," special issue of *Critical Sociology* and Parry, "The Futures Past of Internationalism."

Bibliography

Archives

GARF: Gosudarstvennyi Arkhiv Rossiiskoi Federatsii (State Archive of the Russian Federation), Moscow

RGALI: Rossiiskii Gosudarstvennyi Arkhiv Literatury i Iskussktva (Russian State Arhive for Literature and Art), Moscow

RGANI: Rossiiskii Gosudarstvennyi Arkhiv Noveishei Istorii (Russian State Archive for Contemporary History), Moscow

RGASPI: Rosiiskii Gosudarstvennyi Arkhiv Sotsial'no-Politicheskoi Istorii (Russian State Archive for Socio-Political History), Moscow

RGAKFD: Rossiiskii Gosudarstvennyi Arkhiv Kino-Foto Dokumentov (Russian State Film and Photo Archive), Krasnogorsk

VGIK: Vserossiiskii Gosudarstvennyi Universitet Kinematografii (All-Russian State University of Cinematography), Moscow

Akademie der Künste (Academy of the Arts), Berlin

Nationalna Agentsia Arkhivi (National Archival Agency), Sofia

Interviews

Alarcón, Sebastián. 18 April 2018, Moscow.

Bessmertnaya, Olga. 13 September 2017, Moscow.

Gordon, Alexander. 23 March 2019, Moscow.

Livergandt, Aleksandr. 11 December 2008, Moscow.

Ngũgĩ wa Thiong'o. 19 May 2017, Skype.

Sidorov, Yevgeny. 18 June 2018, Moscow.

Vasilieva, Liudmila. 28 March 2018, Moscow.

Vlasova, Olga. 18 June 2018, Moscow.

Filmography of Solidarity Documentary

Battleship Potemkin (Sergei Eisenstein 1925)

A Sixth Part of the World (Dziga Vertov 1926)

The Roof of the World: Pamir (Vladimir Erofeev 1928)

The Shanghai Document (Yakov Bliokh 1928)

The Heart of Asia: Afghanistan (Vladimir Erofeev 1929)

Moscow-Karakum-Moscow (Roman Karmen and Edward Tisse 1930)

Far in Asia (Vladimir Erofeev 1931)

Song of Heroes (Joris Ivens 1933)

Fighters (Joris Ivens and Gustav von Wangenheim 1933)

Three Songs about Lenin (Dziga Vertov 1934)

Ankara – the Heart of Turkey (Sergei Yutkevich and Leon Arnshtam 1934)

The Land of the Lion and the Sun: Iran (Vladimir Erofeev 1935)

Abyssinia (Ilya Kopalin 1936)

Spain in Flames (Helen van Dongen and Joris Ivens 1937)

Spanish Earth (Joris Ivens 1938)

Heroic China (Vladimir Erofeev 1938)

Spain (Roman Karmen and Esfir Shub 1939)

The 400 Milllion (Joris Ivens 1939)

Our Russian Front (Joris Ivens and Lewis Mileston 1941)

Indonesia Calling (Joris Ivens 1946)

The First Years (Joris Ivens 1948)

The Tale about the Oil Workers of the Caspian Region (Roman Karmen 1953)

The Song of the Rivers (Joris Ivens 1954)

Vietnam (Roman Karmen 1955)

Indian Morning (Roman Karmen 1956)

Sunday in Peking (Chris Marker and Alain Resnais 1956)

The Windrose (Joris Ivens, Gillo Pontecorvo et al. 1956)

Letter from Siberia (Chris Marker 1957)

Austria Greets Peace Visitors (Roman Karmen 1960)

Travel Notebook (Joris Ivens 1961)

A People in Arms (Joris Ivens 1961)

Valparaiso (Joris Ivens 1961)

Cuba Yes! (Chris Marker 1961)

Island in Flames (Roman Karmen 1961)

Death to the Invader (Santiago Álvarez and Thomas Gutierrez Alea 1962)

A Visitor from the Island of Freedom (Roman Karmen 1963)

The Victory Train (Joris Ivens 1964)

Now! (Santiago Álvarez 1965)

The Threatening Sky (Joris Ivens 1966)

Until Victory, Always (Santiago Álvarez 1967)

79 Springs (Santiago Álvarez 1967)

Grenada, My Grenada (Roman Karmen, 1967)

The Forgotten War (Santiago Álvarez 1967)

Far from Vietnam (Chris Marker, Joris Ivens et al. 1967)

LBJ (Santiago Alvarez 1968)

The Hour of the Furnaces (Octavio Getino and Fernando Solanas 1968)

17th Parallel (Joris Ivens 1968)

The Battle of the Ten Million (Chris Marker 1970)

How, Why, and For What General is Killed (Santiago Álvarez 1971)

The Hot Wind of Freedom (Vitaly Komarov 1971)

The Continent in Flames (Roman Karmen 1972)

The Tiger Jumped, but It Will Die, It Will Die (Santiago Álvarez 1973)

The Train Rolls On (Chris Marker 1973)

Chile: Time of Struggle, Time of Discontent (Roman Karmen 1973)

Camarados-Comrades (Roman Karmen 1974)

The Battle of Chile, Part I (Patricio Guzmán 1975)

The Battle of Chile, Part II (Patricio Guzmán 1976)

Maputu: The Ninth Meridian (Santiago Álvarez 1976)

Corvalan's Heart (Roman Karmen 1976)

A Grin without a Cat (Chris Marker 1977)

My Brother Fidel (Santiago Alvarez 1977)

The Battle of Chile, Part III (Patricio Guzmán 1979)

Chile, Obstinate Memory (Patricio Guzmán 1997)

The Last Bolshevik (Chris Marker 1992)

Nostalgia for the Light (Patricio Guzmán 2010)

Literature

Abarinov, Vladimir. "Plamennaia Andzhela." *Radio Svoboda* (blog), 27 January 2017. https://www.svoboda.org/a/28262953.html.

Abdullaev, A., ed. *Mezhdunarodnyi Forum Kinematografistov v Tashkente.* Tashkent: Izdatel'stvo Gafura Guliama, 1978.

Adi, Hakim. *Pan-Africanism and Communism: The Communist International, Africa and the Diaspora, 1919–1939*. Trenton, NJ: Africa World Press, 2013.

Afiani, V. Iu. et al., ed. *Apparat TsK KPSS i Kul'tura, 1953–1957: Dokumenty.* Moscow: ROSSPEN, 2001.

– *Ideologicheskie Komissii TsK KPSS, 1958–1964: Dokumenty*. Moscow: ROSSPEN, 1998.

Agosin, Marjorie. *Pablo Neruda*. Boston: Twayne, 1986.

Ahmad, Aijaz. "Jameson's Rhetoric of Otherness and the 'National Allegory.'" *Social Text*, no. 17 (1 October, 1987): 3–25.

Aitmatov, Chingiz. *The Day Lasts More than a Hundred Years*. Bloomington: Indiana University Press, 1983.

Alimzhanov, Anuar. "Pylaiushchee Kop'e." In *Sobranie Sochinenii. Vol. 2*, 297–344. Almaty: Zhibek zholy, 2013.

Alter, Nora. *Chris Marker*. Urbana, IL: University of Illinois Press, 2006.

Anand, Mulk Raj. *The Sword and the Sickle: A Novel*. Indian Writers Series. Liverpool: Lucas Publications, 1986.

– *Across the Black Waters*. New Delhi: Vision Books, 1978.

– *The Village, a Novel*. London: Jonathan Cape, 1939.

– *Untouchable: A Novel*. London: Wishart Books, 1935.

Anderson, Benedict. *Imagined Communities: Reflections on the Origin and Spread of Nationalism*. London: Verso, 1983.

Anderson, Kevin. *Marx at the Margins: On Nationalism, Ethnicity, and Non-Western Societies*. Chicago, IL: The University of Chicago Press, 2010.

Anderson, Perry. "Internationalism: A Breviary." *New Left Review* 14 (2002): 5–25.

Andrew, Dudley. "An Atlas of World Cinema." *Framework: The Journal of Cinema and Media* 45, no. 2 (2004): 9–23.

Applebaum, Rachel. *Empire of Friends: Soviet Power and Socialist Internationalism in Cold War Czechoslovakia*. Ithaca, NY: Cornell University Press, 2019.

Apter, Emily. *Against World Literature: On the Politics of Untranslatability*. London: Verso, 2013.

Artemeno, V., and L. Pavliuchik. "Net Prazdnika Bez Zvezd." *Pravda*, 31 May 1988.

Asturias, Miguel Ángel. *The Eyes of the Interred*. New York, NY: Delacorte Press, 1973.

– *The Green Pope*. New York, NY: Delacorte Press, 1971.

– *Strong Wind*. New York, NY: Delacorte Press, 1968.

Azeb, Sophia. "Dar El-Odaba: Afro-Asian Writers Remapping Blackness and Afro-Arab Identities." MA thesis, State University of New York, Buffalo, 2011.

Aznar Soler, Manuel, ed. *Secundo Congreso Internacional de Escritores para la Defensa de la Cultura, Vol. 1&2*. Valencia: Generalitat Valenciana, 1937.

Babiracki, Patryk. *Soviet Soft Power in Poland: Culture and the Making of Stalin's New Empire, 1943–1957*. Chapel Hill, NC: The University of North Carolina Press, 2015.

Babiracki, Patryk, and Austin Jersild, eds. *Socialist Internationalism in the Cold War: Exploring the Second World*. Cham: Springer International Publishing, 2016.

Bachman, Jessica. "Bollywood and Bolsheviks: Indo-Soviet Collaboration in Literature and Film, 1954–1991." http://bollywoodandbolsheviks.com/.

Baer, Brian. "From International to Foreign: Packaging Translated Literature in Soviet Russia." *Slavic and East European Journal* 60, no. 1 (2016): 49–67.

– *Translation and the Making of Modern Russian Literature*. New York, NY: Bloomsbury Publishing USA, 2015.

Baer, Brian, and Susanna Witt, eds. *Translation in Russian Contexts: Culture, Politics, Identity*. New York, NY: Routledge, 2018.

Baldwin, Katherine Anne. *Beyond the Color Line and the Iron Curtain: Reading Encounters Between Black and Red, 1922–1963*. Durham, NC: Duke University Press, 2002.

Balogun, F. Odun. "Russian and Nigerian Literatures." *Comparative Literature Studies* 21, no. 4 (1984): 483–96.

Banerjee, Anindita, and Jenifer Presto, eds. "Geopoetics." Special issue of *Slavic Review* 75, no. 2 (summer 2016).

– "World Revolution." Special issue of *Slavic and East European Journal* 63, no. 3 (fall 2017).

Barberis, Patrick, and Dominique Chapuis. *Roman Karmen: Documentaire Arte*, 2002.

Barnhisel, Greg. *Cold War Modernists: Art, Literature, and American Cultural Diplomacy*. New York, NY: Columbia University Press, 2015.

Bartol'd, Vasilii. *Istoriia izucheniia Vostoka v Evrope i Rossii: lektsii*. Leningradskii vostochnyi institut imeni A.S. Enukidze. Leningrad: Leningrad, 1925.

Baskakov, Vladimir. "Boriushchiiisia Ekran." In *Kinoiskusstvo Azii i Afriki*, edited by S.A. Toportsev, 4–20. Moscow: Nauka, 1984.

– ed. *Kino v bor'be za mir, sotsial'nyi progress i svobodu narodov (tvorcheskaia diskussia na [II, III, IV, V, VI, VII, VII, or IX] Mezhdunarodnom kinofestivale v Tashkente)*. Moscow: VNII Kino, 1972 [1974, 1976, 1978, 1980, 1982, 1986].

Batalov, Eduard. *"Novye levye" i Gerbert Markuze*. Moscow: Znanie, 1970.

"Baza Dannykh Aktov Nasiliia, 2007–2018." SOVA Center for Information and Analysis. Accessed 13 March 2019. http://www.sova-center.ru/database.

Beliakova, Elena. *"Russkii Amadu" i brazl'skaia literatura v Rossii*. Moscow: Institut Latinskoi Ameriki, 2010.

Bell-Villada, Gene H. *Gabriel García Márquez's One Hundred Years of Solitude: A Casebook*. Oxford: Oxford University Press, 2002.

Belodubrovskaya, Maria. *Not According to Plan: Filmmaking under Stalin*. Ithaca, NY: Cornell University Press, 2017.

Berg-Pan, Renata. *Bertolt Brecht and China*. Bonn: Bouvier, 1979.

Bethlehem, Louise, and Gül Bilge Han. "Cultural Solidarities: Apartheid and the Anticolonial Commons of World Literature." *Safundi* 19, no. 3 (3 July 2018): 260–8.

Bhabha, Homi. "A Question of Survival: Nations and Psychic States." In *Psychoanalysis and Cultural Theory: Thresholds*, edited by James Donald, 89–103. New York, NY: St Martin Press, 1991.

Bird, Robert. "Medium Intimacy: The Correspondences of Chris Marker and Aleksandr Medvedkin." presented at the Institut National d'histoire de l'arte, Paris, 18 April 2018.

Boltovskaja, Svetlana. *Bildungsmigranten aus dem subsaharischen Afrika in Moskau und St. Petersburg: Selbst- und Fremdbilder*. Herbolzheim: Centaurus Verlag & Media, 2014.

Bonfiglioli, Chiara. "Cold War Gendered Imaginaries of Citizenship and Transnational Women's Activism: The Case of the Movie Die Windrose (1957)." In *Gender and Citizenship in Historical and Transnational Perspective*, edited by Ann R. Epstein and Rachel G. Fuchs, 166–85. London: Palgrave McMillan, 2017.

Bourdieu, Pierre. *Distinction: A Social Critique of the Judgement of Taste*. Trans. by Richard Nice. Cambridge, MA: Harvard University Press, 1984.

Brashinevskii, Mikhail, Petr Shepotinnik, and Aleksandr Kiselev. "S Militseiskoi Migalki v Poiskakh Kino": A Report on the Tenth Tashkent Festiva." *Iskusstvo Kino*, 1988.

Brasken, Kasper. *The International Workers' Relief, Communism, and Transnational Solidarity: Willi Münzenberg in Weimar Germany*. London: Palgrave Macmillan, 2015.

Brandist, Craig. "Varieties of Ideology Critique in Early Soviet Literary and Oriental Scholarship." *Przegląd Filozoficzno-Literacki* 2 no. 47 (2017): 53–67.

Brennan, Timothy. "Postcolonial Studies Between the European Wars: An Intellectual History." In *Marxism, Modernity and Postcolonial Studies*, edited by Crystal Bartolovich and Neil Lazarus, 185–203. Cambridge: Cambridge University Press, 2002.

Brutents, Karen. *Tridsat' Let Na Staroi Ploshchadi*. Moscow: Mezhdunarodnye otnosheniia, 1998.

Buck-Morss, Susan. *Dreamworld and Catastrophe: The Passing of Mass Utopia in East and West*. Cambridge, MA: MIT Press, 2000.

Budiak, Liudmila. *Kino Indii*. Moscow: Iskusstvo, 1988.

– *Tashkentskii Mezhdunarodnyi Kinofestival'*. Moscow: Nauka, 1985.

– *Kinematograf razvivaiushchikhsia stran*. Moscow: Znanie, 1981.

"Bulgarski Kinematografisti." Cinema.bg, 26 April 2016. Cinema.bg/български-кинематографисти.

Burns, Grant. *The Railroad in American Fiction*. Jefferson, NC: McFarland & Company Publishers, 2005.

Caffee, Naomi. "Between First, Second, and Third Worlds: Olzhas Suleimenov and Soviet Postcolonialism, 1961–1973." *Russian Literature* 103 (2019).

– "Russophinia: Towards a Transnational Conception of the Russian Language." PhD thesis, UCLA, 2013.

Casanova, Pascale. *The World Republic of Letters*. Cambridge, MA: Harvard University Press, 2004.

Casula, Philipp. "Two Soviet Responses to Franz Fanon by Rostislav Ulianovskii and Aleksandr Gordon." In *Arab-Russian Sourcebook*, edited by Margaret Litvin, Eileen Kane, and Masha Kirasoriva. Manuscript.

Chakrabarty, Dipesh. *Provincializing Europe: Postcolonial Thought and Historical Difference*. Princeton, NJ: Princeton University Press, 2000.

Chan, Jessica Ka Yee. *Chinese Revolutionary Cinema: Propaganda, Aesthetics and Internationalism 1949–1966*. London: I.B. Tauris, 2019.

Chan, Sylvia. "Realism or Socialist Realism? The 'Proletarian' Episode in Modern Chinese Literature 1927–1932." *The Australian Journal of Chinese Affairs*, no. 9 (January 1983): 55–74.

Chanan, Michael. *Cuban Cinema*. Minneapolis, MN: University of Minnesota Press, 2004.

– "The Changing Geography of Third-World Cinema." *Screen* 38, no. 4 (Winter 1997): 372–88.

Cheah, Pheng. *What Is a World? On Postcolonial Literature as World Literature*. Durham: Duke University Press, 2016.

Chen, Jian et al., ed. *The Routledge Handbook of the Global Sixties: Between Protest and Nation-Building*. London: Routledge, 2018.

Chernetsky, Vitaly. *Mapping Postcommunist Cultures: Russia and Ukraine in the Context of Globalization*. Montreal: McGill-Queen's University Press, 2007.

Chertok, Semen. *Festival' trekh kontinentov*. Tashkent: Izd-vo lit-ry i iskusstva imeni Gafura Guliama, 1978.

– *Tam-tam XX veka: ocherk o kino Chernoi Afriki*. Moscow: Biuro propagandy sovkinoiskusstva, 1977.

– *Tashkentskii festival'*. Tashkent: Izd-vo lit-ry i iskusstva imeni Gafura Guliama, 1975.

– *Nachalo: kino Chernoi Afriki*. Moscow: Biuro propagandy sovetskogo kinoisskustva, 1973.

– "Kino Chernoi Afriki: Problemy i Nadezhdy." In *Mify i Real'nost': Zarubezhnoe Kino Segodnia*. 3. Moscow: Iskusstvo, 1972. http://scepsis.net/library/id_819.html.

Chibber, Vivek. *Postcolonial Theory and the Specter of Capital*. London: Verso, 2013.

Cho, Heekyoung. *Translation's Forgotten History: Russian Literature, Japanese Mediation, and the Formation of Modern Korean Literature*. Cambridge, MA: Harvard University Press, 2016.

Chomentowski, Gabrielle. *Filmer l'Orient: politique des nationalités et cinéma en URSS (1917–1938)*. Paris: Éditions Petra, 2016.

– "L'experience sovietique des cinemas africains au lendemain des independances/African Cinemas: The Soviet Experience after Decolonization." *Temps des médias* 26, no. 1 (2016): 111–125.

– "State Modernization in the Time of Decolonization: How the Soviet Government Helped African Countries Develop Film Infrastructure." presented at the Socialist World, 'Third World', Media Worlds: An Exploratory Workshop, University College, London, 6 November 2018.

Clark, Katerina. "Eurasia without Borders? Leftist Internationalists and Their Cultural Interactions, 1919–1943." Manuscript.

– "Indian Leftist Writers of the 1930s Maneuver among India, London, and Moscow: The Case of Mulk Raj Anand and His Patron Ralph Fox." *Kritika: Explorations in Russian and Eurasian History* 18, no. 1 (2017): 63–87.

– "The Representation of the African American as Colonial Oppressed in Texts of the Soviet Interwar Years." *The Russian Review* 75, no. 3 (1 July 2016): 368–85.

– "European and Russian Cultural Interactions with Turkey 1910s–1930s." *Comparative Studies of South Asia, Africa and the Middle East* 33, no. 2 (2013): 201–13.

– *Moscow, the Fourth Rome: Stalinism, Cosmopolitanism, and the Evolution of Soviet Culture, 1931–1941*. Cambridge, MA: Harvard University Press, 2011.

– "The Mutability of the Canon: Socialist Realism and Chingiz Aitmatov's I Dol'she Veka Dlitsia Den'." *Slavic Review* 43, no. 4 (1984): 573–87.

Claudin, Fernand. *The Communist Movement: From Comintern to Cominform.* Harmondsworth: Penguin Press, 1975.

Comaroff, Jean. *Theory from the South: Or, How Euro-America Is Evolving toward Africa.* Boulder, CO: Paradigm Publishers, 2012.

Condee, Nancy. *The Imperial Trace: Recent Russian Cinema.* New York, NY: Oxford University Press, 2009.

Currey, James. "Ngugi, Leeds, and the Establishment of African Literature." *Leeds African Studies Bulletin* 74 (December 2012): 46–62.

– *Africa Writes Back: The African Writers Series and the Launch of African Literature.* Oxford, Athens, OH: Ohio University Press, 2008.

Curto, Roxanna. "Technology Transfer, Railway, and Independence in Ousmane Sembène's Les Bouts de Bois de Dieu." In *Trains, Literature, and Culture: Reading and Writing the Rails,* edited by Steven D. Spalding and Benjamin Fraser, 53–75. Lanham, MD: Lexington Books, 2012.

Daly, Nicholas. *Literature, Technology, and Modernity, 1860–2000.* Cambridge: Cambridge University Press, 2004.

Damrosch, David. *How to Read World Literature.* Malden, MA: Wiley-Blackwell, 2007.

– *What Is World Literature?* Translation/Transnation. Princeton, NJ: Princeton University Press, 2003.

David-Fox, Michael. *Showcasing the Great Experiment: Cultural Diplomacy and Western Visitors to the Soviet Union, 1921–1941.* New York, NY: Oxford University Press, 2014.

Davidson, Apollon. "Chto takoe Mavritaniia: 50-letie sozdaniia Sovetskogo komiteta solidarnosti stran Azii i Afriki." Interview by Vladimir Tolz. Radio Svoboda, 11 June 2006. https://www.svoboda.org/a/160802.html.

– ed. *Stanovlenie otechestvennoi afrikanistiki: 1920e – nachalo 1960kh.* Moscow: Nauka, 2003.

Davis, Clarence B., Kenneth E. Wilburn, and Ronald Robinson. *Railway Imperialism.* New York, NY: Greenwood Press, 1991.

Deckard, Sharae, Nicholas Lawrence, Neil Lazarus, Graeme Macdonald, Upamanyu Pablo Mukherjee, Benita Parry, Stephen A. Shapiro, and WREC. *Combined and Uneven Development: Towards a New Theory of World-Literature.* Liverpool: Liverpool University Press, 2015.

Denning, Michael. *Culture in the Age of Three Worlds.* London: Verso, 2004.

– *The Cultural Front: The Laboring of American Culture in the Twentieth Century.* London: Verso, 1998.

Desai, M.V. "The Asian Writers' Conference December 1956: New Delhi." *Books Abroad* 31, no. 3 (1 July, 1957): 243–5.

Dickinson, Kay. "Cinematic Third Worldism: 'Resolutions of the Third World Filmmakers Meeting' (Algeria 1973)." In *Arab Film and Video Manifestos: Forty-Five Years of the Moving Image Amid Revolution*, edited by Kay Dickinson, 49–80. Cham: Springer International Publishing, 2018.

– *Arab Cinema Travels: Transnational Syria, Palestine, Dubai and Beyond.* London: British Film Institute, 2016.

Dirlik, Arif. "The Postcolonial Aura: Third World Criticism in the Age of Global Capitalism." *Critical Inquiry*, no. 20 (Winter 1994): 328–56.

"Distributors' Database of New Film Releases on Russian Screens, 2004–2019." Biulleten' kinoprokatchika. Accessed 13 March 2019. http://www.kinometro. ru/kino/analitika.

Djagalov, Rossen. "Literary Monopolists and the Forging of the Post-World War II People's Republic of Letters." In *Socialist Realism in Central and Eastern European Literatures under Stalin: Institutions, Dynamics, Discourses*, edited by Evgeny Dobrenko and Jonsson-Skradol. London: Anthem Press, 2018.

– "The Red Apostles: Imagining Revolutions in the Global Proletarian Novel." *Slavic and East European Journal* 62, no. 3 (Spring 2017): 396–422.

– "Antipopulizm Postsotsialisticheskoi Intelligentsii." *Neprikosnovennyi zapas* 75, no. 1 (2011). http://magazines.russ.ru/nz/2011/1/d17.html.

– "'I Don't Boast About It, but I'm the Most Widely Read Author of This Century': Howard Fast and International Leftist Literary Culture, ca. Mid-Twentieth Century." *Anthropology of East Europe Review* 27, no. 2 (2009): 40–55.

Djagalov, Rossen, and Masha Salazkina. "Tashkent '68: A Cinematic Contact Zone." *Slavic Review* 75, no. 2 (1 June 2016): 279–98.

Djagalov, Rossen, and Christine Evans. "Moskau, 1960: Wie man sich eine sowjetische Freundschaft mit der Dritten Welt vortstellte." In *Die Sowjetunion und die Dritte Welt: UdSSR, Staatssozialismus und Antikolonialismus im Kalten Krieg 1945–1991*, edited by Andreas Hilger, 83–106. Munich: R. Oldenbourg Verlag, 2009.

Dobrenko, Evgeny. "Naideno v Perevode: Rozhdenie Sovetskoi Mnogonatsional'noi Literatury Iz Smerti Avtora." *Neprikosnovennyi Zapas* 4, no. 78 (2011).

– *The Making of the State Writer: Social and Aesthetic Origins of Soviet Literary Culture.* Palo Alto, CA: Stanford University Press, 2001.

– *Making of the State Reader: Social and Aesthetic Contexts of the Reception of Soviet Literature.* Translated by Jesse M. Savage. Palo Alto, CA: Stanford University Press, 1997.

Dobrenko, E.A., and Natalia Jonsson-Skradol, eds. *Socialist Realism in Central and Eastern European Literatures under Stalin: Institutions, Dynamics, Discourses.* London: Anthem Press, 2017.

Dobrenko, Vladimir. "Conspiracy of Peace: The Cold War, the International Peace Movement, and the Soviet Peace Campaign, 1946–1956." PhD thesis, London School of Economics and Political Science (LSE), 2016.

Dovlatov, Sergei. *Inostranka.* New York, NY: Russica Publishers, 1986.

Drews-Sylla, Gesine. "Ousmane Sembène's Hybrid 'Truth': Social(Ist) Realism and the Postcolonial Writing Back." In *Realisms in Contemporary Culture: Theories, Politics, and Medial Configurations,* edited by Dorothee Birke and Stella Butter, 70–89. Berlin: Walter de Gruyter, 2013.

Drobashenko, Sergei. *Kinorezhisser Ioris Ivens.* Moscow: Izd-vo "Iskusstvo, 1964.

Dubovikov, A.N, and L.R. Lanskii, eds. *Iz Istorii Mezhdunarodnogo Ob"edinenia Proletarskikh Pisatelei (MORP).* Moscow: Nauka, 1969.

Dudziak, Mary. *Cold War Civil Rights: Race and the Image of American Democracy.* Princeton, NJ: Princeton University Press, 2002.

Ďurišin, Dionýz. *Theory of Literary Comparatistics.* Bratislava: Veda, PubHouse of the Slovak Academy of Sciences, 1984.

Durovicova, Natasa, and Kathleen E. Newman, eds. *World Cinemas, Transnational Perspectives.* New York, NY: Routledge, 2010.

Earle, Edward Mead. *Turkey, the Great Powers, and the Bagdad Railway: A Study in Imperialism.* New York, NY: Macmillan, 1924.

Ebbrecht-Hartmann, Tobias. "Socialist Competition or Window to the World?: East German Student Films at International Festivals in the Context of the Cold War." In *Cultural Transfer and Political Conflicts: Film Festivals in the Cold War,* edited by Caroline Moine and Andreas Kötzing, 15–30. Göttingen: V&R Press, 2017.

Eby, Marek. "Global Tashkent: Imagining the Soviet East in the Cold-War World." Manuscript.

Echevarría, Evelio. "Bolshevism and the Spanish American Social Novel." *Latin American Literary Review* 4, no. 8 (1976): 89–95.

Echevarria, Roberto Gonzales. *The Voice of the Masters: Writing and Authority in Modern Latin American Literature.* Austin: University of Texas Press, 1985.

Edwards, Brent Hayes. *The Practice of Diaspora: Literature, Translation, and the Rise of Black Internationalism.* Cambridge, MA: Harvard University Press, 2003.

– "The Shadow of Shadows." *Positions: Asia Critique* 11, no. 1 (1 February 2003): 11–49.

Ehrenburg, Ilya. *Liudi, Gody, Zhizni.* Vol. 3. Moscow: Sovietskii pisatel', 1990.

Eisenstein, Sergei. *The Film Sense.* London: Faber and Faber, 1943.

Engerman, David. *The Price of Aid: The Economic Cold War in India.* Cambridge, MA: Harvard University Press, 2018.

– "The Second World's Third World." *Kritika: Explorations in Russian and Eurasian History* 12, no. 1 (2011): 183–211.

– *Know Your Enemy: The Rise and Fall of America's Soviet Experts.* Oxford: Oxford University Press, 2009.

English, James. *The Economy of Prestige: Prizes, Awards, and the Circulation of Cultural Value.* Cambridge, MA: Harvard University Press, 2008.

Erley, Laura. "Reclaiming Native Soil: Cultural Mythologies of Soil in Russia and Its Eastern Borderlands from the 1840s to the 1930s." PhD thesis, University of California, Berkeley, 2012.

Ertürk, Nergis. "Baku, Literary Common." In *Futures of Comparative Literature: ACLA State of the Discipline Report*, 141–4. London: Routledge, 2017.

– "Toward a Literary Communism: The 1926 Baku Turcological Congress." *Boundary 2* 40, no. 2 (2013): 183–213.

Ertürk, Nergis, and Özge Serin. "Marxism, Communism, and Translation: An Introduction." *Boundary 2* 43, no. 3 (2016): 1–26.

Etkind, Aleksandr. *Internal Colonization: Russia's Imperial Experience.* Cambridge, UK; Malden, MA: Polity Press, 2011.

Evans, Christine. *Between Truth and Time: A History of Soviet Central Television.* New Haven, CT: Yale University Press, 2016.

Fanon, Frantz. *The Wretched of the Earth.* New York, NY: Grove Press, 2005.

– *Black Skin, White Masks.* New York, NY: Grove Press, 1982.

– *Toward the African Revolution (Political Essays).* New York, NY: Grove Press, 1969.

Fédération panafricaine des cinéastes. "Niamey Manifesto of African Filmmakers: First International Conference on Cinema Production in Africa, Niamey, Niger, March 1982." Translated by Louise Jefferson. *Black Camera* 1, no. 2 (2010): 111–16.

Fedorova, Anastasiia. "Formirovanie Shkoly Montazhnoi Vyrazitel'nosti v Iaponskom Dokumental'nom Kino 1930x–50x godov: Tvorchestvo Kamei Fumio." PhD thesis, VGIK, 2017.

Feinstein, Adam. *Pablo Neruda: A Passion for Life.* London: Bloomsbury, 2004.

Feldman, Leah. *On the Threshold of Eurasia: Revolutionary Politics and the Caucasus.* Ithaca, NY: Cornell University Press, 2018.

Ferrer, Jorge. "Around the Sun: The Adventures of a Wayward Satellite." In *Caviar with Rum Cuba–USSR and the Post-Soviet Experience*, edited by Jacqueline Loss and Jose Manuel Prietto, 95–108. New York, NY: Palgrave Macmillan US, 2012.

Filatova, Irina. "Indoctrination or Scholarship? Education of Africans at the Communist University of the Toilers of the East in the Soviet Union, 1923–1937." *Paedagogica Historica* 35, no. 1 (1999): 41–66.

Floyd, Nikki Dejan. "Bridging the Colonial Divide: Japanese-Korean Solidarity in the International Proletarian Literature Movement." PhD thesis, Yale University, c2012.

Fomin, Valerii, ed. *Istoriia Kinootrasli v Rossii: Upravlenie, Kinoproizvodstvo, Prokat.* Moscow: VGIK, 2012.

– *Kinematograf ottepeli: dokumenty i svidetel'stva.* Moscow: Materik, 1998.

– *Kino i vlast': sovetskoe kino, 1965–1985 gody: dokumenty, svidetel'stva, razmyshleniiā.* Moscow: Materik, 1996.

Fomin, Valerii, V.A. Zhdranova, and M.I. Kosina. *Letopis' rossiiskogo kino, 1981–1991.* Moscow: Reabilitatsiia, 2016.

Fore, Devin. *Realism after Modernism: The Rehumanization of Art and Literature.* An October Book. Cambridge, MA: MIT Press, 2012.

Frank, Susie, and Franziska Thun-Hohenstein, eds. *Translatio. Begründungen Und Erbschaften Des Imperialen.* Berlin: Kadmos, 2018.

Frezinskii, Boris. *Pisateli i Sovetskie Vozhdi: Izbrannye Siuzhety 1919–1960 Godov.* Moscow: Elis Pak, 2008.

Friedberg, Maurice. *Literary Translation in Russia: A Cultural History.* University Park: Pennsylvania State University Press, 1997.

– *A Decade of Euphoria: Western Literature in Post-Stalin Russia, 1954–64.* Bloomington, IN: Indiana University Press, 1977.

Friedman, Jeremy Scott. *Shadow Cold War: The Sino-Soviet Competition for the Third World.* Chapel Hill, NC: University of North Carolina Press, 2015.

Fürst, Juliane, Silvio Pons, and Mark Selden, eds. *Cambridge History of Communism, Volume 3, Endgames? Late Communism in Global Perspective, 1968 to the Present.* Cambridge: Cambridge University Press, 2017.

Gabriel, Teshome H. *Third Cinema in the Third World: The Aesthetics of Liberation.* Ann Arbor, MI: UMI Research Press, 1982.

Gachev, Georgii. *Chinghiz Aitmatov i Mirovaia Literatura.* Frunze: Kyrgyzstan, 1982.

Gamsa, Mark. *The Reading of Russian Literature in China: A Moral Example and Manual of Practice.* New York, NY: Palgrave Macmillan, 2010.

– *The Chinese Translation of Russian Literature: Three Studies.* Leiden: Brill, 2008.

Genova, James E. *Cinema and Development in West Africa.* Bloomington, IN: Indiana University Press, 2013.

Gerasimova, A.S. *Russkaia klassika v Afganistane: otkrytie i priznanie.* Moscow: RAN, 2015.

Ghouse, Nida. "'Lotus Notes': A Series on the Afro-Asian Writers Association, Part A, B, C." *Mada Masr* (blog), August 2014. https://madamasr.com/en/topic/afro-asian-writers-association/.

Gikandi, Simon. *Ngugi Wa Thiong'o*. Cambridge: Cambridge University Press, 2000.

Gilburd, Eleonory. *To See Paris and Die: The Soviet Lives of Western Culture*. Cambridge, MA: The Belknap Press of Harvard University Press, 2018.

Gilmore, Glenda Elizabeth. *Defying Dixie: The Radical Roots of Civil Rights, 1919–1950*. New York, NY: W.W. Norton & Co., 2008.

Gladkov, Fedor. *Cement*. New York, NY: International Publishers, 1929.

Göksu, Saime. *Romantic Communist: The Life and Work of Nâzım Hikmet*. New York: St Martin's Press, 1999.

Gorky, Maksim. *Mother*. New York, NY: D. Appleton and Co., 1907.

Gorsuch, Anne E. "'Cuba, My Love': The Romance of Revolutionary Cuba in the Soviet Sixties." *The American Historical Review* 120, no. 2 (2015): 497–526.

Gould, Rebecca Ruth. *Writers and Rebels: The Literature of Insurgency in the Caucasus*. New Haven, CT: Yale University Press, 2016.

Gramsci, Antonio. *Selections from the Prison Notebooks of Antonio Gramsci*. London: Lawrence & Wishart, 1971.

Gray, Ros. "Haven't You Heard of Internationalism? The Socialist Friendships of Mozambican Cinema." In *Postcommunist Film – Russia, Eastern Europe and World Culture: Moving Images of Postcommunism*, 53–74. London: Routledge, 2013.

Guettel, Jens-uwe. "The Myth of the Pro-Colonialist SPD: German Social Democracy and Imperialism before World War I." *Central European History* 45, no. 3 (2012): 452–84.

Gustavino, Luis. *Caen Les Catedrales*. Santiago, Chile: Hachette, 1990.

Guzmán, Patricio. "What I Owe Chris Marker." https://www.bfi.org.uk/news/what-i-owe-chris-marker. BFI (blog), 10 February 2015.

Haber, Erika. *The Myth of the Non-Russian: Iskander and Aitmatov's Magical Universe*. Lanham, MD: Lexington Books, 2003.

Haen, Theo d', David Damrosch, and Djelal Kadir, eds. *The Routledge Companion to World Literature*. New York, NY: Routledge, 2012.

Halim, Hala. "Afro-Asian Third-Worldism into Global South: The Case of *Lotus* Journal." *Global South Studies: A Collective Publication with the Global South*, 22 November 2017. https://globalsouthstudies.as.virginia.edu/key-moments/afro-asian-third-worldism-global-south-case-lotus-journal.

- "*Lotus*, the Afro-Asian Nexus, and Global South Comparatism." *Comparative Studies of South Asia, Africa and the Middle East* 32, no. 3 (1 December 2012): 563–83.

Han, Gül Bilge. "Nâzım Hikmet's Afro-Asian Solidarities." *Safundi* 19, no. 3 (3 July 2018): 284–305.

Hart, Stephen. *Latin American Cinema*. London: Reaktion Books, 2015.

- *César Vallejo: A Literary Biography*. Woodbridge: Boydell & Brewer, 2013.

Haywood, Harry. *Black Bolshevik: Autobiography of an Afro-American Communist*. Chicago, IL: Liberator Press, 1978.

Herzig, Edmund, and Stephanie Cronin, eds. "Russian Orientalism to Soviet Iranology: The Persian-Speaking World and Its History through Russian Eyes." *Iranian Studies* 48, no. 5 (September 2015).

Hicks, Jeremy. *Dziga Vertov: Defining Documentary Film*. London: I.B. Tauris, 2007.

Hikmet, Nâzım. *Life's Good, Brother*. Translated by Mutlu Konuk Blasing. 1st ed. New York, NY: Persea Books, 2013.

- *Human Landscapes from My Country: An Epic Novel in Verse*. Translated by Randy Blasing and Mutlu Konuk. New York, NY: Persea Books, 2002.

- *Poems of Nâzım Hikmet*. Translated by Randy Blasing and Mutlu Konuk Blasing. New York, NY: Persea Books, 1994.

Hilger, Andreas, ed. *Die Sowjetunion und die Dritte Welt: UdSSR, Staatssozialismus und Antikolonialismus im Kalten Krieg 1945–1991*. Schriftenreihe der Vierteljahreshefte für Zeitgeschichte. Munich: Oldenbourg, 2010.

Hirsch, Francine. *Empire of Nations: Ethnographic Knowledge & the Making of the Soviet Union*. Culture and Society after Socialism. Ithaca, NY: Cornell University Press, 2005.

Hirst, Samuel. "Soviet Orientalism across Borders: Documentary Film for the Turkish Republic." *Kritika: Explorations in Russian and Eurasian History* 18, no. 1 (2017): 35–61.

- "Anti-Westernism on the European Periphery: The Meaning of Soviet-Turkish Convergence in the 1930s." *Slavic Review* 72, no. 1 (2013): 32–53.

- "Transnational Anti-Imperialism and the National Forces Soviet Diplomacy and Turkey, 1920–23." *Comparative Studies of South Asia, Africa and the Middle East* 33, no. 2 (2013): 214–26.

Hughes, Langston. *Autobiography: I Wonder as I Wander*. Hughes, Langston, 1902–1967. Works. v. 14. Columbia, MO: University of Missouri Press, 2003.

Humphreys, Laura-Zoe. *Fidel between the Lines: Paranoia and Ambivalence in Late Socialist Cuban Cinema*. Durham, NC: Duke University Press, 2019.

Ibragimov, N. and U. Oripov. *Pisateli Azii i Afriki v bor'be za mir i sotsial'nyi progress: (k 30-letiiu I Tashkentskoi konferentsii pisatelei Azii i Afriki)*. Tashkent: Izd-vo "Fan" Uzbekskoi SSR, 1989.

Inostrannaia Komissia Soiuza Pisatelei. *Literaturnaia Zhizn' Za Rubezhom*. 19. Moscow: Soiuz sovetskikh pisatelei, 1990.

International Union of Revolutionary Writers. *Second International Conference of International Writers: Reports, Resolutions, Debates*. Moscow: Izdatel'stvo inostrannoi literatury, 1931.

Iordanova, Dina. "Indian Cinema's Global Reach." *South Asian Popular Culture* 4, no. 2 (1 October 2006): 113–40.

Iordanova, Dina, David-Martin Jones, and Belen Vidal, eds. *Cinema at the Periphery*. Contemporary Approaches to Film and Television Series. Detroit, MI: Wayne State University Press, 2010.

Iovene, Paola. *Tales of Futures Past: Anticipation and the Ends of Literature in Contemporary China*. Palo Alto, CA: Stanford University Press, 2014.

Ismailov, Hamid. *The Dead Lake*. Translated by Andrew Bromfield. H. London: Peirene Press Ltd, 2014.

Ivens, Joris. *The Camera and I*. New York, NY: International Publishers, 1969.

Jackson, Jeanne-Marie. *South African Literature's Russian Soul Narrative Forms of Global Isolation*. London: Bloomsbury, 2015.

Jameson, Fredric. "Third-World Literature in the Era of Multinational Capitalism." *Social Text* 15, no. 15 (1986): 65–88.

Juraga, Dubravka, and M. Keith Booker. *Rereading Global Socialist Cultures after the Cold War: The Reassessment of a Tradition*. Westport, Conn.: Praeger, 2002.

– "The Reds and the Blacks: The Historical Novel in the Soviet Union and Postcolonial Africa." *Studies in the Novel* 29, no. 3 (1997): 274–96.

Kaiwar, Vasant. *The Postcolonial Orient: The Politics of Difference and the Project of Provincialising Europe*. Historical Materialism Book Series; vol. 68. Leiden: Brill, 2014.

Kalashnikova, Elena. *Po-russki s liubov'iu: besedy s perevodchikami*. Moscow: Novoe literaturnoe obozrenie, 2008.

Kalinovsky, Artemy. *Laboratory of Socialist Development: Cold War Politics and Decolonization in Soviet Tajikistan*. Ithaca: Cornell University Press, 2018.

Kalliney, Peter. "Modernism, African Literature, and the CIA." Library of Congress, 13 June 2013. https://www.youtube.com/watch?v=FG3nKy1oSwM on 5 February 2019.

Karmen, Roman. *No Passaran! (Memuary)*. Moscow: Sovetskaia Rossiia, 1972.

Kassamali, Sumayya. "Faiz Ahmed Faiz in Beirut." *The Caravan*, 31 May 2016. https://caravanmagazine.in/reviews-essays/you-had-no-address-faiz-beirut.

Katsakioris, Constantin. "The Lumumba University in Moscow: Higher Education for a Soviet-Third World Alliance." *Journal of Global History* 14, no. 2 (July 2019), 281–300.

– "Burden or Allies? Third World Students and Internationalist Duty through Soviet Eyes." *Kritika: Explorations in Russian and Eurasian History* 18, no. 3 (2017): 539–67.

– "Creating a Socialist Intelligentsia." *Cahiers d'études africaines* 226, no. 2 (2017): 259–88.

– "Soviet Lessons for Arab Modernization: Soviet Educational Aid towards Arab Countries after 1956." *Journal of Modern European History* 8, no. 1 (6 April 2010): 85–106.

Kelley, Robin D.G., and Betsy Esche. "Black like Mao." *Souls* 4, no. 1 (Fall 1999): 6–41.

Kemper, Michael, and Stephan Conermann. *The Heritage of Soviet Oriental Studies*. New York, NY: Routledge, 2011.

Kepley, Vance. "The Workers' International Relief and the Cinema of the Left 1921–1935." *Cinema Journal* 23, no. 1 (1983): 7–23.

Kepley, Betty, and Vance Kepley. "Foreign Films on Soviet Screens, 1922–1931." *Quarterly Review of Film Studies* 4, no. 4 (1 September, 1979): 429–42.

Khalid, Adeeb. *Making Uzbekistan: Nation, Empire, and Revolution in the Early USSR*. Ithaca, NY: Cornell University Press, 2015.

– "Introduction: Locating the (Post-) Colonial in Soviet History." *Central Asian Survey* 26, no. 4 (1 December 2007): 465–73.

Kharitonova, Natalia. "K istorii zhurnala *Internatsional'naia literatura* i ego ispanskogo izdaniia." *Vestnik RGGU*, no. 1 (2015).

Khotimsky, Maria. "World Literature, Soviet Style: A Forgotten Episode in the History of the Idea." *Ab Imperio* 2013, no. 3 (2013): 119–54.

Kim, Yun-Sik, and Sun Yang Tr Yoon. "KAPF Literature in Modern Korean Literary History." *Positions: East Asia Cultures Critique* 14, no. 2 (2006): 405–25.

Kirasirova, Masha. "The 'East' as a Category of Bolshevik Ideology and Comintern Administration: The Arab Section of the Communist University of the Toilers of the East." *Kritika: Explorations in Russian and Eurasian History* 18, no. 1 (2017): 7–34.

– "The Eastern International: The 'Domestic East' and the 'Foreign East' in Soviet-Arab Relations, 1917–68." PhD thesis, New York University, 2014.

- "'Sons of Muslims' in Moscow: Soviet Central Asian Mediators to the Foreign East, 1955–1962." *Ab Imperio*, no. 4 (2011): 106–32.

Klein, Christina. *Cold War Orientalism Asia in the Middlebrow Imagination, 1945–1961*. Berkeley, CA: University of California Press, 2003.

Knight, Claire. "Enemy Films on Soviet Screens: Trophy Films during the Early Cold War, 1947–52." *Kritika: Explorations in Russian and Eurasian History* 18, no. 1 (2017): 125–49.

- "Stalin's Trophy Films (1946–1956): A Resource." *Kinokultura* 56 (January 2017). http://www.kinokultura.com/2015/48-knight.shtml.

Komisssia po mezhdunarodnym sviaziam. *III Kinofestival' Stran Azii i Afriki v Tashkente (Otkliki Zarubezhnoi Pressy)*. Moscow: NII KINO, 1975.

Korchagov, Yuri, and Mrinal Sen. *Mrinal Sen*. Moscow: Iskusstvo, 1987.

Kosinova, M.I. "Mezhdunarodnye Otnosheniia Sovetskoi Kinematografii v Epokhi Ottepeli." *Sovremennye Issledovaniia Sotsial'nykh Problem* 50, no. 6 (2015): 631–48.

Kozlov, Denis. *The Readers of Novyi Mir: Coming to Terms with the Stalinist Past*. Cambridge, MA: Harvard University Press, 2013.

Kristal, Efraín. *The Cambridge Companion to the Latin American Novel*. Cambridge: Cambridge University Press, 2005.

Kudaibergenova, Diana. *Rewriting the Nation in Modern Kazakh Literature: Elites and Narratives*. Lanham, MD: Lexington Books, 2017.

Kudriavtsev, Sergei. "Poseshchaemost' Otechestvennykh i Zarubezhnykh Film'ov v Sovetskom Kinoprokate," 22 April, 2007. https://kinanet.livejournal.com/689229.html.

Kulik, Elena. *Mogolikii mir afrikanskogo kino*. Moscow: Vostochnaia literature, 1993.

Kurant, I.L. and B.M. Parchevskaia. *"Inostrannaia literature," 1975–1984: ukazatel' soderzhaniia zhurnala*. Moscow: Izvestiia, 1985.

- *"Inostrannaia literatura", 1955–1974: ukazatel' soderzhaniia zhurnala*. Moscow: Izvestiia, 1975.

Kuteishchikova, Vera. *Moskva-Meksiko-Moskva: doroga dlinoiu v zhizn'*. Moscow: Akademicheskii proekt, 2000.

La Guma, Alex. *A Soviet Journey: A Critical Annotated Edition*. Lanham, Maryland: Lexington Books, 2017.

- *In the Fog of the Season's End*. London: Heinemann, 1972.

- *A Walk in the Night, and Other Stories*. Evanston, IL: Northwestern University Press, 1968.

- *The Stone-Country*. Berlin: Seven Seas Publishers, 1967.

– *And a Threefold Cord*. Berlin: Seven Seas Publishers, 1964.

Lahusen, Thomas, and Evgeny Dobrenko, eds. *Socialist Realism without Shores*. Duke, NC: Duke University Press, 1997.

Laikwan, Pang. *Building a New China in Cinema: The Chinese Left-Wing Cinema Movement, 1932–1937*. Lanham, MD: Rowman & Littlefield Publishers, 2002.

Lal, Priya. *African Socialism in Postcolonial Tanzania: Between the Village and the World*. New York, NY: Cambridge University Press, 2015.

Larsen, Neil. "The 'Boom' Novel and the Cold War in Latin America." *Modern Fiction Studies* 38, no. 3 (1992): 771–84.

Latynina, Iuliia. "Kod dostupa: Avtorskaia peredacha." *Echo of Moscow* (blog), 7 and 14 December. https://echo.msk.ru/programs/code/.

Layton, Susan. *Russian Literature and Empire: Conquest of the Caucasus from Pushkin to Tolstoy*. Cambridge Studies in Russian Literature. New York, NY: Cambridge University Press, 1994.

Lazarus, Neil, ed. *The Cambridge Companion to Postcolonial Literary Studies*. New York, NY: Cambridge University Press, 2004.

Lee, Christopher. "Addressing an Afro-Asian Public: Alex La Guma's Report to the 25th Anniversary Conference of the Afro-Asian Writers Association in 1983." *Safundi* 19, no. 3 (3 July 2018): 269–83.

– ed. *Making a World after Empire: The Bandung Moment and Its Political Afterlives*. Athens, OH: Ohio University Press, 2010.

Lee, Steven. *The Ethnic Avant-Garde: Minority Cultures and World Revolution*. New York, NY: Columbia University Press, 2015.

Lee, Steven, and Amelia Glaser, eds. *Comintern Aesthetics*. Toronto: University of Toronto Press, 2019.

Leyda, Jay. "Filme aus Asien und Afrika." *Die Weltbuehne*, 31 December 1968.

Li, Weijia. *China Und China-Erfahrung in Leben Und Werk von Anna Seghers*. Oxford: Peter Lang, 2011.

Lipkov, Aleksandr. *Indiiskoe kino: sekret uspekha: razmyshleniia, interv'iu, vstrechi*. Kiev: Mystetstvo, 1990.

– *Iz festival'nogo bloknota*. Tashkent: Izd-vo lit-ry i iskussstva im. Gafura Guliama, 1984.

Litvin, Margaret. "Fellow Travelers? Two Arab Study Abroad Narratives of Moscow." In *Illusions and Disillusionment: Travel Writing in the Modern Age*, 96–119. Cambridge, MA: ILEX/Harvard University Press, 2018.

– *Hamlet's Arab Journey: Shakespeare's Prince and Nasser's Ghost*. Translation/Transnation. Princeton, NJ: Princeton University Press, 2011.

Liu, Lydia. "After Tashkent: The Geopolitics of Translation in the Global South."
    Institute for Cultural Inquiry-Berlin, 22 June 2018. Accessed on 10 July 2019
    at https://www.ici-berlin.org/events/lydia-h-liu/.

Lorde, Audre. "Notes from a Trip to Russia." In *Sister Outsider Essays and
    Speeches*, 13–35. Trumansburg, NY: Crossing Press, 1984.

Loss, Jacqueline. *Dreaming in Russian: The Cuban Soviet Imaginary*. Austin, TX:
    University of Texas Press, 2013.

– *Cosmopolitanisms and Latin America: Against the Destiny of Place*. New
    Concepts in Latino American Cultures. New York, NY: Palgrave Macmillan,
    2005.

Loss, Jacqueline, and Jose Manuel Prietto, eds. *Caviar with Rum: Cuba–USSR
    and the Post-Soviet Experience*. New York, NY: Palgrave Macmillan US, 2012.

Lovejoy, Alice. "The World Union of Documentary, the Early Cold War, and
    International Documentary Between East and West." Manuscript.

– *Army Film and the Avant Garde: Cinema and Experiment in the Czechoslovak
    Military*. Bloomington, Indiana: Indiana University Press, 2015.

Lukács, Georg. *The Theory of the Novel; a Historico-Philosophical Essay on the
    Forms of Great Epic Literature*. Cambridge, MA: MIT Press, 1971.

– "Narrate or Describe?" In *Writer and Critic, and Other Essays*, translated by
    Arthur David Kahn, 110–48. London: Merlin Press, 1970.

Lukács, Georg, Theodor W. Adorno, Walter Benjamin, Ernst Bloch, and Bertolt
    Brecht. "Realism in the Balance." In *Aesthetics and Politics*, 28–59. London;
    New York, NY: Verso, 2007.

Lunacharsky, Anatoly. "Mezhdunarodnaia Konferentsiia Proletariskikh i
    Revoliutsionnykh Pisatelei." *Na Literaturnom Postu*, December 1927.

Luppol, Ivan, ed. *Mezhdunarodnyi kongress pisatelei v zashchitu kul'tury, Parizh,
    iun' 1935: doklady i vystupleniiia*. Moscow: Gos. izd-vo khudozh. lit-ra, 1980.

Lupton, Catherine. *Chris Marker: Memories of the Future*. London: Reaktion
    Books, 2005.

Mahler, Anne Garland. *From the Tricontinental to the Global South: Race,
    Radicalism, and Transnational Solidarity*. Durham, NC: Duke University
    Press, 2018.

Majumdar, Rochona. "Debating Radical Cinema: A History of the Film Society
    Movement in India." *Modern Asian Studies* 46, no. 3 (May 2012): 743.

Mal'tsev, O.M. *Tashkentskie vstrechi; literaturnye portrety uchastnikov
    Tashkentskoi konferentsii–pisatelei stran Azii i Afriki*. Tashkent: Gosizd-vo
    khudozhlit-ry UzSSR, 1960.

Malaka, Tan. *From Jail to Jail*. Athens, OH: Ohio University Center for International Studies, 1991.

Malik, Hafeez. "The Marxist Literary Movement in India and Pakistan." *The Journal of Asian Studies* 26, no. 4 (1967): 649–64.

Malitsky, Joshua. *Post-Revolution Nonfiction Film: Building the Soviet and Cuban Nations*. Bloomington, IN: Indiana University Press, 2013.

Mally, Lynn. *Culture of the Future: The Proletkult Movement in Revolutionary Russia*. Berkeley, CA: University of California Press, 1990.

Manela, Erez. *The Wilsonian Moment: Self-Determination and the International Origins of Anticolonial Nationalism*. Oxford: Oxford University Press, 2007.

Mani, B. Venkat. *Recoding World Literature: Libraries, Print Culture, and Germany's Pact with Books*. New York, NY: Fordham University Press, 2017.

Marquez, Ismael. "The Andean Novel." In *The Cambridge Companion to the Latin American Novel*, edited by Efrain Kristal, 142–61. Cambridge: Cambridge University Press, 2005.

Martin, Michael T. *New Latin American Cinema*. Contemporary Film and Television Series. Detroit, MI: Wayne State University Press, 1997.

Martin, Terry. *The Affirmative Action Empire: Nations and Nationalism in the Soviet Union, 1923–1939*. Ithaca, NY: Cornell University Press, 2001.

Marx, Karl, and Friedrich Engels. *Collected Works. Vol. 12*. Moscow: Progress Publishers, 1979.

Massip, José. "Una Lección de Cine: Crónicas de Un Viaje." *Cine Cubano* 1, no. 3 (1960): 24–8.

Matusevich, Maxim. "The Red and the Black: The Riddle of Post-Soviet Racism." *LeftEast* 25 September 2017. http://www.criticatac.ro/lefteast/red-black/.

– *Africa in Russia, Russia in Africa: Three Centuries of Encounters*. Trenton, NJ: Africa World Press, 2007.

– *No Easy Row for a Russian Hoe: Ideology and Pragmatism in Nigerian-Soviet Relations, 1960–1991*. Trenton, NJ: Africa World Press, 2003.

McGuire, Elizabeth. *Red at Heart: How Chinese Communists Fell in Love with the Russian Revolution*. New York, NY: Oxford University Press, 2018.

McKay, Claude. *Amiable with Big Teeth: A Novel of the Love Affair between the Communists and the Poor Black Sheep of Harlem*. New York, NY: Penguin Random House LLC, 2017.

– "Soviet Russia and the Negro (Conclusion)." *The Crisis* 27, no. 3 (1924): 114–18.

– "Soviet Russia and the Negro." *Crisis* 27, no. 2 (1923): 61–5.

Mëhilli, Elidor. *From Stalin to Mao: Albania and the Socialist World*. Ithaca, NY: Cornell University Press, 2017.

– "Globalized Socialism, Nationalized Time: Soviet Films, Albanian Subjects, and Chinese Audiences across the Sino-Soviet Split." *Slavic Review* 77, no. 3 (2018): 611–37.

Mehmood, Tariq. "The Lotus Project." American University in Beirut. Accessed 15 March 2019. https://www.aub.edu.lb/fas/ampl/Pages/lotus.aspx.

Mestman, Mariano. "Algiers-Buenos Aires-Montreal: Third-Worldist Links in the Creation of the Latin American Filmmakers Committee (1974)." *Canadian Journal of Film Studies* 24, no. 2 (2015): 29–40.

Meyer, James H. "Children of Trans-Empire: Nâzım Hikmet and the First Generation of Turkish Students at Moscow's Communist University of the East." *Journal of the Ottoman and Turkish Studies Association* 5, no. 2 (2018): 195–218.

Mikheev, Aleksei. "Mezhdu Drumia Ottepeliami: Inostrannaia Literatura: Istoriia i Istoki." *Inostrannaia Literatura*, no. 10 (2005).

Miller, Henry K. "The Fog of War." *Sight and Sound* 27, no. 6 (Jun 2017): 14–15.

Miller, Jamie. "Soviet Politics and the Mezhrabpom Studio in the Soviet Union during the 1920s and 1930s." *Historical Journal of Film, Radio, and Television* 32, no. 4 (December 2012): 521–35.

– *Soviet Cinema: Politics and Persuasion under Stalin*. KINO. I.B. Tauris, 2009.

Moine, Caroline. *Screened Encounters: The History of the Leipzig Film Festival, 1955–1990*. New York, NY: Berghahn, 2018.

Moore, David Chioni. "Colored Dispatches from the Uzbek Border: Langston Hughes' Relevance, 1933–2002." *Callaloo* 25, no. 4 (2002): 1115–135.

– "Is the Post- in Postcolonial the Post- in Post-Soviet? Toward a Global Postcolonial Critique." *PMLA* 116, no. 1 (2001): 111–28.

– "Local Color, Global 'Color': Langston Hughes, the Black Atlantic, and Soviet Central Asia, 1932." *Research in African Literatures* 27, no. 4 (1996): 49–70.

Moretti, Franco. *Distant Reading*. London: Verso, 2013.

– *Graphs, Maps, Trees: Abstract Models for a Literary History*. London: Verso, 2007.

– *Atlas of the European Novel, 1800–1900*. London: Verso, 1999.

Morozov, Vyacheslav. *Russia's Postcolonial Identity: A Subaltern Empire in a Eurocentric World*. Basingstoke: Palgrave Macmillan, 2015.

Mukharjee, Tutun. "Writing as Activism: Mulk Raj Anand's Commitment to His Ideology." In *The Lasting Legacies of Mulk Raj Anand*, edited by Rizwan

Khan, 53–64. New Delhi: Atlantic Publishers, 2008.

Mukherji, Ani. "'Like Another Planet to the Darker Americans': Black Cultural Work in 1930s Moscow." In *Africa in Europe: Studies in Transnational Practice in the Long Twentieth Century*, edited by Eve Rosenhaft and Robbie John Macvicar Aitken, 120–41. Liverpool: Liverpool University Press, 2013.

Murphy, David. *Sembène: Imagining Alternatives in Film & Fiction*. Trenton, NJ: Africa World Press, 2001.

Musser, Charles. "Utopian Visions in Cold War Documentary: Joris Ivens, Paul Robeson and the Song of the Rivers (1954)." *Cinemas* 12, no. 4 (2002): 109–53.

Naimark, Norman, Silvio Pons, and Sophie Quinn-Judge, eds. *Cambridge History of Communism: Volume 2, The Socialist Camp and World Power 1941–1960s*. Cambridge: Cambridge University Press, 2017.

Neruda, Pablo. *Canto General*. Translated by Jack Schmitt. Berkeley, CA: University of California Press, 1991.

– *Ispania v Serdtse*. Translated by Ilya Ehrenburg. Moscow: Goslitizdat, 1939.

Wa Thiong'o, Ngũgĩ. *Decolonising the Mind: The Politics of Language in African Literature*. Studies in African Literature. London: Heinemann, 1986.

– *Writers in Politics: Essays*. Studies in African Literature. London: Heinemann, 1981.

– *Petals of Blood*. London: Heinemann, 1977.

– *A Grain of Wheat*. London: Heinemann, 1967.

– *The River Between*. London: Heinemann, 1965.

Nikiforova, I.D., E.P. Chelyshev, and S.V. Prozhogina. *Sovremennye literatury stran Azii i Afriki: tipologicheskie priznaki natsional'nykh i mezhnnatsional'nykh literaturnykh sistem*. Moscow: Izd-vo "Nauka," 1988.

Novodvorskaia, Valeriia. "Ne Otdadim Nashe Otechestvo Nalevo." *Novyi Vzgliad*, 28 August 1993. https://www.ds.ru/vnstat.htm.

Nowell-Smith, Geoffrey. *Making Waves: New Cinemas of the 1960s*. London: Bloomsbury Publishing, 2013.

– *The Oxford History of World Cinema*. Oxford; New York, NY: Oxford University Press, 1996.

Ostrovskaya, Elena, and Elena Zemskova. "Between the Battlefield and the Marketplace: International Literature Magazine in Britain." *Russian Journal of Communication* 8, no. 3 (2016): 217–29.

Ostrovsky, Nikolai. *How the Steel Was Tempered: A Novel in Two Parts*. Library of Selected Soviet Literature. Moscow: Foreign Languages PubHouse, 1952.

O'Toole, Gavin, and Georgina Jimenez, eds. *Che in Verse*. 1st ed. Wiltshire, UK: Aflame Books, 2007.

Oushakine, Serguei Alex. "How to Grow out of Nothing: The Afterlife of National Rebirth in Postcolonial Belarus." *Qui Parle* 26, no. 2 (December 2017): 423–90.

Panizza, Tiziana. *Joris Ivens en Chile: el documental entre la poesía y la crítica = Joris Ivens in Chile: documentary between poetry and social critic.* Providencia, Santiago: Cuarto Propio, 2011.

Panteleev, Mikhail. "Repressii v Kominterne (1937–1938gg.)." *Otechestvennaia Istoriia*, no. 6 (1996): 161–68.

Páricsy, Pál. "Research in Black African Literature in the European Socialist Countries." *Research in African Literatures* 3, no. 1 (Spring 1972): 36–50.

Parry, Benita. "The Futures Past of Internationalism." *Viewpoint Magazine* (blog), 1 February 2018. https://www.viewpointmag.com/2018/02/01/futures-past-internationalism-conversation-benita-parry/.

Pedemonte, Rafael. "Birches Too Difficult to Cut Down: The Rejection and Assimilation of the Soviet Reference in Cuban Culture." *International Journal of Cuban Studies* 9, no. 1 (1 April 2017): 127–41.

Pervyi Vsemirnyi Kongress Storonnikov Mira. Praga-Parizh. 20–25 Aprelia 1949: Materialy. Moscow: Gosudarstvennoi izdatel'stvo politicheskoi literatury, 1950.

Petersson, Fredrik. "'We Are Neither Visionaries Nor Utopian Dreamers': Willi Münzenberg, the League against Imperialism, and the Comintern, 1925–1933." PhD thesis, Abo Akademi, 2013.

Petrov, Petr. *K Istorii Izdatel'stva Progress.* Moscow: Progress Publishers, 1987.

Pitcher, M. Anne, and Kelly M. Askew. "African Socialisms and Postsocialisms." *Africa: Journal of the International African Institute* 76, no. 1 (2006): 1–14.

Platt, Kevin M.F., ed. *Global Russian Cultures.* Madison, Wisconsin: The University of Wisconsin Press, 2019.

– "Occupation versus Colonization: Post-Soviet Latvia and the Provincialization of Europe." In *Memory and Theory in Eastern Europe*, edited by Uilleam Blacker, Alexander Etkind, and Julie Fedor, 125–45. New York, NY: Palgrave Macmillan US, 2013.

Pollock, Sheldon. *The Language of the Gods in the World of Men: Sanskrit, Culture, and Power in Premodern India.* Berkeley, CA: University of California Press, 2006.

Pons, Silvio. *The Global Revolution: A History of International Communism, 1917–1991.* 1st ed. Oxford Studies in Modern European History. Oxford: Oxford University Press, 2014.

Pons, Silvio, and Stephen A Smith, eds. *Cambridge History of Communism: Volume 1, World Revolution and Socialism in One Country 1917–1941.* Cambridge: Cambridge University Press, 2017.

Popescu, Monica. "On the Margins of the Black Atlantic: Angola, the
    Eastern Bloc, and the Cold War." *Research in African Literatures* 45, no. 3
    (1 September 2014): 91–109.
– *South African Literature beyond the Cold War*. New York, NY: Palgrave
    Macmillan, 2010.
Prashad, Vijay. *Red Star over the Third World*. New Delhi: LeftWord Books,
    2017.
– *The Poorer Nations: A Possible History of the Global South*. London: Verso, 2012.
– *The Darker Nations: A People's History of the Third World*. New York, NY: New
    Press, 2007.
– ed. *The East Was Read: Socialist Culture in the Third World*. New Delhi:
    LeftWord Books, 2019.
Pratt, Mary Louise. "Arts of the Contact Zone." *Profession*, 1 January 1991,
    33–40.
Prendergast, Christopher, and Benedict Anderson, eds. *Debating World
    Literature*. London: Verso, 2004.
Pudovkin, Vsevolod Illarionovich. *Film Acting: A Course of Lectures Delivered
    at the State Institute of Cinematography, Moscow*. London: George Newnes,
    1980.
– *Film Technique; Five Essays and Two Addresses*. London: GNewnes, ltd, 1933.
Puzikov, A.I., V.R. Shcherbina, and I.E. Elsberg, eds. *Velikii Oktiabr' i Mirovaia
    Literatura: Sbornik Statei*. Moscow: Khudozhestvennaia literatura, 1967.
Pym, Anthony, and Nune Ayvazyan. "The Case of the Missing Russian
    Translation Theories." *Translation Studies* 8, no. 3 (September 2, 2015):
    321–41.
Qiubai, Qu. *Superfluous Words*. Translated by Jamie Greenbaum. Canberra:
    Pandanus Books, 2005.
Rajagopalan, Sudha. *Indian Films in Soviet Cinemas: The Culture of Movie-
    Going after Stalin*. Bloomington: Indiana University Press, 2009.
Ram, Harsha. "City, Nation, Empire and the Russian-Georgian Encounter."
    Manuscript.
– *The Imperial Sublime: A Russian Poetics of Empire*. Publications of the
    Wisconsin Center for Pushkin Studies. Madison, WI: University of Wisconsin
    Press, 2003.
– "Imagining Eurasia: The Poetics and Ideology of Olzhas Suleimenov's
    AZ i IA." *Slavic Review* 60, no. 2 (2001): 289–311.
Ramsay, Gail. *The Novels of an Egyptian Romanticist: Yūsuf Al-Sibāʿī*. Edsbruk:
    Akademitryck AB, 1996.

Rasberry, Vaughn. *Race and the Totalitarian Century: Geopolitics in the Black Literary Imagination*. Cambridge, MA: Harvard University Press, 2016.

Ravandi-Fadai, Lana. "'Red Mecca' – The Communist University for Laborers of the East (KUTV): Iranian Scholars and Students in Moscow in the 1920s and 1930s." *Iranian Studies* 48, no. 5 (2015): 713–27.

Razlogov, Kirill. *Moi Festivali*. Moscow: B.S.G. Press, 2015.

Razlogova, Elena. "The Politics of Translation at Soviet Film Festivals during the Cold War." *SubStance* 44, no. 2 (2015): 66–87.

– "Listening to the Inaudible Foreign: Simultaneous Translators and Soviet Experience of Foreign Cinema." In *Sound, Music, Speech in Soviet and Post-Soviet Cinema*, edited by Lilya Kaganovsky and Masha Salazkina, 162–78. Bloomington, IN: Indiana University Press, 2014.

Reilly, Catherine. "Remains of Red Letters: Mediating World Literature in the Eastern Bloc." presented at the Remapping European Media Cultures During the Cold War, University of Minnesota, Twin Cities, 31 March 2017.

"Resolutions of the Third World Filmmakers Meeting, Algiers, December 5–14, 1973." *Black Camera* ii (2010): 155–65.

Riddell, John, ed. *To See the Dawn: Baku, 1920–First Congress of the Peoples of the East*. 1st ed. The Communist International in Lenin's Time. New York, NY: Pathfinder, 1993.

Riddell, John, Nazeef Mollah, and Vijay Prashad, eds. *Liberate the Colonies: Communism and Colonial Freedom, 1917–1924*. New Delhi: LeftWord Books, 2019.

Rimer, J. Thomas. *A Hidden Fire: Russian and Japanese Cultural Encounters, 1868–1926*. Palo Alto, CA: Stanford University Press, 1995.

Roberts, Graham. *Forward Soviet! History and Non-fiction Film in the USSR*. KINO, the Russian Cinema Series. London: I.B. Tauris, 1999.

Rogers, Holly. *Music and Sound in Documentary Film*. New York, NY: Routledge, 2015.

Roman, Meredith. *Opposing Jim Crow: African Americans and the Soviet Indictment of U.S. Racism, 1928–1937*. Lincoln, NE: University of Nebraska Press, 2012.

Roth-Ey, Kristin. "We, as Commercial People, Understand: Soviet Cinema and Markets in the Global South." Presented at the ASEEES, Boston, MA, 7 December 2018.

– *Moscow Prime Time: How the Soviet Union Built the Media Empire That Lost the Cultural Cold War*. Ithaca, NY: Cornell University Press, 2011.

Rouland, Michael, Gulnara Abikeyeva, and Birgit Beumers, eds. *Cinema in*

Central Asia: Rewriting Cultural Histories. London: I.B. Tauris, 2013.

Rubins, Maria. *Russian Montparnasse Transnational Writing in Interwar Paris.* London: Palgrave Macmillan, 2015.

Rupprecht, Tobias. *Soviet Internationalism after Stalin: Interaction and Exchange between the USSR and Latin America during the Cold War.* Cambridge: Cambridge University Press, 2015.

Sahni, Kalpana. *Crucifying the Orient: Russian Orientalism and the Colonization of Caucasus and Central Asia.* Oslo, Norway: Institute for Comparative Research in Human Culture, 1997.

Said, Edward. *Culture and Imperialism.* New York, NY: Knopf, 1993.

– "Third World Intellectuals and Metropolitan Culture." *Raritan* 9, no. 3 (1 January 1990): 27–50.

– *Orientalism.* 1st Vintage Books ed. New York, NY: Vintage, 1978.

Salazkina, Masha. "Eisenstein in Latin America." In *The Flying Carpet. Studies on Eisenstein and Russian Cinema in Honor of Naum Kleiman,* edited by Joan Neubeger and Antonio Somaini, 343–67. Paris: Editions Mimes, 2017.

– "Translating the Academy: Conceptualizing the Transnational in Media and Film." In *The Multilingual Screen: New Reflections on Cinema and Linguistic Difference,* edited by Lisa Patti, 17–36. New York, NY: Bloomsbury Academic, 2016.

– "Moscow-Rome-Havana: A Film-Theory Road Map." *October,* no. 139 (1 January 2012): 97–116.

– "Soviet-Indian Coproductions: Alibaba as Political Allegory." *Cinema Journal* 49, no. 4 (2010): 71–89.

– *In Excess: Sergei Eisenstein's Mexico.* Cinema and Modernity. Chicago, IL: University of Chicago Press, 2009.

Salti, Rasha, ed. *Saving Bruce Lee: African and Arab Cinema in the Era of Soviet Cultural Diplomacy.* Berlin: House der Kulturen der Welt, 2018.

Samarin, R.M., ed. *Velikaia Oktiabr'skaia sotsialisticheskaia revoliutsiia i mirovaia literatura: Sbornik statei.* Moscow: Nauka, 1970.

Sarkisova, Oksana. *Screening Soviet Nationalities: Kulturfilms from the Far North to Central Asia.* KINO, the Russian Cinema Series. London: I.B. Tauris, 2017.

Saunders, Frances. *The Cultural Cold War: The CIA and the World of Arts and Letters.* New York, NY: New Press, 1999.

Sauvy, Alfred. "Trois Mondes, Une Planète." *L'Observateur,* 14 August 1952.

Schanzer, George O. *Russian Literature in the Hispanic World: A Bibliography. La Literatura Rusa En El Mundo Hispánico: Bibliografía.* Toronto: University of Toronto Press, 1972.

Schild, Kathryn. "Between Moscow and Baku: National Literatures at the 1934 Congress of Soviet Writers." PhD thesis, University of California, Berkeley, 2010.

Schimmelpenninck van der Oye, David. "The Curious Fate of Edward Said in Russia." *Études de Lettres*, no. 2–3 (15 September 2014): 81–94.

– *Russian Orientalism: Asia in the Russian Mind from Peter the Great to the Emigration*. New Haven, CT: Yale University Press, 2010.

Schoots, Hans. *Living Dangerously: A Biography of Joris Ivens*. Amsterdam: Amsterdam University Press, 2000.

Schroeder, Paul. *Latin American Cinema: A Comparative History*. Oakland, California: University of California Press, 2016.

Scott-Smith, Giles, and Charlotte A. Lerg, eds. *Campaigning Culture and the Global Cold War: The Journals of the Congress for Cultural Freedom*. London: Palgrave Macmillan, 2017.

Semanov, V.I. *Literatura dvukh kontinentov (sbornik statei)*. Moscow: Izd-vo MGU, 1979.

Sembène, Ousmane. *Black Docker*. London: Heinemann, 1987.

– *The Last of the Empire: A Senegalese Novel*. London: Heinemann, 1983.

– *God's Bits of Wood*. Translated by Francis Price. Garden City, NY: Anchor Books, 1970.

Serebriannyi, Sergei. "Comparative Literature and Post-Colonial Studies: An Outsider's View from Post-Soviet Moscow." In *Building Bridges between India and Russia: A Festschrift for Prof. J.P. Dimri*, edited by R.D. Akella, 63–82. Kolkata: Power Publishers, 2012.

Shashkova, Olga A., and Marina A. Shpakovskaya. "The Communist University of the Toilers of the East (KUTV): Its Establishment under the Comintern in 1920s–30s." *Herald of an Archivist* 3 (2018): 704–16.

Shcherbina, V.R., ed. *Mirovoe Znachenie Russkoi Literatury 19–go Veka*. Moscow: Nauka, 1987.

Sheng, Yueh. *Sun-Yatsen University in Moscow and the Chinese Revolution: A Personal Account*. Lawrence, KS: University Press of Kansas, 1971.

Sherry, Samantha. *Discourses of Regulation and Resistance: Censoring Translation in the Stalin and Khrushchev Era Soviet Union*. Edinburgh: Edinburgh University Press, 2015.

Sheshukov, Stepan. *Neistovye revniteli: iz istorii literaturnoi bor'by 20-kh godov*. Moscow: Khudozhestvennaia literatura, 1984.

Sho, Konishi. *Anarchist Modernity: Cooperatism and Japanese–Russian Intellectual Relations in Modern Japan*. Cambridge, MA: Harvard University Asia Center, 2013.

Shridharani, Krishnalal. "Pisateli Stran Azii i Afriki v Tashkente (Russian Translation by V. Zimin)." *Amrita Bazar Patrika*, November 9, 1958. RGALI f. 631, op. 2, ex. 6100, l. 1–8.

Shubin, Vladimir. *The Hot "Cold War": The USSR in Southern Africa*. London: Pluto Press, 2008.

Sibichus, B.Iu. *Kul'tura Meksiki*. Moscow: Nauka, 1980.

Sidenova, Raisa. "The Topographical Aesthetic in Late Stalinist Soviet Documentary." Manuscript.

Siliunas, Vidas, ed. *Osvoboditel'naia i revoliutsionnaia bor'ba v zerkale latinoamerikanskogo iskusstva*. Moscow: VNII Iskusstvoznania, 1988.

Sinha, Subir, and Rashmi Varma. "Marxism and Postcolonial Theory: What's Left of the Debate?" *Critical Sociology* 43, no. 4–5 (July 2017): 545–58.

Slezkine, Yuri. "The USSR as a Communal Apartment, or How a Socialist State Promoted Ethnic Particularism." *Slavic Review* 53, no. 2 (Summer 1994): 414–52.

Smith, Stephen A. "The Bolshevik Revolution from a Global Perspective." Oxford University, 20 November 2017.

– ed. *The Oxford Handbook of the History of Communism*. Oxford: Oxford University Press, 2013.

Smola, Klavdia, and Dirk Uffelmann. *Postcolonial Slavic Literatures After Communism*. Frankfurt: Peter Lang, 2017.

Sobolev, Romil Pavlovich, N.M. Sumenov, and Miron Chernenko. *Aktual'nye problemy kinematografa sotsialisticheskikh stran: sbornik nauchnykh trudov*. Moscow: Goskino SSSR, 1982.

Sobolev, Romil. *Kinematografiia razvivaiushchikhsia stran*. Moscow: Nauka, 1985.

Solanas, Fernando. "Interview with Louis Marcorelles." *Cahiers Du Cinema* 210 (March 1969): 62.

Spiers, Edward. *Engines for Empire: The Victorian Army and Its Use of Railways*. Manchester: Manchester University Press, 2015.

Spivak, Gayatri. "Can the Subaltern Speak?" In *Marxism and the Interpretation of Culture*, edited by C. Nelson and L. Grossberg, 273–313. Urbana, IL: University of Illinois Press, 1988.

"sssr: Samye Kassovye Fil'my." Kinpoisk.ru. Accessed 15 March 2019. https://www.kinopoisk.ru/top/lists/184/filtr/all/sort/order/.

Stam, Robert, Barry Keith Grant, and Jeannette Sloniowski, eds. "The Two Avant-Gardes: Solanas and Getino's Hour of the Furnaces." In *Documenting the Documentary: Close Readings of Documentary Film and Video*, 271–86. Detroit, MI: Wayne State University Press, 2014.

Steiner, Evgenyi. "Orientalistkii Mif Ili Mif Ob Orientalizme." *Polit.Ru*, 22 January 2009. https://polit.ru/article/2009/01/22/oriental/.

Stejskalová, Tereza, ed. *Filmaři všech zemí, spojte se!: zapomenutý internacionalismus, československý film a třetí svět = Filmmakers of the world, unite!: forgotten internationalism, Czechoslovak film and the third world.* Prague: Tranzit.cz, 2017.

Stronski, Paul. "Exporting Modernity: Tashkent as a Cold War Model of Decolonization in Asia." Presented at the ASEEES, Washington, DC, November 2006.

sujs. "Zarubezhnye Fil'my v Prokate SSSR i RF, 1933–1993." *Fenixclub.Com* (blog), July 27, 2018. http://fenixclub.com/index.php?showtopic=187315.

Suleimenov, Olzhas. *Az i Ia: kniga blagonamerennogo chitatelia: "Slovo o polku Igoreve."* Alma-Ata: Zhazushy, 1975.

– *No Liudiam Ia Ne Lgal.* Almaty: Daik Press, 2006.

Suny, Ronald Grigor, and Terry Martin. *A State of Nations: Empire and Nation-Making in the Age of Lenin and Stalin.* New York, NY: Oxford University Press, 2001.

Szeman, Imre. "Who's Afraid of National Allegory? Jameson, Literary Criticism, Globalization." *South Atlantic Quarterly* 100, no. 3 (2001): 803–27.

Tamari, Salim. "Najati Sidqi (1905–79): The Enigmatic Jerusalem Bolshevik." *Journal of Palestine Studies* 32, no. 2 (2003): 79–94.

Taylor, Richard. *The Battleship Potemkin: The Film Companion.* London: I.B. Tauris, 2000.

Telepneva, Natalia. "Our Sacred Duty: The Soviet Union, the Liberation Movements in the Portuguese Colonies, and the Cold War, 1961–1975." PhD thesis, London School of Economics, 2014.

The First Congress of the Toilers of the Far East. Held in Moscow, Jan. 21st–Feb 1st, 1922. Closing Session in Petrograd, 3 Feb., 1922. Petrograd: Communist International, 1922.

Thornberry, Robert S. "Writers Take Sides, Stalinists Take Control: The Second International Congress for the Defense of Culture (Spain 1937)." *Historian* 62, no. 3 (1 March 2000): 589–606.

Tihanov, Galin. *The Birth and Death of Literary Theory: Regimes of Relevance in Russia and Beyond*. Standord: Stanford University Press, 2019.

– "Ferrying a Thinker Across Time and Language: Bakhtin, Translation, World Literature." *Modern Languages Open* 1 (2018): 1–10.

– "The Location of World Literature." *Canadian Review of Comparative Literature / Revue Canadienne de Littérature Comparée* 44, no. 3 (2017): 468–81.

– "Foreword." In Antal Szerb, *Reflections in the Library: Selected Literary Essays, 1926–1944*, ix–xi. Cambridge: Legenda, 2017.

Timofeeva, Natalia. "Kommunisticheskii universitet trudiashchikhsia Vostoka (KUTV): Ideinyi tsentr podgotovki kommunisticheskikh i revoliutsionnykh kadrov Vostoka." PhD thesis. Institut Vostokovedeniia AN SSSR, 1988.

Tlostanova, Madina. *What Does It Mean to Be Post-Soviet? Decolonial Art from the Ruins of the Soviet Empire*. Durham, NC: Duke University Press, 2018.

– *Postcolonialism and Postsocialism in Fiction and Art: Resistance and Re-Existence*. Cham: Springer International Publishing, 2017.

– *Gender Epistemologies and Eurasian Borderlands*. New York, NY: Palgrave Macmillan, 2010.

Todorova, Maria. *Imagining the Balkans*. New York, NY: Oxford University Press, 1997.

Tolz, Vera. *Russia's Own Orient: The Politics of Identity and Oriental Studies in the Late Imperial and Early Soviet Periods*. Oxford: Oxford University Press, 2011.

Tseitlin, B. *Puteshestvie v Abissiniu*. Moscow: Molodaya Gvardiya, 2018

Tyerman, Edward. "Sino–Soviet Confessions: Authority, Agency, and Autobiography in Sergei Tret'iakov's Den Shi-khua." *The Russian Review* 77, no. 1 (1 January 2018): 47–64.

– "Resignifying the Red Poppy: Internationalism and Symbolic Power in the Sino-Soviet Encounter." *Slavic and East European Journal* 61, no. 3 (Autumn 2017): 445–66.

– "The Search for an Internationalist Aesthetics: Soviet Images of China, 1920–1935." PhD thesis, Columbia University, 2014.

Tyulenev, Sergey. "Vsemirnaia Literatura: Intersections between Translating and Original Literary Writing." *Slavic and East European Journal* 60, no. 1 (2016): 8–21.

Unkovski-Korica, Vladimir. *The Economic Struggle for Power in Tito's Yugoslavia: From World War II to Non-Alignment*. London: I.B. Tauris, 2016.

Usova, Anastasia. "Kommunisticheskii universitet trudiashchikhsia vostoka, 1–3." *Magazeta* (January 2017). https://magazeta.com/2017/01/chinese-moscow-4.

Valck, Marijke de. *Film Festivals: From European Geopolitics to Global Cinephilia*. Amsterdam: Amsterdam University Press, 2007.

Vallejo, César. *Tungsten: A Novel*. Translated by Robert Mezey and Kevin J. O'Connor. Syracuse, NY: Syracuse University Press, 1988.

Vetrova, Tatiana. "Territoriia Latinoamerikanskogo Kino Na Rossiiskom Ekrane." *Latinskaia Amerika*, no. 8 (2015).

Viany, Alex. "The Old and the New in Brazilian Cinema." *The Drama Review* 14, no. 2 (1970): 141–4.

Vinson, J. Chal. "The Drafting of the Four-Power Treaty of the Washington Conference." *The Journal of Modern History* 25, no. 1 (1953): 40–7.

Vogüé, Eugène-Melchior. *The Russian Novel*. Translated by Herbert Anthony Sawyer b. London: Chapman and Hall, ltd, 1913.

Volland, Nicolai. "Clandestine Cosmopolitanism: Foreign Literature in the People's Republic of China, 1957–1977." *Journal of South Asian Studies* 76, no. 1 (2017): 185–210.

– *Socialist Cosmopolitanism: The Chinese Literary Universe, 1945–1965*. New York, NY: Columbia University Press, 2017.

Vorontsov, Iurii, ed. *Sotsiologicheskie Problemy Prokata*. Moscow: VNII Kinoiskusstva, 1988.

Vtoroi Vsemirnyi Kongress Storonnikov Mira. Varshava, 16–22 Noiabria 1950: Materialy. Moscow: Gosudarstvennoi izdatel'stvo politicheskoi literatury, 1951.

Vvedenskii, B.A., ed. "Vostokovedenie." *Bol'shaia Sovetskaia Entsiklopedia*. Moscow: Moscow, 1951.

Waugh, Thomas. *The Conscience of Cinema: The Films of Joris Ivens 1912–1989*. Framing Film (Amsterdam, Netherlands), 2016.

– "Loin Du Vietnam (1967), Joris Ivens and Left Bank Documentary." *Jump Cut*, no. 53 (2011). https://www.ejumpcut.org/archive/jc53.2011/WaughVietnam/index.html.

– "*The 400 Million* (1938) and the Solidarity Film: Halfway between Hollywood and Newsreel." *Studies in Documentary Film* iii, no. 1 (2009): 7–17.

– "Travel Notebook – A People in Arms: Joris Ivens' Work in Cuba." *Jump Cut*, no. 22 (1980): 25–9.

Wayne, Mike. *Political Film – The Dialectics of Third Cinema*. London: Pluto Press, 2001.

Wells, Sarah Ann. "Parallel Modernities?: The First Reception of Soviet Cinema in Latin America." In *Cosmopolitan Film Culture in Latin America, 1896–1960*, edited by Rielle Edmonds Navitski and Nicolas Poppe, 151–75. Bloomington, IN: Indiana University Press, 2017.

Westad, Odd Arne. *The Global Cold War: Third World Interventions and the Making of Our Times.* Cambridge: Cambridge University Press, 2007.

Willemsen, Paul. "The Third Cinema Question. Notes and Reflections." *Framework* 34 (1987): 4–38.

Williams, Raymond. *Keywords: A Vocabulary of Culture and Society.* New York, NY: Oxford University Press, 1976.

Witt, Susanna. "Institutionalized Intermediates: Conceptualizing Soviet Practices of Indirect Literary Translation." *Translation Studies* 10, no. 2 (2017): 166–82.

– "The Shorthand of Empire: Podstrochnik Practices and the Making of Soviet Literature." *Ab Imperio* 2013, no. 3 (2013): 155–90.

– "Between the Lines: Totalitarianism and Translation in the USSR." In *Contexts, Subtexts, and Pretexts: Literary Translation in Eastern Europe and Russia*, edited by Brian Baer, 149–70. Amsterdam: John Benjamins Publishing Company, 2011.

Woll, Josephine. "The Russian Connection: Soviet Cinema and the Cinema of Francophone Africa." In *Focus on African Film*, edited by Josephine Pfaff, 223–40. Bloomington, IN: Indiana University Press, 2004.

Wong, Wang-chi. *Politics and Literature in Shanghai: The Chinese League of Left-Wing Writers, 1930–1936.* Manchester: Manchester University Press, 1991.

Wright, Richard. *The Colour Curtain: A Report on the Bandung Conference.* London: Dobson, 1956.

– "The Initiatives." In *The God That Failed*, edited by Richard Grossman, 115–62. New York, NY: Harper, 1950.

Xun, Lu. "China's Debt to Russian Literature." In *Selected Works of Lu Hsun, Volume III*, translated by Gladys Yang, 180–5. Peking: Foreign Languages Press, 1959.

Yashen, Kamil. "Tashkent-Kair." In *Gody, sud'by, knigi: stat'i, ocherki, vystupleniia*, translated by Grigorii Mar'iaanovskii, 117–22. Tashkent: Izd-vo literatury i iskusstva, 1973.

Yoon, Duncan. "'Our Forces Have Redoubled': World Literature, Postcolonialism, and the Afro-Asian Writers' Bureau." *The Cambridge Journal of Postcolonial Literary Inquiry* 2, no. 02 (2015): 233–52.

– "Cold War Africa and China: The Afro-Asian Writers' Bureau and the Rise of Postcolonial Literature." PhD thesis, UCLA, 2014.

Young, Robert J.C. *Postcolonialism: An Historical Introduction.* Malden, MA: Blackwell Publishing, 2001.

– "Ideologies of the Postcolonial." *Interventions* 1, no. 1 (October 1998): 4–8.

Yountchi, Lisa. "Between Russia and Iran: Soviet Tajik Literature and Identity, 1920–1991." PhD thesis, Northwestern University, 2011.

Yudin, Greg. "'Scratch a Russian Liberal and You'll Find an Educated Conservative': An Interview with Sociologist Greg Yudin." *Lefteast*, 23 March 20107. http://www.criticatac.ro/lefteast/scratch-a-russian-liberal-and-youll-find-an-educated-conservative-an-interview-with-sociologist-greg-yudin/.

Zade, Elmira ali-. *Russkaia Literatura i Arabskii Mir (k Istorii Arabo-Russkikh Literaturnykh Sviazei).* Moscow: Institut Vostokovedeniia, 2014.

Zaheer, Sajjad. *The Light: A History of the Movement for Progressive Literature in the Indo-Pakistan Subcontinent.* Oxford: Oxford University Press, 2006.

Zemskova, Elena. "'Gaining Literary Citizenship': Translators in the Soviet Literary Bureaucracy of the 1930s." SSRN Scholarly Paper. Rochester, NY: Social Science Research Network, 8 December 2014.

Zholkovsky, Alexander. "Istorii Vcherashnego Dnia." Accessed 13 March 2019. http://www-bcf.usc.edu/~alik/rus/ess/semid.htm.

Zubel, Marla. "Literary Reportage and the Poetics of Cold War Internationalism." PhD thesis, University of Minnesota, 2017.

– "Toward a Second World Third Cinema: Anti-Colonial Internationalism in Tadeusz Jaworski's 80 Days of Lumumba." *Studies in Eastern European Cinema* 7, no. 3 (1 September 2016): 190–207.

Zvegial'skaia, I. *Vitalii Naumkin: Mchashchiisia Skvoz' Vremia (Al'bom k 70-Letiiu).* Moscow: Institut Vostokovedeniia, 2015.

Index